Gospel Versus Gospel

Gospel Versus Gospel

Mission and the Mennonite
Church, 1863-1944

**THERON F.
SCHLABACH**

Wipf & Stock
PUBLISHERS
Eugene, Oregon

Wipf and Stock Publishers
199 W 8th Ave, Suite 3
Eugene, OR 97401

Gospel Versus Gospel
Mission and the Mennonite Church, 1863-1944
By Schlabach, Theron
Copyright©1980 Herald Press
ISBN: 1-57910-211-5
Publication date 2/2/1999
Previously published by Herald Press, 1980

GOSPEL VERSUS GOSPEL

Studies in Anabaptist and
Mennonite History
No. 21

CONTENTS

Introduction by Wilbert R. Shenk—9
Author's Preface—13

1 New Drumbeats—19
2 Whose Mission?—54
3 The Urge to Make Institutions—83
4 The Pure Gospel: Orthodoxy and Evangelism...
  and Benevolence?—109
5 The Pure Gospel: Teaching the "All Things" (I)—148
6 The Pure Gospel: Teaching the "All Things" (II)—167
7 Helping Gospel Take Root—195
8 Gospel at Home (I)—224
9 Gospel at Home (II): The Rural Gospel—263

Chapter Notes—290
Essay on Sources—331
Index—344
The Author—352

INTRODUCTION

This study attempts to describe and interpret an emerging movement in mission which began in the Mennonite Church about 1860. In doing his work, the historian can follow various paths. Theron F. Schlabach and the Mission History Project advisory committee agreed that the aim of this book would be to discover the dynamics at work. Chronologies and descriptions of organizations have their place, but to understand the forces which drove Mennonites to missionary action—after generations of self-protective inactivity—involves listening to a multitude of voices speaking in their own times and places to the issues of the day. The boards and committees which they organized represent little more than scaffolding and mechanisms. More instructive for us is to know what troubled and what inspired our great-grandparents, grandparents, and parents. What was their frame of reference and how did they go about finding answers to their questions within that frame?

Various themes run through the history of these eight decades. This was a time of beginning as well as of recovery. The period 1863-1944 represents an era of both self-discovery and world-discovery. The wider world was experiencing major jolts and turmoil. By the end of the nineteenth century Western colonial empires had reached their vainglorious heyday, only to have their overweening self-confidence dashed in 1914-17 by a major war. The reader will spot these and other motifs. Schlabach forcefully points to the tensions that played a basic role in shaping the Mennonite missionary movement.

Another theme is worth noting. The great exemplar of the Christian missionary, the Apostle Paul, had forged certain convictions about God's action through the church. Thoroughly aware of weaknesses and immaturity in the church, he nevertheless labored on loyally because he discerned a greater power at work. The paradox which Paul observed in the primitive church is visible in recent church history: the treasure is entrusted to earthen vessels. One must be seen in relation to the other.

Schlabach carries his study of Mennonite missions to 1944. Several reasons justify the decision to stop at that point. The period up to World War II represents a time of gradual growth. World War II was a watershed and the fifteen years immediately following unleashed a flood tide of activity. It soon became apparent that the abundant primary documentation for the years 1863-1944 deserved more complete treatment than would be possible if the study were extended to include the years since 1944. Finally, the advisory committee deemed it prudent to leave the writing of the history of the post World War II era to a future committee. We believe it will be a better history for having had the benefit of more perspective than any historian—regardless of his competence—can bring to events that happened only yesterday.

The story of the first stirrings and gradual emergence of missionary action among Mennonites is intimately bound up with a renewal movement that swept through the Mennonite community toward the end of the last century. Revivalism brought a fresh dynamic and reminded Mennonites of the gospel treasure. Missions became a major means to release this new dynamic. This set in motion a chain of developments, including the formation of boards, committees, schools, and conferences. Even a casual reading of the events of the period reveals how complex and multifaceted the movement was.

A major focal point for Mennonites was the question of identity. Identity always becomes a question when context is changing and new challenges arise. For several hundred years Mennonites had had a strong tradition. Both revivalism and a growing desire to accommodate to the larger culture undercut the tradition. Revivalism introduced new theological emphases and patterns of church life, some of which ran counter to Mennonite traditional understandings. Unfortunately this was as true for the basics of Mennonite theology as for secondary issues. Indeed, as Schlabach has emphasized, the very meaning of the Christian gospel itself was at issue.

Many Mennonites found it difficult to listen with discernment to voices coming from other quarters. Some were inclined to accept at face value what these Christian leaders said. They did not raise the questions their sixteenth-century forefathers had put to the Protestant and Roman Catholic churches. Men as dissimilar as Reinhold Niebuhr and Donald McGavran have told Mennonites patronizingly that the larger Christian cause benefits from the presence of minority groups who practice an ethic of nonresistance even though it is socially and politically irresponsible. Schlabach's study shows what unfortunate results such influences have produced for the integrity of Mennonite identity and witness.

To remain a committed minority with a prophetic message demands more than a strategy of accommodation—either to dominant social values or to another theological tradition. It involves living in constant tension. The period 1863-1944 was a time of many tensions for Mennonites, but they were not always tensions of the right sort. These were often the tensions caused by the demoralization of disintegration rather than the tensions of missionary responsibility in the world and dialogue with other traditions.

Affirming one's identity does not have to lead to isolation from other Christians. Mennonites have not hesitated to borrow and baptize methods and strategies first developed and used by other groups. Problems arise, however, when this happens thoughtlessly, when people do not ask whether the method is consistent with biblical mission or is merely a reflection of the prevailing culture. Surely this is true in the case of racism. It is unfortunate that Mennonites, along with many other Christians, did not listen much sooner to missionary statesmen such as J. H. Oldham and Robert E. Speer who more than fifty years ago were calling on both sending church and missionaries to face racism and deal with it. A mature identity is not based on secondhand assumptions and strategies. It is free to interact, question, and respond out of deeply held convictions which can be shared respectfully with others.

An important lesson which most churches still have to learn is the extent to which mission is an agent of change. At first glance that statement may seem puzzling. The whole point of the Christian message is to change men and women. An earlier generation of missionary leaders went much farther and insisted that the missionary's task was also to remake entire cultures to conform to Christian standards. Few missionaries today—although their species is not entirely extinct—are sufficiently self-assured about Western civilization that they want to make it normative for the rest of the world. But the fact remains: we have been self-centered and have assumed a one-way, outward flow of influence. Change, we have thought, is what happens out there.

But really, change has been a two-way movement. Mission has challenged some of the provincialism of the sending church. Mission has disabused missionaries of cheap solutions to ancient problems. Mission has dignified other cultures and peoples and thereby forced the sending church to see itself in a new light. The process of conversion is far from finished, but it is flowing two ways. In the act of sharing the message, the message-bearer is caught up in the process of transformation. Together missioner and missionized are incorporated into the new creation.

Granted that the treasure is entrusted to earthen vessels. Granted that these eight decades in the nineteenth and twentieth centuries brought momentous changes. What happened to the Mennonite tradition? Did anything uniquely Mennonite remain by the time World War

II arrived? Schlabach carefully traces the sore testing the tradition underwent. The Fundamentalist formula tempted many, but at a crucial point Fundamentalism did not fit. Fundamentalism perpetuated evangelicalism's weak doctrine of the church. Even without a sophisticated theology, Mennonites knew by experience what the church-as-community ought to be. At the same time, the mainline churches' activism and social concern resonated with Mennonite convictions about ethics. Here too the match was not perfect. Mennonites could not accept the increasing "horizontalism" of Protestantism. The result was that the Mennonite tradition did survive—albeit chastened and modified.

If a study of this kind is to have any value beyond that of satisfying a historian's curiosity, it must help the heirs to the Mennonite tradition understand more clearly the ways of God with His people so that they can follow Him in greater missionary obedience. May it be so!

Wilbert R. Shenk
Elkhart, Indiana

AUTHOR'S PREFACE

In the final decades of the nineteenth century, Mennonites in North America joined the modern missionary movement. Those were decisive times in the Mennonite Church, for its people were catching a worldwide vision and in many other ways borrowing heavily from evangelical Protestantism. This book tells a story that began in those days and continued until another decisive time, World War II. World War II made vast changes in the world into which to carry gospel, and for Mennonite Church people the changes were probably greater than for most Christians. For as matters turned out, the war and extensive postwar relief work pulled quite a few able young Mennonites out of secure, parochial communities and sent them abroad to become involved around the world as few North American Mennonites up to then had been.

Moreover, during the Second World War the Mennonite Church selected a new kind of leader for its mission effort. From 1921 to 1944 the chief executive officer of its general mission board, the Mennonite Board of Missions and Charities, had been Sanford C. Yoder. While an able mission leader, Yoder had been first of all a college president through most of those years, serving the mission cause only part time and without salary. Now, in 1944, the board appointed Joseph (J. D.) Graber, a man who was much more dynamic than Yoder in style and above all a professional in the field of mission, with full training at Princeton University and two decades of missionary experience in India. As befitted a professional, Graber was allowed to devote full time to his post as his church's top mission leader, and he received a salary. Such changes brought an end to the first era of Mennonite Church mission, and to the story this book tells.

Much of the book is not only about mission but about developments in the Mennonite Church more generally. As Mennonite Church people shaped their early missions, they did so by no means entirely in response to conditions and needs and voices they encountered on their fields, but very often in response mainly to changes and new assumptions in the church at home. Some of those homeside changes were "theological," having to do with what Mennonites were beginning to believe about salvation and similar questions. Other changes were more "sociological," reflecting who the people of the Mennonite Church were as a subgroup reacting to currents in the North American nations in which they lived. Theological and sociological changes intertwined, until they were almost indistinguishable. Out of that intertwining came a tangle of beliefs, aspirations, strategies, and perceptions about the missionary task. That tangle was what Mennonite Church people took with them as they went, or as they sent, into mission. And so the mission story was not only, perhaps not even primarily, the story of what took place on the field, but largely the story of the Mennonite Church itself.

Some readers will want the story to be heroic, full of giants walking from land to land. Or if they perceive that the vessels God uses are but human, they will still want the story to tell of the Holy Spirit at work to bring to fullness the plan of God in history. Others, surely, will want the opposite: tales, perhaps, of missionaries as villains, robbing hitherto unspoiled primitives of their innocence. Or if they do not want the missionaries portrayed as personally villainous, they may yet want missionaries to appear as pawns of an arrogant, imperialistic, White Western culture that has constantly found new ways to impose not only its armies and governors and trade but even its belief systems on less powerful peoples. Still others, no doubt, will want the story to promote one concept of mission and to put all others down.

I have not set out to produce any of those stories. Yet unabashedly I have come to my task with certain commitments. I am a Christian believer, and by choice a member of the Mennonite Church. Being such, I believe that Jesus offered the Gospel to be communicated, that His followers should be about the task, and that those of His people who bear the label "Mennonite" might even have a particular mission. And I assume that religious conviction and motivation are, or at least can be, real. Whatever forces I may find at work in history, I doubt that economics, sociology, psychology, or other expressions of modern scientism can fully explain religious people's behavior.

On the other hand, as the reader will soon see, I have not particularly intended to be a spokesman for the missionary cause. I have been trained, after all, to be a professional historian, and so I try to recognize cultural and other forces that press upon a people such as Mennonites. I want to be analytical, and I hold at arm's length the claims and slogans of people (even apparently sincere claims and slogans, even of religious people). Professionalism has its snares. Yet I assume that applying whatever skills I have learned of the historian's craft is the best way for me to serve the cause of truth—whether of historical truth, or possibly of some further truth about how Jesus' people do or do not communicate gospel.

Author's Preface

One judgment that I consider to be historical truth is that the pre-World War II missioners of the Mennonite Church were on the whole quite able people, often the cream of their communities' talent. They were remarkably careful, honest, and competent in practical matters. In commitment and motive they were apparently about as sincere as humans can be. By any but the most absolute standards they were neither devious nor ruthless in the pursuit of their goals. And far more than suggested by stereotypes that circulate among some otherwise clever people, they were sensitive toward the peoples to whom they went and toward the problems of cross-cultural contact and communication. On that last score they seem to have been well ahead of most Mennonite Church people in North America, and probably of most North Americans.

Perhaps my appreciation for those Mennonite Church missioners will not always seem very evident. Some missionaries, ex-missionaries, and other readers may well find, with good reason, that in my attempt to be analytical I have often judged too harshly. Yet I believe that those who read carefully will sense that I have seldom needed to cast any doubt on the character or ability of the missionaries themselves. My reservations have been about the assumptions underlying the mission *movement*. I have raised questions, but mainly the questions call for examination of what Mennonites borrowed from the larger Protestant movement. And it was the whole Mennonite Church, not only her missionaries, who was doing the borrowing.

The questions have a positive point, even if they sometimes come in negative guise. With my commitments, I have worked generally from what may be termed the "Anabaptist vision" school's understandings of gospel, understandings that some leading Mennonite thinkers were more or less clarifying at just about the time this book's story ended. Further, I have proceeded from the idea that Jesus shaped His Gospel from the full-orbed vision of human well-being that runs through the Bible as *shalom*. The deeper I delved into this study and into missionary-movement assumptions, the more I became convinced that the modern missionary movement has not very effectively communicated Jesus' full vision. Mennonites had long spoken fondly of a "gospel of peace," and in retrospect their idea seems to have at least suggested *shalom*. So I became ever more convinced that mission-minded Mennonites might have communicated more of Jesus' message if instead of borrowing wholesale from Anglo-American Protestantism they had worked more consciously from some of their own long-held understandings, especially their peace emphasis. That idea became the organizing one, the central thesis, of the book. Its point is the positive one of gospel of peace and *shalom*.

I offer that thesis for thought and reflection, not as any claim of having divined God's plan in history. As a person of faith I do have convictions about God's historic ways, one of which is that if Jesus is Lord those who proclaim gospel should do so consistently with His examples of servanthood and pacifism. Despite my questions about the modern missionary movement (let no one misunderstand) I even suppose that God, working as He always must through human imperfection, was indeed at work in that movement and in the Mennonite Church's version of it. Yet I would not wish to claim too much for either the conviction or the supposition. The fact is, the historian's methods do not include any way of testing which occurrences have been the will of God or the work of His Spirit.

The book is not, of course, an effort of the author alone. Goshen College allowed me to use a sabbatical trimester to finish it, and even more, the Mennonite Board of Missions at Elkhart, Indiana (formerly the Mennonite Board of Missions and Charities, often mentioned in this book) underwrote my time for a year of research and paid various other research and writing costs, including wages of student assistants. In addition, for one year the board hired John S. Miller, then a graduate student and now on the staff of Washburn University at Topeka, Kansas, to conduct a closely related project very helpful to this study. That project was to interview numerous people connected with the mission activity of the Mennonite Church in decades past, and to record their remarks. Later it also financed him for another summer to do the statistical research represented in chapters 8 and 9. From an author's point of view, the relationship with the Board of Missions has been a model one. Never did board officials try in any way to turn the study into something designed to put their own institution and its people in an especially favorable light; indeed, quite the opposite, from the beginning they asked not for a house history but for a reflective work. Yet Ernest Bennett, the board's executive secretary, did offer wise suggestions from time to time. And Wilbert Shenk, its overseas missions secretary, has been supremely helpful, being my chief liaison with the board and a mission-history scholar in his own right.

As part of that help, Shenk organized and chaired an advisory group made up of J. C. Wenger, Melvin Gingerich (until his death in 1975), John S. Oyer, and John A. Lapp. In occasional meetings and

Author's Preface

between times, these persons helped clarify what questions I ought to pursue, they read chapters as I wrote them and gave me very useful criticism and suggestions, and even if now and then they differed mildly with me they were always encouraging and constructive. I hope that my responses have already convinced these able friends and fellow-historians of my warm appreciation for their role. Equally appreciated have been the aid and suggestions from key archivists and librarians, particularly those of two research centers on the Goshen College campus—Leonard Gross, Sharon Klingelsmith, and Rachel Yoder of the Mennonite Church Archives, and Nelson Springer and Lena Lehman of the Mennonite Historical Library. Their help was of a different kind, of course, but probably even more crucial.

And then there were those student assistants who researched certain sources, checked out obscure facts, compiled footnotes, and brought me up short when they caught me being inaccurate. Ah, those student assistants!—Rich Kremer, John Bauman, Steve Reschly, Steve Denlinger, Mark Ramseyer, and Dan Hertzler. If only they could have caught *all* my errors! But that would have been humanly impossible and anyone familiar with Goshen College students in the 1970s knows that in them and in John S. Miller I had, by good fortune, the benefit of some of the very "best and the brightest." To work with them has been a great pleasure. Their caliber is such that they often seemed to be not so much students and assistants as junior colleagues.

A few words about code phrases, capitalization, and the like. This book deals with the mission story not of all Mennonites in North America, but only with that of one branch—called herein "the Mennonite Church" (with upper-case C), but often designated by others as "the Mennonite Church (MC)" or "the (Old) Mennonite Church." Those who find these codes mysterious should consult notes 16 and 34 of chapter 1. On another matter, I did not capitalize words such as "bishop" or "secretary" even when they appear before a person's name as if to be titles. That is not for want of knowing the rules, but because, however much deference Mennonites might have accorded their authorities, especially their bishops, I am convinced that they themselves meant to use such words only as descriptions, not as formal titles to ascribe status. Even more confusing might be my seeming inconsistence in sometimes using upper case, and sometimes lower, on the word "gospel." My point is that there were various "gospels" but, I assume, one "Gospel." I have meant, whether or not I succeeded, to use upper case when referring to Jesus' Gospel, and lower case when the subject is some human version, as of course all gospels actually transmitted have been. The exception to that rule is upper case in the title "Social Gospel." When referring to the historic theological and religious movement that flourished about seventy-five years ago, one capitalizes just as one capitalizes the label of another movement, Fundamentalism.

I only wish that the reader might find no confusions in the book greater than those of labels and capitalization.

Theron F. Schlabach
Goshen, Indiana
January 28, 1978

1
NEW DRUMBEATS

In 1631 a twenty-seven-year-old English Puritan, educated in one of England's best universities, migrated to Massachusetts and soon began to preach to Red "Indians." Fellow-Englishmen who were unable to appreciate people of another culture scoffed at the idea of evangelizing "savages," and the new missionary himself sometimes referred to the Reds as "dregs of mankinde." Yet John Eliot took the "Indians" gifts, learned their language, translated the scriptures, and taught them White people's ways of reading, writing, medicine, fence-building, town-living, law-making, and government.[1] When Eliot died in 1690, a Protestant mission movement was under way.

On August 21, 1732, a young count in Germany rose before dawn and gave two men a send-off from his estate to begin a trip to the island of St. Thomas, in the Caribbean. The nobleman, Nicholaus Ludwig von Zinzendorf, was leader of the "Unitas Fratrum" (seed of today's Moravian Church), a pietistic group that dated back to the fifteenth-century Czech reformer John Hus. As Pietists Zinzendorf's group emphasized conversion, experience, discipleship, love above knowledge, simplicity of life, and service—not so much *doing* service, their apologists would say, as *being* in a servant attitude. In 1727 they had experienced an outpouring that members could describe only as another Pentecost. Thereupon they had begun to speak more and more of sending out missionaries, and had turned to St. Thomas because of contact with a Black slave from there. That predawn departure for St. Thomas was only a beginning. By 1760 when Zinzendorf died, 266 Moravian missionaries had gone out to various places.[2] Another strong mission tradition was under way.

By 1750 quite a few Protestants in Great Britain and her colonies were undergoing a religious awakening. Though the movement was broader than Methodism, the Methodist founders, John and Charles Wesley, represented its epitome. Born in 1703 and 1707 into an intensely religious and mission-minded family, by 1738 these two brothers had led a religious movement among university students, served briefly as missionaries in the North American colony of Georgia under the Anglicans' Society for the Propagation of the Gospel in Foreign Parts (formed 1701), and come into intimate contact with the Moravians.[3]

Early in 1738 the Wesleys underwent new, Pietist-style religious conversions. Soon they had under way across the British Isles an active program of fervent preaching and music, distributing religious literature, and forming classes and cell-sized "bands" and "societies" that profoundly changed British church life, especially among the middle and lower classes. By 1769 they sent missionaries to North America and likewise touched off a lively, missionary-minded movement there.[4]

From the beginning John Wesley advocated social service as well as personal religious experience.[5] Soon evangelical-minded Britons were spawning a variety of good works organizations: a Sunday School Society, schools for various of the underprivileged, a prison reform society, a colony in Africa for freed Black slaves, antislavery organizations, a Baptist Missionary Society in 1792, an interdenominational (but later Congregational) London Missionary Society in 1795, the Religious Tract Society in 1799, the (Anglican) Church Missionary Society the same year, the British and Foreign Bible Society in 1804, and Methodist missionary organizations in 1790, 1813, and 1817-1818.

In North America, also, similar agencies appeared, most notably the American Board of Commissioners for Foreign Missions, formed by a group of New England Calvinists in 1810. An American Bible Society followed in 1816, an American Tract Society in 1825, and soon a plethora of evangelically dominated good works and reform organizations.[6] Activist Protestant piety was expanding and reaching across the seas.

Behind that expansive piety was the prestige of Great Britain, the mightiest imperial nation of the nineteenth century. In May 1792 one

William Carey preached a stirring sermon at Nottingham, England. Carey was a shoe cobbler and Baptist chapel-pastor who as a lad had loved to read about men of adventure, from Columbus to Captain Cook. Now he inspired listeners with the thrilling advice to: "Expect great things from God. Attempt great things for God." Carey followed his sermon with a landmark book, and English Baptists shortly organized a society "for Propagating the Gospel Amongst the Heathen." The society, soon renamed the Baptist Missionary Society, sent Carey to India along with his family and, before long, two more missionaries. Within a few years after he arrived in 1793, Carey typified very well what the Protestant missionary movement would become in the nineteenth century. He had plunged into a study of Hindu thought and culture, and translated Christian scriptures into several of India's languages. Although he had gone as a representative of a denomination, by 1810 he proposed a grand interdenominational missionary conference. He lived by a vision that was global, sweeping, bold.[7]

Carey moved toward that vision even though he was not from the elite of British society but from its artisans and craftsmen. Indeed, an Anglican clergyman, one Sydney Smith, once dismissed him and his fellows as nothing more than "delirious mechanics" who had been bitten by "the nasty vermin of Methodism." Yet even in his social origins Carey was quite typical of nineteenth-century missionaries who followed him. Most of those were people who were looking for new opportunities to be useful and to make religion practical. Few had university degrees or titles. But they were very sure that their cultural ways were superior, at least to those of the "lower orders" of poor at home and the heathen abroad. They were nothing if not culturally self-confident.[8]

The motives of those who made up the nineteenth-century missionary movement were mixed. Missionary outreach went hand in hand with European, and especially British, imperialism. To be sure, missionaries and the British government were uneasy with each other at first. Many officials agreed with Smith who further charged that these "consecrated cobblers" would "deliberately ... expose our whole Eastern empire to destruction for the sake of converting half-a-dozen Brahmins." But missionaries replied that their work was good for the empire and cheaper than war for pacifying natives.[9]

With political went commercial imperialism, and missionaries often approved. In 1857 a most famous one, David Livingstone, declared quite unabashedly, "I go back to Africa to try to make an open path for commerce and Christianity."[10] Cultural imperialism certainly existed also as a mission motive, for many missionaries assumed, as Eliot had, that to Christianize was to teach European and White North American ways. And another motive surely was romanticism, as would-be missionaries suddenly heard calls to far-off continents, distant sea islands, and exotic peoples.[11]

Some motives, however, had more to do with genuine, biblical religion: humanitarianism, as in campaigns against slavery and other oppressive evils; asceticism, sacrificing oneself and achieving saintliness; uneasiness and indebtedness for wrongs White people were perpetrating against others; doing one's duty and bringing honor to God, especially as most missionaries were to some degree Calvinist; and, simply, love and compassion. Love and compassion were apt to shade off into condescending attitudes of uplifting one's inferiors. Yet surely nineteenth-century missionaries often expressed genuine love for Christ and concern for both the temporal and the eternal welfare of fellow humans.[12]

Finally, there were other motives: planting churches (though emphasis on church sometimes got lost in preoccupation with individual soul-saving); eschatology, from missionaries' conviction that the reign of Jesus and His kingdom were at hand; and, though seemingly less often expressed, obedience to Christ's Great Commission to go forth and teach and baptize all nations. Such were the classic motives of the modern missionary movement.[13]

Despite Smith and any other hecklers, Carey's global vision caught on. By the middle of the nineteenth century, names such as Robert Moffat and David Livingstone excited and inspired generation after generation of schoolboys—and schoolgirls, for women were very diligent in mission. By century's end college and university campuses in Britain and North America were scenes of a lively Student Volunteer Movement, with the ringing slogan—full of bombast, great faith, or both—"Evangelization of the World in This Generation!" So strong did the movement become that by 1900 the classic issues surrounding missions had emerged: What place, for instance, did education have in mission? Should money go instead to more direct forms of evangelism? Did one have to educate in English in order to dislodge heathen habits of thought? How and when might new churches become indigenous to their own peoples? And so forth.[14]

By mid-nineteenth century, in fact, Henry Venn and Rufus Anderson, one the secretary of the Church Missionary Society and the other of the American Board of Commissioners, had developed what became the classic ideals for emerging churches: self-support, self-government, and self-propagation. Mission advocates at home might teach young children to look down on the heathen, as in a British Sunday school poem of about 1845:

> The heathen are foolish and brutish and blind,
> They are mortals in body, but demons in mind.
> Yet their souls we must seek though their sins be abhorred,
> For our labour shall not be in vain in the Lord.

Yet at least a few of the best missionary thinkers from Carey's day forth studied foreign cultures appreciatively and planted the seeds of a less self-centered approach to cultural questions.[15]

By century's end the missionary movement had thus matured, to the point in fact of being a matter for self-conscious study. But not, in North America, for the people of the Mennonite Church.[16] For most of the century the whole ambitious movement, to say nothing of careful study of what it was about, passed the Mennonite Church by.

* * *

Until the late nineteenth century, one hundred years after Carey's sermon, Mennonites in North America were still very much a people apart—not only from the modern missionary movement but from evangelical Protestantism itself. Mennonites had a history of their own. Their origin had not been in the mainline Protestant Reformation. Rather their history began among a few "Swiss Brethren" who broke with Reformer Ulrich Zwingli in 1525, and among people around their namesake Menno Simons, who led a parallel movement in northern Germany and the Low Countries beginning about 1530.

Because they baptized believers whose previous baptisms as infants they considered of no account, people such as the Swiss Brethren and Menno had gotten labeled "Anabaptists" (Rebaptizers). They rejected not only infant baptism but also what infant baptism implied: that the church embraced entire populations without much regard to personal commitment, and consequently that church and state were logically to be in union. For these and other deviations both Catholics and mainline Protestants considered them extremists and treated them as outlaws. Whether or not the particular Anabaptists whom Mennonites count as forebears were really extreme is debatable, for often they had to bear the reputation of other Anabaptists who were much more spiritualist or chiliastic than they, or even bloody and violent. Whatever the case, already in the sixteenth century the Swiss Brethren and those around Menno found themselves pushed out of the Protestant mainstream, or standing apart from it voluntarily.[17]

Logically, Anabaptist origins should have made North American Mennonites more, not less, missionary than their Protestant neighbors. In the sixteenth century Martin Luther, John Calvin, and other Reformers had hardly more than the germ of the idea of a church active in mission,[18] while Anabaptists swarmed over Europe with their message.

On many central doctrines—such as authority of Scripture, salvation by faith, the Trinity—Anabaptists scarcely differed with the Reformers. On other points, often with missionary implications, they did:

> *Baptism only of believers*, upon a voluntary confession of faith. This called for personal conviction, which in turn motivated preaching to unbelievers.
>
> *Concept of the Church*: voluntary, made up only of clearly committed believers; pure and disciplined in its inner life; organizationally distinct from government, not depending on force to sustain it; aiming to be the visible people of God, openly living as such, rather than emphasizing the mystical and the invisible. Some interpreters have seen in the understandings of church the essence of Anabaptism.[19] In any case, committed and disciplined members made excellent missionaries. Disconnection from government went along with a broader disconnection from the medieval *corpus christianum* notion of total union of Christianity and culture. That of course had the potential of releasing missionaries from the heavy weight of confusing gospel with European culture.[20] Seeing the church as God's people in new community offered the seeker hope of salvation in one's immediate human relationships as well as in a future world.
>
> *The ethic of love, made specific in various ways*. The Swiss Brethren, those around Menno, and like-minded Anabaptists refused to go to war, to participate in the police function, and to hold offices involving use of government's coercive power. Their ethic fostered extensive mutual aid and in Moravia even communalism, as well as self-conscious good deeds reaching beyond the inner group. In mission terms, conversion had to be by word and deed, not by force.
>
> *Serious acceptance of the Great Commission*. The command to be missionary does not appear formally in Anabaptist confessions of faith; but in Anabaptist defenses before inquisitors' courts no scriptural passage appeared more frequently. Often the immediate purpose was to support adult baptism, with the Great Commission

cited to prove that teaching was to *precede* the baptismal rite. On other occasions Anabaptists quoted the command to prove that they were not irresponsible when they left occupation and family to spread their message. However cited, the Great Commission was very much a part of Anabaptists' language—in contrast to that of the Reformers who largely ignored it, or applied it only to the apostolic age or office, or used its references to "all nations" to defend *corpus christianum* and infant baptism.[21] A 1527 meeting of some sixty Anabaptist leaders at Augsburg, Germany, sent out missioners in twos and threes and divided Europe into districts for evangelization. This produced what was apparently the first plan in the Reformation era for carrying out the Great Commission.[22]

In addition to obvious differences from Reformers' doctrines, there were more subtle ones. For instance, Anabaptists believed with Reformers in the need for regeneration by grace through faith, yet came with a different emphasis. Reformers spoke more of the ongoing sin and depravity of humans. Their movements, therefore, turned more and more around theologies of how one escaped not so much sin itself as the guilt and condemnation that sin brought. Anabaptists connected regeneration more with the subsequent new life in Christ—"life" in not a mystical but a here-and-now, day-to-day sense. Where Reformers looked mostly to the sin that went before, Anabaptists looked mostly to the new creature whom regeneration created. The Reformers asked, "How may a sinner be saved?" The Anabaptists asked, "How do saints walk in Christ's resurrection?"[23]

This in turn produced a difference in style, with Anabaptists somewhat contemptuous of Reformers' abstractions about theology.[24] Rather than formulas of belief, they emphasized the fruits. They lived "on the resurrection side of the cross" and therefore assumed that a holy life was possible and indeed expected of true Christians. Not that they expected some unreal world where evil no longer did its work. In contrast to later Pietism, Anabaptists emphasized not sweet repose in Jesus so much as the harshness and suffering that came with following Him (a subject on which they rapidly accumulated experience).

Thus the Mennonites' forebears strongly taught a very practical kind of yieldedness and discipleship (*Gelassenheit* and *Nachfolge* were their much-used German words). Indeed Harold S. Bender, chief twentieth-century interpreter of Anabaptism, thought the discipleship concept was the essence of the Anabaptist movement.[25] When Anabaptists went forth as missioners, they did not go primarily to spread a body of abstract belief, and certainly not to impose faith by political means and coercion. Rather, they went forth with an invitation to a new kind of living in a new kind of group: as serious, suffering disciples in God's visible new community.

Go forth they did. Church historian Roland Bainton has speculated that Anabaptists' missionary zeal might have made their faith the dominant one of Germany had not authorities impeded them with the sword. Not every Anabaptist went forth, of course, but enough did to spread the faith very rapidly at first. Most Anabaptist witness-bearers were not specially designated persons, and certainly not sent by mission societies semi-separate from the church. To be sure, there was that 1527 meeting of leaders that sent missioners in twos and threes throughout Europe (eventually known as the "Martyrs' Synod" because before many years almost all of the participants were executed). In Moravia, where a degree of tolerance allowed Anabaptist communities to become more stable, organized sending of missionaries emerged in the 1530s and lasted until about 1600, when war badly disrupted community life.[26] Sometimes the sending language grew expansive. Already in 1526 Swiss Anabaptists may have thought of taking their message to Red people in America, but the meaning of that reference is uncertain.[27] Later a missionary from Moravia spoke of the "primary and greatest task" of the church as being to bring God's "counsel to the unknowing nations."[28] His language seemed to imply going beyond Europe.

In practice, however, all Anabaptist activities were in European countries (by Anabaptist lights, most Europeans were as pagan as anyone). Throughout the Continent not only commissioned elders but also laymen—and, significantly, women—went forth to witness in the natural course of living the disciple life. "We preach as much as possible," explained Menno, "both by day and by night, in houses and in fields, in forests and in wastes, hither and yon, at home or abroad, in prisons and dungeons, on the scaffold and on the wheel, before lords and princes, through mouth and pen, by possessions and blood, with life and death."[29]

But Mennonites did not continue to be Anabaptist-style missioners. A confession of faith that some Mennonites at Dordrecht in Holland formulated in 1632, and that Mennonites in many places including North America affirmed over and over thereafter, spoke of God having foreordained Jesus for the "reconciliation," "comfort," "redemption," and "salvation" of the whole human race. But on the whole that influential statement did not emphasize Christians' responsibility to take the message forth, while it spoke very much of their keeping themselves free from sin.[30] Within a century after the Swiss Brethren and Menno, the Mennonite story had changed to one of looking mainly inward, to one's own group. And that is how it continued.

Partly, no doubt, the loss of missionary zeal and the inward turning reflected a typical problem of groups who try to transmit first-generation zeal to later generations. Also, Mennonites were responding to constant discrimination and persecution, banishment, and migration. Those in Switzerland and South Germany, ancestors of most Mennonites in nineteenth-century America, retreated to various rural areas and became people of the soil. Near the end of the seventeenth century some began to move to North America. From 1707 to 1756 perhaps three to five thousand went, settling in Pennsylvania. In the nineteenth century more emigrated, often to Ohio, Indiana, Illinois, and Ontario. Mennonites had become part of North America's westward migration.

In eighteenth century Europe Pietists influenced Mennonites and reinforced certain attitudes—especially biblicism, imitation of the New Testament church, and a sense of being a separated, persecuted people.[31] An even stronger influence was a major Mennonite book, the *Martyrs Mirror*. First published in 1660 to recount the stories of some eight hundred nonresistant Anabaptists who had gone victoriously to the death for the faith, the book went through various translations and printings in Europe and in North America throughout the generations.[32] Its impact upon the Mennonite mind-set was immeasurable.

Imperfectly under these influences, Mennonites in North America retained some crucial elements of their earlier church life: conviction that church and world served different masters, discipline within a peoplehood, much sharing, and the ethic of nonresistant love. They kept alive the ideas of practical discipleship and of literal faithfulness to Jesus, to His ethical teachings, and to the scriptures.

But only very imperfectly. Persecutions, migrations, and time took their toll of faithfulness. Gradually almost all concern for sharing the message of God's work among His people eroded away. Occasionally Mennonites did speak out, for instance with peace testimony in time of war. But often they distorted the quest for faithfulness into legalism and schism. Already in Europe they had quarreled over wigs, shoe buckles, and the like. In 1693 in Switzerland, South Germany, and Alsace a deep rift resulted in the formation of the Amish group—one of many unfortunate schisms to come.

Clustering, usually in agrarian settings, Mennonites and Amish

Mennonites unconsciously perverted the vision of transformed community more or less into ethnic enclaves. Pietism's emphasis on sweet retreat from outer world to inner union with Christ surely reinforced the process, although just as surely there had been separatist tendencies inherent in Anabaptism from 1525 onward.[33] In North America persistent use of German language and dialects generation after generation put still more bricks in the separating wall. By mid-nineteenth century the mainstream of North America Mennonites and Amish Mennonites had long since lost virtually all will to call other people to faith and the faithful community across the dividing wall.[34]

* * *

By the third quarter of the nineteenth century a few Mennonites did have the missionary vision. In the 1820s Mennonites in Holland and in the Palatinate began to support Baptist mission work. In 1847 the Dutch, who had never gone far in the direction of separatism, transformed their wing of that effort into the first modern Mennonite missionary association. Soon they sent out the first Mennonite foreign missionary: a teacher to Java in 1851. Two decades later Mennonites in Russia began to help the Dutch mission with money and workers. Particularly zealous were the "Mennonite Brethren" in Russia, a group which had originated under strong Pietist and Baptist influences.[35]

About the same time, in North America also, a few Mennonites caught the vision. About 1821 an immigrant deacon in Lancaster County, Pennsylvania, named Martin Möllinger had relatives in the Palatinate send him what would have been, if translated into English, "9 copies of the *Magazine of the Evangelical Mission and Bible Society*."[36] But neither Möllinger nor other mainline Mennonites seem to have acted on such interest—at least not nearly as much as did some who later broke with the main Mennonite Church and Amish Mennonite fellowships in North America. By 1860 some of those groups and some recent immigrants joined with each other to create what would become the General Conference Mennonite Church. Eventually large numbers of "Russian" Mennonites also joined, after a historic migration out of the Czar's land beginning in 1873-1874. (Actually the "Russians" were thoroughly German in language and culture.)[37]

A very strong motive behind the General Conference coalition in 1860 was to organize for mission. Some who joined were already beginning to support Dutch Mennonite missions, in 1866 some began city mission efforts in Philadelphia, and in 1880 others began what became a vigorous program of evangelism, schools, and acculturation among Native American tribes in the U.S. West.[38] On the other hand, some in the coalition showed not only interest in mission but also a tendency in other ways to become more typically American. That was especially true of a number of congregations in eastern Pennsylvania who had parted with others of their faith in 1847 (sometimes considered the beginning date of the General Conference Mennonite Church) over questions such as proper dress and church organization. These Mennonites were rapidly becoming more like American Protestants, by raising the questions they raised, and by accepting, for instance, lodge membership, higher education, and interdenominationalism.[39]

The pioneer foreign missionary for all North American Mennonites went out from still another group. He was Eusebius Hershey, a member of the "Evangelical Mennonites"—revival-oriented congregations who left the main Mennonite body from 1849 to 1855 and eventually became part of the Mennonite Brethren in Christ, now the Missionary Church. A visionary, Hershey gazed long and hard at the larger missionary movement's romantic specter of taking gospel to "poor naked heathen." Not until he was sixty-eight did he realize his dream of going, and then he had to go independently because his church refused to commission so old a man. But he went, sailing to Africa in 1890. Within six months he died there.[40]

More auspiciously, in the same year two Mennonite Brethren missionaries went to India under Baptist sponsorship and by 1899 were allowed to take over a district as a field for their own church. Meantime in the 1890s several Mennonites and Amish Mennonites also went overseas. J. R. Godshall of Bucks County, Pennsylvania, and Alice Yoder of Lititz, Pennsylvania, went to India under the Christian and Missionary Alliance. Sara Alice Troyer of Milford, Nebraska, proceeded to China under China Inland Mission.[41] Such beginnings apparently resulted less from anything within Mennonitism than from contact with the Protestant missionary movement.

On a different pattern, meanwhile, some others of the Mennonite and Amish Mennonite Churches reached out to neighbors at home. Ontario congregations, for instance, drew enough that in the latter half of the nineteenth century they even ordained a number of ministers from among those whom they attracted. Also, according to an oral tradition, about 1874 a western Pennsylvania Mennonite bishop named H. H. Blauch began preaching in the hills of western Maryland.[42] But the strongest outreach of that kind was by some in the Shenandoah

Valley of Virginia, who went to neighboring mountain people. And in contrast to individual Mennonites who went overseas with organized Protestant missions, the Virginians followed a pattern that grew more from the life of their own congregations.

To be sure, the Virginia Mennonites, in migrating from Pennsylvania into the Shenandoah Valley, had lost some of their separatism. Often lacking adequate church facilities, they occasionally cooperated with other denominations in sharing meetinghouses and in other ways. Some of their leaders became quite proficient in English. One of these, Joseph Funk, became a noted printer; and in a Mennonite confession of faith that he published in 1837, he included a missionary challenge. "The different denominations," he said, should "lay aside their disputes about external things of minor importance and unite together to promote the redemption of Christ, by the spread of His glorious Gospel and the extension of His Kingdom from shore to shore." Also, two leading nineteenth-century Virginia Mennonite bishops, Peter Burkholder and his son Martin, helped make the transition to English, preached occasionally in non-Mennonite churches, and taught the Great Commission.[43]

Martin Burkholder then went on to help begin a new mission work: preaching in the mountains of Virginia and what became West Virginia. The methods that he and fellow-ministers used were much like Methodist-style circuit riding. Yet they were also in keeping with Mennonites' inner life, and indeed were somewhat like Anabaptist evangelism.

In the years 1858 to 1860 Burkholder and bishop Samuel Coffman went occasionally by horseback to preach in mountainous Pendleton County. During the Civil War they apparently stopped their visits; but a layman known as "Potter John" Heatwole, fleeing as a conscientious objector to another mountain in the county, made friends who wanted Mennonites to come and preach. After the war ministerial visits resumed, and expanded as well into Randolph, Tucker, and Hardy counties. Contacts came naturally. Mountain people coming down into the valley for seasonal work asked that preachers come. Invitations came to conduct funerals. So it went. People met in homes, groves, and especially schoolhouses—humble surroundings, like many an earlier Anabaptist or Mennonite meeting. In 1885 Mennonites of Virginia, Maryland, and Pennsylvania helped one mountain group build a meetinghouse for its own and other denominations' use. By the 1880s in Hardy County the church ordained two men with non-ethnic-

Mennonite names to serve as minister and deacon.[44]

The sending Mennonites scarcely thought of all this as mission work: Missions to them meant city and foreign work, and of those they were still skeptical. In fact they resisted moves toward a more organized missionary-agency pattern. In 1883 Coffman began to call for a special home missionary fund, but the Virginia Mennonite Conference refused. When Coffman persisted, the conference decided that bishops should take the issue back to their people and ask congregations to devise ways for "carrying the gospel to other fields within reach of our ministers." The next year, 1892, the conference did establish the fund, but not until after 1900 did it resort to the standard missionary pattern of sending specialized, full-time workers. Finally, in 1919 it took the final step of creating a conference mission board, removing the work still a bit further from direct congregational initiative.[45]

For over half a century Virginia Mennonites had succeeded in carrying on natural, authentic mission among a humble, neighboring folk. Theirs was not a perfect model; they left too much of the work to traveling ministers and failed to challenge lay members sufficiently to communicate what life as God's transformed people could be. Yet ministers who went did so as agents of real congregations. There was little of the programming that has often made missions into something quite removed from the life of God's gathered people.

* * *

Most North American Mennonites and Amish Mennonites were far behind the Virginia congregations in missionary vision. Nevertheless, in the decades from 1860 to 1900, many of their congregations and communities experienced an exhilarating quickening of religious life. The quickening brought with it widespread concern for mission and raised questions of what patterns Mennonite missions might take.

In 1863 two Mennonite leaders, John M. Brenneman and John F. Funk, each published a pamphlet calling on Mennonite people to remember their anti-war convictions.[46] Brenneman, a bishop at Elida, Ohio, was very much a link between an older Mennonitism and a newer. With the old he retained a piety that constantly warned against "pride"—code word for whatever seemed to violate the spirit of a quiet, sober walk with Christ. With the new, he stemmed from a family well-equipped with English. He welcomed new patterns in church life. He constantly traveled to serve and encourage isolated members, and he won deep affection from self-styled "progressives." Funk, a younger man, had been reared Mennonite in eastern Pennsylvania, gotten a bit of advanced education, and in 1857 migrated to Chicago and a lumber business. There he had been converted in a Presbyterian revival, and joined the Young Men's Christian Association. He returned to the Mennonites in Pennsylvania for a time to receive baptism, church membership, and a wife, but then went again to Chicago to become active in city Sunday school work in the same circles with Dwight L. Moody, the soon-to-be-famous evangelist.[47]

In 1864 Funk made a momentous move: He began to publish a Mennonite church paper, the *Herald of Truth* (and the German *Herold der Wahrheit*). In 1867 he formed a "Mennonite Publishing Company" at Elkhart, Indiana, and moved there, close by a Mennonite community. The paper and the company were private ventures, but soon they functioned as quasi-official church agencies. Funk himself was ordained minister in 1865 and bishop in 1892, and for decades in the Mennonite Church and often among Amish Mennonites his was clearly the most powerful voice at conference meetings and the like, as well as in print. Informally he made Elkhart the center of the new quickening, with many younger leaders serving some time on his staff and thereby establishing contacts and reputations among congregations and district conferences. (Until 1898 Mennonite Church and Amish Mennonites had no general conference or other overall body to tie their districts and congregations together.) Funk's leadership lasted until about the turn of the century. By then younger leaders were chafing under it, and in 1902 the Indiana church took away his bishop responsibility for alleged highhandedness. In 1908 his paper merged into a fully official organ, the *Gospel Herald*.[48] Funk lived on until 1930, but his great influence had been from 1863 to the mid-1890s.

In 1863 also the first permanent Mennonite Sunday school began. As early as 1841 or perhaps 1831 Mennonites here and there had tried Sunday schools; but not until 1863, at West Liberty, Ohio, did one begin that established a continuous record of existence. From 1865 to 1875 three dozen such schools began. By 1890 most congregations west of the Alleghenies had them, and eastern ones often did or soon would.[49] In that year Mennonite Church people in Ontario held the first of their group's Sunday school conferences, modeling it on local or regional conferences in the larger, interdenominational Sunday school movement and among General Conference Mennonites. In 1892, 1893, and 1894 there were grand Sunday school conferences for all Mennonite Church and Amish Mennonite people. In fact, the 1892 and 1893 meetings were more than Sunday school gatherings: They were general rallies for all of a new generation's activism and "progressivism."[50] Sunday schools were centers of the quickening.

So also were revival meetings. Traditionally Mennonites had held to a "quiet in the land" kind of piety and had rejected revivalism. That rejection caused several schisms between 1775 and 1860, yet various conferences continued to forbid "protracted" (that is, series of) meetings. Mennonites had no equivalent mechanism for gathering their own youth into the church. Consequently, in 1872 Funk and bishop Brenneman's brother Daniel held a series in western Pennsylvania that had some earmarks of a revival campaign. Their revivalism did not take root. In 1874 the Indiana conference expelled Daniel Brenneman, partly for defending a revival in Ontario and baptizing converts there when the local bishop had refused. Funk quickly retreated until more propitious times and, in fact, was always cautious about revivalistic excesses. Genuine revivalism in the Mennonite Church began in 1881, at Bowne, Michigan, with John S. Coffman preaching.[51]

Though always deeply and loyally Mennonite, Coffman was another leader from a family quite in touch with non-Mennonites.[52] Sunday school opponents accused his father, none other than bishop Samuel Coffman of Virginia, of sending his children to Sunday school in "fashionable" Presbyterian and Methodist churches and then arguing that Mennonites must have their own schools to prevent such apostasy. The younger Coffman, after being ordained minister in 1875, helped preach to the West Virginians. After a bout of schoolteaching and farming, he moved to northern Indiana, where he became Funk's associate editor and a major contributor to Mennonite Sunday school and other materials. Until he died in 1899, probably no Mennonite preacher traveled more than he. Certainly none led so many youths and others into the fold.[53]

Coffman fit no revivalist stereotype. He preached in natural speech, not flamboyantly. With invitations to salvation he also taught Mennonite doctrine. When church authorities in traditional communities opposed him, especially in eastern Pennsylvania, he proceeded cautiously with a delicate sense of how to be a true brother in a peoplehood church. Warm and reconciling, he was effective.[54] By 1899 most Mennonite and Amish Mennonite congregations had accepted revival meetings, and a generation of their English-speaking sons and daughters had heard Coffman's preaching. Many of the youths had declared themselves Christ-followers and felt the pulse of active, occasionally even full-time, Christian service.

To adult literature, Sunday schools, and revival meetings, by century's end Mennonite Church people had also added Young People's Bible Meetings in 1881, periodicals for children and youth in 1876 and 1894, periodic Bible conferences about 1890, and a college in 1894. The tempo had quickened.

* * *

By 1900 also, Mennonite Church people had established an evangelizing board, several home missions, a children's home, an old people's home, a relief committee, a board of charitable homes, and a mission in India. With the greater activity had come a new interest in the Great Commission. It all began softly, the drumbeat of the quickening descending only quite slowly on the older, more somber piety.

Was anyone keeping himself unspotted from the world, and practicing the pure and undefiled religion as James had taught? bishop Brenneman asked a friend, Mennonite minister Peter Nissley of Lancaster County, Pennsylvania, early in 1865. "Dear Brother,..." he confided, "I sometimes am afraid that we Mennonites are too slack in seeking souls. Nearly all other denominations, and a good many of whom we do not hold to be truly orthodox, are busy in traveling through the whole known world, to make Prosalites, yea they are spending millions of Dollars, to spread the Gospel among the Heathens. And we who hold that we have yet the Doctrine of Christ and His apostles more pure than most others we will not even go abroad as we might do, among the civilized; nay many of our own church members are too much neglected, and how then comes this to be so?... Are we," Brenneman asked pointedly, "consistent with our profession? If our doctrine is more Evangelical than others, why shall we not make it known?"[55]

The obvious answer almost frightened the good bishop. "I do not mean to say," Brenneman quickly qualified, "that we Mennonites should start out now among the Gentiles." Even if Mennonites tried, they "could not speak to them in their tongue." Therefore the course to take, the bishop explained, was to become active in spreading the good news at home. Through that "the Lord might also bless us with talented and gifted men, who might go on still farther to distant lands, to spread the Gospel in its Purity." But the present generation was not ready. There were few like Nissley, Brenneman lamented, with whom he could even share such thoughts.[56]

Philip Moseman, son of a Lancaster County, Pennsylvania, Mennonite bishop who had immigrated from Germany, also was quite aware of how unready most Mennonites in North America were. Carefully avoiding the standard language of benevolence and mission, Moseman pointed out to *Herald of Truth* readers early in 1865 that Mennonites in Germany had been distributing "to the necessity of saints" and even further had invited other people to "the great marriage supper of the Lamb." Some American Mennonites were wealthy, Moseman reflected, and they might want to help the "dear brethren in Germany." It was after all the duty of all to labor at the work of the Lord. Moseman professed to know of some who were already giving to "aid the work of the Lord among the heathen," and they were doing it with the approval of their "dear ministers." Yet he was cautious. Any contributions, he was sure, should be "entirely voluntary." Would such giving offend any of the "ministers and brethren," he asked, "so long as brotherly love is still exercised toward them that have not this conviction?"[57]

Moseman's caution reflected Mennonites' intense commitment to move only as a body, never as unbridled individualists. It also, no doubt, reflected church politics. This being a question "of great importance," Funk agreed editorially, it should go "to the older and more experienced ministers and bishops for a just decision." But Brenneman, being a bishop, could be more bold. Certainly "it is right and the will of God that the gospel should be preached also to the heathen," Brenneman assured *Herald* readers in response to Moseman. The Great Commission commanded it. The Apostle Peter had shown that God is no respecter of persons. Christians should support the right kind of missionaries without worrying too much that someone might take offense.[58]

Less boldly Brenneman warned that it was true, some missionaries went only for personal gain. And then the bishop pointed to another danger: going with a gospel that was not Gospel. A Chinese emperor, he said, had complained that wherever Christians went " 'they make the ground white with the bones of men.' " Mennonites should take care and support only those who preached "the pure and true gospel of Jesus Christ and its non-resistant principles."[59]

Thus began the public discussion of mission, cautiously, the new blending into the old. For a decade and a half it moved slowly. *Herald* writers might use themes such as "Ye Must be Born Again" or "Let Us Be a Light to the World" but pass up the opportunity to present them as missionary texts, turning them instead into admonitions for the humble, quietly pious Mennonite style of life and appearance. Brenneman did not follow with articles similar to his response to Moseman. Instead he wrote various exhortations against pride, or calls for unity among the brethren, or treatises on subjects such as the nature of the soul.[60]

Funk printed missionary pieces from other religious papers or perhaps a verse from *The Sunday School Times*:

> How many sheep are straying
> Lost from the Savior's fold,
> Upon the Lonely Mountains?
> They shiver with the cold ....
> Say will you see to find them?
> From pleasant bowers of ease,
> Will you go forth determined
> To find the least of these?[61]

Yet the *Herald* gave an item about a Moody convert who had won 300 souls in Africa scarcely more play than, for instance, one about a fire on a steamship. The *Herald* probably gave it less coverage than one about a Mennonite brother getting his hand in a threshing machine.[62] Hardly a vigorous discussion of mission.

There was discussion, however. In 1869 "D." (Daniel Brenneman, before his fall from Mennonite grace?) pointed out that if brethren had missionary zeal, they would quarrel less among themselves. Instead they would call for "one united band of preachers, going forth in real earnestness proclaiming the tidings of salvation." About the same time Funk wrote at length about the duty to teach the church's "way of life, and truth, and holiness unto all men." The church, Funk declared, should "not only teach and instruct her own children or members, but all the world—all men, of all nations, tongues, colors, and conditions." To do that, the editor wrote in words that recalled Carey's, she needed "to use means," working systematically as Christ had when He sent out the seventy.[63]

Other *Herald* writers wanted to go beyond the Mennonite circle in benevolent work, as well as in evangelism. In 1872, for instance, they called for aid to victims of the great Chicago fire. Jesus' reference to the poor being always with us, wrote Jonathan K. Hartzler, a layman from Ohio, did not "refer *only* to the poor *among christians*."[64]

By 1880, as the fusion of old and new continued, the Great Commission and the idea of obeying it became more and more a part of

Mennonite piety. As early as 1866 what would become a favorite Mennonite formula appeared: Christ, a *Herald* writer pointed out in that year, had not only commanded us to teach and baptize throughout the world, but had also instructed us to teach *all things* that He had commanded—in other words, the peculiar doctrines of Mennonites. It became possible for writers to begin in the older tone of exhorting humility and faithfulness and then, as they moved to specifics, to call upon Mennonites to "labor in the vineyard of the Lord," help preach the gospel, and use any means or make any efforts to secure the salvation of souls.[65]

Or Funk might tie the mission command with the Mennonite concept of church. "We are to live in one another's society," he wrote in 1882, "so that we may ... be a help to each other, and ... glorify God together. This is what the Church of Christ is." But its purpose was not to keep God's teaching "to ourselves only. God designs all men to be saved" and His religion "to be made known and proclaimed everywhere."[66]

By one formula or another, in the 1860s and 1870s Great Commission language once again became part of Mennonite Church people's thought.

* * *

Practice, however, fell short of talk. In the Mennonite Church through most of the quickening period, "evangelism" and sometimes even "mission" connoted the sending of itinerant ministers to scattered church members, much more than it meant outreach to others.[67] In the 1860s and 1870s the process was extremely informal. Recognized leaders, almost always ordained and often bishops, made extended trips to outlying Mennonite communities or scattered settlers. They preached, held communion, perhaps baptized a few, brought news of others in the peoplehood, and tried very much to reinforce Mennonite ways of believing and living. This they did in the face of intense influence from aggressive revivalism and preaching of nonpacifist and, to Mennonite thought, "popular" or "fashionable" denominations.

Such ministers went mainly on their own initiative. Now and then a district church conference discussed the need and advised that someone take up the work. Certainly, pleas from the scattered ones themselves or from *Herald* writers were frequent enough. No doubt an upcoming leader, Menno (M. S.) Steiner, was quite correct when he observed in 1890 that these "few earnest brethren" had been practically driven to the work, faced as they were with churches closing in many places and with loss of young people where churches met only once or twice a month without any really "apostolic" preaching or methods.[68] In any case, the traveling ministers went on their own time and often at their own expense.[69] For except the deacons' role of collecting for Mennonites and some others in need, Mennonites had no regular offerings or other system for raising and disbursing money.

Eventually, however, the ideas of system and "means" began to take root. Mennonites of the 1860s and 1870s were unsure about what tasks in God's vineyard laymen could properly do, and they were sure, as Menno had insisted, that salaries for ministers would quickly attract a swarm of degenerate "hirelings." But increasingly they suggested that laymen should certainly help with the traveling ministers' *expenses*. In 1881 the Missouri-Iowa Conference resolved officially that since "missionary work is a matter of great importance, and demands the immediate attention of the church," all members should feel the duty to help. Upon learning of a place with "especial need of the preaching of the gospel," they should "send ministers upon the means contributed for that purpose." To get such contributions, the conference recommended, each congregation should "have a treasury into which each member contribute [sic] on the first day of the week as the Lord has prospered him."[70]

Nor was the Missouri-Iowa Conference alone in moving toward providing more "means" for the ministers' work. In 1880 Coffman, by then located in Indiana as associate editor of Funk's paper, wrote in his diary that "what we need is home mission work." Conferences, he thought, should send ministers to places that seemed promising for building up churches. In 1881 the Indiana Mennonite Conference agreed, at least to the point of saying its ministers should visit all scattered members and their small congregatons during the following year. And for ministers who could not afford the expense, each congregation was to "take a collection every three months, or as often as may be deemed proper and necessary."[71]

With such recommendations district conferences were moving not only toward support of Christian workers, but also toward another conviction that Coffman, in 1880, confided to his diary: that "a mission board should be created and evangelists should be under the care of the board."[72]

Finally on December 28, 1882, a group in the congregation at Elkhart met and formed a committee. Funk was one of the committee's three members, and became its chairman, or "moderator"; included also was Henry Brenneman, another brother of the Ohio bishop. Early in 1883 the new group took the name "Mennonite Evangelizing Committee" and indicated that its purpose was not only to serve its own congregation but to reach out to other people. It declared that the "means collected" should go to cover expenses of ministers traveling to scattered Mennonites "not supplied, or only partly supplied with laborers"—and also, "to preach the Gospel in places where our church and doctrines are not known."[73]

Technically, for almost a decade the group was nothing more than a self-perpetuating committee of the Elkhart congregation; but in fact, it began almost immediately to serve as a rudimentary mission board for the larger Mennonite Church. Publicized in the *Herald*, the Mennonite Evangelizing Committee quickly drew gifts from individuals, Sunday school classes, and congregations in many places. Amounts were small: many gifts of one dollar or even less, and total disbursements per year rising from less than one hundred dollars in early years to a scant nine hundred dollars in the tenth year. Most went to help the traveling ministers, although the committee did forward money to various other causes, including some overseas missions, when donors requested.[74]

"Evangelism," that is, the traveling ministers' work, continued to mean going to scattered Mennonites, not to others—except to Amish Mennonites, who more and more cooperated with and worked through the committee. Amish Mennonite cooperation was part of a gradual broadening of the committee's base, a broadening that led it to reorganize in 1892. Taking the name "Mennonite Evangelizing Board of America," the committee began to invite each district conference of Mennonites, and then of Amish Mennonites, to keep a representative on the board. By 1893 it included members from all major Mennonite and Amish Mennonite areas in the U.S. and Ontario except eastern Pennsylvania.[75]

In eastern Pennsylvania, Mennonites of the Lancaster Conference, centered of course in Lancaster County, began about 1890 to send evangelists of their own, especially to people who had emigrated west from their own congregations. In those efforts they cooperated loosely at least with Funk, yet pretty well kept their distance from what was developing at Elkhart.[76] So the evangelizing committee and evangelizing board failed to get anything like full cooperation in the region where Mennonite Church people were most concentrated, most numerous, and quite wealthy. It was a large failure. Still, with that reorganization of 1892, the Mennonite Church had finally gotten at least a semiofficial mission board.

Even so weak a board was clearly a step toward specialized missionary agencies and away from what could have been a greater effort to have *congregations* meet the missionary challenge. But the latter approach was also alive, if not entirely well. Mission-minded Mennonites of the late nineteenth century were often optimistic that as their people scattered in search of land, warmer climate, or whatever, they might be missionaries as they went. Several families moving into a new area might form a seedling congregation that would attract non-Mennonite neighbors for its growth and maturity. In fact, non-Mennonite neighbors especially in church-starved frontier areas did come and listen to Mennonite preaching often enough to keep the hope alive.[77]

Ministers could do more if they scattered out, advised the Ohio conference in 1899. Laymen ought to go out and get farming or school-teaching jobs in scattered places, then help with church and Sunday school work there. One often heard complaints when members moved away from a Mennonite settlement, agreed a *Herald* writer in 1902. Yet "how can a greater evangelization work be done than by having our people scattered throughout the world?"[7b]

But scatter how thin? In 1893 one "D. Kauffman" offered an answer. Probably it was Daniel Kauffman, before many years to be the Mennonite Church's foremost leader. "It is true," D. Kauffman advised *Herald* readers, "that some have moved into communities where our faith was unknown and succeeded in building up prosperous churches; but where one has been thus successful, dozens of families have been lost sight of [and] their children carried off into popular churches." Kauffman thought Mennonites should go only in groups of twenty-five or more.[79] By the mid-1890s many Mennonites agreed. Perhaps partly reflecting the example of "Russian" Mennonites who had recently migrated to North America's Great Plains, a new watchword became "colonization." The idea was to buy land only in large tracts and then resell it principally to Mennonites. Yet not all were convinced. In 1900 Jacob (J.A.) Ressler, newly minted missionary to India, declared that "if our religion is what we claim for it, it cannot suffer from exposure." The "idea that *we must move in colonies in order to keep our people together*," thought he, was "deadly" and "insidious."[80] Ressler had a valid point. Some who promoted colonies did seem more interested in repairing the walls of Mennonite separatism than in being missionary.

New Drumbeats   41

Others, however, had kept at least some vestige of the insight that living together as a loving people might be a church's strongest message. By 1896 the missionary commitment of M. S. Steiner was beyond question, for he was a prominent evangelist and the main founder of the Mennonite Church's first formal mission (the Home Mission in Chicago, begun in 1893). Yet Steiner could argue in that year that "it is all right for us to go out to 'all nations' and preach the Gospel, but it is *not* all right for us to remain out, quit preaching, and possibly allow the world to rope in our children." And against that danger, Steiner thought going as a group was the safeguard. "...Where a company go together," he observed, "hearts that are tender, possibly sad, and lonesome soon find such about them as are full of sympathy and compassion." "The watchword of the Mennonite Church should be, Evangelize!" added one Samuel Kurtz, a young minister in Idaho, in 1900. And Kurtz believed that at least in the rough West in which he lived, colonization could do it better than either formal missions or itinerant preaching. To call the wayward back to their childhood religious training, nothing could serve so well as real examples of Christian living. "Live, LIVE, *LIVE*!" Kurtz exulted. "Christlike living preaches more powerful sermons than most ministers." Thus Kurtz put forward an ideal of communicating gospel not so much by words as by establishing colonies and then living faithfully as congregations.[81]

With their new evangelizing board and their low-key discussions about whether to scatter individually or in colonies, Mennonite Church and Amish Mennonite people were groping for ways to proceed.

Yet action still fell far short of talk, for in the 1880s and 1890s those Mennonites and Amish Mennonites greatly increased their talk about mission. Prodding the discussion were many stimuli. Coffman and others were busy conducting revivals. With Coffman helping to edit it after 1879, the *Herald* took on a bolder tone. In 1886 the evangelizing committee began sponsoring annual sermons that offered Funk, Coffman, and others opportunity to develop semiofficial treatises on mission.[82] Broadened contacts via Sunday schools, religious literature, education, and general living made Mennonites more aware of their neighbors and of the world. The *Herald* continued to print missionary pieces from the broader evangelical Protestant press. People of the Mennonite Church constantly watched other denominations—as examples of missionary activism and as competitors who would snatch away their most able youth unless their church matched the others' style.[83] They also watched other Mennonite groups, especially General

Conference Mennonites with their work among Red people in America.[84]

By the 1880s it was no longer necessary to be delicate and cautious when broaching the subject of mission. The more conservative of the mission-minded continued to fuse the Great Commission with traditionally pious, self-effacing Mennonite language. Obedience-minded and legalistic Mennonites seemingly depended more on Jesus' direct command as a motive than had Protestant pioneers of modern missions.[85] As for the less conservative, by the early 1890s they could say boldly that their fathers had erred. Coffman in 1892 openly lamented the failure of previous generations of Mennonites in North America "to spread the precious Gospel beyond their immediate boundaries." He could only "say with one of old," he thought, "'Both we and our fathers have sinned.'"[86] His words signaled a marked shift.

* * *

"Our fathers have sinned." To be sure they had, even by their own lights. Not only had they kept to themselves the good news of being people of God, but far too many had also fallen into a formal, legalized, ingroup religion that was a grotesque caricature of what they claimed to believe. Yet rejection of the fathers often went further than rejecting only their distortions. More than they knew, the most quickened and avidly mission-minded of Mennonites in the 1880s and 1890s tended also to discard some authentically "Mennonite" perceptions of what the gospel was, and to replace them with general American Protestant understandings.

Or they replaced them with secular American understandings. Much was happening that was not strictly religious. A massive shift to using the English language was one symptom. Another was occupation. Funk's going into the lumber and then the publishing businesses is illustrative. Innumerable Mennonite leaders corresponded on business (even if only chicken, egg, and cheese sales) stationery. By the 1890s many of the younger ones were trying book selling and even printing. These were no doubt stimulated by Funk's example, by growing Mennonite appetites for reading, and by the church's conviction against salaries for its workers. Even more taught public school, at least for a time.

Hand in hand with occupational change went higher levels of education. Normal schools such as Millersville in Pennsylvania and Smithville and Ada in Ohio became gathering-spots for bright Mennonite sons and daughters. Moody's institute in Chicago (its evangelicalism not yet fully developed into twentieth-century Fundamentalism) attracted some. Others were here and there in medical school. It was as a medical doctor in Chicago, for example, that Solomon (S.D.) Ebersole projected the vision for Mennonite mission in Chicago. That mission's first superintendent, Steiner, had attended Ada and then Oberlin College. When a few Mennonites opened Elkhart Institute in 1894, they argued with some force that it was no longer a question of whether Mennonite youth would get higher education. They would get it somewhere.

Among quickened young leaders the motive of serving Christ and church was strong. Present also, however, was a mood of ambition quite different from that reflected in older Mennonite warnings against pride. Coffman, negotiating with Funk in 1879, hoped very much that he was "not moved by any vain aspiration." He wanted "to serve my Master in the best way and place that I can." The church needed "other members than alone farmers," he thought, and he hoped to interest his sons in church publishing.[87]

From there on ambition became even more clear. As a minister, Coffman said, he did not feel needed in Virginia, going "around in my own neighborhood" and preaching to people who had "heard until they are tired" and took "but little interest." The church needed preachers who "excite interest and command attention." Being on Funk's staff would provide Coffman with "abundant opportunity to improve myself" and also to make the whole Mennonite Church his forum. Finally Coffman wanted "to better my worldly circumstances, though I crave only a comfortable living." Steiner, negotiating with Funk a decade later, offered almost a replay except that he seemed even less than Coffman to fear "vain aspirations." He hoped to "make something of himself." He would work for the church at financial sacrifice, but if nothing opened "in the church circle," he was confident a "respectable position" would open elsewhere.[88]

That mood was prevalent. In 1893 George (G.L.) Bender, evangelizing board treasurer, exulted privately but unabashedly that certain eastern people thought Steiner, him, and their close friends to be "just the stuff." Isaac Hershey, soon to be a deacon and a leader of mission interest in Lancaster County, Pennsylvania, was one of those eastern people. In 1894 he confided to Steiner that as a lad he "could not conceive why Mennonite boys were nobody... in the family of Christ"—"nor can I yet." So much for the older Mennonite fear of pride.[89]

God works in mysterious ways. Without question the quickening was a genuinely religious movement that brought many into the circle of God's people that Mennonites were trying to be—many who otherwise would have departed much further from their fathers' faith. Indeed at points the quickening reminded Mennonite Church and Amish Mennonite people about their Anabaptist beginnings and beliefs. In 1871 Funk published the first English-language edition of Menno Simons' *Complete Works*. In 1886 he and his staff produced a new and widely heralded *Martyrs Mirror* in English. In 1887 a young German Mennonite named John Horsch joined Funk's staff and was soon writing prolifically on Anabaptist and Mennonite history and doctrine. (However, since at first Horsch wrote mostly in German, his pre-1900 writings seem largely to have passed the younger generation by.) Funk's biographer has calculated that one fifth of the Mennonite Publishing Company's output was Anabaptist works.[90] And time after time advocates of mission pointed to Anabaptists' missionary zeal.

Yet even religiously the activists were in some ways becoming less "Mennonite" and more like North Americans in general. The Mennonite Church's quickening was hardly an Anabaptist revival and certainly not a "recovery of the Anabaptist vision."[91]

At some points the quickened generation rediscovered Anabaptism, but that rediscovery was hardly the underlying rhythm of the new drumbeat. During the 1890s J. A. Ressler moved into full adulthood, had a conversion experience (albeit a mild one), and formed the commitments that led to his appointment in 1898 as leader of the Mennonite Church's first team of foreign missionaries. Keeping a diary through much of the decade, he made one reference to the evangelists who went out from the 1527 synod of Anabaptists. But he showed almost no consciousness that being Mennonite meant having a peculiar message or heritage of mission. Meantime Allen Erb, born in 1888 and in the twentieth century a deeply committed minister, church hospital administrator, moderator of his denomination's general conference, and home missionary, surely got his nurture from the Mennonite Church that emerged from the late nineteenth century. Yet Erb has told of 1925 being the year when he became deeply impressed with the meaning of the Anabaptist example.[92]

The fact was, when mission-minded Mennonites in the late years of the nineteenth century pointed to Menno and other Anabaptists as examples, they often seemed to be making the Anabaptists into modern-style missionaries rather than to be asking how the Anabaptists had gone about communicating gospel.

Moreover, while Mennonites were learning bits of their own faith, evangelical Protestantism was finding weak points in traditional Mennonite defenses. Formal separation of church and state in America, and the passing of the notion that all within a territory were part of an official church, made Mennonite concepts of church and believers baptism seem less unique. So also did revivalists' demands for personal commitment. Much of American Protestantism accepted Calvinistic ideas of human depravity and worthlessness, at least mildly; and Mennonites could easily confuse those ideas with their own emphasis on lowliness and humility. Virtually all American revivalists preached some version of pietism and holiness. Apparently to some Mennonites, that sounded like their own kind of discipleship and obedience. Evangelicals rested their case on direct appeals to scripture. Apparently it was difficult for Mennonites to see how that differed from their own tradition of biblicism. Not least, the vast majority of American Protestants put their theology into language well suited to younger Mennonites' levels of education and intellect.

Quickened Mennonites sometimes expressed the wistful belief that Protestants were beginning to embrace pacifism.[93] In the long run, however, few of the most "evangelical" and biblically literalist among them, those with whom Mennonites increasingly identified, would come close to Mennonite nonresistance. Neither did they come very close to Mennonite beliefs regarding nonconformity or lifestyle. If nonresistance and nonconformity were really central to Mennonite understandings of gospel, the breaches in Mennonite defenses were quite serious. If, in addition, Mennonites misunderstood some of the evangelicals' other assumptions—say about church and state—the breaches were even greater. Nevertheless the onslaught could come in a way that seemed hardly more than shifts in emphasis. Had not Mennonites always believed in some sense in the doctrines that revivalistic Protestants emphasized: the reality of sin, salvation by Christ's sacrifice through faith, Jesus as Savior, personal decision and commitment, etc.?[94] The defenses were down.

A powerful stimulus to the quickening was interdenominationalism. A Methodist might still find the *Herald* uncomplimentary toward his church, as at least one did in 1887. But in their quickening period Mennonites cooperated more with members of nonpacifist churches (they had always had some fellowship with Quakers and Dunkards) than ever again until at least the 1950s. J. A. Ressler and Isaac Hershey, in Pennsylvania's Lancaster County, were examples. Not wanting Mennonites to be nobodies in Christ's family, Hershey declared emphatically to Steiner in 1894 that from his youth he had thought separate denominations to be like so many lodges (in Mennonite circles the ultimate put-down!). Recently he and Ressler had worked with Presbyterians, United Brethren, and Methodists to arrange a temperance lecture by a man whose denomination he did not know. Also, Hershey had drawn much criticism by advising members of his family who were in trouble with their Mennonite bishop to go to the local United Brethren minister for spiritual counsel. Ressler, for his part, was a warm friend of several U. B. ministers. Like a number of other Mennonites of the time he worked with the Young Men's Christian Association, an excellent example in the 1890s of revivalistic Protestant interdenominationalism.[95]

An even earlier and much broader case was Mennonite presence in interdenominational or union Sunday schools. Funk had attended one as a boy in eastern Pennsylvania before teaching in them in Chicago. By the 1870s and into the 1890s many, many Mennonites, from well-settled eastern communities to struggling frontier ones, participated.[96]

Conservatives protested. "The highest, the proudest, and the dressiest classes" of Americans supported the Sunday school movement, several Virginia Mennonites pointed out in an 1871 article, which Funk refused to print. By giving prizes for merit, the schools taught "pride and exaltedness." They mixed Mennonites with "other societies," some of which taught "almost a worldwide way to heaven," and they taught not the Bible but selective portions of the Bible along with materials "by societies not opposed to war, bloodshed," and lawsuits. "The Mennonite Church," the conservatives emphasized, "was to be a people of God, separate from the world."[97] Nor did only conservatives give warning. In 1863 bishop Brenneman and his friend Peter Nissley visited the Sunday school where young Funk was working in Chicago. Afterwards Nissley advised Funk that he had been glad to hear the children repeating "Suffer the little children to come," and "Love your enemies"; but he hoped that the children were not learning Calvinism, and the Sunday school [in those civil war times] was not teaching them that they would get glory in heaven if they died in battle."[98]

Unfortunately, not all Mennonites' warnings against Sunday schools rested quite so much on concern for godly living and sound gospel. The conservatives argued also that Sunday school was "something new," not "practiced by our forefathers." Mixing such weak

New Drumbeats 47

arguments with the strong, opponents could not counter the will among many Mennonites to attend Sunday school, in union schools if need be.[99]

Mennonites did try to inject their doctrines into union schools. And almost everywhere they left the union ones as soon as they had the strength to go it alone. Indeed by the 1890s, through developing their own schools and materials, they probably had made the institution into an insulation against outside teachings more than a point of contact. But for a significant time, many Mennonites had gone interdenominational with their children. "We have a Union S.S. here," an Ohio Mennonite wrote to Steiner in 1892, "and dare not put to[o] much stress on any one way." Nevertheless, "we get along nicely," and "I think we are planting the right kind of principals [sic] into the young minds."[100]

Despite a certain pigheadedness, the Sunday school opponents had a point. Some historians of religion in America now say that interdenominational Sunday schools in the nineteenth century helped confuse religious faith with the American nation and American cultural ways. The author of a book ironically entitled *A Christian America*, Robert T. Handy, has argued that this confusion really was a new formula for the old *corpus christianum* concept of uniting church and national culture.[101] To quite an extent, the general Sunday school movement taught a Protestant-blessed Americanism.

Mennonites' participation in union Sunday schools illustrated a larger fact: *Revivalistic Protestantism offered outward-looking Mennonites a pipeline to American ideas and American ways. It presented a formula for becoming respected Americans and becoming so quite comfortably with the sanction of faith and religion.* To the extent that Mennonite quickening came from such a source, it was not exactly a revival of Mennonites' own beliefs and surely not a new vision or expression of Anabaptism. Yet it brought many Mennonites' and Amish Mennonites' sons and daughters to faith, a faith with a new kind of vitality. And it was the key to Mennonites' recapturing a missionary vision.

* * *

Along with the quickening, there seemed to come a change in the very gospel Mennonites wanted to proclaim.

By the 1890s Mennonites had new code words. Terms such as "active" were replacing the old, solemn warnings against "pride." Writing from his travels, Coffman in 1894 told of Mennonites "fretting like

caged birds," just waiting to be released "into active Christian effort....
It is not freedom for the world they want, but freedom to work
actively."[102]

"Aggressive work" became the catch phrase for all the new activities. Steiner decided that Mennonites had stressed humility to the point of losing symmetry, and he preached on the "manliness of God." Despite Mennonites' pacifism, military analogies and the term "church militant" became common. Topics such as "The Sunday School an Aggressive Power" were the order of the day. So prevalent, even obnoxious, did this nervous activism become that in 1898 Abram B. Kolb, associate editor of the *Herald*, complained that Christianity was now "all work—one continued earnest, active, hurrying, rushing, hustling, pushing whirl of active work." Youth, he advised his readers, should "go to the closet" and "hold communion with God." When their hearts were filled "with divine grace and power," then they should go forth. Kolb still wanted the youth to go, but in effect he was calling on them to go a bit more in Mennonites' pre-quickening mood of being the "quiet in the land."[103]

If the activism was a departure from earlier Mennonitism in North America, was it nevertheless a return step toward Anabaptism? Hardly. The "Onward Christian Soldiers" mentality of quickened Mennonites seemed to have more in common with the cultural self-confidence and imperialism of the modern Protestant missionary movement than with Anabaptism. One writer has pointed out that modern missions have evoked two kinds of "asceticism": mission work as withdrawal from the world's mainstream into one of its more humble corners, and mission work as giving oneself to a grand world-conquering cause. Late nineteenth-century Mennonites mainly chose the latter.[104] The former was probably nearer to Anabaptist discipleship, yieldedness, and suffering.

Similarly, quickened Mennonites blurred the Anabaptist insight that church and world, gospel and national culture were radically different. Bishop Brenneman had been determined to keep the distinction clear. Lamenting the U.S. Civil War in 1864, he hoped that at least war might sift the conscientious from the worldly, or strike a "Line Between the kingdom of Christ and the kingdom of this world. These two opposite kingdoms," he thought, "have been too much Blended and mingled together." To be sure, Mennonite writers in Funk's paper in the late nineteenth century confused the two realms much less than did the authors of many non-Mennonite pieces that the *Herald* reprinted.[105]

New Drumbeats 49

The new activists did confuse them however.

Thus in 1872 Jonathan K. Hartzler, a promoter of Mennonite Sunday schools in Ohio, wrote how glad he was that China and Japan were building railroads and sending sons to study in the United States so they could "see that Christian civilization is better than the idolatry and darkness which abound in their own countries." Coffman asked editorially in 1882 whether, without missionaries, China, India, and Africa could become "Christian countries [sic]."[106] Perhaps the most notable examples of such thinking came in two addresses by Ebersole of Chicago in 1892 and 1893. They are notable because Ebersole was speaking at landmark Sunday school conferences that very much epitomized the new activism, and because young activists responded enthusiastically and went on from these speeches to shape the Mennonite Church's first formal mission in Chicago.[107]

When Ebersole spoke, his words certainly were not in the traditional Mennonite idiom. To be sure, he made a few remarks tailored to his Mennonite audience, including a reminder that the Anabaptists had been mission-minded. But upon being asked to speak in 1892 he admitted that of late he had gotten out of touch with Mennonite Sunday schools; and the tone of his addresses came from outside Mennonitism. He breathed the assumptions of bringing cultural uplift to the ignorant poor. He used standard language of upper-class American philanthropy that called upon Christians to see themselves as "trustees" of the less fortunate. More specifically, he blurred the distinction between church and surrounding society. "Do you believe it," he asked in 1892, "that this subject of Sunday schools and missions is the greatest, the most important subject confronting the churches to-day, as well as all sound-minded men?" Without missions "this world is doomed to destruction." On missions hung "the destinies of the nation." Immigrants in Chicago, he lamented in 1893, were "not becoming naturalized, Americanized, or Christianized. ... We know that our cities rule the nation," he warned, "and as our cities are, so our government will be."[108]

Thus did the grand call that inspired Mennonite Church youth to begin their church's first formal mission effort blur the two realms. Some older persons left the 1892 meeting crying in discomfort, and by 1894 district church conferences warned "that the S.S. Conference work should not be left too much in the hands of the younger members." One can well imagine how alien the young activists' language seemed.[109]

Among the profoundest changes was a shift away from references to the "non-resistant gospel."

Early in the quickening, advocates of Mennonite Church mission constantly used the nonresistant-gospel phrase or others such as "the gospel of peace." And to be sure, thirty years after Brenneman's response to Moseman, one might still hear sentiments like his warning to support only those who preached "the pure and true gospel... and its non-resistant principles." "What a boon we are denying the poor heathen" by letting "lovers of war" take God's message to them, declared one *Herald* writer in 1892, and "by withholding from them the true non-resistant doctrine of Jesus." None could set forth pacifism as a message that the world needed more eloquently than could Steiner, leader of the younger generation of quickened Mennonites at the turn of the century.[110]

Nevertheless, by Steiner's time the quickened in the Mennonite Church were mostly losing the concept that nonresistance was at the very heart of the gospel, letting it disappear in a flood of standard revivalistic-Protestant talk. A careful study of the *Herald*'s borrowings from other church papers would almost certainly reveal that Funk's paper gradually used Quaker writings less and less and nonpacifist sources more and more. In Funk's reporting of religious statistics, he also seemed to shift away from bracketing Mennonites with other pacifists and toward perceiving them as another Protestant denomination.[111] By the 1890s it seemed as natural for Funk and the *Herald* to refer to "truths held common by Evangelical Christians" or to laud a Mennonite Bible conference for throwing "valuable light on many points of Evangelical doctrine"[112] as it was to refer to "our non-resistant gospel" and the "gospel of peace."

These latter phrases had quite clearly communicated a perception that the gospel message and the nonresistant ethic were one and the same. Their loss was more than a mere change of words. Not that the quickened Mennonites were losing their pacifism, or, more broadly, their belief in distinctive ethics and lifestyle. The quickened who stayed with the Mennonite Church were very conscious of being "Mennonite," and the leading ones were very loyal.[113] Coffman had set the tone when in his revival meetings he constantly preached doctrinal sermons— Mennonite in content—as well as invitational ones. A youth such as Edward (E.J.) Berkey, attending college in Illinois and soon to be a worker in the Chicago mission, could write in 1893 that "I attend the Methodist Church & Sunday School but grow stronger in the plain Mennonite doctrine every week." Yet Berkey was a prime example of one who could speak on and on in the language not of traditional

Mennonitism but of revivalistic Protestantism.[114]

Such sons of late nineteenth-century Mennonitism did not completely lose Mennonite distinctiveness so much as develop a new formula. While that formula did not at once destroy the older ethical convictions, for many it laid out alongside those convictions a different track to salvation.[115] No longer was the *very content of salvation* to be found in yieldedness, obedience and discipleship, living separated as God's people, living by the love ethic, and depending humbly on Christ (however much the fathers had distorted these). Now salvation became a matter of the Reformers' preoccupation with guilt of past sin, a revival-style acknowledgment of that sin, and a turning to a Christ who had fulfilled the ritual of sacrifice to a judging God. The call was to that, more than to following the Lord who offered instruction, example, and a new community for a life of suffering love.[116] Redemption came not so much in a new kind of living as in a formula, the formula captured in the borrowed phrase, "plan of salvation."

Mennonites thereafter had some struggle with how to lay out the two tracks. How did their ethical convictions relate to God's saving work? After all, if nonresistance and simplicity of life and appearance had nothing to do with the salvation process, nothing to do with humankind's fallen condition and basic needs, why bother?

A superficial solution, but one very tempting to Mennonites with their strong emphasis on obedience, was to consider the ethical convictions as something extra that God demanded more or less arbitrarily: as commands and little more. But of course that answer presented God as a capricious and demanding taskmaster, and fostered a legalism that could become as grotesque as the fathers' caricatures. Equally distorting was another concept, "restrictions." When planning a Bible conference program, for instance, or writing on Bible doctrine, Mennonites might make the "Plan of Salvation" the first topic, then include topics on ordinances and such matters. Somewhere then down the list one would appear on "restrictions"—the love ethic and distinctive lifestyle relegated, of course, to that negative and repulsive category. By the early twentieth century that formula was standard.[117]

When Mennonites faced the question less superficially, however, they had to work harder at the process of separating salvation from living. In 1894 G. L. Bender began to wear the distinctive Mennonite coat. He did so, he said, because he thought that Christian workers so attired would make "the most powerful army of Christian soldiers to be found anywhere on the face of the earth." The following year he consented to defend plain dress before a group of quickened Mennonites whom he knew to be somewhat skeptical. "I want to be understood that I do not put any religion in the attire of the body, so far as salvation is concerned," Bender declared at the outset. "The blood of Christ is what cleanseth us ... and unless we have that blood applied to our hearts ... though we practice simplicity to perfection, we will never enter the pearly gates." But, Bender went on to declare, "while attire has nothing to do with our getting saved, it has ... a great deal to do with our remaining saved.... There are two words that cover all: 'Blood' and 'Obedience.' The blood of Christ saves us, and obedience to His Word keeps us saved."[118]

How odd! Mennonites had once worn plain attire as a very natural expression of the humble quality of life that *was* the salvation that God had offered through Jesus. Now plain attire applied only *after* salvation. Bender still referred to plainness as expression of inner humility,[119] but mostly he presented it now as one more thing for the activist to *do*, as an act of obedience and even as a show of militance. It had nothing any more to do with salvation itself, nothing to do with answering fundamentally where humankind had gone wrong. It was only to help the Christian keep his grip on an elusive, abstract formula of salvation by proving in one more way that he was an "aggressive worker." For Mennonites salvation and release from human sin were no longer to come by the very living of the new life to which God had called. They were no longer to come by the kind of living to which Jesus, by His ethical teachings and by His own self-sacrifice, had shown the way. Salvation and release from sin were to come on another, alien, more standard Protestant track, through a theological formula.[120]

Bender had spoken to more than just clothes. He had said much more than he knew. He had captured the entire process by which the late nineteenth century's newly activated Mennonites imposed the drumbeat of revivalistic Protestantism onto the quiet Mennonite faith. Largely separating ethics from salvation, he had laid down a two-track formula that did much to spell out the gospel Mennonites would carry when they went as missionaries.

* * *

By the 1890s Mennonites were ready to venture forth. Had they listened to stiller, smaller sounds, they might have gone forth not quite so much to the drumbeat of Anglo-American Protestantism, and therefore less in step with the West's larger march of energetic imperialism.

Had they listened more to Jesus' low-key rhythm, to the modest congregations of Christians of Paul's time, to the Anabaptists, to the best words of their Mennonite fathers—ah, but what was, was. The drumbeat was next to deafening. And its rhythm did call Mennonites to mission.

Yet at century's end Mennonite Church people were not completely in step. Just where their march might still differ, where they might have to remain aloof and move by their own special convictions—these would be tough questions for mission-minded Mennonites in the early twentieth century. The new formula brought Mennonites close to the missionary movement, where they could hear the band play and unconsciously move with its beat. Still, they moved stiffly, cautiously, and a bit aloof.

2
WHOSE MISSION?

In the 1890s Mennonite and Amish Mennonite missionary talk became action. Quickened youth in the Midwest turned cityward and in 1893 opened a home mission in Chicago. Eventually the mission got firmly established, but only after some great difficulties, and after almost closing for a time. City work, following general Protestant patterns as the Chicago mission did, too often seemed alien to the Mennonite Church's people. Meanwhile, in eastern Pennsylvania, other young activists went into action, but began closer home. In some ways they were more successful.

* * *

To begin in the city was not really necessary. In the 1880s and 1890s country Mennonites from East to West often reported that neighbors who had heard their preaching or read Mennonite literature had shown interest. Those near a new Mennonite colony at Denbigh, Virginia, seemed "much impressed with our doctrine and appearance," declared one such report in 1898, some of them freely expressing confidence "that we were the true church of God." In 1887, from the continent's other end, one John Christolear of near Red Bluff, California, wrote Funk that he had seen copies of the *Herald*. How could he join the Mennonite Church? Funk published Christolear's story, and one

Herald reader answered: Have some wealthy Mennonite give $200, or 4,000 Mennonites each give 5¢ to send Christolear a minister. If a minister went, agreed Jonathan Smucker, prominent Amish Mennonite bishop in northern Indiana and "evangelist" to the scattered, he might organize a church that would attract many others. Californians might be rough and wicked but Jesus had suffered for them also, and "why should not the gospel of peace and good will to all men be preached to them?"[1]

Nearer Smucker's home, also in the 1880s, were Andrew and Mary Crook, husband and wife on a farm in Dubois County, southern Indiana. Early in the decade Mr. Crook had come upon something John Brenneman had written, liked it, and visited Brenneman in Ohio and Funk in Elkhart. Soon he and Mrs. Crook had joined the Mennonite Church, and would remain faithful to it until they died in 1911 and 1913. They seemed to have captured Mennonites' understandings of gospel quite well. Crook wrote in 1890 of advising a neighbor "never to sue, but just forgive. . . ." He lamented that churches in his area did not understand "our non-resistant doctrine" and hence did not preach "true Christianity." Neighbors' pursuit of fashions, intoxicants, and elections seemed to him quite futile. Mennonite ministers visited and found the couple longing for more fellowship with Mennonite brothers and sisters, and, despite ridicule, dressed humbly in Mennonite garb. The *Herald*'s editors observed in 1890 that those who became Mennonites without Mennonite rearing often defended the church's beliefs "more intelligently than others who have grown up in the heart of our strongest church centers." The editors almost certainly had the Crooks in mind.[2]

The Crooks hoped, at least at first, to be a nucleus of mission. Especially when Mennonite ministers occasionally visited, they gathered neighbors in the local schoolhouse to hear the Word. There was in Dubois County "a hunger and thirst after righteousness," agreed one of the ministers, John Shenk of Ohio, in 1881. In 1882, the *Herald*, under the title "A Mission to Southern Indiana," observed that a proper effort, with God's blessing, might well "result in building up a church at that place."[3]

Yet quickened Mennonites did not respond with a mission strategy to Dubois County or any similar place. Even the precedent of West Virginia did not move them to that. No doubt they attracted non-Mennonite neighbors to their churches, here and there. And in 1889 Smucker went to California and prepared the way for Indiana Amish Mennonites the next year to receive Christolear as a member in absentia.⁴ But Smucker's vision for a larger mission in Christolear's community apparently came to nothing. Nor did anyone move to help the Crooks in any ongoing way. Someone should have. The Crooks were not far from scattered Mennonites in neighboring counties, and not impossibly far from strong Mennonite churches in Ohio and northern Indiana.

Dubois County simply did not stir the blood of activist youth. Those who visited the Crooks were established ministers and bishops, sent in part by somewhat cautious district conferences. True, most ministers who traveled were at least halfway quickened, but they were too middle-aged and too rooted to move very boldly. So the mission that might have been, never happened. Instead, activists went to the glittering city and imitated Protestant mission.

* * *

"Why, in the name of our Holy faith does not our church send out missionaries into such places" as Chicago? asked thirty-year-old Daniel Shenk, active Ohio layman and nephew of John Brenneman, in 1884. There the church could "seek out the poor and downtrodden, the despised and the erring, and invite them and welcome them into the fold of Christ." By the early 1890s young Mennonites were in Chicago. Early in 1891 M. S. Steiner apparently visited there, with missions in mind. By then Dr. Ebersole was already there, and along with him a Mennonite student at Moody Bible Institute, Menno S. Miller. These two urged Steiner on.⁵ But congregations at home did not seem very interested. "It takes a blast from the Ram's Horn that would waken the dead it seems," Steiner would observe in 1895, "to bring out the church that has slept for centuries."⁶

A pattern was already forming: youthful leadership, influence from Moody's, and tension with the home church.

At a district church conference of Amish Mennonites in Indiana, in 1891, serious public discussion of city mission did begin. Steiner, Coffman, and Funk, among other visitors, were there. The question came up formally only late in the day. "What ought we do toward furnishing a church home for the converted poor of our large cities?" the conference finally asked. The answer: "Some warm sympathy was expressed, and the question somewhat discussed," but "for want of time" it was tabled.⁷

So leadership for mission did not come from an established conference. The conferences saw themselves too much as defenders of the fortress—"watchman on the walls of Zion," to use a favorite phrase of traditionalist Mennonite ministers. To be sure most conferences, especially those west of the Alleghenies, were letting Sunday schools, revivals, and the idea of missions come in. And when they did, their sermons and resolutions commonly retained "gospel of peace and simplicity" language much better than did many young activists. Indeed, the Indiana Amish Mennonite conference was among the most progressive. It was under the influence of Elkhart. And it had as leaders men like Smucker, like Daniel J. Johns, the bishop of the Clinton Frame congregation near Goshen where the great Sunday school conference and rally for mission occurred in 1892, and like an intellectually inclined minister from the "Haw Patch" district of Lagrange County, Jonas (J. S.) Hartzler. But even the Indiana Amish Mennonites tabled the city mission matter in 1891, "for want of time."

A conference might table, but activists continued to discuss. In some respects theirs also was a very "Mennonite" discussion.

It reflected the tension of withdrawal versus going into the world. Mennonites should not flee from the "modern Ninevehs" to their "remote and quiet country homes," Steiner argued in the *Herald* in June of 1891. Early Christians had preached mostly "to the *poor*," and now most of the poor were in the cities. The real challenge of modern life, agreed two pieces the *Herald* printed in July, was to be "in the world" and "yet not defiled by it." It *was* possible to be a Christian in the city, and anyone who thought cities too wicked to evangelize needed a larger gospel. Yes, agreed Reuben (R. J.) Heatwole, a remarkable lay leader in Kansas. As in New Testament and in Anabaptist times, Mennonites should go "*wherever* a field may open, whether among Mennonites or other classes." How many people had modern Mennonites sent "from city to city to preach," or for that matter to "foreign (heathen) lands?"[8]

Some predicted that in mission, Mennonite distinctives would help. In real fact, once the Chicago mission became reality, not all of its workers would care very much for plain dress.[9] But for a time mission crusaders argued that the cities' poor would feel attracted to Mennonites' plainness, for it was cheaper to be Mennonite. City people would respond, thought one *Herald* writer in 1892, if plain people showed them they were interested in their souls and not in money, and that nonconformity was biblical. Steiner emphasized that Mennonites were down-to-earth and practical, and did not spend for elaborate church buildings. Even Ebersole suggested that Mennonites would preach "the religion of Jesus Christ in its *simplicity*," in settings where the poor would not have to spend all they possessed to keep up "with extravagances, vanities and expenses of the popular churches."[10]

But on other points, the Mennonite Church's activists simply followed Protestant ideas and models. Steiner, as he called for city work, quoted at length from learned Presbyterian and Methodist divines. Ebersole explicitly urged Mennonites to imitate other denominations, and the *Herald* pointed approvingly to his considerable experience in other churches' missions. In January of 1893 William Page, a young Mennonite from Elkhart, moved to Chicago in search of printing-house work, quickly made contact with Miller, and was soon deep in Sunday school work and other activities of Moody's church and institute. It really fired him up, he wrote Steiner. In February, William Coffman, an employee of Funk and a son of the evangelist, visited Chicago. Page and Miller took him on Saturday evening to a mission run by a former drunkard-blacksmith; on Sunday to a sermon and Bible class at Moody's church, an unruly Sunday school conducted by a Moody Mission Band, and a new nurse-and-deaconess-training center run by a free-lancing General Conference Mennonite, John A. Sprunger; and on Sunday evening to a Salvation Army meeting. Later in 1893 Steiner again visited Chicago, and among other activities attended a Christian Alliance Convention and a round of meetings at Moody's. In September the *Herald* published a lengthy piece on city mission work from a leading Protestant missionary journal, the *Missionary Review*.[11]

Such doings formed the background for the Sunday school conference of 1893 where, it would develop, Steiner would receive a charge to open the mission in Chicago. To activist young people in the Mennonite and Amish Mennonite churches it was clear that other denominations and their missions had shown how to proceed, and to quite an extent had formulated the message. What was not clear was the authority, in a peoplehood church, to proceed.

No conference or other established church authority had given a mandate. Nevertheless by autumn of 1893 the Chicago group and Steiner were moving ahead, calling themselves the "Mennonite Mission Committee" or the "Mennonite City Mission Committee." Early in October, Ebersole, in his second Sunday school conference address, presented Chicago as a Sodom or a Gomorrah and then announced that the committee had already chosen a site, and would open a Sunday school, a medical dispensary, gospel meetings, Sunday services, and eventually perhaps a kindergarten. A group of the most interested among the conferees then met informally and appointed Steiner to superintend the new venture. Within a month Steiner took a room in Chicago, visited missions, addressed a Moody-connected one, and soon had located a new site with a hall near Eighteenth and Halstead Streets.[12]

Later in November he and others of the committee held a deeply spirited consecration meeting, and appointed Ebersole as their secretary and treasurer. At first they lacked even the $50 for the first month's hall rent, but soon, by Steiner's interpretation, a "higher power" intervened: the Mennonite congregation at Cullom, Illinois invited Steiner to speak and collected $36.15 for his work. On Sunday December 3 the mission held its first service and by January it had added the medical dispensary and the Sunday school. Soon the workers were carrying on a variety of services to help people religiously, physically, and materially.[13]

Contributions and encouragement flowed in. A Logan County, Ohio correspondent wrote that "quite a number" in his congregation wanted "to do at least something," and were sending $5.00. A twenty-year-old woman from Ontario declared that for her the mission was an answer to three years of prayer that the Lord "might wake us up to a sense of duty"—"to snatch the ruined & degraded of the great Cities, from everlasting death." A Flanagan, Illinois woman reported that her congregation had a Woman's Aid Society: what kind of clothing should it send?[14] A shaky-handed grandmother sent $5.00. J. S. Hartzler wrote from the Haw Patch that his congregation had been glad to hear that a mission would preach the pure, simple gospel to the poor, including "Non-resistance, Non-conformity and other neglected doctrines"; even the bishop, Michael Yoder, had heartily approved. At Smithville, Ohio, bishop John K. Yoder reportedly was "the First One to give his mite." In eastern Pennsylvania bishops were more skeptical, but young activists of the Isaac Hershey and J. A. Ressler stripe began immediately to raise and send money. Foodstuffs and clothing arrived from as far as Maryland and Virginia in the East and Kansas and elsewhere in the West—not to mention substantial amounts from Illinois, Indiana, and Ohio.[15]

By late 1894, to be sure, the first excitement was past. Criticism had set in, and support was dropping off. Yet a core remained faithful. In December mission worker Samuel (S. F.) Coffman, son of evangelist Coffman, could still report that "contributions have been coming in nicely."[16]

The Mennonite Church now had a mission. Or did it?

If those who began the Chicago Home Mission in 1893 looked outside of their own church so much for inspiration, and if they got their mandate from themselves or from an unofficial rump session of a Sunday school conference about which the church at large was uneasy, was the mission really a venture of the Mennonite Church? Both Funk and J. S. Coffman, the two people who might bring young activists and the larger church together, qualified their support. After the 1893 Sunday school conference, bishops in Indiana considered the developments and neither endorsed nor opposed them. Funk's attitude thereafter, Coffman advised Steiner early in 1894, was warm but cautious. The older man, Coffman reported, had said only, " 'All right *if*,' etc."[17]

Coffman himself decided that the Indiana bishops had not done or said anything to stop the mission. As for his own support, "My heart is in it." But Coffman also had his "if." "A great part of the church would support the mission," he advised, if the workers proceeded "in the order of the church" and upon "the principles of the Bible as held by our people." Steiner should be careful of mistakes. Warned Coffman: "I see many chances for defeat."[18]

Coffman was right. Critics thought Steiner was proud, especially of his education. That might have been somewhat true, although it was hardly more than the speck in a brother's eye. Others thought the Chicago workers lazy, and out to find support without working.[19] Such suspicion of economic-nonproducers was understandable from people of the soil, but it hardly showed brotherly good faith.

Perhaps most unfair was persistent distrust of the Chicago workers for their youth—unfair because the middle generation had after all not led the youth, to Dubois County or to Chicago. Steiner, in his late twenties, was in effect the mission's elder, but for personal and church reasons he moved to Ohio in the fall of 1894 and turned the superintendency over to S. F. Coffman, who was only twenty-two. Youthful treasurers hurt the mission: earlier Ebersole had raised eyebrows by running a restaurant at the World's Fair in Chicago, and he also got mission accounts badly confused; another, Edward J. Berkey, had raised a stir with a chain-letter scheme to raise 10-cent contributions.[20] Moreover, having young unmarried workers of both sexes living at the mission aroused suspicion, especially when a couple of romances flourished. Yet, except for a time when the rising church leader Aaron Loucks lived there with his family while he studied at Moody's, the mission for some years was not able to attract a married couple to supervise, even though it tried. Mature people of the Mennonite Church just were not responding to the Chicago challenge. And that made criticisms of workers' youthfulness quite unfair.

Another source of criticism was more justified: Did the mission communicate what Mennonites understood to be gospel?[21] To keep pocketbooks open and prayers flowing, J. S. Coffman advised Steiner in 1894, the work must be "pretty thoroughly Mennonite." Steiner should be especially careful of what sisters the mission took on as workers. To keep the work Mennonite might mean slower progress at first, but, observed Coffman, "the church, I find all along, will stand by you if you stand by the church."[22]

Some workers' dress, the rule-of-thumb test many Mennonites used for orthodoxy, seemed out of line. At least one woman worker, Alice Thut, had already drawn criticism back home in Ohio for violating the codes, and it took time to convince even her fellow-workers in Chicago that she was a "solid Mennonite." As for male workers, Page drew criticism with a mustache, while DeWitt Good, a Virginia Mennonite studying in Chicago for foreign mission service, wore a ring. Such matters, to most Mennonite Church people, clearly symbolized one's attitude toward the world's ways and values. By August of 1894, Steiner, wanting Funk formally to organize a congregation at the mission, could assure the bishop that the workers were ready to follow Mennonite practice. Yet their attitudes surely hurt the mission.[23]

Broader than just dress, there was a question of general style. "A good many of our people ... are afraid we are drifting into Methodism," admitted mission worker Barbara Sherk early in 1895.[24] The Methodism charge was shrewd, for when Mennonites' ethical piety combined with the quickening's revivalism it did produce something close to Methodist-style holiness. The mission's stronger and more direct connections, however, were with the nondenominational Moody Bible Institute. Again, Moody's in 1894 was not the Moody's of three decades later. But the mission was an arm of Moody's about as much as of the Mennonite Church. At least ten workers studied there during the 1890s. Steiner and others attended Moody functions often, and the nickname for some of the mission's workers was "Moody boys." At least one, John Greaser of Wooster, Ohio, was not a Mennonite but a Presbyterian.[25]

Some of the sharpest criticism of the mission came from one John (J. K.) Brubaker, a fifty-year-old Lancaster County, Pennsylvania veterinarian and minister. Brubaker visited the Chicago mission in mid-1894, claimed to have support west of the Alleghenies, and vigorously urged his views upon church leaders there as well as in the East. In 1896 he was large enough to admit that it had been wrong to hurt the mission cause, but for a time in 1894 and 1895 his tone was very different. In addition to criticisms such as mishandling of money, he added another: general suspicion of cities. The mission's promoters were, of course, turning the badness of cities into a challenge. "Souls hovering around the Furnaces of Iniquity. The Boiling Caldrons of sin. The Craters of Hell open to receive souls by wholesale. ... Struggling masses of humanity pushing and crowding each other on to certain death." With these words Steiner's friend Christian (C. K.) Hostetler, for example, called for greater effort, in 1894. But Brubaker, although he agreed that God loved city dwellers, thought that missionaries should go to "other and better fields." City people had "so entirely abandoned every good principle" that they ignored the Sabbath, so they could no longer expect God's favor. Thought he: "Chicago like Sodom is no field for the Gospel to Succeed."[26]

Some objections were even more "Mennonite" than was distrust of cities, which many rural Americans of course shared. Brubaker (although his own style was hardly self-effacing) saw Steiner as lacking in humility, and admonished him on the point when he visited Chicago. Mennonites of Brubaker's region also distrusted the studying at Moody's. According to a powerful Lancaster conference bishop, Jacob (J. N.) Brubacher, it was bound to bring a "studied and salaried ministry."[27] Surely Brubacher was right in sensing that such influence would deeply change the Mennonite Church.

Indeed, much of the unease about the Chicago mission turned on a question of what authorities would call the tune in the Mennonite Church.

Authority for the Chicago home mission was much confused. Mennonite Church people, especially in Lancaster County, were nervous about what was proper activity for lay people. At Chicago laymen even preached, a fact offending even some friends of the mission.[28] Moreover Funk had ordained Steiner in 1893, and then in 1895 ordained S. F. Coffman for his work at the mission, without the traditional selection by lot. "Vox populi," bishop Brubacher scolded; and J. K. Brubaker thought Funk should have gotten the consent of the Illinois Conference. Funk, in self-defense, invoked words of the New Testament's Paul, Indiana Conference policy, and the fact that in young Coffman's case the congregation of a dozen workers at Chicago had given its voice. To that, however, J. K. Brubaker replied that the workers were not a formally recognized congregation, under conference authority.²⁹

Some district church conferences—in 1894 the Indiana Amish Mennonite one, and the Missouri-Iowa, the Southwestern Pennsylvania, and the Illinois Mennonite ones—endorsed the mission, but always with reservation. The Indiana body's language set the tone: the mission "should be encouraged and supported by prayer, counsel, helpers and finances" provided the workers "teach and practice" Bible doctrines "as accepted, taught and practiced by" the conference's congregations. The Illinois Mennonites added to their reservations that a bishop, Emmanuel (E. M.) Hartman, should visit the mission and report back.³⁰ The strong reservations meant that the mission continued to run on shaky authority.

So the question remained: was the Chicago work really the Mennonite Church in mission, or merely a rump group?

Pressures were building up until finally in the latter part of 1895 authorities would close the mission home, and for a time in 1896 the mission would cease officially to hold services. Behind all that were many immediate questions and short-term maneuvers, but the large question was still that one of authority. Or more broadly, it was the question of how a peoplehood church can marshal its resources for mission.

In Christian missions generally, the relation of church to mission has been troublesome. At one extreme have been Christians so preoccupied with the church's own life that they have forgotten mission—for instance, the Protestant Reformers, and most mid-nineteenth-century Mennonites. At the other extreme have been "faith" missions—private ventures, unhooked from any real church, looking more like secular business and voluntary organizations than like a gathered people of God. The faith mission has lacked counsel from the church in doctrine, in the use of God's money, and in other important matters. Between the extremes, most denominational mission boards have operated. But while they have been tied responsibly to the church as denomination, they have connected only tenuously to church as congregation. That pattern might fit traditions whose people consider church to be organization and hierarchy, but it is a questionable one for Mennonites. For to Mennonites church has meant above all the people—gathered for worship, for common life, for mutual support, and for doing God's work.

Torn loose from grass-roots church, missions have often tended to become exalted holy orders, and missionaries a special kind of saint. So appeals for grass-roots money and support have too often had to be contrived and artificial—at best leaving wide gaps in understanding and involvement, at worst lurid and unfair to peoples of other cultures. And so the question of relation of church and mission, or really of how church mobilizes to carry on its mission, has persisted. And of course it has posed an especially poignant challenge to a peoplehood church that emphasizes holiness and full obedience for all of its members, with no special holy orders.

As if to highlight the church-mission issue, in 1896 the Mennonite Evangelizing Board managed to expand itself and take control of the Chicago mission. In the more immediate sense, the Board's actions involved questions of who controlled, of who got what money, of whether it was better to use resources in the city than among scattered Mennonites, and—inevitably—of personality.

Funk at Elkhart and some who supported him could be most determined, while Steiner no doubt wanted too much to have his own organizations. Neither side worked very much to involve Mennonite congregations, as congregations, in mission. Very early Funk warned privately against the Chicago committee's considering itself a board. He urged Steiner to have the Chicago work clearly under the Elkhart-based and semi-official Mennonite Evangelizing Board of America instead of, in his words, "only connected with the Church by imaginary ties."[31] Early in 1894 the Evangelizing Board endorsed only missions "such as" the Chicago project, not clearly the Chicago mission itself, and pledged no hard cash; yet it wanted the mission to report to it on finances and activities.[32] That put Steiner in a glum mood and very soon, with cooperation from evangelist Coffman and others, he organized a new, alternative "Benevolent Organization of Mennonites." The Benevolent Organization's Illinois charter set forth an expansive set of goals: home and foreign missions, a Bible training school, deaconesses' and nurses' training, hospitals, and homes for children and for the old.[33]

Taking form was a most unfortunate and unsavory struggle, which during the next dozen years would put Funk always on one side and Steiner on the other. Various quickened Mennonite leaders took positions between, but gravitated generally toward Steiner. And far too often the struggle put all concerned into unbrotherly moods. During 1894 the Chicago mission's finances fell into such disarray that by March of 1895 Steiner himself talked of closing the mission. At first Funk, along with J. S. Coffman, expressed hope that it could continue. And in April the

Elkhart bishop went ahead and ordained the younger Coffman, and also baptized the first new believer so received at Chicago, a young man named Otto Boelke.³⁴ But in July he used his *Herald* to let loose a most unbrotherly blast.

Because of contributions for Chicago, Funk complained publicly in sharp language, gifts for sending evangelists among scattered Mennonites had dropped off sharply. In its dozen years the Evangelizing Board had, at very modest expense, brought hundreds of souls into the church. The Chicago mission, Funk continued by contrast, was using money three times as fast, with little result. Moreover, "the Chicago Mission is not under the control of the Evangelizing Board."³⁵

Funk overreached, for in his next issue he scaled his charges about expenses down from three times to one-and-one-half times, and confessed that the mission had done some good. But meantime, with his blast and the many other complaints as background, an apparently self-appointed group—older or middle-aged men ranging from Funk to Illinois bishop Hartman to Ohio minister J. M. Shenk to evangelist Coffman—met with Steiner and S. F. Coffman on July 25 and considered what to do. Their decision: close the mission home, where the workers lived. Later, in March of 1896, Steiner went to Chicago and more or less closed down the mission itself—although especially some women workers, particularly Lina Zook, Melinda Ebersole, and Mary Denlinger, stayed on and continued some of the programs, mainly those for children. Steiner's action, Funk asserted privately, was abrupt and "without authority."³⁶

Just then, somehow, the directors of the Benevolent Organization let the Evangelizing Board absorb their agency and reconstitute itself, in 1896, as the Mennonite Evangelizing and Benevolent Board (MEBB). Although not totally uncooperative, Steiner seemed unenthused, and soon busied himself with setting up an orphans' and an old people's home in Ohio. His aloofness from the MEBB, he suggested to a friend in 1897, grew from fear of being used by certain forces at Elkhart. In October of 1896, with Steiner thus all but out of the Chicago picture, the MEBB moved in, "reopened" the mission at a new location, and began to rebuild staff.³⁷

That finally put the mission on a continuous course. Moreover, it made it less a faith mission and more a denominational one. The Evangelizing Board had long had the various conferences sending representatives to serve on it. So when as MEBB it adopted the Chicago work, it brought the Mennonite Church very close to the denominational board pattern. At that time nobody was asking how a church with strong peoplehood traditions might make the congregation the main unit for mission.

As for results at Chicago, there was some reason for Funk to charge in his July, 1895 blast that they were small. Yet the youngsters at least had more to show than the middle generation could show in Dubois County.

"Where the sick are healed, the needy clothed, the hungry fed, and to the poor the Gospel is preached," declared the mission's letterhead. The workers were carrying on a fairly standard Protestant mission program. They provided a reading room. By February, 1894 they began to place needy children out into country Mennonite homes. By August they claimed a Sunday school attendance of 170 or 175, and dreamed of 300. Meantime they commenced a kindergarten, and expanded their dispensary to include fourteen inpatient beds. Faced with slum poverty plus a sharp depression in 1893, they distributed much food, clothing, etc., gleaned from country Mennonites. Combining preaching and social service was apparently no great problem. "Preaching is mighty poor comfort to an empty stomach & shoeless feet," Ebersole had said in 1893. But of course workers did preach and testify—in gospel meetings at their hall, in street meetings, in house visits, and by giving tracts. "A large amount of religious work has been done," Funk admitted as he retracted some of his criticism.[38]

"...And," Funk concluded, "a number of young people are encouraged and helped out of their sinful and corrupt ways."[39] In reality, however, new believers actually brought into the church were few. By late August 1894 workers claimed eighteen "converts," pointing to the lives and testimonies especially of four young men; and soon Steiner urged Funk as bishop formally to organize a congregation. But no one hurried. There was, quite clearly, an honest concern to count as converted only those who really seemed to understand the Christian life—to consider quality, not merely quantity. Steiner instructed the new ones on "Conditions of Discipleship" and Funk, in a September, 1894 visit, preached on "Separation from the World." Coffman advised Funk to move slowly if the new believers did not seem entirely sincere. It was safer not to be "too eager for numbers," Coffman thought. "We need to receive only the truly converted to our doctrine, and we are safe." But Funk should recognize that souls *were* being saved.[40]

That concern for "safety" was partly a fear that new believers might create further difficulty between mission and church, and the pace remained slow. In August 1894 Funk pleaded a throat ailment, and advised the applicants to wait a few weeks until he could come and baptize them. But he did not do so on his September visit, nor during the following winter. To complicate matters, the four young men were themselves unsure. Each had been baptized as an infant, and rebaptism meant defiance of their parents. Finally in April, Funk did baptize Boelke. But then attendance at the mission slumped. The slump, S. F. Coffman thought, came because families now realized that the mission was serious about proselytizing. Moreover, young Boelke soon quit the mission.[41]

Christian mission calls for planting churches, not just convincing individuals. Most missionaries have recognized this, and Mennonites with their understanding of church should recognize it the more.[42] Nevertheless, Funk did not organize a congregation as Steiner requested in mid-1894. By the time he baptized Boelke and ordained S. F. Coffman, the mission's troubles were of course coming to a head. In September, soon after the closing of the mission's home, young Coffman left. While those women workers gave the mission some continuity, male workers, including acting superintendents, came and went. Finally in September of 1897 the Evangelizing and Benevolent Board put nineteen-year-old A. Hershey Leaman of Lancaster County, Pennsylvania, in charge.[43]

Even then the mission did not become really secure and permanent until 1902, although meanwhile there were at least six or eight more baptisms.[44] Much of the problem was apparently in Elkhart. In January of 1902, for complex reasons, Funk's church and conference finally suspended his powers as bishop. In April, Illinois conference officials stepped in and ordained Leaman, and soon officially organized the mission congregation. Leaman was superintendent until 1920. By then the congregation numbered 75, and the mission had spawned another in Chicago with a congregation of 69.[45] Some members were country Mennonites who had gravitated to the city, and of course some were the mission workers. But the work had taken root.

The first formal venture of the Mennonite Church in mission was not a failure, but its beginning had been slow. Partly it was a case of youth against entrenched conservatism, but that was only at the surface. More deeply, the way of working in Chicago was foreign to the Mennonite Church's soul. To be sure, at least the women workers in Chicago wore and taught distinctive dress, while Steiner and others taught discipleship and separation. Moreover, at one point when rowdies were disturbing services, E. J. Berkey called on workers to respond nonresistantly. And when Lina Zook felt deeply attracted to a Baptist doctor who served the mission's dispensary, she yielded to the counsel of her church and waited for a Mennonite husband. All this was indeed quite "Mennonite."[46]

Yet in 1894, one Charles C. Shoemaker of Freeport, Illinois, sensed a deep problem in the Chicago Home Mission. Shoemaker, thirty-three, was a director of Steiner's Benevolent Organization and a brother of "J. S.," the bishop who in 1906 would be the first to serve as executive secretary of a new Mennonite Board of Missions and Charities. "We younger members should give ear to our older brethren, and not be stubborn," C. C. Shoemaker advised Steiner as the mission's troubles were beginning to build. Not Steiner, but some other young church workers were careless about working peaceably within the brotherhood. And precisely the people who supported the Chicago mission often seemed to be the least Mennonite in spirit. "I must say," Shoemaker continued, "that so far as I have met and conversed with the (I would say) staunch Mennonites, they do not approve of" the mission. Why did not "some good thorough bred [sic] Mennonite take hold of that Institution[?] If it was run right I would be in it heart and hand." As it was, Steiner's friend lamented, "I shrink from it."[47]

Shoemaker's remarks were of course in some ways narrow and unfair. But he was right in this: there was something about the mission that was not much a natural expression of Mennonites' faith. Surely the mission produced some good results. But it was not well rooted in Mennonites' own experience of trying to live as people of God.

* * *

Away from the Chicago scene, there was stirring also in eastern Pennsylvania. Some good might "come out of Nazareth yet" declared young evangelist D. H. Bender to Steiner in 1895; for "the mission spirit is running high in Lancaster County."[48] Bender's words were not entirely fair. The fact was, the mission movement in the Lancaster Conference kept itself closer to the Mennonite community and its life than did the Chicago mission.

Lancaster Conference Mennonitism was deeply conservative—as much socially as religiously. Its was the conservatism of communities that were, as North America and North American Mennonitism went, deeply rooted, in 180 years of stable history. Authorities were strong:

tradition, and a bishop system that was already becoming a legend among Mennonites. The authorities had been slow to accept Sunday schools. In the 1890s they mainly stood against revival meetings, church-sponsored higher education, formation of a general conference, and the like.

On the other hand, in some respects Mennonites in Lancaster County and elsewhere in Pennsylvania wove their lives far more deeply into the fabric of their larger communities than did many Mennonites farther west.[49] Language was for them no barrier against the world, for many of their non-Mennonite neighbors spoke the same Palatine or "Pennsylvania Dutch" dialect; and they knew English better than did Mennonites more recently arrived from Europe. In civic politics, they probably voted more than did their midwestern brethren.[50] Classwise, to trans-Allegheny Mennonites the wealth of eastern Pennsylvania Mennonite farmers and small businessmen was as legendary as the authority of their bishops. Indeed for the mission-minded, that wealth seemed a bottomless pit, smelling of perdition perhaps, but also suitable for deep mining.[51]

Here was the conservatism of well-placed peasants and burghers— deeply rooted in soil, family, and tradition, and fixed firmly in place with the glue of religion. Whatever its merits and demerits (it had both), the Lancaster Conference outlook affected the beginning of Mennonite mission there. It kept mission firmly under the control of the church (though whether of a peoplehood church or of an episcopacy is a question[52]). It brought intelligent caution. "To fully understand the work, and to learn the best methods" in mission might take the church years, declared a Lancaster County activist, Abram Metzler, Jr., in 1895. And, at best, it brought soundness. "It does not depend so much on what we say, or how we say it, as on what we really are," Metzler went on.[53]

Metzler, who had visited the Chicago mission in 1894, was among a group of "progressives" in Lancaster County—the same group who, according to G. L. Bender, thought that Steiner and his kind were "just the stuff." A leader of the group was John H. Mellinger, eventually executive secretary of the Eastern Mennonite Board of Missions and Charities after its creation in 1914, and among Lancaster Conference Mennonites the symbol of mission. Prospects for mission were growing brighter, reported another of the group, Christian (C. M.) Brackbill, to Steiner in 1894; some Amish and Mennonite brethren in Brackbill's neighborhood had started a Bible meeting and planned to send offerings to Chicago. The sentiment for mission was "quite a movement" and held "bright prospect." Yet, Brackbill observed, at present advocates of mission had to move "very cautiously."[54]

Cautiously, perhaps, but move. On a Saturday evening in September of 1894 twelve progressives met, all laymen, eight of them under thirty-five years of age, and spoke of organizing for action.[55] Some of their inspiration came from outside Mennonitism. In the group was the interdenominationally minded Isaac Hershey. So also was J. A. Ressler and his brother Amos; J. A., at least, was very friendly to several U. B. ministers, and about that time attended a Presbyterian meeting on missions in Japan. As a committee of the progressives began to draw up a constitution, they held one crucial meeting in a U. B. meetinghouse. On the other side, the group was careful to consult the prominent bishop in their district, Isaac Eby, and not to move without his approval. Eby on a Sunday pointedly preached on "Take Heed How Ye Build." Yet he apparently gave a nod, for on January 12, 1895, calling themselves the "Mennonite Home Mission Advocates," the group sponsored a public meeting. Some 150 persons attended, and gave $42.35 for mission.[56]

Then came opposition, complicated apparently by tensions among progressive laymen, the ordained ministers, and the close cadre of bishops. The tension was not new. In the winter of 1893-1894, for instance, the bishops had been advising evangelist Coffman, who privately called them the "Lancaster Sanhedrin," to stay out of the district for the time being. Eventually Coffman went, but advised the progressives to bear with their bishops. In Brackbill's opinion, the bishops spoke too much of "custom law rule, and *Conference*. O how sad to hear so much rule and *conference* and so little of *Grace*."[57] Bishop J. N. Brubacher was, for mission advocates, the main obstacle. In his younger days Brubacher had helped to innovate Sunday schools, but with his ordination he had become more cautious.[58]

Yet control by Brubacher and others who thought like him was not absolute. The people had begun "reading and thinking for themselves," declared the astute Metzler soon after the public meeting; and on the day following the meeting minister John Ranck, of the Paradise Mennonite Church in Eby's district, preached what Ressler thought was "with a little straining ... a mission sermon." Metzler thought quite a few ministers favored mission, but lacked "individuality and religious courage" to say so.[59] Then there was Eby. Eventually the progressives

Whose Mission? 71

learned that for some years Eby and his wife had quietly contributed to mission causes. Publicly Eby observed that he would not oppose what he had no scripture to cite in opposition. In his own way Eby served as the advocates' protector. After all, among the progressive group three Mellinger brothers were his nephews, while Isaac Hershey was nephew to Eby's deceased wife and would soon become son-in-law of Eby's second wife! Still, Metzler observed, if a layman did not want to "be set down on pretty heavy, he had better not do much suggesting, or do much practical work."[60]

Just as with Sunday schools, opponents could seem downright pigheaded. Soon after the Advocates' public meeting the *Herald* received a report which it refused to print on grounds that it was not signed.[61] With lapses of spelling and syntax, but in an old-style and beautiful handscript, the piece probably spoke for many Mennonites the *Herald* was ignoring.

It was not a matter of opposition to mission, professed the anonymous writer. Indeed, "to be daily engaged and try to draw the unconverted to Jesus" was the Christian's duty. But many who had attended the Advocates' meeting and given their names were now "sorry" and "feel to resign." For they now saw they were "going against the laws of the Mennonites," and that they were making church trouble. The Advocates should have consulted with the ministers, so "all things could be done in peace." Instead, they had opened "the door for the world"; for, declared the writer, "we hear say why the Mennonites are having a society," when "I thought they do not believe in anything of that kind. O let us cling to what we profess to be plain followers of that meek and lowly lamb Jesus Christ."[62]

Further, declared the writer, "We need not appoint special men to do mission work"; for "we all have enough mission work right at home first at our own families," and in giving words of encouragement to those one meets. So, "let us watch and pray that we walk more together hand in hand which the word of God teaches. Be kind to the poor" did not mean "send my money to some brother about 20 miles away." For "there are many poor ones in our villiage [*sic*] so if I have some remaining till I have supported myself then I can distribute among the needy."[63]

Marvelous provincialism! Yet however nearsighted and deadweighted, the writer's folk wisdom offered some corrective against merely copying the mainline missionary movement. As Coffman had written to Steiner a few months before, the church needed the East's "fearful, conservative disposition. ... We need the East and the East needs the West."[64] The anonymous author's concern for ministerial authority and Mennonite "laws" reflected, however distortedly, the idea of the people moving together, with discipline. Astonishment at a Mennonite "society" no doubt reflected Mennonite antipathy for lodges; and that in turn bespoke the conviction that the follower of Jesus did not divide his loyalties. Besides, fear of "societies" could become a bulwark against a tendency in the general mission movement to spawn organization that was unhooked from real church life. Similarly, fear of appointing "special men" could become a defense against setting missionaries up as a special kind of saint. And despite the writer's twenty-mile shortsightedness, was the principle of starting at home amiss? How many Christians have loved the heathen, but not their neighbors?

Whatever its value, the "conservative disposition" for which Coffman saw a need soon made itself felt. In April the bishops in their semiannual conference asked the Advocates to disband—expressing with the anonymous writer a mistrust of innovation, concern for church harmony and authority, and preference for beginning near home. Mission activity being "new in the Mennonite Church in the East," the bishops declared, we ... do not feel inclined to approve of all things that are connected with it, for the present at least." They did "not wish to condemn it;" but as "the great body of the church" was "not reconciled with it" (the progressives' version was that the people were afraid of their church authorities), it were best to wait until the church were more ready.[65]

"We do not wish to be understood that we do not favor mission work," the bishops continued, double-negatively. To visit the fatherless and widows, to distribute good religious literature, "to secure proper opportunities for our ministers to preach the Word of God," to visit neighbors and invite them to Christ and His church—these were surely "commendable and very highly appreciated." Ministers appreciated laymen's help in them. But as for the Advocates, "we would kindly and most sincerely wish to advise not to continue the above named society."[66]

The Advocates avoided confrontation. Informally J. A. Ressler might jokingly spell "bishop" as "Bis-hop," but later in 1895 the group voted unanimously to disband the "Mennonite Home Mission Advocates"[67] Yet harmless as doves, the group was wise like serpents. "You just can't get a hold on them," a critic reportedly said; they were too shrewd and "careful not to violate any ruling of conference or the church."⁶⁸ As the group recognized, the bishops had left a loophole by endorsing work close to home. Moreover, Brubacher had earlier championed Sunday schools, and someone passed the word that a broader Sunday school effort would be all right. So as the group made the motions of disbanding, it appointed a committee to draw up new resolutions. While the rest sang, the committee framed a plan for a "Mennonite Sunday School Mission" devoted to "practical Sunday school work." The full group approved, and by January of 1896 the erstwhile Advocates were back, with scarcely a lapse, as the "Mennonite Sunday School Mission."⁶⁹

In that form the progressives succeeded. Soon they were operating a half-dozen Sunday schools in rural and city areas of Lancaster County.⁷⁰ Leading with Sunday schools may have been questionable for a group committed to the believers church. The bishops' preference for such child-oriented work was perhaps a hint that their peasant-and-burgher sense of rootedness had brought a subtle version of *corpus christianum*. Indeed, Brubacher in 1862 had first gotten interested in Sunday schools by happening to attend an Episcopal one,⁷¹ and what tradition has represented *corpus christianum* ideas more than the Episcopal? In any case, at least three Mennonite congregations eventually grew out of the Mennonite Sunday School Mission.⁷²

And the activists in Lancaster County were made to work close to where ordinary Mennonites were trying to live their version of discipleship and peoplehood. And they were made to work. "Serves us right that they closed us Advocates down," Hershey admitted. "Let's stop advocating and start doing." Thereafter the group did seem less concerned with politicking, and more with quiet working.⁷³

Actually, the authorities did not confine the group to Sunday school work. At their Sunday school outpost in a mining district, Hershey and his wife, Ada, soon were giving clothing to poor children; and that soon led to creation of a Women's Sewing Circle at Paradise Mennonite Church. Before long John Mellinger was bringing "Fresh Air" children from New York City for periods in summers. And although mission offerings were at first dangerous, no one objected when donors quietly laid money on a certain table at the quarterly MSSM meetings. In 1897 the group began collecting money for India. and broadened its constitution to allow giving to any deserving Christian work or charity in the U.S. In 1899 it opened a city mission in Philadelphia on the Chicago pattern. In 1901 it began a discussion of charitable homes, so that a Mennonite old people's home was opened in the county in 1905, and a children's home in 1911. In the latter year, the group incorporated legally.[74]

Meanwhile there were strong side effects for Mennonite church life. MSSM quarterly meetings became highlights, with large crowds sometimes overflowing into churchyards. Groups hired special rail cars to travel to and from, and en route home lustily sang new songs learned at the meetings, such as "Send the Light,"[75] Thus Lancaster area Mennonites got a carefully measured dose of camp meeting, and reinforcement of the mission idea. By 1913 even bishop Brubacher participated. The gatherings continued until 1917. By then they had helped spawn the Eastern Mennonite Board of Missions and Charities, and thereby made themselves somewhat obsolete.[76]

Besides all that, in 1898 the Lancaster progressives generated the first Mennonite Church mission to a Black community. It was an industrial and educational project that quite unconsciously used a philosophy much like that which Negro leader Booker T. Washington had absorbed at Hampton Institute in Virginia and was trying out at Atlanta. In the Welsh Mountain Mission, named for a district in eastern Lancaster County where some poor Blacks lived, Lancaster district Mennonites did *not* emphasize church-building. Neither did they put simple "preaching of the Word" ahead of social service, at least not at first. They used a social service approach of a certain kind. And the kind demonstrated that the peasant-and-burgher Lancasterians, whatever their symbols of cultural separation, were very much in tune with some basic attitudes in U.S. life.

The concepts underlying the mission had nothing discernible to do with effort to create a community of radical faith, Anabaptist-style. Rather, those who promoted the mission spoke the language virtually any philanthropically inclined person in the U.S. would have spoken at that time: emphasis on self-reliance and self-help, on cleanliness and hard work, and on the better classes uplifting the lower ones while avoiding outright charity. To "Christianize" and to produce useful citizens got confused. "The temporal, moral, and spiritual condition of many of these mountain people," declared one John Buckwalter at an 1895 Advocates meeting, was a "mocking shame to our religion and boasted civilization."[77]

The result was that when a committee formed and opened the mission early in 1898, it used programs and methods of payment designed to teach the work ethic. It put twenty-two Black men and boys to clearing land, as a beginning; placed out pigs to be raised; attempted to operate a stone quarry; did run a shirt factory, where by the end of 1899 Black women and girls worked at twenty-three sewing machines in a new, solid, stone building; promoted broom-corn raising, broom-making, and strawberry raising; and not least, introduced a public school in the area, at which an upcoming Mennonite leader, and eventually prominent bishop, Noah H. Mack, taught for some years. For work done the Mennonite philanthropists were careful to pay in scrip, or IOUs, not in money. When storekeepers accepted the scrip, and exchanged it for cash collected from Mennonites and their neighbors, the mission required a record of what the recipients had bought.[78] Soon the mission operated its own store. In mid-1898 Jacob Mellinger, one of the original Lancaster County progressives, declared that although the recipients did not always spend the scrip judiciously, at least they were not buying whiskey. To Mellinger the refusal to give gifts and goods outright made the mission a "business" rather than a charity. Or at least to his way of thinking it was "a charitable institution in business garb."[79]

Mellinger's words spoke more of one class or caste in society teaching a "lower" one its own ways than of a new brotherly and sisterly community of God's people. Almost any North American, particularly a well-heeled one, would have found such words congenial. So did the editors of the *Herald*. The Welsh Mountain's "class of people" were "as nearly heathen as it is possible to find them outside of the foreign mission field," they declared in July of 1898. "Our Lancaster brethren have adopted a highly practical plan. . . . They are teaching them to *live*, which is one of the first requisites of mission work."[80]

Was it the color of the Welsh Mountain people in the mission's district that kept Mennonites from thinking of real Christian community with them? "The Mennonite church has been strictly a white man's church," a *Herald* writer from Illinois had declared sarcastically in 1892. "The idea of a negro or a Chinaman being a Mennonite, such an innovation would certainly make trouble, we being so dignified (?) [*sic*]"[81]

The public attitudes of Lancaster County Mennonites were mixed on the color question. At two of their quarterly mission meetings in 1898 they pointedly included talks on God's revelation to Peter that He was no respecter of persons, and on equality in Christ—the first by the astute Metzler, the second by the outstanding pastor of a General

Conference Mennonite Church in Philadelphia, Nathaniel B. Grubb. We must not "consider ourselves better than the black race," wrote a twenty-two-year-old Lancaster County resident, David Wenger, in the *Herald* in 1899. "We as Christians ought to have no respect to persons whether they be white, black, or yellow." Nevertheless, Wenger and other writers continually emphasized that the Welsh Mountain people were a "worthless" class, to use the word of a Mennonite history written in 1905 by educator-minister J. S. Hartzler and church leader Daniel Kauffman.[82]

Sometimes the statement was that Blacks had learned dissolute ways from a gang of white outlaws on the mountains. But all too often mission spokesmen emphasized the Blacks' pre-1898 habits of stealing, begging, and creating expense to the county with their irresponsibility. And while Wenger believed that Blacks could rise to Whites' levels, he thought, as did so many North Americans, that "of all the races, the white has reached the greatest perfection." "There is much to do," he urged, "to change the negro's manner to a more Godlike character"; and, confusing nation and church, he added that "great will be the reward to the nation or individual through whom it may be done."[83] Thus mission-minded Mennonites spoke condescendingly toward Blacks-as-they-were even while they expressed abstract faith in Blacks-as-they-could-be.

Although eventually Lancastrians would avidly invite Blacks to become Mennonites, in the early days at Welsh Mountain they apparently did not. "The Welsh Mountain Mission is an industrial rather than a religious institution," observed the minutes of a 1906 meeting for the creation of the Mennonite Board of Missions and Charities at Elkhart. "What will you do with the colored man when he is converted?" ran a typical question at quarterly MSSM meetings.[84] For some years the mission answered with a handy formula: while Mack, his wife Elizabeth, and other workers taught school and did their industrial work, they left church-formation to African Methodist Episcopal and Presbyterian ministers who worked in the area. Especially, they cooperated with an educated Black Presbyterian, Rev. Malford Hagler, scrutinizing him closely, letting him speak in their meetings, and allying with him in the work.[85] It was a formula that neatly avoided the question of Black Mennonite membership—and of course the question of what it meant to build a true community of faith.

Eventually the Lancastrians left their early formulas. From the early days they had conducted some Bible study and other such activities in the shirt factory. In 1906 Mack was speaking the language of "saving souls," not just that of moral uplift. John Mellinger, outstanding Mennonite mission leader of the region, came to speak especially eloquently of soul-saving as "the supreme object" of mission effort.[86] In 1914 the mission opened its own Sunday school. In 1917 C. M. Brackbill, now a bishop (despite his anti-bishop remarks in 1894), baptized the first Black to be received at the mission as a brother, one Elmer Boots. In 1920 the mission sponsored its first series of evangelistic meetings, and by mid-decade it had a standard mission program of Sunday school, Sunday preaching, Bible study meetings, and the like—with, in 1926, four Black members. Gradually the more direct-evangelism approach was replacing the industrial. A tragic incident in January, 1924 hastened that shift: the mission lost its superintendent, Arthur Moyer, when a Black whom he caught stealing corn shot him fatally. Later that year, as it abandoned industrial work, the mission began to provide a home for the invalid and aging, and in October it became the Welsh Mountain Mission and Samaritan Home.[87] It was in that form, quite changed from its original, that the mission continued in the late 1920s and beyond.

The form had changed. Meantime the attitudes by which mission-minded Mennonites judged Blacks and the work changed a degree, but not entirely. Reduction of crime and begging and thereby lowering expenses for Lancaster County's taxpayers had always been one strong criterion for judging the mission's success. In 1926, in a public report, Samuel H. Musselman, a mission leader among the county's Mennonites, still judged partly by that test. But he declared that lowered expense to the county was not as important as the reduction of lawlessness; also, he pointed to the fact of the four Black (or "colored," the term then in use) members.[88] Condescension and the attitude of moral uplift had by no means ended by the 1920s. Yet there was perhaps a bit more concern for the individual's regeneration and a bit less emphasis on convenience to the community. And Mennonites were beginning—imperfectly no doubt, but beginning—to accept Blacks as part of their own church.

Whatever their progress or imperfections along those lines, the Lancaster progressives in their Welsh Mountain Mission, and generally in all their activities, had demonstrated an important fact: it was not necessary for mission advocates to cut themselves off from their home congregations to make a start. In a deeply conservative conference, the most populous one of the Mennonite Church, mission-minded Mennonites could act on their convictions and do it under the discipline and counsel of the church.

* * *

On February 22, 1899, three missionaries sailed from New York for India, to establish what would become the Mennonite Church's first foreign mission. Their going depended much on Mennonite Church people's responding to dramatic stories of famine. For a time they depended heavily not on a regular income but upon getting gifts wherever they could, and the gifts often came to them directly rather than via a board.[89] So the India mission was at first something of a faith mission. On the other hand, there were those in North America who hoped at the outset that there could be a mission in which Mennonites of various branches—Mennonite Church, General Conference Mennonite Church, and others—might cooperate. In the end Mennonite Church people began their own India mission (and the General Conference Mennonites started another, in 1900). It became a going concern—this time of course not because it was close to home, but more probably due to other causes. The mission was far enough away not to be under constant scrutiny. By 1899 Mennonite Church people were more used to the idea of mission than they had been in 1893. Moreover they got caught up in the drama of famine, and of sending missionaries to a far-off land.

By the 1890s people in the Mennonite Church, as they paged through the *Herald* and other literature, were reading more and more about India's unsaved millions. In 1894 an Ontario Mennonite named Levi Groff even told of a heavenly message in which five huge letters, I N D I A, appeared before his eyes wherever he looked, and of the Lord's telling him plainly that the Mennonite Church would soon begin work there. In response he sent the Benevolent Organization of Mennonites $5.00, and then $1.25 more, to begin the work. By early 1896 when the evangelizing board swallowed the benevolent organization and formed the MEBB, it had about $100 in hand to open foreign work.[90]

Then in 1896 famine struck India, a severe one in which eventually some three million persons died. Various agencies in North America put out calls for funds to help, especially a Protestant weekly printed in New York, the *Christian Herald*, which by April 1, 1897, had raised $50,000. In that climate, early in March, Funk and others at Elkhart created a Home and Foreign Relief Committee under the MEBB. By the end of March the HFRC had pledges and gifts of some $4,000 in money or grain for India. By the end of 1898 it would raise $40,000.⁹¹

Before 1897 Funk's paper and the evangelizing board had been cooperating with other Christian groups to send money to sufferers for instance in Armenia and in Russia, and now the HFRC cooperated with the *Christian Herald* and others to send its grain.⁹² But this time the Mennonites sent a representative, to buy still more grain abroad and to oversee distribution. Their man was George Lambert. A free-lancer in style, Lambert would eventually fall out badly with Mennonite Church missionaries in India, who (fairly or unfairly) charged him with everything from self-promotion to smoking cigarettes. But already before 1897 Lambert had taken a trip around the world, published a book about it, kept up an interest in orphan work in India, and continued to correspond with some Protestant missionaries there.⁹³

In 1897 and 1898 Lambert was a Mennonite Church hero. He helped found the HFRC, and in April it sent him to India. The *Herald* was soon publishing dramatic letters from him about conditions there, and Protestant missionaries sent glowing reports to the HFRC of his businesslike methods. In November he returned to North America and went about telling Mennonite congregations of India's plight. In 1898 he published a book. *India: The Horror-Stricken Empire*, he called it, and the inside of the book had the same tone.⁹⁴ Mennonites, being a people who lived close to earth and food, responded. Perhaps, as the Mennonite Church's foremost mission leader in mid-twentieth century, Joseph (J. D.) Graber, would suggest, for Mennonites thus to respond to physical need when they had not yet risen to India's spiritual condition showed immaturity.⁹⁵ But at least the Mennonite Church in 1897 did not make the opposite mistake: to deliver only theological abstractions when people desperately needed food.

Late in 1897 the Elkhart group cut the HFRC loose from the Mennonite-Church MEBB, and renamed it a "Commission" instead of a Committee. Apparently they wanted to make it more inter-Mennonite. For in fact a number of Mennonite branches were already channeling their aid to India through it, and even furnishing a few of its directors and officials.⁹⁶ In 1898 the agency faced two major questions: Would it be really inter-Mennonite? And would it, in India, move on from only relief to united Mennonite effort in mission?

Andrew B. Shelly, secretary of the General Conference Mennonites' mission board at Berne, Indiana, wanted it to do both. Twice he helped arrange meetings to accomplish it. But in 1898 Mennonite

Church leaders were launching their own general conference, and at least one such leader, D. H. Bender, feared that any "combining with the Berne people" via HFRC would hurt the general conference cause. In August the HFRC's directors decided that "under existing circumstances, it is not deemed advisable to attempt to organize a united mission work." They hoped, however, "that the Lord may direct the work according to His will."[97] Whether or not it was the Lord's will, there was thereafter some inter-Mennonite cooperation. But in 1899 the General Conference branch formed its own relief agency, and from 1901 onward all HFRC officers were people of the Mennonite Church. As for the HFRC becoming a mission board, in the sordid quarrels around Elkhart there were charges that it tried to force India missionaries to recognize it as one of their supporters alongside the MEBB, and that it did not route money through the MEBB when it should have.[98] Finally in 1906 Mennonite Church leaders formed a new denominational board with clear authority over missions such as in India; and with that both the HFRC and the MEBB ceased to exist.

Meanwhile Mennonite Church leaders moved in other ways to make the India work more clearly a mission of their church. When Lambert was in India in 1897 he expressed doubts about how some Protestant missions were using relief monies, but he became a warm champion of others and encouraged Mennonites to help, especially their orphanages. Other leaders, however, thought differently. In 1898 C. K. Hostetler, as secretary of the MEBB, wanted "all the future Orphan work in India done through our own missionaries," and a stop to "dumping Mennonite money into Methodist and other channels." And in the same year Daniel Kauffman complained that the "Elkhart doings" were sapping the revenues of the church" for missions that taught "everything but Mennonite doctrine." Asked he, obviously referring to some accolades the *Herald* had published: "Why should we cripple the force of our organization that other denominations should say nice things of us?"[99]

In that mood some Mennonite Church leaders finally appointed their first foreign missionaries. Funk, in the habit of making such decisions for his church, wrote privately in August of 1897 that he was hoping to find someone to go. During 1898 Scottdale, Pennsylvania minister Aaron Loucks seriously thought of volunteering—a thought encouraged by his attending a rally of the most vigorous organization going for recruiting missionaries, the interdenominational Student Volunteer Movement, whose conventions younger Mennonites at the turn of the century were often attending. By midyear Loucks was giving up his idea; his wife's health was none too good, and the couple had three children. But the district conference of his area, the Southwestern Pennsylvania, was by then stirred up. When it met in October someone challenged members to pray every day until someone of the conference volunteered to go. The conference itself appointed a committee to help the MEBB make a selection.[100]

A few weeks later, in November, the Mennonite Church's brand-new general conference met at the Holdeman meetinghouse in the country near Elkhart for its first sessions. With it, the MEBB and the HFRC also held meetings. Enthusiasm for finding someone for India was running high, and went even higher when M. S. Steiner called a special meeting for November 4.[101] Among those at that meeting was J. A. Ressler, by then a minister closely associated with Loucks at Scottdale. Ressler did not have Loucks' family ties, since his wife had recently died and left him with only a small daughter.

Almost without forethought, Ressler found himself volunteering. That evening fifteen of the church's leading bishops met as an examining committee, and approved him. On the same day the committee also accepted William D. Page and his wife, the former Alice Thut, both of them of course former missionaries in Chicago.[102] By now Page was trained and ready to go as a medical missionary. In mid-1900, with the India mission barely underway, the Pages would have to return from the field because he suffered two serious bouts of illness. But for the moment the Mennonite Church had its first three foreign missionaries. In February they sailed, and on March 24, 1899, they arrived at Bombay.

At least the Mennonite Church sent Ressler and the Pages more or less. The mandate of the three missionaries was none too secure, for the general conference was new and controversial, and a number of important district conferences had not joined. For a few years, given those continuing frictions mainly between the Steiner group and the Elkhart forces, there was still some confusion about the lines by which the mission really connected to its church.[103] On the other hand the India mission surely grew out of a popular outpouring of concern among Mennonite Church people, albeit in the dramatic and temporary crisis of famine. Examination and approval of the missionaries by fifteen bishops who had come together for important churchwide meetings clearly constituted some kind of mandate from the church. And time would show that, although the India mission would suffer some lean times, the home church people kept it going with far more certain support than they gave the Chicago Mission in its early days.

From 1899 onward, the Mennonite Church was a church in foreign mission.

* * *

Whether or not midwestern Mennonites could have succeeded in the 1880s had they begun naturally and authentically in some place such as Dubois County, will always remain a puzzle. And would the easterners have succeeded so nicely had Steiner and others not broken ground further west, borne the brunt of hostility, and shown what to avoid? Or would Mennonite Church people have sent missioners to India simply out of concern for carrying the good news, without the drama of famine and a book on a "horror-stricken empire"? "Who can understand His ways?"

Whatever the answers, the Chicago venture got into trouble because it was removed from what Mennonites knew as church and community life, yet close enough for homeside Mennonites to see and criticize. The progressives in Lancaster began closer to their church, its authorities, and its people, and they succeeded better. The India mission had help from dramatic human need, plus the exotic aura of foreign work. Moreover, although there was still some confusion about just how the Mennonite Church could mobilize to send missionaries, by 1899 the idea was firm that the Mennonite Church would have missions. So the mission in India got underway, and continued.

As they began in each location, Chicago, Lancaster County, and India, the Mennonite Church's new missioners very much copied general American and Protestant attitudes and methods. As they continued they kept up that imitation by making their church and its work more institutional.

3
THE URGE TO MAKE INSTITUTIONS

Every schoolchild knows that in the late nineteenth and early twentieth centuries the Andrew Carnegies and the John D. Rockefellers were building new business institutions on a modern design. But not everyone realizes that others were doing much the same with almost every kind of institution from government bureaucracies to welfare agencies to schools to churches. In fact from its beginning the modern missionary movement reflected such changes in the Western world. The changes were leaving less and less of life to natural family, neighborhood, and similar groupings, and making more and more of it a matter of deliberately planned, geographically far-reaching organizations, which spelled out human relationships in constitutions and by-laws, contracts, professionalized offices, and organizational charts.[1] Hence the mission movement's many Bible, tract, and other societies, its mission boards, and its benevolent institutions such as schools and hospitals.

By the time of the Mennonite Church's quickening, the changes had begun to sweep Mennonites along. For instance in 1847, in eastern Pennsylvania, a major schism occurred around a preacher named John Oberholtzer when he demanded mainly that the Franconia Mennonite Conference keep formal minutes and have a constitution. Eventually the Oberholtzer group and others formed the General Conference

Mennonite Church, so named because its people formed an overall, denomination-wide governing body. In 1866 some of these organizing Mennonites created a missionary society, which they made over in 1872 to be a mission board. In 1884 a group formed an orphans' aid society. In 1896 one of their district conferences began an old people's home. Et cetera. Boards, institutionalism, and more formal and modern-style organization were coming closer and closer to the Mennonite Church.

Though they followed the new trend more from afar, people in the "old" Mennonite and Amish Mennonite churches began to march along. In the 1870s many of their members participated in an inter-Mennonite "Board of Guardians" to help some fellow-Mennonites immigrate from Russia. There seems to be no hard evidence of that experience touching off the Mennonite Church's movement into mission and benevolence in any direct way, but it all fit the organizing mood. In the 1870s and 1880s Mennonite Church people in Pennsylvania, Indiana, and elsewhere, with their district conferences' permission or sponsorship, formed organizations for mutual aid against fires.[2] A Mennonite Evangelizing Committee appeared of course in 1882 and evolved into the Mennonite Evangelizing and Benevolent Board. J. S. Coffman, Steiner, and some other quickened leaders organized a "Mennonite Book and Tract Society," in 1889. That was a step onto the turf of Funk's publishing house, still another example of institution-building. By the 1890s almost all of the Mennonite and Amish Mennonite churches' district conferences were keeping formal minutes, however ironically in light of the Oberholtzer story. And in 1898 their leaders, after much pulling and hauling, created a general conference of their own, which (although the populous and powerful Lancaster Conference as well as the Franconia and some others refused to join) held biennial sessions thereafter. Thus did people of the Mennonite and Amish Mennonite churches step with the trend.

Some were more or less conscious of the process. "In all our work system is necessary," declared an 1881 *Herald* editorial on "church extension." A year later a frequent *Herald* contributor, a Michigan layman named John O. Smith, agreed: "Proper and effectual system," he wrote, was as important for spreading the gospel as a farmer's using a threshing machine instead of a flail. In 1892 evangelist Coffman argued that when it came to giving people the Word of God, Mennonites were "too slow, too indifferent and too unsystematic."[3]

In 1895, at a Sunday school conference, rising church leader Jacob (J. B.) Smith put it right into the language of late-nineteenth-century business. Mennonites should concentrate forces, he argued, for "concentration is the secret of strength in all the management of human affairs." Also in business language the *Herald* editors, in 1898, eulogized an Englishman's support of orphanages with a remark that "every penny was carefully accounted for and expended with that strict conscientiousness" which came from seeing that all belonged to God. Concerned that Mennonites were giving to non-Mennonite orphanages in 1906, Aaron Loucks asked rhetorically why they did so, when Mennonites' own projects "make a dollar go much farther than many other Missions." "It costs $1 a soul by the evangelizing board to convert them," reflected J. A. Ressler privately in 1897. "Do missions pay?" the Kansas-Nebraska-Oklahoma district conference asked itself in 1898. Yes, it answered, it paid those who were saved, and it always paid to obey God. So the conference concluded, still in business-style language, that "missions pay largely."[4]

Usually those who commented did not carefully examine their language or the trends they were following. But some raised questions. Not always did they borrow the business outlook uncritically. As Steiner became increasingly disillusioned with Funk, for instance, he accused the powers at Elkhart of "monopolizing."[5] (Of course in making that charge, Steiner was borrowing another North American theme of the 1890s.) Frequently those who called for more system stopped long enough to say that *too much* machinery could be a curse, or to warn against machinery without the Spirit's leading.[6] And already in 1881 the *Herald* editor who called for more system reflected what was perhaps the most profound issue for Mennonites: he hoped, he said, system could come in a manner "that will not conflict with our quiet, humble ways, with our time-honored usages and customs, and with our rules of order."[7] Apparently the editor—probably Coffman—did not fully understand what profoundly different attitudes he was trying to mix.

Despite some questions, quickened Mennonite leaders were usually quite sure that institution-building was good. None was more sure than Steiner, who in 1891 made a deliberate appeal for the Mennonite Church to do it. "The most prosperous periods of the children of God under the Old Covenant are marked by the preparation for and building of the synagogues and temple," the young quickened leader asserted. And Christ had taught in those institutions, as well as in the field. Primitive Christians had held goods in common, and now church institutions could be the common endeavors. An institution such as a

Church publishing house could help spread the " 'peace doctrine' of Christ." "There are orphan homes to be built," and "mission stations to be planted in the dark regions of the earth." There were "Bible institutes to be established for the training of teachers, missionaries and evangelists ... that the doctrines and teachings of Christ may be circulated far and wide." "Much good is to be accomplished through various institutions," Steiner was sure; "and why are we not at it?"[8]

The words were a ringing call. Yet, probably more than Steiner ever recognized, they were a call to follow a way of North American culture—once again, of course, in a religiously sanctioned manner.

* * *

By 1896 a group around Steiner began to heed his words. Even before his challenge, in 1889 an anonymous *Herald* writer had called on Mennonites to do something for the "thousands and thousands of dirty, ragged, friendless, and homeless children" growing up under evil influences in city, town, and countryside. That writer thought Mennonites might support existing, non-Mennonite children's aid societies. But the *Herald* editors wondered instead: "Would it not be doing the work of the Lord, if the Mennonite church would establish and maintain an Orphan's [sic] Asylum?" Soon *Herald* reader J. K. Zook of Missouri quietly offered Funk $100 toward an orphanage fund.[9]

The orphanage idea lay dormant for a couple of years, and then Steiner revived it in the *Herald's* pages. Immediately there was the question of how that kind of institution would relate to the church. Quite a few brethren favored an orphanage, Steiner declared in 1892, but they thought the church should own and control it; so they were waiting for the church to act. To that Steiner replied that "every new enterprise, or every reformation or revival in religion" began with individuals leading out. "The church as a body moves slowly in any direction." The apostle Paul had moved ahead of the church, and so had Menno Simons. So why did not some "well-to-do brethren" build an orphanage and "then solicit the interest and patronage of the church?"[10]

Steiner had argued well. However, he overlooked two points. When he called on "brethren," he ignored a fact that women were sending some substantial bequests to budding church organizations. Second, Steiner might have examined more closely whether his way was really the way for a people of God to find God's will, or whether it smacked merely of Anglo-American individual enterprise.

As matters turned out, in 1893 the Southwestern Pennsylvania district conference endorsed the orphanage idea, before free-lancing individuals built any. Then in 1894 or 1895 an evangelist from northern Indiana, David Garber, moved to a Rittman, Ohio farm his father-in-law Solomon K. Plank had offered to begin such a home. Early in 1896 an Amish Mennonite woman in Illinois bequeathed $500. In mid-1896 the orphanage opened. The Ohio conference endorsed it, and appointed committees to oversee it and raise money.[11]

Not all Mennonites were ready to give. Garber assured *Herald* readers in 1896 that the project depended on free-will gifts and self-support; nobody would be "taxed" for it. The *Herald* announced that the Evangelizing and Benevolent Board also stood ready to receive gifts and pass them to the orphanage, and pointed to the example of Seventh-Day Adventists, who in less than fifty years had developed "numerous Sanitariums, Hospitals, Colleges, Publishing Houses, etc." in North America and even abroad. "Thorough organization brings success," the editors commented; and above all, every Adventist member was an earnest worker and gave a tithe.[12] Despite such pep talks, finances at the Mennonite orphanage were tight. Women's groups and others furnished plenty of bedding, clothing, and other gifts in kind, but for some years cash was short.[13]

Nevertheless, in 1897 a Wayne County, Ohio, couple named Daniel and Fannie Amstutz willed a farm for another step in Mennonite benevolence, an old people's home.[14] As it developed, that institution raised some interesting issues. *Regionalism:* People far from Ohio were often understandably reluctant to give support. When they did, eastern Pennsylvanians with a mentality of permanence wanted a very substantial stone building while midwesterners, less wealthy and less rooted, wanted a frame structure. (The board decided on frame construction with brick veneer!)[15] *Professionalization:* In 1897 and 1898 the board paid its treasurer, G. L. Bender, to solicit funds[16]—this from Mennonites who refused to salary ministers. *The nature of the church:* Bender scarcely seemed to assume that congregations were decision-making units. Instead he tended to go to reputedly wealthy individuals—without reflecting on what it meant to let a wealthy class, rather than the whole church, make the church's decisions. Some Amish Mennonites in Illinois, however, insisted on bringing the old people's home matter to their congregations before contributing to Bender's cause.[17]

Mostly however the issues remained below the surface, and activists moved forward on the easy assumption that to build the institutions was surely the Lord's work. The old people's home opened in 1901, with five inmates from five states. In 1900 the orphans' home moved to West Liberty, Ohio. In 1917, with some sponsorship from Elkhart but initiative mostly from farther west, Mennonites began a children's home at Kansas City, Missouri, in connection with a mission they had begun there in 1905. In 1919 the old people's home burned; in 1922 the board at Elkhart helped open another at Eureka, Illinois, and in 1939 reopened the Ohio one. Meantime, east of the Alleghenies, Mennonites of the Lancaster, Pennsylvania area opened an old people's home in 1905, and Maryland Mennonites one in 1923—plus children's homes at Millersville in Pennsylvania and at Grantsville in Maryland in 1911 and 1914, and that old people's home in connection with the Welsh Mountain Mission in 1924. Eastern progressives, such as John Mellinger, would surely have been willing to work more closely with westerners.[18] But for complex reasons—controversy surrounding Funk, distaste for a budding college at Goshen, Indiana, and the like—easterners chose to operate to quite a degree independently not only from Elkhart but also from the Steiner group.

But one way or another, often by passing lightly over some of the issues and the regional divisions their actions touched, quickened Mennonites began to create and operate benevolent institutions.

* * *

All of that did not happen without some sharp factionalism, mainly with Steiner and people of his rising generation who accepted his leadership clashing against elements at Elkhart still more or less loyal to Funk. In 1906 creation of a Mennonite Board of Missions and Charities, with clearer denomination-wide sponsorship than any previous board, finally did much to end those frictions. In the narrowest sense the MBMC was a product of tugging and pulling within the Mennonite Church. More broadly, however, it reflected the standard Protestant model of a denominational mission board, Western culture's institutionalizing trend, and desire to get the lines of new institutions' authority to run clear and straight and more under the authority of the church.

For a time in the 1890s it appeared that the Evangelizing and Benevolent Board created in 1896 would be the denominational agency. It assumed control of the previous evangelizing board's work and the Chicago mission, took charge to open work in India, and in 1897 appointed a group of Ohioans, including Steiner, to oversee the orphanage and the old people's home.[19] But Steiner soon turned the Ohio group into a board rivaling the MEBB. The reasons were complex:

growing unhappiness with Funk's publishing; troubles at the Elkhart church and Funk's losing bishop authority; hurts—on the one side Steiner's position since at least 1891 that the church should have a publishing house really its own,[20] and on the other the Funk group's summary dismissal in 1895 of Steiner as editor of a *Young People's Paper*.[21] More generally, Funk seems to have been increasingly high-handed, and certainly Steiner was ambitious. In 1899 the Ohio Board got itself legally chartered as the Mennonite Board of Charitable Homes, with Steiner as president; in 1903 it reincorporated, adding "and Missions" to its name. Its jurisdiction got entangled with that of the MEBB, until in 1904 workers for instance at the Ft. Wayne, Indiana mission complained that they were not sure who was responsible for their work. In 1905 J. A. Ressler had sharp words for Steiner for what he perceived as effort to wean the India mission from MEBB to MBCHM, maybe even withholding donations for the purpose. The exchange got so sharp that John Mellinger felt like spanking both Steiner and Ressler.[22]

Although very unfortunate, the friction did set off some thinking about how the church should conduct mission and benevolence. Yet even that often reflected the cultural trends toward organization and professionalism more than careful questions about what it meant to be people of God doing His work.

In 1904 Noah E. Byers, president of the new Goshen College, called for both clearer organization and in effect the beginnings of professionalism. The Mennonite Church had everything needed for "strong and effective" mission work, he argued in the *Herald*: high per capita wealth; a "sacrificing, consecrated and obedient" people; and youth "well trained in industry, economy, and sincere morality." But, Byers lamented, efforts remained fragmented among several boards who played on "selfish motives and prejudices," while each region wanted its "own board officers, titles and fees." The mission cause needed a well-qualified, full-time person: "an organizer, a leader, a director who makes this one thing his chief concern in life." In other words, the Mennonite Church needed one "General Missionary and Evangelizing Board" with a full-time, paid executive secretary.[23]

To that, others such as D. H. Bender and C. K. Hostetler somewhat agreed. But Hostetler, as secretary of the Elkhart-based MEBB, emphasized the problems. The Mennonite Church had "no recognized 'head,' " he wrote publicly. Mission work was no mere local affair, yet district conferences were locally oriented. Easterners and westerners in the church were not ready to cooperate in "general organization" (clearly Hostetler had in mind Lancasterians' and others' choice not to affiliate with the church's general conference). And Hostetler knew of no man "into whose hands all sections would be willing to commit their mission interests." That last point Hostetler probably aimed at Steiner; in any case, he went on to assert that the basic organization of MEBB was good, with nine directors and various field-workers more or less representing district conferences. To strengthen it he would have each district conference form its own mission committee, and then annually have the central board meet, with each committee sending a representative, to achieve general cooperation.[24]

Solomon (S. B.) Wenger, an Iowa layman who was president of the Missouri-Iowa district conference's mission board, wanted clearer centralization. "We need our publishing interests under the direction of the church," thought Wenger; "a church paper ordered and controlled by the church, our educational work the same way." The "system of work" should be "uniform" with every member feeling "he is connected in a direct line." For that Wenger had a plan, which he considered to be as nicely systematic as God's own solar system: have a general, churchwide mission board made up of representatives of district conference ones, and the district ones made up of representatives of congregations.[25]

With Wenger's plan, Byers enthusiastically agreed. Several Elkhart people argued however that in essence their MEBB was already what Wenger was calling for. Hostetler suggested further that after the general conference had reorganized the MEBB, it should see that all the church's mission work was brought under it. (So much for Steiner's MBCHM!) Meanwhile from solid experience on the field Ressler warned against either too much or too little central direction—but especially, just then, against too many organizations. He surely did not want separate district conferences appointing missionaries, for he thought such a pattern would soon create "a lot of independent missions" and for the missionary on the field "require all the grace possible ... to keep out of trouble." Not only did Ressler want orderly organization; he hinted also at professionalism, for he added that he wanted to be sure a central board retained power to screen missionary candidates.[26]

More on the other side were views of two Amish Mennonites—reflecting, perhaps, fidelity to the Amish group's less centralized, more congregational understanding of church. Not that the two rejected all system: "All should be done systematically in harmony with love to one another," said one of them, Samuel (S. D.) Guengerich of Iowa. "Order is one of God's first laws; let us abide in the same." And Pius Hostetler of East Lynn, Missouri, generally supported Byers' call for a new central board.[27]

But, Pius Hostetler asked, could one board draw as much total financial support as the several boards were now getting? Moreover, should the church put both mission and benevolence under one body? Were the same officials capable of overseeing diverse kinds of work? And, wondered Hostetler—in effect raising another issue regarding professionalism—should the church really take men qualified and ordained to preach the gospel and use them to direct organizations? To all that, Guengerich added a warning against the business models. In business, he reasoned, central directors might sit back and make key decisions; but mission board members should be people directly involved. In mission, results came by involvement. "The more brethren we have at work, old and young, ... the more efficiently can the work be done for the Master's cause."[28]

Discussion continued, and by the spring of 1905 a movement was on to amalgamate MEBB and MBCHM into something more certainly a denominational board. Regionalism was apparently the chief hindrance. "You know" how in the East "anything about Elkhart is looked upon rather suspiciously," John Mellinger advised Steiner. Reformers were well advised not to "attempt to lasso the East," agreed Noah H. Mack of the Welsh Mountain Mission, in 1906. Daniel Kauffman, in his lawyerlike way, thought the solution was for the church's general conference to take over both MEBB and MBCHM, giving the former the responsibility for evangelism and the latter for benevolence: "Two distinctive Church Boards, one to feed the mouths of the needy and the other to feed the souls of the needy."[29] Kauffman's plan had nice symmetry, in keeping with the idea of system in organization. It also fit the separation growing in Mennonite thought between salvation and ethical concern.

But that plan did not take root. Kauffman was soon emphasizing the danger of rival boards, and calling for somehow joining the two old ones. Then, he advised, let each mission station and each benevolent institution have a local governing board under that central board, to keep the central board's work down to the point where it would not need salaried officers.[30] With that suggestion Kauffman was of course resisting professionalization. He would also keep mission organization somewhat loose from the whole district and general conference structure. That looseness might provide some freedom from the church's many-sided politics; but it also left some ambiguity as to how answerable missions and institutions would be to their church.

Whatever the merits or demerits, something close to Kauffman's second plan became reality. On November 15, 1905, at an MEBB meeting held in conjunction with general conference sessions at Berlin (later renamed Kitchener), Ontario, interested persons decided upon a committee of nine to work out an MEBB-MBCHM amalgamation. On May 19 and 21, 1906, the nine met and approved a plan drafted largely by Steiner and Illinois bishop Joseph (J. S.) Shoemaker. The central idea, as in Kauffman's second model, was local boards under a central board. One refinement was for the central board to have, in addition to its main treasurer, a regional one for the "East" and another for the trans-Allegheny "West"—reflecting, of course, the Mennonite Church's deepest regional fissure. The plan gave the mission and charities enterprise a certain degree of self-perpetuation and autonomy. On the central board was a core of eight members that the organization itself would appoint to four-year terms. General conference appointed, by contrast, only three members, and those for only two-year terms. Each district conference appointed two for one year. Institutions' and missions' local boards were each able to name one board member. So while the enterprise was partly answerable to church government via the conferences, it had strong features of an independent, self-contained enterprise.[31]

Nevertheless, the Mennonite Church had finally gotten its denominational board, or "Mennonite Board of Missions and Charities." MEBB and MBCHM officially approved and on June 20 the organization received an Ohio charter. Steiner became its first president, Shoemaker secretary, and G. L. Bender treasurer. In 1907 the church's general conference gave its official blessing. At first the new board's legal place of meeting was the old people's home in eastern Ohio, but in 1915—after Funk's company and power base at Elkhart had ceased to be—it established permanent headquarters at Elkhart. Also in 1915 it granted a living allowance for Bender and his family, and he became the board's first full-time official.[32]

The MBMC, often referred to as the "General Board" or the "Elkhart Board," succeeded, but not absolutely. Its members seemed to work together well, so at least it represented a resolution of the old factionalism. To some degree, despite the independence built into its organization, it did put missions and benevolence more clearly under the auspices of the church. On the other hand, for years it did not enjoy the full confidence of the numerous and relatively wealthy Mennonites of the "East"—even though the increasingly prestigious John Mellinger helped create it and served as a board member, and another Lancastrian named Samuel Musselman was its eastern treasurer. Nor apparently did one board draw as many donations as two. In 1910, not long before he died at the age of only 44, Steiner noted both a decline in giving and a tendency for regional leaders for instance in eastern Pennsylvania and in Ontario to move ahead on their own rather than accepting leadership from people farther west. He did not entirely oppose local responsibility, for he thought it should give people second thought before beginning some expensive new project.[33] But the fact was that the early years of the board were difficult, financially.

Whatever its successes or difficulties, the board represented trends toward organization and system to be found in North America generally and in the modern Protestant mission movement. At its outset it made "to systemize and extend the work of evangelization" its first object, and "to systematize as much as possible the evangelistic work of the church" a main duty of one of its leading committees.[34] Apparently no strong voice asked whether Mennonites, from their historical experiences and their understandings of how God works, ought to proceed differently. Steiner, in that reflective mood before his death, did have some second thoughts. The impulse to organize was getting out of hand, suggested the once eager champion of institution-building. "We are now in the 'organization' period of our church life." As soon as several hundred or thousand dollars appeared, "someone is ready to propose the incorporation of a board." "Everybody seems to have been taken with the fever.... The thing is being overdone.... The Church is in fact at present 'organization poor.'"[35]

Steiner's warning was surely one his church could well ponder. Yet even he was objecting mainly to too much scattering of energies and finances. In part at least he was calling for still more system and coordination. He was not asking whether modern-style organization, with its rational planning and its designs for wielding power, fit the nature of God's church. Was it in keeping with Jesus' nonresistance, with His way of working through what the world calls weakness?

* * *

The organizing trend operated, willy-nilly, in the building up of the India mission. By a year after J. A. Ressler and Alice and William Page arrived on their field in 1899, they had an extensive work-relief program going so smoothly that a British official thought the missionaries seemed not even to work very hard, since everything went like clockwork.[36] Within a decade the mission had many institutions: orphanages, a dispensary, schools, a lepers' asylum, even an entire village. Behind them was no master plan. The missionaries just plunged—into the wake of a famine, and into currents started by other missions.

Beginning a mission in the wake of famine led quite naturally to organizing of institutions. George Lambert, the *Herald*, and others who had spoken loudly for sending missionaries to India had made much of the needs of orphans. The missionaries arrived in March, and by September's end had charge of their first eight.[37] For adults their answer was work-relief. Crops failed again in 1899, and mass hunger increased. When two sixteen-year-olds came begging for food, Ressler advised *Herald* readers in September, he decided they would work for it. "I have no work but will invent" it, he wrote resignedly, and then added, in a standard Anglo-American attitude: "I don't want to make paupers of them."[38]

Thus began a work-relief program, almost unplanned. Soon the missionaries and the district government struck up a scheme whereby the government provided food and pay for workers while Mennonites supervised, paid for building materials, and got new mission buildings. Ressler had some reservation about the scheme, but reasoned: "We keep from 500 to 1,500 people under our influence for the greater part of a year and in the end have a set of mission buildings. Is our investment bad?"[39] By December he was supervising also some 9,000 people working in government projects to build roads and reservoirs, and eventually he took charge of such work in some thirty-eight villages. Meantime Dr. Page, in addition to medical work, ran a government-sponsored poorhouse and a government-financed kitchen that fed as many as 1,500 people twice daily. Alice Page initiated a milk-feeding program for children. And by late 1900 the orphanage had grown to 150.[40]

Thus, responding to famine, the American Mennonite Mission (as it named itself) quickly had extensive buildings, programs, and institutions. Nobody resisted the trend; during the next decade a score of new missionaries arrived and most went to work in ways that continued it. Not that they ignored Bible teaching, preaching, and church-formation. About December of 1899, Ressler and the Pages and several Indian Christians began a Sunday school and street preaching. Late in 1900, with the famine crisis past, the missionaries set about instructing and receiving would-be church members—having waited until then, they later explained, so as not to attract "rice Christians." By 1902 the Mennonite Church in India had 320 members and by 1910 about 500, a plateau it then held for about a decade. Meantime the mission developed an evangelistic department with colporteur work, village preaching, and the like. Yet in 1912 missionary J. Norman Kaufman wanted new missionaries sent over on grounds that only two of the sixteen already there were full-time in direct evangelism.[41]

The ultimate expression of the institution-building mentality was to buy a village. In 1906, after much discussion, the missionaries paid $2,600 for an eight-hundred acre tract that included a settlement called Balodgahan.[42] It was somewhat like buying a large plantation and with it getting a force of farm workers or sharecroppers. But what irony! Mennonites, historically a humble and unassuming folk, were now in a lordly role. And since the village was a unit of civil government, the purchase had overtones of *corpus christianum* of a kind Mennonites' forebears had stoutly rejected. Yet the missionaries defended their move. It would, they said, make for permanence: the people would find that "if they want to object to the Christian religion they must combat a *permanent thing*." It would help support the mission, to the tune—at least one estimate ran—of $700 of profits a year. Most of all, it would help give the emerging Christian community a solid economic base. That last argument the missionaries used also to defend industrial schools and other programs to teach orphans and other Christian youth various farming, business, and craft skills.[43]

Whatever the merits of such arguments, the projects cost money. In the latter part of 1906 the mission found itself floundering in financial crisis, borrowing at 12 percent interest to pay part of the price of the village, and putting out emphatic appeals to the home church just when the new board there was scarcely on its feet. Matters eased a bit in 1907, yet remained difficult enough that in the remainder of the decade some officials and others in North America began to ask whether the mission was not costing too much, and particularly whether it had not ought to work more by "direct" evangelism, less through institutions.[44] The board's response, however, was mainly more system. For instance, in 1907 it began to send regular monthly checks to the mission instead of just forwarding donations that came in, and then trying to raise extra money when mission appeals grew urgent. To forestall another 1906-style crisis it also set up emergency funds, both at home and in India. And where at first the India group had operated almost as a faith mission, getting more than half its money directly from homeside contributors rather than through any board, now both board and missionaries worked to get more and more of the money channeled through the board.[45]

Still, while the India missionaries and the new board at home made some changes, there were many questions they did not face. Some they would face eventually, especially in the 1920s in a crisis surrounding institutional work in India and homeside support for it. Was institutionalized permanence really an ideal for God's church, as missionaries assumed? To build God's Kingdom, was administering institutions the best use of a missionary's time? Would ownership and control of a village—a civil community—make for the kind of church that Mennonites understood Jesus' church to be? And did the institutions and the village put white foreigners and brown Indians into contacts that best demonstrated the spirit of Jesus, and made for a church where all met truly as brothers and sisters?

Hardly pausing for such questions, the missionaries in India forged on—despite the financial crisis of 1906, and despite what seems to have been a general crisis of missionary health at the same time. In 1906 one of them, Jacob Burkhard, died of blood poisoning from a carbuncle. Another, Mahlon (M. C.) Lapp, suffered a jackal bite. There were other health problems. But problems became occasions to rally people at home to the heroic work, and to send more missionaries. Calls for new buildings continued, especially schools. "The orphan children are nearly all grown and need to be trained for special work of various kinds," George Lapp argued, cogently, in 1908. Despite lack of funds M. C. Lapp built a chapel at Balodgahan in 1909, using his own money and hoping that the home board might make a "small donation to finish it, ha ha." Kaufman called (unsuccessfully, in this case) for purchasing more villages, saying they would be centers of evangelism.[46]

A great momentum for developing institutions was at work in the American Mennonite Mission in India. It was a momentum that would create problems for the mission in the decades ahead.

* * *

At the same time, in the U.S. West, especially Kansas and Colorado, zeal of Mennonites to operate welfare institutions was moving to a high point. By 1928 the Mennonite Church through its missions and charities board owned and operated a hospital at La Junta, Colorado.

Once again, nobody much thought about institution-building as a strategy. A sanitarium, then a nursing school, and then a general hospital all seemed like Good Things. Besides, westerners quite clearly wanted their own project. And, as board member J. S. Hartzler said in 1917, reverting to the Pennsylvania German that still warmed Mennonite cockles, the board's policy was "*das siehe du zu.*"⁴⁷ In other words, the board's attitude was laissez-faire, and looked to local initiative: go ahead, "*you* carry it through."

Steiner and his circle had of course had visions of hospitals and nurses' training when they began their short-lived Benevolent Organization of Mennonites, in 1894. In 1893 John A. Sprunger, the free-lancing General Conference Mennonite, had already opened a deaconess' school in Chicago. After moving to Cleveland in 1902, Sprunger operated a hospital. From 1900 to 1911 General Conference Mennonites opened hospitals in four of their communities, two with nurses' schools. And in 1902 and 1903 some Mennonite Church members moved to the La Junta area, began a small church, and soon were publicizing the climate as most healthful. Others began to visit for health reasons, and in the winter of 1903-1904 a settler named Daniel S. Brunk suggested that "our people" buy land and erect cottages for convalescents.⁴⁸

Individuals should do it; the church already had enough institutions, another Brunk, J. M., would argue in 1906, as secretary of the Mennonite Sanitarium Association. But district conferences in the West showed interest, and in 1905 the general conference offered "hearty sympathy" and "moral support." La Junta's business community was also in favor. So in 1906 some westerners asked the church to sponsor a sanitarium for tuberculars and at the very meeting in which it organized itself the new board accepted jurisdiction.⁴⁹ By 1908 the sanitarium opened, in a new, substantial masonry building. Patients who could pay were expected to; those who could not were not. Eventually, however, the institution did turn some bills over to collecting agencies.⁵⁰ The Mennonite Church was getting deeper into the running of institutions, and into welfare.

Some in the Mennonite Church meantime called even more ambitiously for a hospital with a nurses' school, and by 1906 had collected $5,000 and a three-acre plot at Goshen, Indiana, toward their dream.⁵¹ In 1906 also George Lambert of India fame bought Sprunger's enterprise in Cleveland and for a time interested some Mennonite Church leaders in taking that over. "Think of a hospital in a large city, conducted by God-fearing men, and supplied with a corps of tried [did he mean "trained"?] Christian nurses," enthused Lancaster progressive

Abram Metzler, Jr. "What an opportunity for doing good, not only for their sick and aching bodies, but also an open door to bring the comforting influences of God's grace to their souls"[52] The Goshen and the Cleveland proposals fizzled. But early in 1914 David S. Weaver, president of the La Junta sanitarium's local board, personally gave $2,000 to expand the sanitarium into a general hospital provided the general board would match the amount.[53]

The board did not act immediately. Nevertheless in 1915 westerners, with board cooperation, added a nurses' training school. One argument was that non-Mennonite schools were luring young Mennonite women away from the faith; a student at such a school told of knowing three would-be nurses lost that way. Moreover, Mennonite-run training would mean graduates for mission work.[54] Whatever the arguments, the training program made a general hospital seem more important than ever. Then in 1916 a young Kansas minister named Allen H. Erb became superintendent at La Junta, and soon was promoting the general hospital idea very effectively. And La Junta city leaders urged the Mennonites to take over and operate the general hospital of the city.[55]

G. L. Bender, as general board treasurer, had doubts. "A hospital," he predicted privately in 1919, "will be a much bigger ELEPHANT to handle than the Sanitarium."[56] Nevertheless, late in 1919 the general board said yes to leasing the city institution. At first its lease was for only eighteen months,[57] but the arrangement continued.

Bender probably was referring to the hospital's becoming a financial and administrative elephant. His fear was not an idle one, for by the 1930s the board found itself carrying a $30,000 debt on the institution. It was a difficult one to pay off, especially in depression times. But some of the deepest issues the institution raised were not financial, nor so easily recognized. Mennonite Church people were somewhat conscious of the question of whether this was the way to do evangelism.[58] But few really raised questions whether it was the church's business to run the institutions of society at large, or even of a local community. Still another issue not really faced was: When the church treads the field of some profession, who sets the rules—church, or professional accrediting agencies and the like?

The last question, for instance, was implied in sanitarium practice as early as 1911. The Kansas-Nebraska Conference asked that year about the propriety of insignia that nurses wore, and of their headgear not being the traditional Mennonite prayer veiling.[59] Apparently the

The Urge to Make Institutions 99

institution's local board, to whom the conference referred the matter, found some satisfactory answer, for the institution continued to run. In any case, while the conference's immediate concerns may have been petty, they involved that profound issue of one's profession beginning to replace one's church. The same issue was even more present in the 1930s when the state of Colorado demanded that supervisors have certain qualifications before it would accredit the nursing school. Sometimes the mission board had to keep nurses off their regular fields—delaying Selena Gamber's return to Argentina after furlough, for example—to meet state requirements.[60] Should a government's demands have dictated a person's place of work in Christ's Kingdom? Running institutions, especially when the church also asked society to give accreditation, could raise profound questions.

Whatever the issues, by mid-1920s there was a strong movement among some Mennonites to have their own hospital building. A planning group looked quickly at suggestions for taking over an existing one in Wichita, or building in some community with more Mennonite clientele—Newton or Harper, Kansas; Waynesboro, Virginia; or Manson, Iowa. But then it recommended La Junta.[61] Promoters, above all Allen Erb, then went on to raise the $100,000 to $120,000 needed beyond some $50,000 realized from selling the sanitarium building and a farm.[62] By 1928 the Mennonite Church built and put into operation at La Junta a new, 67-bed hospital-and-sanitarium.

The project evoked some discussion about strategy, partly because by the mid-1920s Fundamentalism, which stood for "direct evangelism" and against "social gospel," had penetrated the Mennonite Church. But Allen Erb was a premillennialist and Fundamentalist enough.[63] So a Mennonite-run hospital became bricks-and-mortar fact.

* * *

Benjamin (B. B.) King, superintendent of the mission at Ft. Wayne, Indiana, did not like the building project at La Junta. Although he was an outspoken Mennonite Fundamentalist, King professed to have nothing against hospitals and sanitaria. Rather, he wrote in 1924 to Sanford C. Yoder, the general board's secretary, the problem was that present administrators were sponsoring grandiose buildings that later ones might find obnoxious. A case in point was a Mennonite mission building at Youngstown, Ohio.[64]

King's was an apt example. A building at Youngstown had turned out to be large, awkward, and to the board, costly.

Yet the deepest problem was not one of real estate. It was an arrangement for institutional work that put Mennonite mission people working hand-in-glove with persons who held power, political and social, in industrialized Youngstown. Those included city charity officials steeped in prevailing Anglo-American attitudes about benevolence, in a city with 70 percent foreign-born and quite a few Blacks. Rural-based Mennonites were scarcely aware of the class bias in those attitudes, or of what it might mean to work with a city's power elite.

In the late 1890s and ten years following, Mennonite Church people established a half-dozen or more city missions in cities second-rank or smaller in size, from Kansas City, Missouri, to Altoona, Pennsylvania. All the city missions involved at least some social and institutionalized work, in addition to "direct" evangelism. Some would in time do their institutional work quite successfully. In Youngstown, however, mission leaders—people such as local board president Jacob (J. S.) Lehman; the bishop from nearby North Lima, Albert (A. J.) Steiner (brother of M. S.); and Tobias (T. K.) Hershey, mission superintendent at a crucial time—walked innocently into a trap. Youngstown's Associated Charities organization promised the mission financial help, and the Mennonites accepted. The result was that secular, upper-class-oriented officials and promoters convinced the mission to overinvest, and to a degree tried to determine mission policy. That produced strains—strains with an increasingly skeptical board at Elkhart (which also was helping underwrite costs), and strains with the city officials.

Inspiration for the Youngstown mission had grown less from Mennonites' own ways than from outside models. About 1898 or 1900 Lehman, a Mennonite farmer and produce peddler from nearby Columbiana, learned to know a Nettie Westlake through sales to her husband's store. Mrs. Westlake typified a strain of activist, uplift-minded, old-stock American charity people. Descended from New Englanders, a Congregationalist, active in the Women's Christian Temperance Union, she founded and operated a home for wayward young women. Before she got interested in Mennonite work she had helped get support and give advice to at least one other mission in Youngstown, known as the Plymouth Mission. According to Lehman, she learned to appreciate Mennonites deeply—but not, it would seem, for anything unique about their understanding of how to be people of God. Instead she appreciated Mennonites' solid-citizen virtues of "economy," "seriousness and earnestness," and "pure simple life." Lehman in turn admired her "Christian Character" and, in his own words, "became attached to her in a special way." In October of 1908, with her encouragement and help, he and other Mennonites along the Ohio-Pennsylvania border opened a mission in Youngstown.⁶⁵

Chief designer of the mission's institutional program however was T. K. Hershey, installed as superintendent in 1911 at age 32 after studying at Goshen College and before going as a missionary to Argentina. Hershey, as he would always be, was a promoter and a doer. One story had it that a Mennonite farmer once told another that he supposed Hershey's next scheme would be to install a poolroom at the mission.

> "A poolroom? What's that?"
> "It's a place to swim in."
> "Is that so? It's just like him."⁶⁶

Hershey had grown up in Lancaster County, where some of the most wealthy and culturally self-assured Mennonites lived; and he had come within an eyelash of joining the Methodists.⁶⁷ When the elite of Youngstown charity officialdom and some wealthy donors opened their doors to him, with Mrs. Westlake helping as go-between, he was quick to respond.

In 1911 the mission already had a congregation of 26 members, a Sunday school of some 90, sewing classes of about 40, and other activities. Soon Hershey and the local board decided to construct a new edifice, and the general board agreed to chip in $1,500. At first the building was to be 30 x 40 feet, and two-story.⁶⁸ Then Youngstown's charity officials got them to think larger, of a complete set of community social services. The Mennonites promised to raise at least $10,000, and to make the social welfare part of their work nonsectarian; Chamber of Commerce and Associated Charities officials in turn gave permission to raise another $10,000 from non-Mennonites in Youngstown. Mrs. Westlake promised to solicit, and a high charity official, one J. M. Hanson, suggested there would be community money for operating expenses as well as for building. The building grew larger to forty by one hundred feet and three stories, or four counting the basement.⁶⁹

The Mennonites seem not to have asked whether the Youngstown elite's charity was Jesus' kind. Charity Organization Societies or Associated Charities were products of a "charity organization" movement imported from England to North America in the 1880s. The movement was in some sense Christian: disproportionately, ministers or lay people in prominent churches filled its offices and ranks. But its approach smacked more of "Christian nation" and "Christian civilization" concepts than of Jesus' command to give simply to the one who asks, cloak as well as coat.[70]

A central concern of the movement was to abolish "indiscriminate charity." In line with that turn-of-the-century urge toward rational organization, thinkers and officials of the movement tried to introduce system, often to keep the poor from receiving too much. Confident that upper-class people would be fair in judging the poor, they made a great point of never giving to someone without first a careful investigation—of need, but beyond that, also of the needy one's moral worth. There was in the movement a certain compassion for those judged to be "worthy poor." And there was a sense of stewardship. But it was compassion and stewardship that allowed the giver to remember his or her status and superiority as a member of the successful, moneyed classes. It was not the first-shall-be-last way of Jesus.

Mennonites were susceptible to the charity organizers' assumptions. Going cliches about worthy and unworthy poor had surfaced in the *Herald of Truth*, and Mennonite commentators quoted charity organization literature as authority. In 1903 Noah Byers, while studying at Harvard University, published an eloquent treatise in the *Herald* praising organized philanthropy. Sometimes Mennonites did raise some questions (as did charity organization people themselves). At least one reader protested in 1894 when, in a reprint from a non-Mennonite source, the Steiner-edited *Young People's Paper* suggested that some poor were "not worth saving." That same year evangelist Coffman suggested that sometimes the poor were victims of depression or the ability of the rich to manipulate affairs, and called for love for all and equal interest in everyone's salvation. Yet even the gentle Coffman could use the prevailing language, and declare it "true that we have in our country thousands of willfully idle and vicious poor."[71]

Mennonites might have offered more of another approach. In 1899 the Amish Mennonite Conference of Indiana discussed how to help "financially poor and spiritually indifferent" members. Among its answers were "giving them good advice," helping them help themselves, and helping them to earn livelihoods rather than giving them money outright. Thus far the approach was not very different from that of organized charity: lumping the financially poor and the spiritually indifferent together implied that poverty and sinfulness were about the same, and hesitation to give money outright fit the warnings against "indiscriminate charity." But the conference went further. Part of the solution, it concluded also, was in "being humble ourselves," "giving them a welcome among us," and keeping them "in touch with the church" through "visiting, encouraging, and admonishing them" and helping them find homes near to churches.[72]

Those further statements were a formula for breaking down class feelings and for enveloping people with positive caring even for their social and economic problems. Of course the conference was referring to care for its own people. But Mennonites might have drawn from that inner life of their own to see the unloving features that too often appeared in the standard charity approach.

At Youngstown the Mennonite missionaries did not do much to sort out the genuinely loving way from the organized charity approach. They went ahead, entered the relationship with the city's charity officials and other people of power, and built the larger building. In addition to its preaching, Sunday school, cottage visiting, and such "religious" services, the mission by late 1913 was running a day nursery, a kindergarten, a manual training program, a medical dispensary, a sewing school, girls' clubs, and a clothing dispensary. Within another two years its many departments included: "Temporary Shelter for Deserted Wives, and Widows and Children"; English classes for foreigners; and "Relief Work, Etc." Meantime in mid-1914 Hershey lost his voice and suffered general fatigue, so he went to La Junta for a leave of absence. As acting superintendent the boards appointed one John I. Byler, a 33-year-old who had earlier worked at the mission, and had attended Goshen and Toronto Bible colleges.

Without doubt the workers at the mission did much that reflected the genuine love that the Indiana Amish Mennonite Conference had implied. Although Byler and his family took up residence outside of the city in 1916, most of the workers after all lived at the mission, among the people. Their pattern was that of a "settlement house" more than of a charity organization society, and in North America generally, settlement house workers were somewhat more sympathetic and less judgmental toward the poor than were charity organization people. It was as a settlement house that city charity officials conceived the mission, and Mennonites themselves used the term.[73]

On the other hand, when the mission's superintendents articulated mission philosophy, they sometimes seemed to do it less in the spirit of having God's people envelop others with love and help, than in the mood of secularized, uplift-minded, upper-class charity. An annual report booklet that Byler circulated at the end of 1915 was especially so. Downplaying any sectarianism, Byler said that "one of the principal features" of the work was its "being religious without being narrow and fanatical." And the jargon of organized charity saturated the booklet. "Very little is given away promiscuously," it declared for instance of the clothing dispensary, "and none at all without careful investigation." There was nothing about giving cloaks as well as coats.[74]

By a year after that, the mission was moving to a crisis. As happens in real life, mood and philosophy got all mixed with historical accident and practical problem. Hershey's leaving left Byler with the very common problem of trying to retain support that a dynamic predecessor had drawn to himself. At least one official of the central board, secretary Shoemaker, thought Byler inclined to go his own way rather than to take advice,[75] and that may have been at least partly true. In the press of work Byler did get accounts mixed up, in a way that left some city donors fearful that they were not getting proper credit for their gifts. That tightened the hands of Youngstown's financial angels.[76]

Meantime some Mennonite supporters raised doubts about the mission's relations with the city's powerful. Byler's antisectarian language, obviously tailored for the city angels, must have sounded strange to Mennonites who still held to strong convictions that Jesus' way was a narrow one. Besides that, Mennonites who visited the mission found the rectangular, factory-like building too institutional, not warm and inviting.[77] Their unease may have reflected their ruralness; but it was evidence also that the mission had not grown enough out of their own life and experience. In harder terms, Mennonites began to ask who was in control. In 1914 the mission set up an advisory council consisting of city businessmen-donors; at least one Mennonite, David S. Weaver of Colorado, thereupon advised board treasurer Bender that he did not wish to give to a mission not really under Mennonite direction. Bender mollified Weaver for the moment. But in 1918 the Mennonite boards governing the mission abolished the advisory council, although some city donors objected.[78]

Besides all that, interested Mennonites began to feel that the mission simply cost too much. Of that feeling, Byler was victim at least as much as cause. One cause was the church's eternal hope to have missions without too much financial sacrifice. Of course, confusion in Byler's accounts did him no good; but mission boards probably overemphasize an ability to keep good books as a test for whether one is an efficient missionary. Beyond such problems, Byler stayed essentially within the framework Hershey had set up, and governing boards might well have spent less time judging Byler's performance and more time examining assumptions underlying that framework. They might also have asked how well the mission's local board had performed. Local board members seemed much quicker to commit the mission to grandiose plans than actually to find the money for them.

About 1917 the crisis came, and fell mainly on Byler. In that year the governing boards appointed someone else as superintendent. Byler eventually left the Mennonite Church, and became a musician, evangelist, and bishop in the Church of the Brethren. Meantime the superintendent the board installed at Youngstown was none other than C. K. Hostetler, one of the old Steiner circle. Older and more experienced than Byler, Hostetler put the mission's accounts in order, and proceeded to cut operating costs. Yet even he did not find a formula to put the mission on solid footing, financially or philosophically.

Hostetler ran into yet another difficulty: Mennonites' nonresistance, in a time of high emotions for fighting World War I. Quite naturally the alliance with people in power broke down in time of war passion, since such people were not pacifist and did not distinguish as Mennonites did between church and nation. The war focused the central question: If Mennonites were really radical and prophetic enough to be pacifist and aloof from nationalism, was not a cozy relationship with local people of power inconsistent, and as a practical matter unrealistic? At its depth it was a theological question, and one that any Mennonite philosophy of mission had to answer, sooner or later.

It was also an immediate, practical question, as Hostetler soon found. "I saw H. H. Stambaugh & John C. Wick [two of the main financial angels]," Hostetler advised Bender early in 1918, "& tried hard to get them on paper for the same as last year but it won't go. They and other capitalists are buying liberty Bonds [sic], furnishing base hospitals," and giving to Red Cross and YMCA. "Meanwhile Mennonites are getting a black eye. Folks that won't fight" or buy bonds or even work in a war-related hospital—"Why should we support their little old mission?" Hostetler thought probably "that we better [sic] cut down the scope of our work here and get ready to finance it almost entirely through the Mennonite church."[79]

Nor was pacifism the only issue. "The Youngstown Mission has been used ... as a dumping ground for undesirable charity cases," Hostetler decided after a few more months. The city's elite "support it liberally, but their $150.00 a month charity workers would not touch with their fingers some of the dirty, diseased children my wife and the workers here have had to clean up." So "the sooner we cut loose from that bunch entirely ... the better it will be." The mission should "do just the work that the church will support and no more."[80]

The mission did cut back, drastically. Its boards decided to sell the building to the city's charity interests, who wanted it for a YMCA for Blacks. The news made Hershey, by then in South America, unhappy. But Christian (C. Z.) Yoder, an eastern Ohio minister and since 1911 president of the general board, thought it wise. The mission was costing too much, he advised Hershey, and with the war it could not depend on city donors. Two workers, Joseph Detweiler and Mabel Riehl, were thinking of going to work in South America. Even the religious part of the work was not going well. According to Yoder "the good old members have all died," and, to keep mission expenses down, Hostetler was working so much as a carpenter that "the religious work has been neglected." Yoder also added another, rather curious reason: that "Colored" people were moving into the neighborhood and displacing the foreigners with whom the mission had been working. His statement was curious because the mission had worked with Blacks for some time, and although workers segregated them into separate clubs and occasionally invoked the racial stereotypes of the day, none seem to have suggested that the presence of Blacks was any great problem.[81]

In any event, the Mennonites sold their overbuilt edifice and moved into smaller, more homelike quarters. Still the mission did not prosper. Perhaps it had just lost everyone's confidence. Perhaps Hostetler could have used a little of Hershey's and Byler's spirit of promotion. Perhaps Youngstown's population shifts and their various side effects were doing it in. And perhaps Hostetler offered at least part of the truth. Mennonites, he observed, were more persuaded to support foreign missions than to support less exotic work at home. Nor had their home missionaries learned to cope with language and cultural barriers that they faced when they worked among immigrants. Later Hostetler would argue also that Mennonites' dress codes hurt their city missions.[82]

Whatever the explanations, the mission continued to cut its social programs and in 1922 began to look for still smaller quarters. The Hostetlers resigned in that year. A new couple who took charge, Amos and Edna Swartzentruber, although they later had a long and successful missionary career in Argentina, had no luck reviving the Youngstown

The Urge to Make Institutions 107

work. In 1923 the mission closed. Its boards traded the city property for an eastern Ohio farm—an authentically Mennonite decision at last!

Gradually, those responsible for the Youngstown mission had realized they were entangled beyond their depth. In 1915 the general board appointed treasurer Bender, Aaron Loucks, and the board's field representative Samuel (S. E.) Allgyer as a committee formed partly to investigate the problems at Youngstown. Observed Allgyer in 1916, as he elaborated the committee's findings: "Our [Mennonite] people are a rural folk, and not used to the conditions found in the city." In 1918 a major report of the general board, with Youngstown surely in mind, explicitly advised that in all city and rural missions there be "no organized effort to secure regular support from the non-Mennonite population." When in 1921 Hostetler specifically opposed any more efforts to raise money from non-Mennonites in Youngstown, the board's executive committee agreed.[83]

Mission officials were also becoming doubtful about institutional work. "To study the problem of institutional work" was in fact the primary purpose of the Bender-Loucks-Allgyer committee. Before reporting in 1916 the three men visited several Presbyterian, Episcopal, and other establishments in Pittsburgh with vast institutional programs. Such programs could surely do much moral, physical, and social good, they came away saying, but experienced people had told them that unless there was an endowment fund to supply money, and a "well organized church" to provide workers, the programs interfered with "direct Gospel work." Board policy, the three advised, should be to get mission efforts "directed more particularly along the lines of Sunday school and evangelistic work and the establishment of the Church."[84]

Although the general board had tied the three men's institutional-work inquiry to the Youngstown problems, the experience at Youngstown was by no means a full answer. While the mission there rose and fell, a somewhat parallel one in Kansas City succeeded quite well, especially after 1912 when Jacob (J. D.) Mininger, erstwhile superintendent of the old people's home in Ohio, took charge. To be sure, missionaries in Kansas City did not develop the institutional, social-service side quite so ambitiously, for they emphasized street evangelism, jail visitation, neighborhood Sunday schools, and such "religious" work somewhat more.[85] But at least at first they did cooperate to some degree with their city's organized charity forces, and they did offer medical assistance and other benevolent services.[86] They especially emphasized child welfare, so that by 1917 they had established that children's home, with very substantial facilities. The mission's local board and surrounding congregations and conferences supported the work well. Thus Mininger and others demonstrated that vigorous "direct" evangelism and church-formation could combine with institutional work.

As for the Youngstown mission, its problems had not necessarily been with institutional work *per se*. Rather they stemmed from a mixture of historical accident, overexpansion, and mismanagement. And perhaps most fundamentally, they grew from ill-advised entanglement with classes and powers and attitudes that governed the city.

* * *

About 1910 Mennonites finally began to question institutional work, but they did not question very much the larger trend toward system, structure, and organization. There would have been good reason to do so, for the trend was an expression of North American and more broadly Western culture, more than—at least in any clear, direct way—of Jesus' Gospel. The modern mission movement from which Mennonites were taking cues had built upon that trend. That fact suggested how tied to Western ways of thinking the missionary movement was.

Moreover, when Mennonite Church people raised doubts about institutional work, more and more their doubts rested on still other attitudes that they were borrowing from North American Protestantism. They were borrowing Fundamentalistic attitudes, that emphasized "direct" evangelism.

4
THE PURE GOSPEL: ORTHODOXY AND EVANGELISM ... AND BENEVOLENCE?

Concern for people's physical and cultural needs as well as for their souls (probably a false distinction) has ever been a part of the modern missionary movement. Had not Jesus Himself healed the sick and pictured those who clothed the naked and visited prisoners as inheriting eternal life? Yet mission people have not been sure whether such help is something worthwhile in itself or merely a way to get to people with a message about reconciliation with God and eternal life in heaven. Pre-quickened Mennonites and their Anabaptist predecessors did not separate body and soul, did not separate here-and-now needs and eternal salvation, quite so sharply. But with "plan of salvation" language, quickened Mennonites did.

That led to some uncertainty about work to meet physical and cultural needs. If salvation was a "spiritual" matter, should not "direct" (that is, verbal) evangelism be considered much more important than medicine, food, or education? By the latter 1920s that question often had Mennonite Church missionaries on the defensive.

What plan-of-salvation theology had begun, some early-twentieth-century Mennonite changes carried further. That was true especially of an emphasis on correct mental belief, an emphasis bolstered by Protestant Fundamentalism. Temporarily, at least, the emphasis sharpened those issues about "direct" evangelism versus physical and cultural ministries. And along the way it put the Mennonite Church to a very practical test: would the church, as it pursued its goals in mission, act as just another power organization, or act truly as church?

* * *

By the turn of the century, the Mennonite Church was ready for new and clearer definition. The quickening had brought diversity, and strong leaders sensed, probably correctly, that there was danger their people might lose traditional Mennonite understandings entirely. A few Mennonites were looking to Christian Science, some to divine healing, and many more to the "second work of grace" idea of sanctification.[1] By 1903 M. S. Steiner and Daniel Kauffman feared their church's new college at Goshen, Indiana would lead folks into "popular channels of worldliness." By 1908 they thought they saw a threat of theological "liberalism," and agreed that "we need some emphatic teaching" to stem the drift.[2]

For in fact, sons of the quickening such as Steiner and Kauffman were among the most alarmed. Not that they saw all outside influences as threats. They did not see the Reformers' understanding of salvation that way, for instance, and many of them easily borrowed a premillennialist view of future events from a Protestant prophecy-conference movement. Nor would they take alarm at a subtle change in how Mennonites understood scripture's inspiration.

But selectively, the new generation of leaders reacted, especially in two ways. Both ways emphasized authority. The first was to create stronger structures of control. Hence, for instance, from 1904 to 1908 they created those three major church boards (of education, of missions and charities, and of publishing). Hence also they engineered and then dominated a general conference. At the outset in the late 1890s Kauffman promised that it was "not a *law-making* institution."[3] But it more and more became one by, say, the 1920s.

The second way was to emphasize orthodoxy in belief. By 1898 Kauffman boiled the quickening's main theological assumptions down to a small *Manual of Bible Doctrines*. Mennonites in America had from time to time reaffirmed a 1632 Dutch Mennonite confession of faith, yet they had mainly expressed their beliefs piecemeal, in practical-life applications. Now they showed a new concern for stating them abstractly, as propositions. With general conference guidance and other authors' help, Kauffman's *Manual* grew into a larger Bible doctrines book.[4] Published in 1914 and again in 1928 the book was for many

Mennonites the last word on what to believe.⁵ People of Kauffman's generation also wrested control of publishing from Funk and in a complicated set of developments created, by 1908, a quasi-official church paper—the *Gospel Herald*—which Kauffman then edited until 1943. During those 35 years Kauffman was truly, as his successor Paul Erb has written, "the interpreter of the Mennonite Church to itself."⁶ Whatever else these and similar developments did for (or to) Mennonite Church people, they brought more unity of belief.

Meanwhile, of course, on the larger Protestant scene the "Fundamentalist" movement was taking shape. That was a movement too diffuse for anyone to say precisely what were the limits of its main beliefs, or exactly who was in and who out. A very strong root clearly grew from that late-nineteenth-century "prophecy" movement.⁷ Not only were people in that movement "premillennialists" (believers that after the world waxes worse and worse Jesus will return and literally reign on this planet for 1,000 years), many were also "dispensationalists" (interpreters of past, present, and future in terms of epochs, or dispensations, in which God works differently at different times). And as Fundamentalism took shape its concern was more and more to fight liberal and "Modernist" Protestants whom upholders of "fundamentals" perceived (often surely with reason) to be eroding traditional Protestant doctrines. Fundamentalists objected especially to "higher criticism" of biblical texts (study of the culture out of which a biblical writer wrote, etc., etc.). In that last concern millenarian Fundamentalists often got help by allying with non-millenarian conservatives who simply wanted to uphold traditional beliefs in matters such as the virgin birth of Jesus, His miracles, His bodily resurrection, and atonement for sin through His shedding of blood on the cross.⁸

Most important of the non-millenarians were some theologians at Princeton Seminary. Their great contribution was to forge a theory making *all* of the *very words* of the Bible inspired ("plenary" and "verbal" inspiration), at least as originally recorded. So the Bible was absolutely without mistake ("inerrant"). God had dictated, in effect, and biblical writers had been passive scribes whose personalities, cultures, and outlooks had left no mark. For conservatives, that view of inspiration more and more became bedrock upon which they could rest the other orthodox beliefs. For millenarian Fundamentalists the same bedrock seemed to uphold their interpretation of certain "prophecy" passages, as well as those other beliefs. Hence the alliance.⁹

A precise statement of who in the alliance were Fundamentalists and who simply more traditional conservatives seems impossible. But there was, in addition to sets of beliefs, a kind of Fundamentalist style. Fundamentalists and their defenders assumed that God's truth lay in verbalized propositions much more than in, say, justice in human affairs. Most relevantly for mission, they saw God's truth in verbalized propositions more than in the actual life of God's people and in deeds of sharing, mercy, and love. And since they treated truth as having been already delivered, in full and for all times, their style was militant: to defend truth, transmit it unblemished, and brook no compromise. Even in people with their own special ideas of what points were really "fundamental," there could be that defensive, combative, Fundamentalist mindset.[10]

Most importantly for mission, Fundamentalists tended strongly to reject any emphasis on humanitarianism or anything else they thought smacked too much of "social gospel." That fit their view of atonement, the absolute place they gave to the verbalized and delivered word (or Word), and their pessimism about world conditions before Christ's return.

* * *

Mennonites were not automatically Fundamentalist. The quickening had opened them to such currents, but the quickening itself had taken cues from a more nineteenth-century version of evangelical Protestantism, a version that was comfortable with the social reformism of, for instance, pre-Civil War evangelist Charles G. Finney.[11] At the turn of the century quickened Mennonites, including leaders of the movement for missions, could sound very social-gospelish. To be sure, no Mennonite Church leader advocated the full-blown Social Gospel that made salvation primarily a matter of social change rather than of individual regeneration. But J. A. Ressler, for instance, reflected privately in 1892 that "Peace not war, love not hatred, democracy not aristocrisy [sic] is the natural condition urged by our Savior." Funk was much interested in World Peace Congress efforts to promote arbitration of international disputes, and J. S. Coffman in 1896 went so far as to declare that if such efforts succeeded it would mean, "'Behold, at last the Prince of Peace reigneth.' "[12]

Or regarding scriptural inspiration: Mennonites had always read scripture as uniquely inspired, but instead of a formula like the "plenary and verbal" one, they had associated inspiration with the Bible's ability to instruct and guide.[13] "The Bible is the inspired word of God," five church leaders declared simply in an 1896 report, "written for the guidance of saints and the admonition of sinners." In 1897 a *Herald* writer, J. K. Zook of Missouri, even suggested that Paul's words about women had "doubtless originated from custom and social standing"—and that inspiration meant merely that the writings were "just and right in their time" rather than "always alike applicable under all circumstances."[14] Even as late as 1913 a district conference, the Indiana-Michigan, adopted a statement that—although it referred to inspiration as "full and complete"—avoided the "plenary and verbal" phrase, quite deliberately it would seem.[15]

On the other side, pulls toward what would become Fundamentalism were strong. Time after time by the latter 1890s the *Herald* implied that higher criticism was a great evil, as if that judgment were a flat axiom and the case were closed. Steiner, also, was happy in 1897 when a non-Mennonite journal that he called a "fire-brand anti-higher critic paper" complimented Mennonites for interpreting scripture literally. And in 1906 Kauffman warned publicly against modern marks of infidelity, then proceeded to list what a budding Protestant Fundamentalist might have listed—from denial of biblical inspiration, to believing hell a condition rather than a place, to Darwinian evolution.[16]

So by 1906 something akin to the larger Fundamentalist crusade was pulsing in the Mennonite Church. Like the larger one, the Mennonites' movement would put premillennialists and premillennialist-dispensationalists into shifting alliance with some non-millenarian (or "amillennialist," to use a term Mennonites favored) conservatives. Despite Mennonite nonresistance it would have that combative style. It would cause Mennonite Church leaders constantly to favor the words "fundamental" and "fundamentalist," with either small "f" or large. And because such words proceeded from some who were essentially just conservative, with neither the radical millennialism nor the radical style of Fundamentalism, it was and remains impossible to tell precisely who was a Mennonite Fundamentalist and who not.

The limits were imprecise, but there was a Mennonite version of the Fundamentalist crusade, too vociferous and too influential to deny. Its opening shot, one might say, was a 1908 blast entitled "The Danger of Liberalism," by the Mennonite Church's leading scholar, John Horsch. For at least ten years Horsch had wanted Mennonites to be more militant. Now, Kauffman and Steiner also thought the church needed "teaching along that line." So Horsch got his article into the new *Gospel Herald*.[17] Thereafter he went on to publish various further articles, booklets, and books that were rich in anti-liberal and anti-Modernist polemic.[18]

Since by general Protestant definitions there was virtually no real theological liberalism or Modernism in the Mennonite Church, Horsch often seemed to be aiming elephant guns to kill flies. But across the church others rose to help him—most zealously Jacob (J. B.) Smith and Amos (A. D.) Wenger, successively presidents of Eastern Mennonite School; a prominent Lancaster Conference bishop, John H. Mosemann, Sr.; Virginia bishop George R. Brunk, Sr., who in 1929 began a thoroughly Mennonite-Fundamentalist paper with the militant title *The Sword and Trumpet*; plus others perhaps less outspoken. Hardly anyone in the Mennonite Church had technical training in theology, so a phrase such as "Biblical criticism," for instance, must have conveyed not its technical meaning of careful analysis but its popular one implying negativism, rejection, and ridicule.

Misunderstanding of some of the issues did not keep some Virginia Conference leaders from compiling a Fundamentalistic eighteen-point statement of Mennonite beliefs in 1919 and then in 1921 getting the church's general conference to adopt it as a report of a "Committee on Fundamentals." In 1923-1924 the church's oldest college, Goshen, closed temporarily, largely due to Fundamentalistic attacks on it. Reorganized, it opened again in the fall of 1924 with none other than mission board secretary Sanford C. Yoder as its president, chosen apparently because in addition to his abilities he was a moderate, and because he hailed from an Amish Mennonite group in Iowa who had not gotten very caught up in the turmoils of the day.[19] Yoder served as chief executive officer of both mission board and Goshen College until he resigned his college presidency in 1940, and then his secretaryship in 1944.

The Mennonite crusade was not an exact copy of the Protestant one. Like a Protestant Fundamentalist statement might have, that 1921 general conference report began by asserting "plenary and verbal inspiration of the Bible as the Word of God." Yet unlike much Protestant Fundamentalism, it did not rest on Calvinistic assumptions. Nor, on the second coming, did it specify premillennialism. (Too many Mennonite leaders, even militantly anti-liberal ones, indeed even Horsch, remained amillennialist.) And, very typical of the Mennonite crusade, it included many distinctive Mennonite teachings that Protestant Fundamentalists generally would not have made "fundamental" if they believed them at all. Church-state separation, modesty of dress, nonresistance, the footwashing rite, and such matters were identified as Mennonite "fundamentals."[20]

Yet, although Mennonites went forth in their crusade under their own distinctive banners, the Fundamentalist march took them quite a distance further from their own historic understandings. Understanding scripture by the "plenary and verbal," "inerrant" formula rather than finding inspiration in its guidance for living was to go further than they realized. So also was the way they made their distinctives into "fundamentals"—doctrinal propositions, now, to be defended in combat, rather than simply the ways Jesus' followers lived out His teachings and commands. The distinctives were getting pulled from their roots. Even when their form was traditionally Mennonite, tone and spirit and approach to truth had become Fundamentalist.

The most strident of Mennonite crusaders were to the "right" of the Mennonite Church's main path. Squarely on that path, of course, was Daniel Kauffman. Kauffman was simply a theological conservative— orthodoxy-minded, but non-millenarian and (despite some reputation to the contrary) often a reconciler of different views. He was distant enough from the vehement, premillennialist crusading of, say, George R. Brunk, Sr., that in 1918 at the Virginia Conference Brunk vigorously attacked him in all but name for an allegedly liberal taint in his 1914 *Bible Doctrines* book.[21] In another book in 1918 Kauffman still held back from using the "plenary and verbal" formula. As late as 1924, although defending Fundamentalists as defenders of orthodoxy, he conceded a point to a few progressive Mennonites (often called "liberals," but not really liberal in the Protestant theological sense) who were counterattacking people such as Horsch for aligning theologically with some who had zealously supported World War I. Yes, conceded Kauffman, we would not ally with Catholics just because we believed some points *they* believed. Kauffman's distance from some to his "right" was enough that in 1931 board secretary Yoder (lamenting privately about the "politics" he had seen from "Eastern people" and a few others at a general conference session) could suggest that not many years earlier, with some justice, "Dan Kauffman ... and a number of others were classified as radicals"; but "today they have become the liberals in the church and the radical group to the other end is doing their best to unseat them."[22]

On the other hand, Kauffman often used Fundamentalistic language in the *Gospel Herald*, and did so from its beginning. By 1923 he put the "plenary and verbal" formula into a new book that he wrote.

And he could say, as he did in a 1937 Mennonite dictionary: "The Mennonite Church is firmly committed to the Fundamentalist faith." He quickly added that Mennonites held to "some unpopular" fundamentals "which many so-called Fundamentalists reject"—an addendum that was a common one for Mennonite Fundamentalists. In some sense Kauffman, in a time of pressure and confused words, did ally with Mennonite Fundamentalists, and even consider himself one.[23]

In a 1941 book Kauffman emphasized only that some Fundamentalists were "anything but fundamental in some of their tenets of faith." Instead of fundamentalism, with large F or small, he held up a pure "conservative Christian faith."[24] Yet he did not make that into an authentically Mennonite third ground. That was strange, for as early as 1910 he had come close to doing just that. The great failure of Daniel Kauffman was that he never marked out a third ground for Mennonites other than Protestant Fundamentalism or Protestant liberalism.

In 1910 Kauffman had tried in a series of articles to say what Mennonites believed. His titles were Fundamentalistic enough: "In What Fundamentals Do Mennonites Agree?" and "Upon What Fundamentals Should All Christian People Agree?" But he seemed still to understand faith in terms of the life of God's people, rather than in creedal, propositional terms. When he did outline doctrinal points, he emphasized the living as well as the believing, italicizing "*lived and taught.*" Although he came close he did not use the "plenary and verbal" formula, nor did he, as later Mennonite-Fundamentalist statements would, put the point about scripture's authority first, even before ones on God and Christ. Moreover, unlike Protestant Fundamentalists, he was strong on a doctrine of the church, for he declared the "visible Church" to be "the earthly home of God's people on earth who constitute a peculiar people." He began his discussion with Mennonite history, and pointed out that sixteenth-century Anabaptists' faith had been "radically different" from either Catholic or Protestant.[25]

Other language in Kauffman's articles sounded more Fundamentalistic. Yet in 1910 Kauffman had the seeds of what others, in mid-century, would make a third ground for Mennonites: the "Anabaptist vision" effort to understand scripture and faith in light of Mennonites' own history and understandings. "Anabaptist vision" theology, although influenced by conservative Protestantism, would emphasize faithful church and discipleship more than propositional truth. And once more it would treat scripture as if its inspiration and value were in the guidance it gave for living, not as did the "plenary and verbal" formula.[26] But in 1910, in Kauffman and in other church leaders, seeds of Fundamentalism took root while those others lay quite dormant.

* * *

With Fundamentalism's impact, pressure increased on Mennonite Church missionaries to be absolutely correct in verbal formulations of belief. In 1911 the Kansas-Nebraska conference urged the mission board to use "utmost caution" when it selected missionary candidates, accepting only those who believed "in verbal and plenary inspiration of the Bible" and stood "against the modern trend of religious thought." Much similar advice followed. In 1921 bishop Mosemann offered the board a thoroughly Fundamentalist list of criteria for missionaries, saying that the church wanted workers "untainted with the corruptions of higher criticism" and should serve notice that " 'none others need to apply.' "[27]

The board of course was an agency for acting, not especially for defining doctrine. Yet by 1913 it appointed a committee to formulate tests of orthodoxy in mission candidates. Mainly, the group tried to define biblical inspiration. One of the five members was John (J. E.) Hartzler, who on that question stood fixedly against the Princeton-Fundamentalist formula[28] and, after a time as president of Goshen College, would eventually, under accusations of liberalism, change to the General Conference Mennonite Church. The committee's statement, then, did not use the words "plenary and verbal." Yet neither did it emphasize the Bible's value to guide and admonish. Instead it went very near to the standard Fundamentalist view, by saying the minds of biblical writers were "a pliable medium for making known the will of God."[29]

A much extended doctrinal statement by the board in 1918 also avoided the "plenary and verbal" phrase. Yet it was even more Fundamentalistic—beginning with a point on scripture, using the term "infallible," and going on to uphold the literal truth of the creation account in Genesis, the authenticity of miracles, etc. It also upheld many of the Mennonite distinctives, and, more in an older Mennonite vein, warned against "pride" and pursuit of "worldly power." But on a doctrine of church it was not traditionally Mennonite, for it spoke more of authority and organization than of peoplehood and fellowship. God had provided for His visible church's "organization, government and perpetuation." He had given her authority "to interpret Scripture, choose needed officials, discipline members, and establish institutions."

Every member ought to support her loyally, with "willing obedience and ready service."³⁰

It was as if the Bible had replaced Jesus as God's main revelation, and the church had replaced Him as Lord. And it was almost as if there were no Christian community, only troops obeying superior officers. Such were the words. In actual practice, however, the leading mission officials were moderate men who often stepped in to buffer missionaries against crusaders. Yet the doctrinal statements were not just window dressing³¹—as missionary J. W. Shank, for instance, found out.

By about 1910 some people in the Mennonite Church were calling for a new foreign mission in South America, and in 1911-12 the board sent Shank southward to investigate the possibilities. In 1917 Shank, his wife Emma, and T. K. and Mae Hershey would again travel to South America, this time to stay. By early 1919 they would begin a mission in Argentina. But meanwhile some voices, especially in the Kansas-Nebraska Conference (Shank had grown up in Missouri), began to question Shank's views on scripture, on atonement, and on matters such as the prayer veiling for women. In 1913 the board examined him rather thoroughly, asking for instance whether he believed the Bible "contains," or "is," the Word of God. ("Is" of course suited Fundamentalists, while "contains" did not.) In the end he passed the test, after he affirmed in writing a new general-conference resolution that declared the Bible "the one inspired, infallible, inerrant message of God ... inbreathed of God ... free from all human imperfections." Yet attacks continued, and in 1916 he confessed, again in writing, to taking "a wrong attitude" and to having made "radical statements." Such generalities did not satisfy critics, and for a few months the board delayed the Shanks' and the Hersheys' departure. Finally, however, they went.³²

Back on furlough in 1923 and 1924 Shank sought to be ordained for his work. But now there was an additional charge, which Shank was too honest to renounce: on the field, he had worn a necktie. Finally, in 1924, he was ordained, in Colorado. But western officials who first examined him had never before, at least in the memory of one, put a candidate "under more strenuous test and examination than he," especially "on the question of Modernism." And even after his ordination he drew more criticism, when en route to sail he committed the indiscretion of speaking to an Indiana congregation that was on the "liberal" side of church troubles there.³³

The Shanks did sail, without going through the kind of heresy trial that was occurring in some denominations. Yet Mennonite Fundamentalists and their allies had made clear their penchant for correct formulas and purity of belief.

The Mennonite crusade reinforced tendencies to reject anything that seemed like a liberal or too-social approach to mission. When for instance in 1932 a group of Protestant laymen published a report called *Rethinking Missions*, with its main point the liberal one that Christianity ought to enter give-and-take dialogue with other religions, Mennonite mission people—even non-Fundamentalistic ones—felt the need to make almost a ritual of denouncing it.[34] Much the same was true of anything like a full-blown Social Gospel theory of mission. In the 1890s there had been a kind of back-and-forth attitude among quickened Mennonites toward a more or less social gospel. On the one hand there had been those social-gospelish statements. On the other there had been many like an 1899 one of Chicago Home Mission superintendent A. Hershey Leaman (despite social work his own mission was doing), denouncing efforts to solve problems by human science and skill, and declaring that Mennonites knew that "nothing will avail except Jesus' blood." By 1920 or 1925 the give-and-take was essentially over. In 1916 a conciliatory, moderate, non-Fundamentalist such as future board secretary Yoder, then a bishop in Iowa, made the point that "the Church was not instituted to wage a warfare against the civic and political agencies that are corrupting the world." Rather, it existed "that men through the Word might receive a soul-saving knowledge of God."[35]

By no means did all rejection of social gospel run contrary to what Mennonites might believe from their own traditions. In 1920 Horsch castigated a Social Gospel spokesman for suggesting that the Kingdom of Heaven would be realized in the state. And in 1927 Paul Erb, a Mennonite college teacher and future editor of the *Gospel Herald*, warned missionaries to be free from Modernism and the Social Gospel. In the course of his warning he denounced those who would make the spreading of American ideas and civilization their task. Such statements fit well with the distinctions Anabaptists and Mennonites had long made between church and state, and between gospel and national culture. But at the moment the crusading and anti-social-gospel zeal of Fundamentalism was a more dynamic source than Mennonites' concerns about separating church from nation. In 1920 Horsch published a small booklet, in his polemical tone, against liberalism in mission.[36]

And in the next dozen years letterheads of a Mennonite mission at Peoria, Illinois, made clear what dynamics were at work. One in the early 1920s proclaimed the mission's practical aims: "To preach and teach the Gospel/To distribute Gospel literature/To put homeless children into Christian homes/To provide clothing for the worthy poor/To provide free medical aid for the afflicted poor/[and,] To welcome all classes, especially the poor and needy." By 1929 a new superintendent had it declaring "What We Believe," namely: "Divine Inspiration of the Bible/Deity of Christ/Salvation thru the blood of Christ/Complete separation from the world/[and,] Preach the Gospel to all people." In 1930 still another superintendent dropped the point on separation and replaced it with emphasis on belief "in the personal imminent return of the Lord Jesus Christ."[37]

* * *

Despite the Fundamentalistic shift that the letterheads signaled so succinctly, hardly anyone in the Mennonite Church rejected benevolent efforts totally. Virtually all rejected social-gospelism at a philosophical level, and many raised questions for the practical level. In 1927 S. F. Coffman, a staunch premillennialist but one who was moderate in style, made the anti-social-gospel point that "we must preach repentance; not just a reformation." Yet he did not want people to "blame our missionaries because they are not preaching Christ all of the time." Orphanages, schools, and the like, he said, grew from "the life of Christianity, because Christianity is sympathetic and efficient." Missionaries simply could not "let a poor sick man suffer." For, "when people are sick they are sick."[38]

"When people are sick they are sick." That powerful bit of logic was one rationale that helped keep Mennonite benevolence alive even when there seemed to be little theology to justify it. Another logic was bait-the-hook: that the purpose of benevolent work was to make contacts for verbal evangelism. Right in the 1920s, for instance, the medical institution at La Junta, Colorado, expanded magnificently. It drew heavily on both rationales, put forward very effectively by a quite Fundamentalistic superintendent and promoter, Allen H. Erb.

As is usual, the issues surrounding La Junta did not fall neatly along theological lines. Opponents of the hospital project argued that it was overpromoted, or badly situated to serve Mennonites.[39] Supporters were often westerners who, being far from major church centers, quite apparently wanted their own institution. Whatever the merits of Erb's promotionalism, his religious approach was quite Mennonite-Fundamentalist. He was among the first to raise questions about J. W.

Shank, and in 1924 Kauffman published one of Erb's sermons under the title "Fundamentalism Versus Modernism: A Militant Attitude Necessary." Nevertheless Erb did not sharply divide ministry to body from that to soul. In late life, at least, he liked to intertwine the fingers of his two hands and say: "If you love a man's soul, you actually *love* him, why you'll love everything that he needs ... in body, etc." And in the 1920s also, some of his language was in that vein. Moreover, Erb was able to turn the "distinctives" part of Mennonite Fundamentalism into an argument for his institution. "Does it make any difference," he asked rhetorically in 1925, "whether a bobbed-haired flapper waits on you or a veiled Christian woman?"[40]

Other of Erb's arguments started from that forthright logic that the sick must be served, and went on to idealism about Mennonites as servants. Mennonites practiced "love and good will toward all men"— "rich and poor, learned and unlearned, white and black, Christian and infidel, friend and enemy," Erb claimed in 1927. Besides, Mennonite young people were especially well-suited for hospital work. For they came from a "social and industrial and religious background," that kept them from being "hardened by the coarse, flippant, gay attitudes of society."[41]

But those were minor themes. Erb's really steady theme was to de-emphasize the value of humanitarianism for its own sake and to argue that it made opportunity for verbal evangelism. "Of course, we know that the social Gospel does not save," Erb declared in 1926. And Christians did not exist "merely to make the world better to live in nor to keep men's bodies in health." As for what Christians *were* about, Erb recorded for the year 1921 that the hospital staff had given direct personal testimony to 533 souls, and that in sanitarium and hospital together 1,088 cases of personal work had occurred in the forms of prayer, Bible reading, and conversation. To that he added accounts of two people being converted before they died. A decade later the statistics were 4,467 cases of personal work in a year, and four of confessing Christ. The only justification for a mission board to sponsor medical work, the superintendent declared flatly in 1925, was that "it affords to the Church an avenue through which she can reach the world." It might not be the cheapest way; but if "it costs $500.00 to save Sam Jones and $200.00 to save John Smith, shall we neglect to save Sam Jones?"[42]

Was the hospital really such an evangelistic agency? Without question, it was, in some cases. One Maude Buckingham, from Arkansas, was probably all the justification it needed for Erb's philosophy of reaching the Sam Joneses. In 1922 Maude Buckingham and her husband, Edward, traveled to Colorado because he was ill with tuberculosis. They were so poor that they had to hitchhike, but the sanitarium at La Junta took him in. The couple professed a faith in Christ, but he had not been baptized. He soon died. But before he did, he renewed his faith and received baptism; and after his death Maude Buckingham worked for a time at the sanitarium and joined the Mennonite fellowship. Wanting to return to Arkansas and serve there, she attended school at Hesston College and at La Junta, and became a nurse. By 1930 she returned to her native state, soon remarried, and went on at Mountain Home, Culp, and nearby points in Arkansas to be perhaps the Mennonite Church's most versatile and effective rural missioner of her time. In a career that lasted into the 1970s, she served a large area with her medical skills and in many other very practical ways. In the course of her service she attracted Mennonite preachers and lay workers to her area, who helped establish Sunday schools, Bible schools, a mission farm, some small businesses, a twelve-grade Mennonite school, and some five Mennonite congregations, most notably Bethel Springs at Culp.[43] If it cost $500 or even a great deal more to bring Maude Buckingham into the Mennonite fellowship, surely Mennonites could consider the dollars well spent—and the medical work at La Junta an evangelistic success!

On the other hand Selena Gamber, from her experience as a missionary in Argentina and as director of the nursing school at La Junta in the mid-1930s, seemed unsure about La Junta's evangelizing role. While the enterprise did some evangelism, she observed in 1934, its nursing school made people think of it "more as an educational institution." Moreover, Erb himself declared in 1940 that for the Christian church "to maintain [its] institutional work as an evangelistic agency" was perpetually a problem.[44]

Meanwhile did the hospital people proclaim what Mennonites had long understood to be the gospel? In 1925 a committee laid down conditions under which non-Mennonites might enter the nurses' training program. The statement covered dress standards, and that of course expressed a long-time Mennonite concern. Beyond that, it set standards regarding amusement, and others on devotional life and on service attitudes. Still others specified belief in the Bible as God's inspired word, in the virgin birth, and in Christ's atoning death as the sole means of salvation. But the committee said nothing of nonresistance, or a gospel of peace. Were these peripheral, optional? The omission was broader than La Junta: Daniel Kauffman, D. H. Bender, and other church-wide leaders or future ones made up the committee.[45]

Whatever the questions, Fundamentalists and other anti-Modernists in the Mennonite Church did not stop the La Junta institution from growing. The program and its facilities continued to expand to a peak not reached until shortly after World War II. Moreover about 1936 there began a movement for some sort of Mennonite mental institution, that would come to fruition after World War II. On the eve of World War II there was new talk of taking over administration of hospitals in other communities, especially in Wauseon, Ohio; again, such talk came to fruition, not at Wauseon but in some other places, after the war.[46] At World War II, with programs at La Junta, in India, in Africa, and a bit in Argentina, and talk of new ones, the Mennonite Church was still very much in medical work.

Before World War II, Mennonite Fundamentalists and other conservatives made sure that nobody put forward the full-blown Social Gospel. And they made it necessary to defend the humanitarian programs, especially with that contacts-for-soul-winning argument. But such programs survived, and even flourished. Maybe Mennonite Church people were not listening enough to abstract theology and its propositions to kill off what in their bones they felt was good. Perhaps for them it was still enough to say, "When a man is sick he is sick."

* * *

Or else their habits of giving help and relief were just too deeply rooted. From the latter 1920s to the early 1940s a Mennonite Church vision of generosity to the needy remained intact, although as a social vision it remained limited.

By the time they joined the mission movement, Mennonites had long since developed habits both of mutual aid for each other and of relief-giving beyond their own group, especially to victims of war. From Anabaptist days onward their understandings of practical Christian living and of church no doubt had done much to root those habits. Menno Simons, from whom they gradually got their name, had described them as people who not only preached in houses and fields day and night and "know war no more," but also as people who "comfort the afflicted; assist the needy; clothe the naked; and feed the hungry."[47] Even more, historical experience may have rooted their habits. American history is replete with immigrant and other sharply defined subgroups who have provided at least their own members with immigrant-aid, sick, burial, and other mutual-aid funds. By the late nineteenth and early twentieth centuries Mennonites had of course accumulated a remarkable history of fleeing or moving from place to place and land to land and living as aliens. So mutual aid, and perhaps even helping others who suffered, was natural for them as well as central in their understanding of being Christian.

Whatever the impulses that moved them, Mennonites in seventeenth-century Holland sent money to help persecuted coreligionists in Switzerland move northward into the Palatinate. Eighteenth- and nineteenth-century Mennonites in Switzerland and in North America aided fellow-members making the trip across the Atlantic.[48] Meanwhile, in the French and Indian War Pennsylvania "Menonists" offered to pay for gifts to Indians if government would deal with the Red people peacefully rather than fighting them. And as the American Revolution approached, they advised government that they found "no Freedom in giving, or doing, or assisting in any Thing by which Men's Lives are destroyed or hurt." Instead they wanted "to be helpful to those who are in Need and distressed Circumstances," whatever their station, "it being our Principle to feed the Hungry and give the Thirsty Drink...[and] serve all Men in every Thing that can be helpful to the Preservation of Men's Lives."[49]

A century later, in 1873, people of different Mennonite branches cooperated to form a "Mennonite Board of Guardians" and through it gave much aid to fellow-Mennonites who were rather suddenly immigrating into North America from Russia. Indeed the Board of Guardians provided Mennonite Church people with their first significant experience in modern-style mission or philanthropic organization. Funk and other quickened leaders were active in it. Later, of course, in 1897 to meet the famine crisis in India, they organized what became that inter-Mennonite Home and Foreign Relief Commission. Such inter-Mennonite effort gestated until the World War I-era birth of the relief-oriented Mennonite Central Committee, which has continued vigorously since. And in the immediate post-World War I years there was a lively inter-Mennonite unit of volunteer reconstruction workers in France, organized in cooperation with the American Friends Service Committee.[50]

Overall however, inter-Mennonite relations were none too cordial in the early twentieth century, and as Mennonite Church people established their own mission board they more and more preferred to route famine relief and other such monies through it. Then in 1917, responding to World War I, they put together a "Mennonite Relief Commission for War Sufferers" (MRCWS), closely but not clearly tied to the board. In the war and immediate post-war years it was very active especially in sending relief money, goods, and a few workers into the Middle East and southern Russia.[51]

By the mid-1920s the MRCWS was sending funds for earthquake relief in Japan, or responding to a hurricane disaster in Florida, or helping some Mennonites who were managing to move out of Russia and into Canada or Mexico. It had, by 1927, distributed some $1,175,000 collected throughout the Mennonite Church, plus about $900,000 more that others had given. In 1927 however the mission board amended its constitution to take on the job of relief and create a Relief Committee. Thereupon the MRCWS ceased to be.[52] In part the move was response to the fading of its original wartime purpose, and to the feeling that the size of the relief task had shrunk. Apparently it also reflected the concern, at a time when Mennonite Church authoritarianism was running high, that organizational lines be more clear so that something like a relief agency should not be semi-independent.

By creating the Relief Committee the Mennonite Church had kept alive the idea of a ministry not emphasizing direct evangelism, even though Mennonite Fundamentalism was at high tide. Yet the committee's vision in its early years was quite limited: a bit of help after some natural disaster here or there, or even among impoverished coal miners, but mostly aid to fellow-Mennonites. In most years until World War II the amounts of money it gave out were hardly impressive, compared to what the mission board was disbursing for its missions and benevolent institutions. In the late 1920s the board's spending for relief never reached 4 percent of its total cash income, or perhaps 5 percent if value of clothing that women's sewing circles made and distributed were added. In 1930-1931 relief expenditures did reach 10.7 percent of cash income, due to a hefty amount (more than $25,000) given through Mennonite Central Committee for settling Mennonites from Russia in Paraguay. But by 1935, relief had dropped to ½ of 1 percent of the board's cash income, although it may have been as much as 7 percent or more if value of clothing were added.[53]

Strangely, except perhaps somewhat in the disbursement of clothing and other goods-in-kind, the board's relief giving in the 1930s seemed not at all to reflect the severe depression that was taking its toll in North America and all the Western world. Apparently the Mennonite Church was not responding directly to people's physical needs.

Instead it was reacting mainly to two other stimuli: (1) the specter of fellow-Mennonites forced once again to uproot and migrate; and (2) war suffering.[54] The first response was a natural, mutual-aid one, that fit well with Mennonites' deepest historical memories. The second certainly had its admirable side. But it also suggested how much the Mennonite Church's social conscience and its peace testimony were chained to, and limited by, a rather formalized dissent from actual war.

Response to war brought a new spurt of relief in the latter 1930s, and then of course further action in the 1940s. In 1936 and 1937 the Relief Committee had a subgroup investigate how to respond to a harsh and dramatic civil war that had drawn all the Western world's attention to Spain. In November of 1937 the board sent to that country two workers, furloughed Argentina missionary D. Parke Lantz and former Chicago Home Mission superintendent Levi C. Hartzler. The two distributed relief, first under the umbrella of the American Friends Service Committee and later as a more independently Mennonite operation. Eventually several other workers joined them. In the peak year, from April of 1938 to March of 1939, the board dispatched some $14,500 to Spanish relief, plus about $12,500 worth of clothing. That year its giving for all relief reached almost 7 percent of its income, or perhaps about double that if value of clothing were counted. By early 1939, however, the right-wing forces of General Francisco Franco got virtually complete control of Spain, and made the Mennonites' kind of activity next to impossible.[55] In the next year the cash the board put out for relief dropped as low as 1.7 percent of its income, then in the early 1940s it rose again to 7 percent or a bit more as the Relief Committee, cooperating closely with Mennonite Central Committee, gave to relieve victims of World War II.[56]

The direct-evangelism emphasis, pressures from Mennonite Fundamentalists, and the like, had by no means completely destroyed that ancient Mennonite (and of course more broadly Christian and human) impulse to be "helpfull to those who are in Need and distressed Circumstances." Indeed the conservative Lancaster Conference, with some strongly Fundamentalist-leaning leaders, was apparently as willing as any segment of the Mennonite Church to contribute. In 1937-1938 for instance the sewing circles collected at Lancaster nearly $8,900 of a total $13,100 worth of clothing they sent to Spain, compared to only $2,300 worth shipped from Elkhart. In 1941, at a time when the general board was sending $2,250 per month to Mennonite Central Committee for relieving World War II sufferers, the Lancastrians' Eastern Board was

The Pure Gospel

sending an additional $1,250. During World War II, moreover, the Mennonite Church's impulse for relief began to broaden for various reasons into a wider vision of relief-and-service. In 1943 the board responded to an idea that a few Mennonite thinkers such as Guy F. Hershberger had been developing for some years, and gave its Relief Committee a mandate to begin "Mennonite Service Units." The Committee got the first unit underway by the summer of 1944, and went on to lay ground-work for a vigorous Voluntary Service program in the postwar era. In 1953 the committee would get a new name, Mennonite Relief and Service Commitee.[57]

But from the late 1920s to the early 1940s the Mennonite Church was acting from a pretty narrow vision of relief. Specific Mennonite Church missions and institutions and sewing circles may have been responding to people's physical needs in depression times in a limited and piecemeal way. But the board's overall Relief Committee, which might have been developing the larger vision, did little more than respond to those two ancient stimuli, the needs of migrating fellow-Mennonites and the plight of war sufferers. Occasionally, in a lesser way, it responded to some other dramatic event, such as a flood or a hurricane. What the committee did, or rather helped its church's people to do, was surely admirable. Yet against the backdrop of the physical and social needs of people in the Great Depression, the Mennonite Church's relief-and-service vision remained strangely limited, although not dead.

* * *

If the mood of Mennonite Fundamentalism was not very effective against medical work at La Junta, nor fatal to Mennonite relief-giving, it nevertheless made some problems for missionaries in Argentina and in India.

Much of the original discussion for opening work in Argentina, coming as it did just before Fundamentalism took form, sounded somewhat social-gospelish. Shank came back from his investigative trip in 1912 saying that while preaching "Jesus Christ and His message" was most important, a mission should also teach "a higher standard of character" and "a Gospel of right living," probably through institutions such as a boarding school and an orphanage. By appointing the Shanks and the Hersheys, the board began the Argentina work with institution-minded if not actually social-gospel-inclined people.[58]

By the time the two couples actually arrived and began work, however, the home board was more and more emphasizing "direct," that is verbal, evangelism. Once again, the reasons were not only or neatly theological. Board members were deeply disillusioned with the Youngstown experiment,[59] for instance, and of course that same Hershey was now going to Argentina. In the background also was the cost of the rapidly expanded social and educational work in India. Yet the theological concern was there. Mennonite Fundamentalism was just taking shape, and if it could not do away with educational, benevolent, and such programs it could at least put them on the defensive.

So in 1918, just as the four Argentina missionaries were preparing to begin, their home board declared that mission stations' regular services should consist before all else "of preaching, Sunday School, Young People's Meetings, Bible classes, devotional meetings, and such like." Missionaries should begin "other activities" and "lines of service" only if "prayerful consideration" indicated they would be "helpful" and if "workers and means are available." Even then they should begin them only if the board gave permission.[60] The Mennonite Church's mission priorities were now clearer, but they tended to limit the early missionaries in Argentina.

One of the missionaries' major frustrations was the question of buying a farm. Shank and others had very early collected $20,000 to get the Argentina work started, and because a mission farm had been a strong idea among the donors, Shank felt a moral obligation to use the fund for that purpose. But as the mission was beginning, the board's secretary, Yoder, and its Eastern treasurer, Samuel Musselman, visited in Argentina. Board policies were by then hardly conducive to the farm idea, and, after some "real live discussions," the two officials said no. Soon the missionaries were requesting only a *quinta*, a small acreage for truck farming. Their immediate argument turned mainly on practical considerations, not theology—that the *quinta* would help the missionaries to support themselves. The request probably had much to do with the subculture out of which Mennonite missionaries went. How could *Mennonites* live without gardens and truck patches and cows? The meats, eggs, butter, and milk that the missionaries had to buy in the markets were hardly fit to eat, complained the Lancaster County-bred Hershey.[61]

Still the home board simply would not send the money down. It listened quite systematically even to a rather grandiose proposal that Hershey promoted about 1927, to go into partnership with a local businessman, one Walter Hamilton from Canada, for farming and raising cattle on a large scale. Mr. Hamilton, Hershey argued, was "at heart ... a Mennonite," for he had acted nonresistantly in several business dealings. Moreover, said Hershey, Mennonites, "being farmers," could do what other big agriculturalists in Argentina were doing, "rope in the pesos by the thousands, and thousands." But skeptical home board members again answered no. The board continued to hold the $20,000 until the mid-1930s, when it finally released some of it to help finance programs of partial self-support for Argentines who by then had become pastors.[62]

The farm idea was an ambiguous case. While the home board was squelching that one, it did allow the missionaries to build up, to a limited extent, some other service institutions and programs. Hardly had the Hersheys and the Shanks begun their work when they called for the home board to send an agriculturalist, a building contractor, a kindergarten teacher, a nurse, Bible instructors, and school teachers. They by no means got all those. But in 1919 they began a kindergarten. Home folks in the North seemed not to object, perhaps because, as Mae Hershey wrote publicly, a kindergarten was almost like an extension of Sunday school.[63]

Eventually, by the early 1940s, Mennonites had kindergartens in a half-dozen or more Argentine towns. By 1921 there were classes also for some lower elementary grades. The board encouraged the missionaries to limit their program to preschoolers, but for some years the mission operated an all-grade elementary school at the town of Pehuajó. Finally by the early 1940s the missionaries did cut back, but more because of governmental restrictions and expansion of public schools than because of mission theory. Meanwhile by 1924 women missionaries had begun sewing circles for young women. Who in the home church could oppose sewing circles? Yet in fact they were a kind of industrial work, for they existed more to teach skills and help young women better themselves economically and socially than to produce goods for charity.[64]

In 1925, the missionaries began a poor fund, partly because there was a drought, and partly because the church was beginning to have old people who needed support. The next year they started an orphanage. And slowly, they began some medical work. Selena Gamber arrived in Argentina in 1923 to be the mission's first nurse, ministered in various ways informally, and surveyed and pondered how to get something going more systematically. During much of the 1930s she was back in North America on furlough or working at La Junta. But in 1938, again in Argentina, she finally began at Pehuajó a kind of convalescent home where doctors could treat certain patients. In the early 1940s two more nurses arrived, Una Cressman and Calvin Holderman, and the missionaries also began a program to help young Argentine women get nurses' training.[65]

Meantime, of course, the mission's leaders started other institutions: the printery, the several periodicals, and the Bible school to train church leaders. The home board was rather slow in sending hard cash for these, being by the 1920s and 1930s quite skeptical of new institutions and projects. Yet the missionaries rather easily found a rationale for printery and Bible school as direct aids to verbal evangelism and to church-formation. The schools for children and the benevolent programs required more defense.

Often, of course, missionaries just spoke of the inherent good the non-"direct"-evangelism programs would do. Arguing in 1920 for an orphanage, J. W. Shank thought "there is no organization better fitted to take care of such helpless ones" than a missionary society. In a mission orphanage, "the children will find the nearest approach to a good Christian home that is possible."[66] Or there was that handy rationale about contacts the benevolent work would create for verbal evangelism.

The promoters and builders of the Argentina mission seemed to use the contacts-for-verbal-evangelism argument surprisingly seldom, especially if compared with Erb at La Junta. But they used it. However much Yoder and Musselman in 1920 rejected the buying of a farm, the two advisers returned to North America ready to contemplate some benevolent programs. And concerning medical work, they suggested that a missionary doctor "would be able to reach a class of people that an ordinary missionary would not be able to reach." The argument did not always refer to a specific, highly personal kind of testimony. In 1942 for example Nelson Litwiller said of the orphanage that it was a "good investment" because it gave "silent witness to the critical, ungodly, suspicious, and hostile folks around us ... of our good will, practical Christianity, and unselfish service in the name of Christ." He meant a rather general witness.[67]

In saying what he did, Litwiller also touched upon a third theme that the Argentina missionaries used very much, namely that the educational and benevolent programs and institutions helped the missionaries and new Christians to establish their place, a respectable place, in their communities. It was an argument in some ways not very authentically Mennonite, but one much like they used also when they wanted to

The Pure Gospel

build a nice, substantial church building: that it would show that Mennonites were part of the community and were there to stay.[68] To the basic argument they added refinements. Good works, for instance, would help dispel rumors that Mennonite missionaries were in Argentina as agents of the U.S. government. Or benevolent programs and institutions were necessary because Argentine people with their Roman Catholic background expected these from a church and would despise any church that did not care at least for its own people.[69]

In the place-in-the-community argument there was a paradox—surely very similar to a Mennonite one in North America. The paradox was that at the same time the programs and good works were supposed to bring acceptance, missionaries expected them also to give institutional form to a separation from the larger community. When in 1919 the Hersheys and the Shanks called for that long list from building contractor to schoolteachers, they wrote also of building "as rapidly as possible a Mennonite community." Or, arguing in 1926 for the orphanage, Hershey referred to the "great gulf" that existed between Argentina's Catholics and her Protestants. The gulf kept Mennonites out of Catholic institutions, he reasoned, so they had little choice but to build their own.[70] Similar arguments served for schools, or, in the late 1930s, for beginning that convalescent home. Thus Mennonites hoped by their programs to win acceptance and yet to institutionalize a cultural gap.

In all this, surely no Mennonite missionary would admit to any fondness for social gospelism. Shank declared in 1920 that "the missionary ... should not directly attack political, social, commercial, intellectual and physical problems but he must use the Gospel as an indirect method." In 1923 Hershey, a premillennialist, was even clearer: He saw some social-gospelish missionaries in other denominations as "simply going 'daffy,' on this World Betterment movement."[71] Moreover, while the Argentina missionaries were building up their limited programs of benevolence, they were developing a much more impressive array of street and plaza meetings, literature distribution, tent evangelism, Bible coach work, Sunday schools, and young people's meetings and activities. By 1942 they had planted one and a half dozen of what could be considered established congregations, plus more or less regular services in another dozen places.[72]

There was some connection between theological emphasis and method of work, but it was by no means absolute. For instance missionary D. Parke Lantz, who arrived in 1921, had studied at the thoroughly Fundamentalistic Los Angeles Bible Institute and he liked the verbal evangelism strategy it taught: simply to preach, from town to town, more or less as an itinerant. At least one less Fundamentalistic colleague got quite critical, in private, of what he thought was the impermanence of such work. Nevertheless Lantz, when on furlough in 1927, wanted to solicit money for the orphanage and of course in the 1930s he served as a relief worker in Spain. Meanwhile moderates on the home board had reasons other than theological for checking institutions and benevolent programs in Argentina: simple prudence, caution about Hershey's promotionalism, and the like.[73]

Yet the checking of non-"direct"-evangelism programs in Argentina took place within a certain climate. There was that 1918 policy statement of the board giving "direct" evangelism clear priority, and it had come hand-in-hand with Mennonites' growing Fundamentalism and emphasis on verbal formulations.

* * *

Looking back in later life, T. K. Hershey put his finger on another key to opposition against benevolent programs in Argentina. "We were told to go to Argentina and do mission work, and not to spend time in institutional work, he observed. And that was because the India mission, with its many institutions, had run into "certain problems."[74] The India mission, especially in the 1920s, did indeed have "certain problems." Not least among them was homeside criticism that came largely from the crusading of Mennonite Fundamentalists, or their close allies.

As usual the issues were not nice and clear, although the influence of Fundamentalism was unmistakable. Helping create distrust were costs, fear that missionaries were wasting energies on secular activities, suspicion of education, concern for maintaining Mennonite distinctives, and even conviction against organized sports. These fused with fear of higher criticism, preoccupation about Modernism, and a preference for verbal evangelism. Regionalism at home was also a strong factor; most of the distrust lay along an axis from Lancaster, Pennsylvania, down into Virginina's Shenandoah Valley. While the criticisms came partly from an older kind of Mennonite conservatism, that axis just happened to be the major one also of crusading Mennonite Fundamentalism.

Hints of troubles began very early. Why did so many home folks raise questions about the India mission's costs? missionary M. C. Lapp asked publicly in 1908. Was not the money going to lay foundations of a Mennonite Church in India? Returning from a visit to India in 1911, board member J. S. Hartzler found many people asking why missionaries there did not "devote more time to preaching the Gospel and not so much to things secular." In 1912 missionary M. C. Lehman dropped a remark about graduates of the mission high school being equipped for university work; soon the missionaries had to answer people who associated universities with "rank atheism" and "higher criticism."[75]

But what really set off a flurry was a simple game of football. In 1916 Lehman and the editor of the Mennonite paper *Christian Monitor* made a mistake: they published an account of a game between boys in the Mennonite high school in India and a non-Christian team. Because each side had sought divine help for victory, the whole town where the game occurred had gotten excited. And just at the last minute, the Christian boys had stopped the heathen from scoring, and so had won! Lehman's moral: God is God. It had been almost like Elijah against the priests of Baal.[76]

What irony! Home folks apparently confused what was really a game of soccer with more savage American football—and what was hardly more than a sandlot game with organized sports, American-style. And Lehman—often to be accused of liberalism—was asking homeside conservatives to believe in a miracle! Missing the irony, bishops in the north-of-Philadelphia Franconia Conference, whose people were just beginning really to support missions, cut off money to India for more than a year. And as much as five years later missionary P. A. Friesen, on furlough, ran into " 'Football' trouble" as far west as Elida, Ohio.[77]

Football or Fundamentalism? Lehman was a graduate of Goshen College, and soon the charge more and more was that the India mission was "Goshenized." As proof J. L. Stauffer, Bible teacher at Eastern Mennonite School in Virginia, pointed board officials to an article by Lehman in Goshen's 1915 yearbook. Lehman had emphasized that many in India were Goshen alumni, and had told how that to greet Lehman's arrival someone had taught Indian schoolboys to sing Goshen's song in Hindi.[78] Stauffer ignored the purpose for which Lehman had written the article. And since Goshen was suspect as "liberal," his whole charge was decidedly a Mennonite-Fundamentalist one.

Fundamentalism was even more clear in criteria that Lancaster bishop Mosemann, in 1921, suggested for screening missionaries. They were: soundness regarding scripture's inspiration; no taint of higher criticism (higher criticism always "tainted"—somehow it never spotted, smudged, stained, smeared, blotched, or saturated); proper belief in blood atonement; and the like. Except for some imprecise words about living in "humble obedience to Christ and His Word in all things," and about being "uncorrupt in life," the tests did not include nonresistance, or loving, or Christ-likeness. Strangely, they did not even include the Mennonite distinctives, or nonconformity or separation. The list was scarcely even *Mennonite*-Fundamentalist—just Fundamentalist.[79]

It was true, the India missionaries were not generally Fundamentalist. Yet neither were they liberal or "Modernist." Rather, right into the 1920s and 1930s, most spoke the language of an older, non-Fundamentalist Protestant orthodoxy, the language much more of the Mennonite quickening of which most of them (and Goshen College) were products. To be sure, they denounced Modernism from time to time, or the idea of dialogue among the world's religions.[80] And they spoke of winning souls and of bringing people to accept Jesus as "personal Savior." But they did not dwell on such phrases overmuch, and they clung even less to fine points about the nature of scripture or of the end times. They were much more inclined to refer to building a Christian community or to bringing people to the Kingdom of God.[81] "Community" and "Kingdom" were not favorite words of Fundamentalists.

Yet the India missionaries were also borrowing heavily from outside Mennonitism. Not that they (any more than Mennonite Fundamentalists) always did so. Apart from football stories Lehman, for one, was quite inclined to make new applications of Mennonitism for mission. Look how slavery to fashionable dress and other extravagance helped produce the world's poverty, he preached in 1915 when on furlough in North America; Mennonites believed "in a Gospel which has the remedy for the very evil." And (World War I having just begun) he called on his audience to look at Europe and its battlefields and see that the Christianity believed and preached in Europe "was not whole," since it lacked "the principle of peace and non-resistance...that has come to you by your forefathers." Or in 1924, instead of dwelling on the sacrifice-for-past-sin purpose of Jesus' death, Lehman spoke of missionaries doing good works out of "a vision of Jesus hanging on the cross expressing His love to humanity."[82]

Still, the India group did borrow heavily. Compared to most Mennonites they were generally well-read, some of them even scholarly. And—a further sore point with critics—they mixed much with other missionaries and participated in interdenominational missionary organizations. So they clearly absorbed language about church-planting for instance from a mission author such as the Presbyterian Robert

The Pure Gospel

Speer, or in the late 1930s the slogan "mass evangelism" from Methodist J. Waskom Pickett and others. The social values they taught were mostly standard "Protestant work ethic" ones, and in that they happily borrowed also from U.S. Negro leader Booker T. Washington's much admired philosophy of industrial education. In 1923, for instance, Lehman (on furlough) wanted to study at Columbia University but pressure from Mennonite Fundamentalists prevented it. So he spent time instead at Washington's alma mater, Hampton Institute.[83]

In all that, the India group by no means preached the Social Gospel in the sense of emphasizing social values or the building of the Kingdom to the point of downplaying individual sin or the need for personal repentance and atonement. Declared the mission's 1922 annual report, concerning manual training or "industrial work": It would be a grave wrong to make such training "a substitute for preaching the Gospel of salvation and conversion"; the "real motive" was only "to help people who are already converted to get the necessities of life."[84] Nevertheless, within the bounds of a Protestant orthodoxy that was neither Fundamentalism nor the Social Gospel, the India missionaries were borrowing heavily.

By 1919 those India missionaries were clearly becoming defensive about their educational, industrial, and other non-"direct"-evangelism programs. So their 1918-1919 annual report officially stated their case. The mission's tasks, wrote Aldine (A.C.) Brunk, the mission's secretary, were (1) to preach salvation and (2) to organize believers into "self-supporting, self-propagating churches, with capable leaders." Medical work in the mission's four dispensaries was ultimately to help evangelism. It was, Brunk reasoned in language much like Allen Erb's, a way "to the heart and soul." Orphanages, a widows' home, and a leper asylum showed Hindus, whose religion did nothing for unfortunates, "the Gospel of love to the weak and helpless."[85]

As for education, Brunk insisted (obviously responding to home-side critics) that the missionaries did not consider it a means to salvation. But ignorant, unlettered Christians often drifted back to Hinduism, and a Christian schoolmaster had wide influence in a village while teachers in government schools were often militantly Hindu. A Bible school was of course necessary to train workers for village evangelism, etc. And the mission's more advanced, English-language school (the most controversial of all) would help Indian church leaders to be in touch with the home church and its literature. At least other denominations' missionaries so advised.[86]

Brunk agreed that educational and benevolent programs were not as central to the mission's purpose as were village evangelism and actual church work. They were not mainstream but "tributary." (Statistics actually gave a different impression. In 1919 and the early 1920s, only about 10 or 11 percent of the money the board sent the mission for operating expenses went to "direct" evangelism—Bible women, the Bible school, evangelists, literature, etc. Up to about 10 percent went for medical work; about 30 percent supported seven village primary schools, two central primary and middle schools, and the English-language high school; and some 30 to 40 percent went to care for orphans, widows, the old, and lepers.[87]) But those who thought "tributary" programs met only temporal needs, Brunk thought, understood neither the programs nor Indian conditions.[88]

Despite such defenses, homeside critics kept up their questions and by 1926 were creating a crisis. In that year, although he warned against "crowding our missionaries unduly," Fundamentalistic evangelist and *Christian Monitor* editor C. F. Derstine worried that the India mission's "material development" threatened to hinder "the spiritual." In 1926 also, board treasurer Vernon Reiff commented privately that some Virginians had given little for India in recent years because of objections some people at Eastern Mennonite School were raising. Simultaneously, critics in eastern Pennsylvania and elsewhere complained about a book the India missionaries printed entitled *Building on the Rock*, that had pictures of Indian Mennonites wearing mustaches, and, thought the critics, said too much about mission institutions and not enough about evangelism. Others at a Lancaster Conference session and no doubt elsewhere distributed a booklet that the board and missionaries took to be an attack. Probably it was *The Ravages of Higher Criticism in the India Mission Field*, by Watkins Roberts, a British Fundamentalist. At least Daniel Kauffman used *Gospel Herald* space to point out that Watkins had made no charges against the Mennonites' work. Not too accurately, Kauffman insisted that the book upheld "the same standards that our missionaries in India hold."[89]

Kauffman failed to meet an objection on which critics were about to attack in earnest: that Mennonite missionaries in India were consorting too much with those of other denominations. Beginning in April of 1927, Stauffer of Eastern Mennonite School and others objected to a report that missionary George Lapp was helping Baptists hold union evangelistic meetings in southern India. Were not the India missionaries losing their loyalty to the Mennonite Church? Stauffer asked. And if they were overworked and unable to cover their own territory, as often reported, why were they preaching for others?⁹⁰

Soon came a salvo of further questions, and much sparring between board and critics. Mennonite Fundamentalism was about at its zenith. By 1928, for instance, a weak little inter-Mennonite paper called *The Christian Exponent* expired. Anti-Fundamentalist Mennonite progressives had begun it in 1924 (and secretary Yoder, although himself hardly a Mennonite Fundamentalist, had advised the board's missionaries that it was best not to send it news⁹¹). But another paper, *The Sword and Trumpet*, begun by Virginia bishop Brunk in January of 1929, soon flourished. Meanwhile in 1928 the Lancaster Conference's board of bishops wanted to circulate a questionnaire, presumably directly to India missionaries, and they cut off support to India until they would get some satisfactory answers. And the Virginia Conference appointed a committee—Stauffer, A. D. Wenger, and Brunk—to investigate the India work. A bit less drastically, the Virginians threatened to cut off support if they did not get satisfactory answers.⁹²

Most questions came to the board from these two eastern groups. But at one point secretary Yoder was alarmed to get from Iowa a letter that "repeated olmost [*sic*] word for word" one from bishop Mosemann of Lancaster. The board wanted no such alliance. "If there is a possible way of keeping that fence built on top of the Allegheny Mountains," advised Daniel Kauffman, "we should spare no pains to do it."⁹³

Sparring against the Lancastrians' idea of a questionnaire, board officials called instead for meetings between themselves and eastern leaders. From 1928 to 1930 several meetings did occur. In the first, furloughed missionary Ernest E. Miller met with the Lancaster bishops, who came armed with fifty-one questions. There was a similar one with missionary George Lapp, and others with board officials. Also, Mosemann sent questionnaires to at least two missionaries. One was to P. A. Friesen, who leaned somewhat toward Fundamentalism and very much to "direct" evangelism, and was at times critical of "Goshenized" colleagues. But Friesen kept ranks closed. With the strictest of protocol he submitted his reply to J. N. Kaufman who was then the mission's secretary. Kaufman sent it to the board, who sent it to Mosemann.⁹⁴ That apparently was the end of questionnaires directly to missionaries.

Finally by May of 1930 the Lancaster bishops boiled their concerns down into ten points for the mission board itself to answer:⁹⁵

1. The bishops could not have full confidence in the India mission

when ten of its fourteen ordained missionaries were Goshen-trained, and these were training nine ordained Indians.

The board's reply: Missionary training was a problem, and not everything in Goshen's history had been ideal. But the board had tried to send people who were in full harmony with the church, and "would not knowingly allow any unorthodox or modernistic missionary to remain."

2. It was unwise to use resources to educate people who had not yet accepted the gospel. The cost of educating millions of heathen was too much.

Reply: Educational work did present questions, and the India missionaries recognized that they should reorganize the educational work to make it more evangelistic.

3. The mission ought not hire heathens and Mohammedans, or even Methodists or Quakers, to teach in its schools.

Reply: The point was correct, and the mission was gradually replacing such teachers.

4. Foreign missions should be "nearly self-supporting and self-sustaining as soon as possible."

Hearty agreement: The missionaries had studied the matter at length, but were faced with "the prejudices, ignorance, superstitions, poverty, and moral degradation out of which our Indian converts have come."

5. "Too much institutional work is an unwise expenditure of money." Buildings and equipment did not reproduce themselves, while "souls who have been quickened and born again" could witness and win others. Admittedly, some institutional work was necessary but it should be "at a MINIMUM and Evangelistic work at a MAXIMUM."

Reply: Much of the institutional work was the legacy of famines—especially the work with orphans, whom the mission had to provide for, and educate.

6. Missionaries should not work with or use personnel of missions "not of like precious faith" and practice with Mennonites.

Reply: The missionaries might have committed some indiscretions, and they mixed with others during rest periods in the hills. But they worked in a district all their own, and they did not mix extensively. Any association their mission had with any non-Mennonite organization was not an "organic connection."

7. The head covering of Indian Christian women should be different from what other Indian women wore, and Indian brethren should not wear mustaches.

Reply: The missionaries tried to observe every scriptural principle, but different conditions in India meant some different practices. The missionaries had declared themselves willing to work at the problem.

8. To be above suspicion, the board ought to allow missionaries to answer any questions put to them.

Reply: The public was entitled to information, and although the board may have made some mistakes, its aim was not to withhold information. The bishops knew, however, that committee work required "a certain amount of privacy."

9. The board should send out only missionaries trained in institutions "beyond question as to orthodoxy and soundness."

Reply: The board tried to send only those of sound faith, but thought the test was orthodoxy of the person himself, rather than of the school.

10. A large percentage of missionaries who had returned from India had left the Mennonite Church, and someone ought to study why.

Reply: The board had studied the matter, and the causes seemed to be personal ones, with origins in North America, not problems of the mission.

The ten questions represented the substance of the bishops' original fifty-one. Virginians' points differed only in nuance: stronger language, for instance, on freedom from Modernism and on taking an aggressive stand against it; mention of missionary neckties as well as Indian mustaches; and clearer language calling for a distinctive prayer veiling. Such were the issues. At one point Yoder complained privately of having to answer questions that "have been answered so often."[96]

And in fact, the way critics and board interacted was hardly worthy of a Christian church.

The critics often seemed less interested in getting information and a basis for understanding than in finding a forum in which to accuse; and at least one, Mosemann, expressed hurt that the board was not showing bishops the deference due them.[97] On their side board leaders surely treated the critics too seldom as brothers to be heard and understood, and too often as a political faction to maneuver around. Moreover, in making at least one point, that the Mennonite mission had no "organic" connections with interdenominational organizations in India, board officials surely tortured the meaning of "organic," if they did not outright lie.

From its early days the mission had had organizational connections with interdenominational missionary organizations in India,[98] and surely, by any normal meaning, organizational connections were "organic" ones. The India missionaries had not been denying that such connections were "organic." Instead, their defenses had been that they did not let interdenominational bodies legislate for them, allow such ties to compromise any Mennonite positions, or participate in any "union" mission efforts.[99] Some of the missionaries have since made the point that their mission was not really a member of the National Christian Council of India. But that point has only obscured the matter of "organic" connection further—because actually no mission, Mennonite or otherwise, was a member directly of the national council. Rather, missions sent representatives and money to regional bodies, in the Mennonites' case the Mid-India Christian Council. The regional bodies in turn sent representatives who made up the national body. In that kind of connection, surely an "organic" one, the Mennonite mission did participate. And they continued to do so. In 1933 J. N. Kaufman as the mission's secretary advised Yoder that the mission was sending two representatives and the Indian Mennonite Church a third to that Mid-India council, and paying membership fees. The Mennonite delegates had full voting rights, Kaufman said, and moreover were eligible to hold offices in the organization, including the office of representative on the National Christian Council.[100]

With that information in hand a home board committee in 1934 declared it to be "the sense of the Board that our brotherhood in India discontinue organic relations with the National Christian Council and its affiliated organizations." The board printed the report publicly and let the declaration stand as if it were firm policy. But actually it never enforced it. In 1935 Fred Brenneman, a missionary with ties to the critics at home, objected and Yoder said he thought the India mission had no such connections. But he also told Brenneman that he "never knew that it was unbiblical or unmennonite to be friendly toward other denominations." In fact the mission's connections with the various Christian council structures were continuing. Finally in 1938 the mission clarified its policy, partly in response to a further inquiry from Stauffer. Its policy now was: to avoid any "union" efforts, to witness in interdenominational circles against "secularized social uplift programs" that were substitutes for Christianity, to speak in favor of "our distinctive Church principles," and to "refrain from taking prominent positions in the National Council." That of course was a policy that fell quite short of cutting all "organic connection." Nevertheless, the home board's executive committee quietly approved.[101]

The 1938 policy may well have been a wise and good one; surely Yoder's principle that it was not "unbiblical or unmennonite to be friendly" toward others seems to have been a charitable one. Yet the fact was that throughout the 1930s, the board was leaving one impression at home as to what was policy, and letting the missionaries in India do something else. Not only was the mission sending representatives to the council organization, but individual Mennonite missionaries also served, sometimes prominently, on various regional and national council committees.

In December of 1929, right when easterners' criticism was hottest and only a few months before the board disclaimed "organic connection between our own and other Christian organizations" in India, Ernest Miller reported to secretary Yoder that a Mid-India Education Union had made him its secretary-treasurer, a post that meant he was also convener of the Christian Council Committee on Education. He went on to promise that he would "attempt to remain true to Mennonite policies and avoid any entangling alliances" that might increase the board's problems.[102] No doubt Miller was correct in thinking the position would not force him to violate any specific, distinctive Mennonite doctrine such as, say, nonresistance. But he did not seem to ask himself how much such interdenominational involvement had changed Mennonite missionaries' theology generally. And surely what he and other missionaries were doing hardly fit the "no organic connection" phrase.

The critics seem often to have wanted to accuse more than to discern God's leading in mission. In turn, board officials probably treated the critics more as a political faction than as brothers, and in the matter of "organic connections" they practically lied. Thus the exchange between critics and board raised many questions of whether or not the Mennonite Church in mission could rise above its members' humanness. And finally, the entire affair badly mixed questions of how to be faithful with a seeming desire to have missions without much cost. How much did the critics really believe in verbal evangelism as the best way to communicate gospel, and how much did they like it because it was cheaper?

What came of all the sparring? Not as much as might have. Despite her pleading the board declined to return one ex-missionary, Mary Burkhard, to the field, partly it seems because of the pressures. But no other missionary was put to a heresy trial or removed from the field clearly because of the crusade. The Mennonite Church as a whole continued to support the India work. Indeed, many people even in Lancaster County apparently gave money all through the crisis, even for the educational work. S. F. Coffman probably reflected very well the Mennonite Church in general. A board member, he observed that the attitude behind the Lancastrians' ten points "localizes orthodoxy" and made "Theology...more powerful than the Grace of God."[103] Those were shrewd observations about the way Mennonite Fundamentalists looked for truth.

The whole affair brought no great change in policy. It did probably affect Yoder's advice to would-be missionaries on where to study. If they were not already going to a "sound" school such as Toronto Bible College he tended to steer them to Biblical Seminary in New York whose emphasis on inductive Bible study suited all sides—to it, even above a pacifist school such as the Church of the Brethren seminary in Chicago.[104] Also, the India mission reorganized its secondary schools in 1930 and the board emphasized that the new plan reduced educational work in relation to evangelism. From greater distance, however, the changes look more like streamlining. In 1928 missionaries had suggested closing the high school, but Yoder had advised them to look forty or fifty years ahead. The graduates would still be living and working in those years, said Yoder, but the climate would probably be quite different.[105]

Due to some factors such as personnel changes, disagreement among India missionaries themselves about some of the critics' issues got somewhat more intense in the 1930s. Yet the board and the missionaries made no wholesale change of policy. Indeed, in a 1936 book the

The Pure Gospel   143

Methodist mission strategist J. Waskom Pickett presented the "Mennonite Church and Mission" at Dhamtari as a prime example of "the close thinking, careful organization, and heavy institutionalism" typical of many denominations' stations in mid-India. According to Pickett the Mennonites still offered "a comprehensive program of service to the Christian community, and to some extent to the non-Christian public." Pickett believed in a "mass movement strategy" that would not pull new Christians out of their former communities and treat them as a people apart. Because of that, he was critical of the Mennonites' mission (a criticism that the India missionaries soon more or less accepted, perhaps listening to a British Methodist more quickly than to their church brothers in North America!). His criticisms were that the Mennonites at Dhamtari had created, by their institutional programs, a Christian community too much apart from the communities out of which the believers had come, and that the Mennonites' idea of conversion, like that of many other missionaries who thought as Westerners, was too individualistic and did not recognize how that the Holy Spirit could convert whole groups.[106] In key ways Pickett's concerns were just opposite from those of the mission's critics in North America. But he and the critics could agree that the India mission was highly institutional. Nor did he find that condition to have changed by 1936.

In 1934 the same home-board committee that said the sense of board policy was that the India mission should cut off affiliation with interdenominational councils nevertheless defended what the missionaries had done by way of economic and social work. The missionaries had only worked to meet Indians' needs, the home authorities said. What they had done they had done "not as a civilizing influence, but as a method of expression of the Christian life," as means to strengthen Christian experience, and as a way to influence people "to a holy and helpful life in Christ." The committee did not claim that the India mission had lessened very much its social and economic or institutional efforts. And indeed in the 1930s George Lapp, by then one of the mission's elders, was especially enthused with a strategy popular just then, that of "Rural Reconstruction." He served as convener of the National Christian Council's Committee on Rural Work, and in 1938 authored a small volume on the rural reconstruction topic. Published by the YMCA of Calcutta, the book was an expression both of continued interdenominationalism, and of ongoing belief in extensive social and economic efforts.[107]

So the criticisms brought no really clear change in policy. They did, however, bring two other rather definite developments.

One was that the board formulated a doctrinal statement in 1929 for overseas missionaries to sign. It was a mild one, designed, said Yoder, only to cover "*general* practices of the church," not "sectional differences and peculiarities." Missionaries needed hardly do more than to (1) affirm "full sympathy" in general with Mennonite Church doctrine and practice as the 1921 general conference statement defined them (Fundamentalistically enough, to be sure) and (2) specifically "deny and oppose the doctrines of Modernism." Virtually all signed with little hesitation. From his field T. K. Hershey assured home officials that "to my knowledge the Mennonite Mission in Argentina is absolutely free from Modernism."[108]

From Modernism, centainly. But regarding Mennonite practice, not only had Shank worn that necktie on the field, but Hershey—who as an ordained man and bishop certainly could not have worn a necktie at home—felt the need when having his picture taken in Argentina, at least in a later one taken in 1938, to tuck his straw hat strangely under his chin in a way to cover his shirt front. That sort of thing troubled missionary Emma Shank. As she pondered the doctrinal statement in 1929 she was sure that she and her husband J. W. were "fully in accord with" Mennonitism and "in no sense Modernists." She did not doubt that in "simplicity of life and conduct, modesty in dress," and the like, she had never been "more of a Mennonite than I am today." But, she advised Yoder, her bonnet was not like Mennonite ones, and if home-side brethren would come to Argentina without staying long enough to understand, they would surely say "we have all been false witnesses."[109]

In her pain Emma Shank concluded that "for some people it seems so easy to do things for Policy's sake," while for herself "I can't help feeling that it is wrong to just keep quiet and by so doing make people get the wrong impression." That may have been a bit too harsh on most of her fellow-missionaries. But most did sign that 1929 statement without expressing such reservations.[110]

A second definite development was that about 1930 the Lancaster Conference began moving toward opening its own foreign work, under its Eastern Mennonite Board of Missions and Charities. The Eastern Board's president, John Mellinger, suggested quite grandly in 1931 that the Mennonite Church could eventually send 100 missionaries to Africa. An African work, he thought, would be less costly than that in India. The reason? "You can draw your own conclusions."[111]

"Surely," declared another Lancastrian in 1933, "we want to

relieve suffering," to have people able to read God's Word, and to see them have "useful trades, make homes, and in a general way... become self supporting." The speaker was Henry F. Garber, who would soon succeed Mellinger as Eastern Board president. But, Garber continued, those were "by-products," not the "essential message." The church was supposed to take the heathen the gospel, not "our western civilization.... Our question is not how much institutional work can we do, but rather how little need we do and still effectively evangelize."[112]

In 1934 the Eastern Board did send out its first foreign missionaries, four of them, to East Africa's Tanganyika district. Apparently they kept their work less costly than that in India, both absolutely and relatively to the situations. The Africa missionaries in the early years ran nothing comparable to the English-language high school in India, and where they ran institutions they tried hard from the beginning (with some problems) to achieve a measure of African self-support. Also, they were determined to keep education, medicine, etc. strictly subordinate to "evangelism." Nevertheless, they did almost immediately begin village schools, special girls' schools, medical facilities, and a teacher training school. Perhaps out of Fundamentalistic emphasis on verbal gospel, they even made ability to read a requirement for baptism. Of course the bishops had admitted, in that ten-point statement in 1930, that some institutional work was necessary.[113]

The fact was, however, that the Africa work did not look as different from that in India as its founders hoped. And if that was ironic, so also was this: One of those four sent in 1934 was John Mosemann, Jr., son of the crusading bishop; in a later day he would become president of the churchwide, general mission board; and his orientation would not be toward Mennonite Fundamentalism, but toward "Anabaptist vision."

The quarrel between the India mission and its critics had set people who were fusing Mennonitism with traditional Protestant orthodoxy against those who would fuse it to Fundamentalism. Eventually John Mosemann, Jr., perceived that neither of those two ways did much to apply Mennonite understandings to the issues the critics had raised.

* * *

In all the turmoil that Fundamentalism and related issues created, coupled with a goal-orientation that mission itself had tended to bring, the Mennonite Church had difficulty functioning like a loving and sharing people rather than like an agency designed to organize and manipulate power. Surely her leaders wanted to function more as true church, and often did. Yet on the one side critics saw tendencies which genuinely alarmed them, became frustrated, and grew accusatory and inclined to bring pressure. On the other side, board officials at worst staved the critics off with almost outright dishonesty. And short of that, they did not always fully listen. Sometimes their not listening may have come from the kind of fatigue that Yoder expressed. But had they learned how to listen? In 1928 J. N. Kaufman thought that the critics' "unfortunate attitude does provoke a self examination."[114] Self-examination, however, implied that missionaries were in the end to be their own self-judges. Did it really show willingness to hear counsel?

Time and again Yoder expressed hope that the board was responding in a truly Christian way. His hopes and his efforts were surely sincere. But he said it almost too often—as if, really, he felt the board was not. And in 1939 he all but admitted as much. Once again, the Virginia Conference was questioning missionaries' attire. Foreign workers did violate home church standards, Yoder confided to J. D. Graber. And while the board claimed to support the homeside standards, its "unexpressed policy" was really to "allow missionaries to use their judgment." "For a long time I have felt conscience-smitten because of this irregularity," the secretary confessed; the board was "not quite honest with the Church and with the missionaries."[115]

Actually it was more than a question of simple honesty. A major issue was whether the Mennonite Church had found a way, in mission, to work not as power blocs but truly as church. Her leaders by no means failed that test, on the whole. But neither did they pass with highest marks.

Indeed a further major issue went even beyond that of living up to established ideals. That issue was whether the ideals and understandings themselves were not changing. On that one also, answers that mission-minded Mennonites returned were mixed ones. The main question was whether Mennonites were taking into mission one of their most central historic understandings: that faithfulness to Jesus expresses itself in ethics of love and sharing and deeds, at least as much as in correct propositional belief. In the end such deeds did not stop. One scholar, at least, has written of Mennonite home missionaries in rural areas that they "managed to demonstrate a social gospel which truly combined preaching of the gospel with social uplift."[116] That was surely true at least to a point, and could have applied to city and foreign missionaries as well. Crusading Mennonite Fundamentalists and their orthodoxy-minded allies by no means stopped evangelism by deeds. Had anyone asked the question bluntly, they would hardly have said they wanted to. Yet they did manage a shift toward greater priority for verbal evangelism and propositional truth, until the Mennonite Church's missionaries often had to stutter hard to say fundamentally why they should use God's time and money to feed the hungry or educate the unlettered.

Consequently in the 1920s and the 1930s the Mennonite Church, in her missionary endeavors, sometimes floundered. Moreover, much the same happened as her missionaries tried to carry to the mission fields some of her distinctive doctrines and practices —to teach, as Mennonites liked to say from the Great Commission, the "all things."

5
THE PURE GOSPEL:
TEACHING THE "ALL THINGS" (I)

Missionaries inevitably face the question, consciously or unconsciously, of what truly is the Gospel, the Good News message, and what are merely ideas and practices of the missionary's own culture or subculture. Maybe for Mennonite missionaries such questions have been sharper than for most, for Mennonites have carried along many distinctive practices. When it came to more or less external practices, the Mennonite Church's missioners struggled with their distinctives in several different ways. At points they accommodated to the cultures to which they went, if certain considerations governed the situation. And not every peculiar emphasis of Mennonites necessarily made communication across cultural barriers more difficult. Indeed, compared with others in the modern missionary movement, Mennonites probably went with more advantages than disadvantages for cross-cultural communication.

Like many others, the Mennonite Church's early missionaries went to their fields more or less as North Americans. And they taught revivalistic Protestantism's ideas of Christian living, including taboos against smoking, drinking of alcohol, and various other behaviors. But the Mennonite Church also had its own more distinctive teachings and ways. Its people held to "nonresistance," quite often formalized into an almost ritualistic refusal to participate in the military, sue at law, or hold public office. They emphasized "nonconformity," spelled out in detail in matters such as clothes, hairstyles, and the like. They interpreted literally the words in 1 Corinthians 11 about women's veiling during prayer and prophecy, and ofttimes even said that the passage called for a special covering of distinctive design. Jesus' injunction to wash one another's feet they observed as a special Christian rite. They rejected musical instruments at least in formal worship, and opposed life insurance for being a false and worldly way to security. Confusingly, Mennonite Church people in different North American communities practiced various of the distinctives somewhat differently. Yet their missionaries were supposed somehow to carry the distinctives to the mission field.

For Mennonites tended to see in their distinctives the "all things" that Jesus, in his Great Commission, had commanded His followers to teach as they went into all the world.

If that made the gospel harder, Mennonites were used to that. Their own history was full of martyr stories, and of migrations across countries and continents in order to maintain the separated, faith-centered community life their forebears had sought. Theirs after all was not a gospel only of deliverance from guilt, or of sweet repose in Jesus, or of comfortable, priestly benediction upon the nation or upon society's ways. They had long emphasized discipline, obedience, a new and different life, and breaking with one's old ways and with surrounding culture. Of course many other Christians have adhered to a hard gospel, but Mennonites have surely done so more rigorously than most.

With that background, Mennonites in mission could feel quite justified in demanding practical applications that were culturally strange to their listeners. Their missionaries went forth with a concept of teaching an especially pure gospel. As two of them declared in 1911, when they had opened work in India in 1899 they had deliberately chosen a location far enough away from other denominations' missions to avoid contamination from "a lower standard of Christianity."[1] Such thinking weighted Mennonite distinctives with heavy religious meaning. And there was very little room in Mennonite missionary thinking for formulas that might soften new believers' paths by letting the gospel fuse or syncretize with different cultures. Mennonite ways of thinking allowed the missionaries few tools to rationalize and defend adjustment and cultural accommodations.

It was not that all thought and practice in the early-twentieth-century Mennonite Church was absolutely rigid. No doubt there was a surplus of rigid, formalized legalism, especially as Mennonites stiffened their own convictions with an added authoritarianism borrowed from Fundamentalism. Yet Mennonite Church leaders and thinkers also found ways to soften their legalisms. They pointed to their distinctive practices' deeper, spiritual meanings, as for instance when a 1912 committee of the general conference observed that after all, "the body wears what the heart dictates." Or they worked to give a teaching a positive cast, for instance defending nonresistance by pointing out that in World War I Mennonites gave more money per person for relief than did people of any other denomination in the U.S.[2]

Missionaries in particular tended to soften Mennonite legalisms as they fellowshiped with non-Mennonite missionaries. On the field, they did often fellowship with such persons. After all, they had gotten into the mission movement largely through other denominations' influences, and so to do so seemed natural. Hardly had the Argentina mission begun, for example, when missionary Emma Shank confessed privately that at a union-church communion service in Buenos Aires she had been sorely tempted to participate, despite the Mennonite rule of "close" communion. By 1941, seven years after missionaries of the more conservative Eastern Board opened work in East Africa, even they were communing with non-Mennonite missionaries.[3]

Meantime came reports that some missionaries were yielding on other matters. By 1930 Chicago Home Mission practices were such that its supporters were hearing of wedding rings, women's hats, a piano, and other deviations. That made Abner G. Yoder, an Iowa bishop who was mission-minded but otherwise staunchly conservative, feel that the money and the people his congregation had been sending were coming to nothing. (After all, had not advocates sold the mission cause to people such as Yoder with arguments that the world needed Mennonites' distinctive teachings?) Elsewhere, foreign missionaries' children who returned to North America for college suffered cultural shock at the strictness of the home church. And in 1925, during send-off festivities for new missionaries Nelson and Ada Litwiller and Joseph (J. D.) and Minnie Graber, Daniel Kauffman asked jokingly: Was it really true that missionary women threw their bonnets overboard once they were past the Statue of Liberty?[4]

Mission board officials often wanted to be less rigid and legalistic than quite a few others at home. Referring to the lapel-less Mennonite garb for men, secretary Yoder referred in 1933 to certain people's being "on the verge of insanity about the plain coat." A mission congregation in Los Angeles, after evolving from board supervision to being a full-fledged congregation under a district Mennonite conference, asked in 1938 to be brought under the board again because conference discipline seemed too harsh. Writing in later life of the pre-World War II decades Yoder declared that the board had never intended "to insist that converts accept all the traditional modes of dress and other distinctive practices of the church which was then largely rural."[5]

Nevertheless a consciousness of the distinctives was very much a part of the Mennonite Church's mission movement. Teaching of the "all things" gave the church its authority, one Warren Cable of Elkhart, Indiana, advised *Gospel Herald* readers in 1909. The way to extend "the boundaries of Zion" was to "be more zealous in teaching the Gospel in its purity"; therefore, Cable continued, a plain, nonresistant, non-oath-swearing church such as the Mennonite had authority to go forth. In the 1920s and 1930s the "all things" often took on an expanded meaning of anti-Modernism, but that meaning could blend nicely with the old. Belief in the prayer veiling or footwashing or nonresistance was necessary, wrote Eastern Mennonite School president A. D. Wenger in 1931, because those too were fundamentals. "Why omit any? Jesus said, 'Teach them to observe all things whatsoever I have commanded you.'"[6]

The mission board made the distinctives, the "all things," official policy. In 1914, in keeping with a larger movement within the denomination's general conference for more uniformity of standards, the board issued a statement of standards for missionaries. The statement reiterated the Mennonite Church's rationale for the various distinctives. Footwashing and the prayer veiling were, it said, genuine Christian ordinances. Certain other practices, while not ordinances, were clearly scriptural: simplicity of dress and avoidance of jewelry and ornamentation; "non-conformity to the world in business and social relations"; not participating in "secret societies, life insurance, labor unions, and kindred organizations"; avoidance of all military activity, as "antagonistic to the spirit and teaching of the Gospel"; giving one's word without oath; and settling disputes without lawsuits. Very directly, the board enjoined that its workers "shall conform to the order of simplicity of attire." Sisters were to wear "the plain bonnet, and brethren the regulation coat." And the "general appearance and demeanor" of all was to be "exemplary and consistent with a pious devoted Christian character."[7]

Nor was the concern with distinctiveness and separation a matter only of official policy. "We as a people have a unique heritage," wrote one Charity Gingerich in the *Gospel Herald* in 1925, Anabaptism's 400th anniversary year. Did not the forebears' record of living "separate in life and doctrine" inspire Mennonites "to enter the Master's service more wholeheartedly?" Practicing missionaries affirmed the distinctives. From the Canton, Ohio, mission, worker John (J. A.) Liechty reported in 1905 that some new believers had decided to join with other denominations because the mission was not willing to modify Mennonite ordinances and restrictions." But it was John Liechty's stated opinion that, "we cannot afford to sacrifice principle for numerical strength."[8]

Indeed, missionaries quite often presented themselves as *more* faithful than the home churches in maintaining standards. Sometimes, to be sure, the standards in question were not so much Mennonite as the more general taboos of revivalistic Protestantism. In late life T. K. Hershey liked to recount that during a furlough in the 1920s a Mennonite man had quizzed him doggedly on whether he and his colleagues in Argentina were teaching Mennonite doctrine. "Yes," Hershey finally replied, "all you teach here and one more. We teach that our members should not use tobacco." Later he learned that the man was notoriously a tobacco user. But often the question was upholding of the Mennonite distinctives. "We are facing a problem, yea a crisis rather," wrote Earl Miller, superintendent of the mission at Peoria, Illinois, in 1929. When country Mennonites came to visit, women who attended regularly at the mission had taken to counting the hats in the anteroom. Now one new member, formerly a Methodist, was refusing to wear the bonnet. What was a superintendent to do?[9]

Nevertheless, in some ways, Mennonites probably had the advantage over many Protestant missionaries when it came to communicating gospel to people in different cultures.

The advantage was that Mennonites still retained from their history some sense of detachment from Western culture, and skepticism about it. "Are all those that live in (so-called) Christian countries therefore Christians?" an Amish Mennonite of Iowa, Benjamin Eicher, had asked rhetorically in the *Herald of Truth* in 1865, just as Mennonites were beginning to discuss mission. And in 1895 the *Herald* had asserted editorially that nonresistant people ought to espouse "a patriotism that is not confined to the narrow limits of a country, a patriotism that is not bounded by and born of selfishness, a patriotism that acknowledged Christ as Ruler" and nations as "rebels and selfish insurrections."[10]

To be sure, mainline Protestant missionaries might also question the idea that Western meant Christian. "Are all the countries of Europe to be counted as Christian [and]...truly and completely evangelized?" asked a writer in *The International Review of Missions* in 1912. To be sure also, while Mennonites were joining the missionary movement their own sense of separateness from national culture was seriously eroding. In 1914, in the Mennonite Church's *Christian Monitor*, one Lydia LeFeber expressed perfectly what "civil religion" scholars in the 1970s see as ideological union of religion and state in the United States despite organizational separation. A problem for home missions, LeFeber declared, was that immigrants could not understand how there could be separation of church and state "and yet the complete union of religion and national life." Three years later the *Monitor*'s editor, Frank Reist, exulted before a mission meeting audience on how the "Western civilization which followed the preaching of the Gospel" was changing the peoples of Asia. "If genuine civilization is based upon evangelism let us maintain it by evangelism," he challenged. Reist spoke almost as if civilization were the goal, and gospel only a means.[11]

Despite the erosion, Mennonites and their missionaries did often retain a sense of detachment from Western imperial power, nationalism, and culture. In 1915 J. L. Stauffer, at that time mission superintendent at Altoona, Pennsylvania, asserted that Mennonites could preach especially well to Jews, because both peoples were aliens in the nations in which they lived. As World War I began, M. C. Lehman told *Christian Monitor* readers that people in India were troubled because they saw the war as the work of Christian nations. But, said he, Mennonite missionaries explained that while Christianity may have contributed to Western civilization, the two were distinct. The war, said Lehman, strengthened rather than weakened Mennonites' message; for Mennonites taught that the war was "due to a misconception of what real Christianity is."[12]

Such aloofness from Western civilization was an advantage. But in trying to communicate gospel across cultural lines Mennonites surely also had a disadvantage: the heavy religious significance they attached to the cultural ways of their own subgroup. Mennonites saw religious meaning in the smallest acts of life. At best, that was a sign of earnest, practical, minute-by-minute discipleship. But at worst, anything from a collar to an insurance arrangement might carry more religious weight than it could bear. Mennonites could go forth somewhat detached from the chauvinism of Western culture—but not so from the Mennonite distinctives.[13]

* * *

"*Mennonitism*," Daniel Kauffman editorialized in 1910, "—that is what some people call our position on the ordinances and restrictions." Yet, Kauffman asserted, Christ Himself or His apostles had taught every one of them, from nonresistance to footwashing to believers baptism by effusion. So "why not call it *Gospelism*?"[14]

Which Mennonitisms *were* truly Gospelisms? That was of course the central question, underlying Kauffman's argument and indeed all the struggle with the distinctives. But neither Kauffman nor others who commented on mission quite framed the issue so directly. Instead they treated it in various ways indirectly.

One indirect way was to discuss whether the distinctives—especially external ones such as dress codes—helped or hindered the mission cause. Had commentators associated Mennonite practice fully and absolutely with their gospel's inner message, then of course such talk would have been entirely beside the point. But since the quickening had put the distinctives more and more on a different track from the "plan of salvation," making them seem somewhat optional, the discussion ran on and on.

Some commentators continued to believe, as many had argued late in the nineteenth century, that the distinctives helped the cause of mission. In 1923 a writer discussing Mennonite work in West Virginia judged that in the long run Mennonites had been successful because of the way they lived their gospel. Charity Gingerich in her 1925 article reasserted the old point that Mennonites' "simple gospel," preached by humble, unsalaried ministers, had a special appeal to the poor. As late as 1939 Noah Good, superintendent of the Lancaster Conference's mission at Reading, Pennsylvania, argued with similar logic that Mennonites were especially suited to take the gospel to Negroes.[15] But many, especially home mission workers, became preoccupied with problems the distinctives created. Mennonite nonresistance naturally brought rebuff in World War I, not only in a city such as Youngstown, but also in rural communities in the hills of Missouri. And a Mennonite colony at Concord, Tennessee that over the years had attracted an exceptional number of its neighbors found in World War II that people were staying away. In 1941 Frank Raber, mission superintendent in Detroit, pointed to Mennonites' rejection of life insurance as a problem, especially when richer Mennonites seemed none too ready to give aid to needy brothers and sisters. Meanwhile in the 1930s fieldworker S. E. Allgyer faced difficulties in Mennonite rejection of labor union membership. "The work of building up churches with Mennonite principles in the city," Allgyer observed, "is not an easy task."[16]

Attire, especially the Mennonite bonnet for women, caused the most debate. It took an awfully lot of teaching, declared Home Mission workers in Chicago in 1897, to get people to see that the workers' garb was not just that of some special Christian order. Asked in 1910 why so many mission Sunday schools lost their children at about age 15, workers cited among other reasons "our peculiar costume." In 1914 a city worker recounted to *Christian Monitor* readers that one mother had been so against her daughter's wearing the bonnet that she had blurted out: If not wearing the bonnet would send her daughter to hell, the girl would just have to go there! "It seems an awful uphill job, to get those English to see that Mennoniteism [sic] is Christianity," lamented Simon (S. M.) Kanagy, Mennonite mission superintendent in Toronto, in 1918. "We have a half-dozen more who would join, were it not for our bonnet regulation."[17]

In 1931 a General Conference Mennonite scholar, Edmund G. Kaufman, published a book[18] on Mennonite missionary and philanthropic efforts. As his main point he asserted that those Mennonites who were less preoccupied with distinctives were more active in mission work. In other words, laxity on nonconformity aided mission. The point was plausible. Kaufman's book covered the efforts of the various Mennonite branches in North America. His own General Conference Mennonite branch allowed more latitude on dress and some other matters than did "old" or "Mennonite Church" Mennonites. And it had been ahead in establishing formal missions, boards, and institutions.

Kaufman's point was also a joust in an inter-Mennonite battle, and very quickly John Horsch, the Mennonite-Fundamentalist historian, reacted vigorously. Some of Horsch's argument was of the tarbrush variety: He noted, for example, that the General Conference Mennonites had for a time affiliated with the "modernistic" Federal Council of Churches. Other of it was of a higher order: He argued that early Anabaptists and European Pietists had been in the forefront of mission, yet vigorously separatist; and he asserted that the Mennonite Church was currently showing how to be mission-minded and yet faithful to scripture on nonconformity and separatism.[19] But Horsch missed two major fallacies underlying Kaufman's book.

As a compendium of facts of Mennonite mission, Kaufman's book was very helpful. But a fallacy was that in his definition of mission and charitable activity Kaufman had assumed the general Protestant methods and models. Therefore, for example, as Horsch did point out,[20] he failed entirely to mention the Virginians' early work in West Virginia. A second fallacy was the classic one of assuming *post hoc, ergo propter hoc* (if one thing follows another, the first caused the other). Actually the two factors—the more libertarian Mennonites' relative indifference about some of the distinctives, and activism in mission— had resulted largely from a third development: *borrowing from revivalistic Protestantism.* The General Conference branch had taken form partly as a result of quickenings similar to the one that Mennonite and Amish Mennonite Churches experienced in the late 1800s. Having been quickened earlier, its Mennonites were farther on the road both toward abandoning nonconformity and toward mission activism. The one was not the result of the other, but both were largely results of acculturation via revivalistic quickenings.

The fact was that, contrary to what Kaufman suggested, both libertarian Mennonites and conservative ones could succeed in mission. Amos (A. M.) Eash, within a few years after being appointed in 1906 as superintendent of the Twenty-Sixth Street work in Chicago, was in trouble with various critics and the board for laxity on the distinctives. But apparently he was popular and attractive to the people among whom he worked. On the other side, J. D. Mininger of Kansas City was conservative enough to tell in 1921 of one woman whose husband had angrily torn the bonnet off her, while she stood firm and declared that "'None of these things move me.'" Yet Mininger was also a highly popular and even more successful mission superintendent. At the conservative-oriented Altoona mission one Charles Weyandt, newly a Christian through the mission's effort, testified in 1927 that it was "easy to wear plain clothes when the love of God came into my heart." M. C. Lehman declared in 1931 that he had questioned many fellow missionaries on the effect of plain clothes, and not one had declared the distinctive garments themselves to be a disadvantage. "What does create prejudice or even derision," Lehman concluded, "is lack of genuineness revealed in squeamish, half-hearted observance."[21]

Lehman might have added that judgments about the effect of plain clothes and other distinctives depended very little on evidence and very much on a commentator's personal convictions. How Mennonites perceived the effects depended on who was perceiving.

A second indirect way that Mennonite missionaries worked around the edges of the basic what-is-Gospelism-and-what-is-mere-Mennonitism issue was to struggle between the idea of "facsimile" or "replica" churches—mirror images of home churches—and the idea of adapting their patterns to the various cultures. Of course, the instinct of Mennonite missions, as with most missions, was to plant facsimile churches. Thus in 1921 T. K. Hershey quickly assured North American Mennonites that in Argentina new members were baptized in the same way as "at home," and were taught the same doctrines. The booklet *20 Lecciones Bíblicas (Twenty Bible Lessons)* that Argentine missionaries printed for doctrinal instruction was essentially Kauffman's *Bible Doctrines* scaled down and translated, even to the point of treating ethics mainly as "*restricciones.*" Replication extended to forms of worship: To go with certain lessons, *20 Lecciones* suggested songs that were translations of "Hallelujah, Thine the Glory," "Spirit of God, Descend Upon My Heart," "Holy Bible, Book Divine," etc. And not only in Argentina: In 1924 M. C. Lehman, although quite sensitive on intercultural matters, described a heathen celebration with its noises of "pans, horns, drums and guns" as being much inferior to a weekly prayer meeting of Christians singing "Nearer My God to Thee."[22]

The instinct to replicate extended to church structure. Despite some variations to accommodate the fact of mission authority, and in India the introduction of a church council that imitated the traditional village *panchayat*, missions transplanted the whole round of Sunday morning services, Sunday schools, sewing circles, Young People's Meetings, and conferences. (In the 1980s, are they transplanting relief sales?) After a trip to Argentina in 1940 board secretary Yoder noted privately that services in Argentina were so "typically Mennonite" that "the men sit on one side of the aisle and the women on the other side!"[23]

"To what extent should the home Church project its standards into the Church on the field?" Daniel Kauffman asked in 1933. "We answer, one hundred per cent. After all, the principal difference between the home Church and its outposts is a difference in geography. We have the same Lord, the same Gospel, the same Great Commission, and we ought to recognize the same standards."[24] The facsimile church idea was strong.

But even Kauffman saw need for some cultural adaptation. Missionaries often found themselves faced with a choice between standards practiced in America and foreign ones, he said. If the decision was between truly gospel standards and worldly foreign ones, of course there was no choice. But if missionaries upheld standards practiced in America, let them be sure to choose the "standards of the American Christian and not the American worldling"—"the standards of American Mennonitism rather than American worldliness." If Kauffman too easily identified Mennonite with gospel standards, at least he was advising Christians to take cues from the church, which was trying to be people of God, rather than from the nation. And indeed he qualified even further: The "universal standard of the Cross," he declared at another point, "does in no way conflict with the idea of recognizing conditions as they are and adjusting ourselves to them."[25]

From near the beginning of their movement, Mennonite missionaries and mission commentators actually were quite conscious of the need for that kind of adjustment. Of course there were limits. In 1932 when the theologically liberal "Laymen's Report" sent reverberations among Protestant missionaries by strongly advocating dialogue between Christianity and other world religions, almost as if between equals, Mennonite missionaries like many others scrambled to dissociate themselves from that.[26] Yet through the years they sometimes discussed questions of cultural adaptation. Partly, they were again emulating Protestant mission patterns. Early in 1911 Lydia Ellen Schertz, missionary on furlough from India, warned *Christian Monitor* readers against assuming that Americans were civilized when the Chinese were not, or insisting that India's people eat with forks and sit on chairs. Quite clearly she was taking cues from the mission movement at large, for in the same piece she denounced sectarianism in a way that seemed almost to undermine Mennonites' basis for having their own church.[27]

From whatever motive, some Mennonites saw the need to study and understand the nations, cultures, and peoples to whom they went. After all, Mennonite Church people were not going into government, law, big business, university teaching, etc. So for them mission was a major opening into a larger world, and attracted some of their best minds. J. A. Ressler began a tradition of inquiry when in the earliest years of the India mission he wrote back article after article full of remarkably reflective and informative observation. Although not totally free from condescension, Ressler had very little of lurid descriptions and put-down of "benighted heathen."[28]

Mary Burkhard advised *Gospel Herald* readers in 1909 that missionaries needed to study not only language but a nation's history and literature. And indeed, especially in India where she had worked, several Mennonite missionaries dug deeply into the culture's philosophical concepts. J. D. and Minnie Graber studied Hindi scriptures and other literature extensively in the course of mastering the language, and in 1928 J. D. treated *Gospel Herald* readers with a learned discussion of the Hindi concept of salvation, or *Karma*. M. C. Lehman wanted very much to take up oriental studies at Columbia University during a furlough in the 1920s. Because Mennonite Fundamentalists suspected such a university would turn him into a Modernist, he settled instead for industrial education at Hampton Institute in Virginia. Finally in the early 1930s he accomplished his ambition at Yale, writing a doctoral dissertation on a late-nineteenth-century Indian writer named Harishchandra.[29] For various reasons Lehman did not return to India as a missionary thereafter. Yet his interests illustrate how profoundly some of the India missionaries wanted to understand the underpinnings of Indian culture.

The motive for such study seems to have been strongest where the culture was most distinct from the missionaries' own. To be sure, that was hardly true of Eastern Board missionaries in Africa before World War II, for Lancastrians held a deep skepticism about secular learning, a skepticism that made little room for such an approach. To be sure also, various home missionaries were intellectually vigorous. J. R. Shank, missionary in the rural hills of Missouri and Arkansas and brother of J. W. in Argentina, contributed much to Mennonite Sunday school and other literature. Others became teachers in Mennonite colleges, etc. But, understandably, home missionaries did not match the intercultural scholarship of the India group. In many ways J. R. Shank, for instance, was the Mennonite Church's foremost rural missionary, and a model one—helpful to, kind to, and apparently loved by people in the Ozark communities where he made his circuits, self-giving and tireless on behalf of the poor. Yet he seems to have made virtually no adjustments because of cultural background when it came to enforcing the distinctives, lest he sully the purity of the church. Very probably in part because of that (although in part also due to circumstances such as displacement of people when a dam was built) the ongoing, visible results of his work were somewhat meager.[30]

Moreover, in addition to such direct application of the distinctives, home missionaries could make the people they were reaching feel culturally put down. In 1926 Selina Jennings, of a family who had become Mennonites through the colony and church at Concord, Tennessee, pointed out that southern manners and heritage were "decidedly different from those of the Mennonite who is fundamentally northern." She also quoted a Kentuckian's complaint that "you missionary people ...photograph our worst homes and lowest people," never telling "of the good people nor the substantial things of the community." Probably the Kentuckian was not referring specifically to Mennonites. But Selina Jennings was.[31]

The intercultural thinking of the missionaries in Argentina, where the culture was Western but not North American, fell somewhere between. T. K. Hershey, who did so much to shape the Argentine work, was reasonably perceptive but more of a doer than one to stop and reflect. Yet even he warned the mission board (and the board agreed) against the notion that any well-meaning country Mennonite could, with a bit of Bible school training, become an effective missionary. Missionaries, he said, needed systematically to study the country's history and culture.[32] J. W. Shank was more inclined toward scholarship than was Hershey, and wrote several small books and a BD dissertation on South America and Argentina. Yet his writings were largely descriptive and interpretive. A 1945 book *Argentina from Within*, by Lewis Weber who went to Argentina in 1931 and became something of a mission leader, used some scholarly sources but was much like the writings of Shank.[33]

Some Mennonite mission thinkers did think interculturally, and did put their ideas into large frameworks. Helping in the 1920s to get discussion toward work in Africa, Irvin (I. E.) Burkhart, a Mennonite studying theology at a Southern Baptist seminary in Kentucky, presented the call as one to a continent where Western imperialism had broken down old ways but not offered Africans adequate new ones. There was then, he said, much opportunity to help Africans rebuild their lives around the Christian gospel. J. D. Graber, on furlough in 1932, told an audience that he would not present a picture of Indians as "those poor, black heathen," for such language grew out of racial prejudice and "the religion of being white." As for heathendom, Graber thought that the way Indian independence leader Gandhi was emphasizing passive suffering was "a good deal nearer Christianity than some of the imperialistic and capitalistic policies of our own country." And missionary Ernest E. Miller, arriving home from India in 1938, advised that his church thereafter should select its missionaries on the assumption that in the Orient "the day of the white man's superiority has come to an end." Any missionary who went about forever telling "about his wonderful America, her wonderful farms, her wonderful hospitals and schools," Miller warned, would never see nationals as co-workers, but only as " 'my workers' and 'my servants.' "[34]

Miller's comment suggested the ideal of a church that was genuinely an international brotherhood. A number of other missionaries thought in larger or smaller terms about the nature of the cultures in which they worked, and how missionaries ought to respond. So while the ideal of replica churches was very strong, Mennonite Church missionaries at least tempered it by also recognizing some need for adaptation. That was the second way in which the Mennonite Church's mission movement dealt indirectly with the basic issue of what is gospel and what mere Mennonitism.

The third way was to work out various accommodations on the different Mennonite distinctives.

As a group Mennonite Church missionaries did accommodate. They did so differently in different cases. Aside from particular missionaries' personalities and attitudes, the nature and degree of accommodation depended mainly on three interacting variables: How clearcut, if one viewed scripture in quite a literal and obedience-minded way, was the scriptural basis of a teaching? How easy was it to transmit the practice into another culture? And how much did a given practice disrupt the lives of new Christians?

The Mennonite Church in North America did not allow musical instruments in formal worship, for instance. But regarding a scriptural basis for that prohibition it did not have clear enough consensus to maintain the taboo indefinitely in mission congregations. It happened that even one outspoken Mennonite-Fundamentalist leader at home, J. B. Smith, argued from the Greek-language New Testament that scriptures favored use of instruments, and some other church leaders conceded that he had a point.[35] So by the mid-1930s pressure to allow missions to use the instruments in worship was building up, especially for the Argentina field and for Spanish-language work at home.

To such pressure, the reaction was rather odd. Through the entire discussion, for instance, the only alternative anyone seemed to see to homeside Mennonites' *a capella* singing was the North American Protestant method of trying to lead (at worst, blast) a congregation along with a piano or an organ. A second oddity was that in 1933 a home board resolution, possibly by design, discouraged only missionaries' use of instruments, not their use by the people of their congregations.

Finally, less officially, by 1935 secretary Yoder tacitly approved a portable organ for services among Mexicans in Chicago, at least for meetings in private homes.[36]

Finally, when board officials finally did more or less resolve the issue, it was by deflecting it with jokes rather than by facing it head-on. In 1940 Yoder, having just visited in Argentina, reported at a meeting of important board committees that Argentine congregations were using organs. According to Yoder's account, board president D. D. Miller "flared up" briefly but did not get support. Then "Dan Kauffman in his lordly semi-jocularly [sic] way" suggested sending one of the committee members present, Chester (C. K.) Lehman of the Eastern Mennonite School faculty, to Argentina "to teach those people how to sing" and to worship. Thereupon, Yoder has reported, "I told him it would probably be necessary to have J. B. Smith define what constitutes Biblical worship. ...After that everybody smiled and dropped the subject."[37]

From then on the board seems to have let foreign-field missionaries proceed as they wished, and home-field ones also if district conferences did not interfere. Where the scripture behind a distinctive teaching seemed none too clear, Mennonites could gradually relax a rule.

The prayer veiling for women was quite a different case. Most Mennonite Church people took I Corinthians 11:2-13 to say clearly at least that women should veil their heads during prayer. Moreover they required the sisters in the home churches to wear a special "covering," rather than allowing ordinary headgear to suffice. But in missions, to demand some conspicuous pattern of veiling would certainly make new believers appear strange, and thus disrupt their lives. The solution on foreign fields was to transmit the standard, but in more culturally acceptable forms. In short, India missionaries allowed Indian women to do just as their custom had always been, namely cover their heads with a part of their regular garment. Thus the solution was simply to invest ancient Indian practice with new, Christian meaning. Critics at home, especially the Lancaster bishops and the Virginians who confronted the India mission so energetically in the 1920s, objected to a covering that was not uniquely Christian.[38] But the accommodation survived the challenge.

In many places home missionaries, by contrast, found no such satisfactory solution. Practice in a mission congregation usually was supposed to conform to the rules of the congregation's district conference. Moreover, the cultural form that home missionaries might have accepted, the women's hat, was too often a vehicle for the kind of showy display that Mennonites found entirely contrary to scripture. So to one degree or another most newly believing women in home missions had to accept the veil in its traditional form. When in 1936 a Black woman in Lancaster was ready to become a Christian but for the veil and the plain dress, mission workers pointed out that "not every one that saith Lord, Lord shall enter the kingdom of heaven, but whosoever doeth the will of my Father which is in heaven." And in Los Angeles, in 1942, mission superintendent Glenn Whitaker felt "real joy" in seeing "colored sisters with their devotional coverings."[39]

In Argentina the solution was similar to that in India: acceptance of a form familiar in the culture. In this case it was the *mantilla*, or long black veil that Argentine Catholic women used in worship and in mourning. In 1923, in response to uneasiness in North America, the board asked missionary women in Argentina to wear the North American Mennonite "covering." But it only asked them to "encourage" Argentine women to do so, and that only if it "will not cause too much difficulty." Even those qualified directions brought spirited dissent from women missionaries there, and in practice the *mantilla* gradually became accepted. Late in the 1930s board officials accepted the *mantilla* for Spanish-speaking people in Texas, also. Some Mennonites in an established congregation nearby objected; but, wrote Yoder privately, "I told the Executive Committee of the Kansas-Missouri Conference [which had jurisdiction in Texas] that I am not at all interested in starting work among the Mexicans and spending a lot of money if it means that we will have to impose conditions upon them that will make it impossible for them to come into the church."[40] The *mantilla* stayed.

Thus, where missionaries and the board were able fairly easily to translate a Mennonite distinctive into a practice already accepted, adaptation and accommodation proceeded.

Apparently a distinctive such as the rite of footwashing caused scarcely any problem at all, at least on foreign fields. Argentina missionaries for instance, could write in the 1940s that "feet washing for our people is a plain 'thus saith the Lord' and is practiced cheerfully."[41] Not only could mission workers cite a direct command of Jesus, but washing feet was understandable to peoples accustomed to religious ritual, as were Argentines, Indians, and Africans. And being confined to a service inside a church building, the rite apparently did not cause ridicule or otherwise disrupt new believers' lives. Indeed, it could have deep meaning: Missionary George Lapp declared in 1923 that low-caste Indian people appreciated it profoundly as "an emblem of sacrificial service and love," and as a "social leveler."[42] And so missionaries were able to communicate that distinctive into new cultures without great adaptation, apparently even translating something of its deepest meaning.

With other distinctives also, practice depended on how the three variables mixed. The North American Mennonite bonnet for women became highly controversial because there was not very clear scripture for that particular form, and because, being headgear precisely for wearing in public, it was conspicuous and disrupted new believers' patterns of life (or at least their emotions). Consequently by World War II use of the bonnet was beginning to decline. Against the cutting of women's hair Mennonite Church people thought they had clear scripture, also in 1 Corinthians 11. To some their view was convincing: In 1927, for instance, a girl with bobbed hair wrote to thank the Eastern Board for publishing a tract on the subject, and said that she was now trying even to persuade other girls to let their hair grow. But because hairstyle so affected public appearance the prohibition could be quite disruptive and create much tension (especially in Argentina and in home missions). By World War II that rule also was breaking down. Meanwhile most Mennonite Church people considered wedding bands and the counterpart in India—bangles, that is glass armbands that married women wore—to violate scripture's prohibition of adornment with gold and costly array. But again, because the bands had deep cultural meaning for showing marital status, to abandon them would be disruptive. So missionaries accommodated. In India they very early settled on a formula of allowing a woman two bangles, but no more—enough to show marital status, but not enough to be ostentatious.[43] In Argentina the missionaries seem never to have made a great issue of wedding bands.

As for the many problems of marriage itself—plural spouses in India, and elsewhere common-law marriages and reception of people who were remarried and had former spouses still living—Mennonites struggled with the questions much as many other missionaries have. They did not, by World War II, come up with satisfactory solutions.

North American Mennonites were unclear in their own churches about precise answers to divorce-and-remarriage issues. By the 1920s and 1930s most of them were taking the unequivocal position that no currently married person could be received if a former spouse was still living. At least one district Mennonite conference, that in Indiana back in 1875, had once said that a previous marriage contracted when the parties were not church members was no more than a civil matter, and so, if civil authorities then dissolved it, the marriage was no longer religiously binding. But by the 1920s and 1930s the home church had developed a far less accommodating attitude on the question, and boards and missionaries were in a struggle to enforce the unaccommodating attitude on the field. Yet even Lancaster Conference conservatism could not produce absolute answers. In 1938, in Africa, despite help from home-board officials who were visiting the field, Eastern Board missionaries failed to develop clear policy. Soon thereafter one of their medical missionaries, Noah K. Mack, advised an African Christian to divorce her husband—because the husband had other wives, and had thrown the woman out to die of infections which Mack had then been able to heal. However, as for remarriage after divorce, missionary bishop Elam Stauffer reported in 1939 how he and his colleagues had prevented one such union, even though in the divorce the African Christian woman who wanted to remarry had not been the partner at fault, and even though "three or four earnest native Christians" had come with "strong reasons" for allowing her to remarry. "There was no way of granting marriage from God's Word," Stauffer reported; the missionaries had replied to the Africans just by "going back to the Word."[44]

Later, after World War II, there would be more strategy of accommodation and adjustment in such cases on the various fields. By World War II, pressures were building strongly for such a change.[45] But at the end of a half-century of mission work neither the Mennonite Church's missionaries nor their board had found a rationale for such change—despite the fact that their standards on marriage clearly kept quite a few people from entering fellowship in new, mission-planted Mennonite churches.

The marriage question, then, was something of an exception: Mennonites engaged in mission had great difficulty accommodating, despite profound disruptions their standards demanded in the lives of new believers. Apparently marriage seemed just too important for adjustments. But then the marriage question was hardly a distinctively Mennonite one either. On the distinctives themselves Mennonites usually found it possible to make some accommodations if that seemed necessary. The precise patterns depended on the particular mixture of the three variables: clarity of scriptural command, ease of translating into an acceptable cultural form, and amount of disruption caused in new believers' lives.

None of the three ways Mennonite missionaries wrestled indirectly with intercultural questions quite got to the heart of the basic question. The discussion of whether Mennonite distinctives helped or hurt mission went on inconclusively. To the implicit tension between cultural adaptation and facsimile church, Mennonites applied a reasonable amount of intelligence. On specifics, they made many practical accommodations when the variables demanded it, although without very clear theory for doing so. But in none of these ways did Mennonites quite define and deal directly with the central issue: What was really gospel, and what were mere Mennonitisms?

* * *

Compared with the problem of confusing gospel with Western culture, Mennonites' problem of confusing it with their own distinctives probably was preferable. At least the distinctives had grown out of the life of the church itself. And at least they reflected an earnest desire to break with the world to obey God, a principle that it was surely necessary to demonstrate, somehow, in the course of proclaiming gospel. Should a people be judged harshly just because they ventured forth to preach gospel without waiting until they had first become sophisticated in anthropology or in theories of cross-cultural communication? Mennonite Church missionaries had ample problems with preaching gospel across cultural lines. But they were the problems of people who were trying even in the details of life to be faithful to God.

6
THE PURE GOSPEL: TEACHING THE "ALL THINGS" (II)

The more or less external distinctives aside, did Mennonites transmit the central perceptions that, historically, had helped shape their understandings of the gospel? What of a concept of salvation that emphasized the new life as God's regenerated people living on the "resurrection side of the cross," in new relationships, with new ethics? What of an understanding of church as God's voluntarily committed people, receiving counsel and discipline from one another in order to follow Him and to keep from following the world's unregenerated ways and systems? What of the idea that peace was at the very heart of the gospel message—not only inner, personal peace, but peace also as ethic for relationship and action? Of such understandings there were hints, and sometimes more than hints, in the Mennonite Church's mission movement. But the insights came separated, hardly in a well-focused vision of gospel. The understanding of basic gospel was not much different from that of the larger Protestant mission movement.

* * *

For instance, salvation. Mennonite mission people occasionally seemed to get beyond a message mainly of deliverance from past guilt. "The message of Jesus Christ is one of separation," declared the board's field-worker S. E. Allgyer in 1927. It was one "of regeneration; of nonresistance; of non-conformity; of obedience to the whole will and counsel of God." Could Christians claim "close relationship with Christ, unless we are willing to stand for all the things He stood for?" Although Mennonites were by nature no better than other people, Allgyer wrote four years later, they had a faith that enabled them to live uprightly, and that was "something the world needs." Thus Allgyer did bring the obedient Christian life close to the concept of salvation. So also did Daniel Kauffman, in an important "Standard for Missionaries" that he drafted for the board in 1932. Kauffman laid out "The Missionary Message" in very ordinary terms of faith and repentance, substitutionary atonement, and "plan of redemption." But he followed that with a description of " 'Unspotted' " living, striking the vein that "it is but natural that they who have been 'born again' should, in all things, 'walk in newness of life.' "[1]

Yet statements such as Allgyer's and Kauffman's did not spell out clearly that obedient Christian living, as a gift of God's grace, might actually *be* the tangible, here-and-now shape of salvation. Any such suggestion was even more remote in a 1927 attempt of S. F. Coffman to say succinctly what it meant to preach Jesus Christ. Certainly Coffman sensed the meaning of new life as God's people: two years earlier he had written a tender hymn warmly commending the footwashing rite and the Christians' love and service to one another that it symbolized. But the language of his 1927 address was orthodoxly Protestant. To preach Christ was to proclaim "Jesus Christ as God's Witness to the world"; Jesus Christ as God's Lamb, offered for the world's sin; Jesus' dying as the penalty for sin; Jesus' resurrection as the power of new life; Jesus as having ascended, serving now as ambassador before God; Jesus as coming again bearing resurrection power; and "Christ as King in the new heavens and the new earth." Perhaps Coffman's reference to power for new living hinted that obedience was part of God's salvation. And later in his address he called on Mennonites to meet people's physical as well as spiritual needs, for "unconverted people do not call so much for Christ as they call for the fruits of the Christian life." But if he hinted of relationship between salvation and living as God's people, he only hinted.[2]

Some Mennonite statements, for instance a 1924 one by D. H. Bender, scarcely offered even the hint. Bender said the missionary's task was to: "teach men the atonement; baptize them into the Church; teach them to observe all things; teach them the wonderful truth that Christ lived, suffered and died for us; [instruct them] that He arose, went to the

Father and is now our advocate before the Father; [and] teach them the awful price God paid to redeem their souls and wash them white in the blood of the Lamb." Bender dropped no clue of how the "all things" related to the perception of salvation that his other phrases implied. A 1935 statement by missionary Mary Rutt of Argentina, on the other hand, offered some clue. Rutt wrote of sin as transgression for which God justly demanded punishment, of Christ's suffering the punishment, and of His power to cleanse. From there she went on to how Christ delivers from sin's power as well as from its punishment, and to His becoming preeminent in the believer's life. Thus she did emphasize victorious new life, but seemed to separate that from a salvation that came prior: once again the two-track formula. Nor did her concept of new living get beyond the individualistic application that Protestants in the revivalistic tradition have been inclined to give it.[3]

Some such statements tended, once salvation got separated from the track of ethics and obedience, to let the second track deteriorate. Speaking at a 1927 mission meeting on "Things Most Surely Believed Among Us," home missionary Allan Good of Portland, Oregon, listed: Jesus as the entire Bible's central theme; the virgin birth; Jesus' coming to seek and save the lost; our being the Father's ambassadors; water baptism; the fact of temptation; the need to preach the Word; prayer; missionary activity; invitation to God; repentance; and Jesus' resurrection, ascension, and promise to return. The missionary's duty was to "preach, preach, preach"—"preach the Word," "Preach the full Gospel."[4]

Surely Good and others who gave such formulas believed that obedient Christian living was important. But through the 1920s, 1930s, and 1940s the unconscious notion that the salvation message was one matter, and Mennonite teachings about Christian living another, was running deep. In 1937 T. K. Hershey warned strongly against mixing too much "*doctrinal*" teaching with the "evangelistic" message. "Don't deceive the unsaved by announcing revival services" and then pour[ing] into them certain things that may be your hobby," Hershey advised. People "first needed salvation"; doctrinal subjects—matters such as the prayer veiling and according to Hershey even nonconformity and nonresistance—could come later.[5]

J. D. Graber has recalled that during the 1930s the Mennonite Church's missionaries in India assumed that first of all a person had to become a Christian and take up Christian ideals and practices, and then "being a Mennonite was something beyond that." Until about World

War II, according to him, "trying to get people converted, trying to get them to believe in Jesus Christ as Savior," crowded out time to teach something like nonresistance. After all, Graber paraphrased, "If a man hadn't accepted Christ, why should you talk about a lot of other things?"[6]

Such words suggest that Mennonite missionaries did not see such "other things" as central to understanding the Christ whom they were calling people to follow. In adopting a view of salvation so confined to initial conversion and deliverance from past guilt, mission-minded Mennonites tended to separate other principles they considered biblical from having a place in God's basic way of dealing with human lostness.

* * *

That was true for the concept (or concepts) of the church. How the ongoing community of the believing contributed to salvation remained ambiguous. Not that mission-minded Mennonites lacked all vision for creating faithful churches, obedient to God; they kept that vision somehow, even if some of their remarks about the gospel's message failed to mention obedience, and even if they put obedience on a different track from salvation.

Visions of pure church and of faithful, obedient community have of course been strong in Mennonite understandings. Historian Franklin Littell and others have argued that the central point of sixteenth-century Anabaptists was the idea of a voluntary church, living by a new ethic and disconnected from the coercive structures and methods of society. Mennonites throughout the centuries have wandered and migrated to achieve and preserve their visions of community. In recent decades Mennonite scholar Guy F. Hershberger has iterated and reiterated that the Mennonite view is for Christians to live in the world as "colonies of heaven." That, for Hershberger, has been a principle not only for ethics, but for evangelism. "We must remember," wrote he in 1944, "that the most effective testimony of the Mennonites in times past has been given through the group."[7]

As Mennonites from the quickening onward opened themselves to Protestant influences, they opened themselves also to altered views of Christian community and church. Individualism has of course been strong in much of the Protestant missionary movement, so that missionaries have often emphasized individual soul-saving and one-by-one personal acceptance of Jesus to the point of scant recognition that humans are social beings, living in and taking values from groups. In extreme form the individualism has produced those "faith missions" unhooked from church in the organizational sense and often lacking any real concepts of church. Or it has produced those who have emphasized broadcasting the Word to the point of scant concern for follow-up, nurture, and church-building. Meanwhile, others in the Protestant mission movement have been less individualistic, and have emphasized church-planting—for instance, J. W. Pickett with his writings especially in the 1930s emphasizing "mass movement" evangelism, or the idea of measuring success by statistics of "church growth," the emphasis of missionary and scholar Donald McGavran, of whom Pickett was, in the 1930s, a colleague.[8]

Yet even Protestants who have emphasized church and community of belief have often done so rather differently from the way Anabaptists and Mennonites have stressed voluntaristic, regenerated, and obedient new community. Especially in the nineteenth century, some Protestant missionaries thought in group terms precisely because they associated Christianity with the spread of Western culture and empires. Mass movement evangelism in the twentieth century has rested on the theory, perhaps more anthropological than theological, that in some cultures people make decisions not as individuals but as tribes or communities. And Professor McGavran, in his theories of church growth, has used a word such as "disciple," rather differently from Anabaptist and Mennonite usage. For Anabaptists and Mennonites, "discipleship" has very much carried the idea of *ongoing* obedience to God, scarcely to be thought of apart from living within the disciplined, fellowshiping community of faith. In McGavran's emphasis discipling refers much more to the bringing of people to initial commitments to follow Christ, with less emphasis on the church that follows.[9]

In the Protestant missionary movement there has been perhaps, in experience if not in theory, something akin to the Anabaptist and Mennonite understanding of the new fellowship of voluntarily and deeply committed believers. Believers-church theologian John Howard Yoder has suggested that unconsciously many missionaries have found in mission a de facto free-church experience. They entered the movement as volunteers, and discovered in it a fellowship of like-minded and committed Christians. Proclaiming gospel, they drew around themselves people who had broken decisively with their communities in ethics as well as in beliefs, and who had done so voluntarily, as adults. Sometimes the new churches they founded have been very much at odds with political and other community authorities. So, Yoder has concluded, even where Protestant missionaries have not much emphasized the building of the new people of God, they have often experienced it.[10]

All this—Mennonites' own background and traditional emphases plus a variety of voices within the Protestant mission movement on the matter of church—invited confusion in Mennonites' own mission concepts and approaches. Nor was a more individualistic emphasis entirely alien to Mennonites. Certainly in their emphasis on voluntary, believers baptism, Anabaptists and Mennonites from the sixteenth century onward had advocated personal decision and personal faith. Influences from Pietism had strengthened that belief. As their own missionary movement got under way, then, Mennonites scarcely questioned use of language that suggested the evangelizing of persons individually, language such as "soul-saving" and "accepting Jesus as personal Savior."

The two emphases, individual and corporate, could mix and did so quite comfortably in the Mennonite mission movement. For language emphasizing church was common also. As the Lancaster County "progressives" began their activities in the 1890s M. S. Steiner was glad that "the fire of activity in extending the borders of the Church has been kindled." In 1914 C. Z. Yoder, president of the mission board, used the language of "winning souls" in a *Christian Monitor* aritcle; but he added "and building them up in Christ," and called for "hearty cooperation" among "the evangelist, workers, and congregation" to perform the "great work." In 1918 India missionary M. C. Lapp invoked a picture of "Indian brethren and sisters...bringing into the fold of Christ their relatives and friends," and headed that section of his article "Growth of the Church." It was a picture of calling people to Christ in groups, not just one-by-one. "Effective evangelism," declared J. D. Graber in 1932, "consists not only in shouting aloud in the village chauks, '*Yishu Masih ki jai*, Believe on Christ or you'll die.'" Missionaries, said Graber, had not just "to sow the seed but to make disciples." And that meant further "to teach Scriptures in India against Indian custom and a non-Christian background and give it a vital and practical interpretation." "The primary aim and purpose of the whole missionary enterprize [*sic*]," declared India missionary Ernest E. Miller, fresh from the field in 1938, "is the establishment of Christian churches."[11]

The fact was, however, that when Mennonite missionaries used non-individualistic, church-building language, they often borrowed it from the missionary movement at least as much as from their own traditions. In his 1938 statement Miller went on to speak of the Apostle

Paul's "method" of planting a church and then moving on[12]—clearly borrowing from mission thinker Roland Allen, and Allen's classic 1912 *Missionary Methods: St. Paul's or Ours?* Some of the language that Graber and others used, phrases such as "growth of the church," "making disciples," etc., undoubtedly reflected the currents of thought out of which McGavran has developed his emphases. (Indeed McGavran, in India as a missionary in the 1930s, was a warm friend of Mennonite missionaries there.)[13]

Graber explicitly acknowledged the influence on Mennonites of a landmark World Missionary Conference in 1938, sponsored by the ecumenical International Missionary Council and held at Madras, India. In view of the imminent collapse of Western empires and influence, the Madras conferees emphasized the need to foster strong, indigenous churches. The Mennonites at Dhamtari were remote from Madras, Graber declared in a 1939 report, and the Madras conference had promoted the idea of "a universal church fellowship" which was somewhat different from what Mennonites were emphasizing. "But," declared Graber, "the movements that stir men's hearts in the larger India, whether political, social, or religious, come eventually and surely as a ferment into the thinking of our own people. We shall be happy when the Church-centered emphasis of Madras reaches us."[14]

The words of Graber demonstrated an irony: although Mennonites had strong traditions of church to draw upon, they turned quite heavily to the larger missionary movement for their cues even when they considered the corporate dimension of faith.

Older Mennonite instincts that church is a supporting fellowship and community might still come through. When in 1930 Lancaster Conference missionaries at Tampa, Florida, sought membership for the first of their new believers, missionary-minded bishop Noah H. Mack observed that conference authorities "were somewhat at a loss what to reply"—for "the Mennonite Church does not believe in receiving people into fellowship and then afterwards not take care of them."[15] But Mennonites interested in mission also put forward other, less traditionally Mennonite concepts of church.

Mission-minded Mennonites might see church as vast machine for activism, service, and dispensing of salvation: in 1914 D. H. Bender spoke of it as "avenue of Christian activity and divine service...the vehicle used of God to carry His message of grace to a lost world," while H. R. Schertz, Chicago Home Mission superintendent, declared in 1924 that "we are a big corporation," and one that might learn something about united effort from the Ku Klux Klan. Or the mission-minded might see church as guardian of sound doctrine: Lewis Weber, as mission superintendent in Toronto, said in 1927 that the purpose of the church was to "proclaim a full New Testament Gospel" in the face of the "many 'damnable heresies'" of the last days. Another view was, the church as evangelists producing more evangelists: "the two-fold work of every church should be that described in Ephesians 4:12-14," observed Lancaster Conference bishop Henry E. Lutz in a mission sermon in 1940, "namely to win souls, and build up in the faith those who in turn can be sent forth." Still another view followed the two-track formula: to speak of becoming baptized without becoming a member of the church was wrong, declared field-worker Allgyer in 1924; for "every soul should remember that Jesus Christ did not stop when He said go and teach and baptize, but teach them to observe...every commandment in God's life-giving Word. ...There is absolutely no use in saving souls unless we can keep them saved," and teaching the all things was the way to keep them saved.[16]

On the actual mission fields also, the church seemed to be many things. Mennonite missionaries in Argentina seemed to think of it as a solid social institution—hence their desire for owning property and buildings that would create "prestige among the people." In India, missionaries worked constantly to counteract the image that Christian churches were mainly agencies of affluence, dispensing philanthropy. And in Chicago, a daughter of a couple drawn to the Mennonite Church in the 1930s through its mission effort has been sure that her parents responded to relief given by Mennonites in depression time—although two of her brothers have insisted that what the parents saw was not just philanthropy but a broader pattern of kindness and love.[17] Whatever the truth about the Chicago couple, concepts of church in the Mennonite mission movement were many.

Some in the mission movement feared that new believers or even some missionaries did not have a strong enough sense of being called out and living apart from the patterns of the world. In the late 1930s, commenting on political involvements of people in the Indian and the Argentine churches, board secretary Yoder feared that such people were "influenced by the spirit of the times and the situations out of which they come and can not differentiate clearly between 'what is Christ's and what is Caesar's,'" (It was probably easier for a U.S. Mennonite to see that in India or Argentina than in North America.) At about the same time, Mennonite Church missionaries opened a new field in the Bihar province of India and hoped to use (but never really achieved) the "mass movement" strategy. Since that strategy would encourage believers to remain fully integrated into their communities' economic life (instead of building a sub-economy around mission institutions), and since it assumed that the gospel should spread along "natural lines of caste and family relationships," missionary Fred Brenneman objected. It would mean, he argued, baptizing people who wanted to "keep the old earmarks" and not stand out boldly as Christians.[18] Brenneman's criteria for standing out boldly were frequently more Mennonite-Fundamentalist than Anabaptist or traditionally Mennonite. But he was quite correct in sensing that his colleagues, in their enthusiasm for mass movement, could be sanctioning a nonprophetic fusion of faith with culture.

Despite all that, there nevertheless ran through the Mennonite Church's missionary movement a noticeable sense of being Mennonite. Calling in 1927 for more rural workers in several states of the U.S. West, a speaker at annual mission board meeting lamented that there was "not a Mennonite Church or teaching throughout the [West's] rural sections." More happily, a decade later bishop Lutz, returning from a deputation visit to his board's foreign field, rejoiced that "we can truly say that a Mennonite Church has been started in Africa." To be sure, a daughter of the Hershey's, Beatrice Hallman, who herself became a missionary in the Argentine, has said that her parents taught her not to feel a difference in denominations. Yet to instruct new believers, for instance, the Argentina missionaries and church used translations of the North American church's eighteen Articles of Faith and of its *The Confession of Faith and Minister's Manual*. In their Bible school they of course taught a certain amount of Mennonite history and doctrine, and especially in the 1940s they translated and published in Spanish several key works in Anabaptist and Mennonite history and thought. Both Argentina and India missionaries reported that members of their churches were often reluctant to join other denominations if they moved to areas without Mennonite fellowships. There was, then, some sense of a distinctive church with distinctive traditions.[19]

Of course much of that may have been the natural sociology of new churches. And the ultimate value of new believers just "feeling Mennonite" was questionable. But there were signs of something deeper, something reflecting genuine Christian community and church. Orley Swartzentruber has reflected that during his youth as a son of missionaries in Argentina on the eve of World War II, being Mennonite did not mean anything very unique in mission strategy or message: "As far as I was ever aware, we were one of the evangelical missions." Yet on further reflection he thought that Mennonites did have an added sense of separation from the world, and of transmitting not merely a call to conversion but (for better or for worse) a whole lifestyle. John Friesen, second-generation Mennonite missionary in India, has emphasized that a real sense of brotherhood and sisterhood existed between missionaries and Indians, so strong as to transcend whatever unfortunate "imperialistic" master-over-servant attitudes lingered. Moreover Indian members who migrated cityward sometimes drew together spontaneously into Mennonite fellowships. In the Mennonite Church mission movement as a whole there did seem to be a fairly strong sense of the church's being called out, and of its living by values distinct from those at work in worldly cultures and societies.[20]

And the emphasis was on tangible, not only mystical fellowship. When the Argentina missionaries spoke in 1919 of establishing a "Mennonite community" in Argentina, they seemed to imply patterns of economic and social life, not just spiritual. In 1932 Ernest E. Miller, insisting that "the establishment of a Christian Church is the object of all our endeavour," used language from Acts 2 to put forward the ideal of church as a very visible group, living much of their lives in common: a sharing community with all things common; a joyful community, eating meals with gladness; a community worshiping daily with one mind; a respected community, in favor with the people; and a growing community, with the Lord daily adding new members.[21] Such emphases at least hinted of course at what Anabaptists and Mennonites historically had understood, and to an extent experienced, church to be.

More centrally, people in the Mennonite Church's mission movement retained and taught a very strong belief that the church was to be, in unmistakable and practical ways, the *faithful* church. For early-twentieth-century Mennonites, an extra dimension of faithfulness was apparently Mennonitism's central meaning. In a call to follow Jesus in preaching to the poor and brokenhearted, evangelist Clayton (C. F.) Derstine declared in 1921 that "if our past history means anything [the Mennonite Church] will do its duty. Will we go to our limit as the faithful men of the past have?" Criteria for faithfulness might vary. On the mission field they might reflect revivalistic Protestantism as much as anything distinctly Mennonite. "Nobody upheld plain clothes as part of Mennonite witness in Argentina," according to Orley Swartzentruber's recollection, and "pacifism was not the mark of the Argentine Mennonite" either; Mennonites there spoke of nonconformity and separation, "but the phrases were then reduced" to mean the standard ones of "no smoking, no drinking, no theater, no dance"—"these were the great things....These were the marks of true conversion."[22]

The criteria were not always distinctly Mennonite, but from the mission movement's outset the ideal of a rigorously uncompromising church ran strong. Satan tempts us to gain influence by yielding a bit on this point or that, preached J. A. Ressler in 1897, not long before he left for India. "Ah, but at what cost?...Leave all that makes the church worthy of her name in order that we might admit a few unconverted people"? No, said Ressler. "The disciples in early days were separate from the world and a clear and distinct line of demarcation ran between the two." "Preach Christ," agreed Daniel Kauffman in 1905. "Preach the cross. Preach salvation. Preach entire separation from the world. Preach perfect obedience in all things." Then, "having done what you can, don't question the wisdom of God's work if you can not number your converts by the score and by the hundreds." The test of mission success, declared board secretary Yoder in 1927, was "not the number of mission stations, nor the number of members," for many members might not be "soundly converted and may be lost again." The test was "what effect the Gospel has wrought on the lives."[23]

A faithful church, not mere numbers. In practical terms the ideal of faithful church translated into great concern that conversions be tested and new Christians adequately instructed. In 1922, D. H. Bender declared that "the object of true missionary effort is not only to take the Gospel to the lost, but helping [sic] the convert to find the real standard for the new life." The sinner "must be born again," with "thorough repentance, genuine faith, and an implicit trust in the atoning blood of our crucified Savior." But even that was not the whole matter. Converts not properly indoctrinated might soon fall away. Missionaries had to teach them to make the Word of God the rule of life, and to keep separate from the world and "world-compromising entanglements in all...activities—business, social, civil. ...'Blessed are they that do his commandments, that they may have right to the tree of life.' "[24]

Bender's language capsulized Mennonite mission people's habit of moving along with a fairly standard Protestant emphasis on conversion and at the same time with Mennonites' own insistence on almost legalistic obedience. Mennonites might be unclear about how those two tracks were part of the salvation process, but they traveled on both. The words of Bender were representative, and missionaries labored hard to follow the formula he spelled out. In Argentina, Hershey reported in 1924, there were people "now waiting over a year to be brought into the Church. We want to keep the Church pure." Because the missionaries were not accepting people who smoked, for instance, there were "some people we do not take in that would probably be taken in at home."[25]

India missionaries too were cautious in receiving new members. The missionaries wanted a true Christian church and not just a collection of people, J. D. Graber has recalled, so they insisted on new believers' undergoing lengthy Bible instruction before baptism. It is true that in the 1930s, under the influence of mass movement and church growth ideas, Mennonites along with others in India began more to reason that if they delayed baptism too long the new believers would lose enthusiasm and perhaps be dissuaded by militant Hindus. But the overall pattern was one of caution.[26]

On the home field what was asked of new believers varied; but with guardians of the faith nearby in established Mennonite churches, home missionaries also had generally to be quite cautious. And when the Eastern Mennonite Board opened new work in Africa in the 1930s, its missionaries tried especially hard to maintain rigorous standards for membership. Africans might attend an inquirers' class for some months and still not be accepted for baptism; instead, there evolved a further time of seeking, a "wants to believe" stage lasting for another year, during which the seeker had to attend catechism classes regularly, demonstrate a grasp of the teaching, live a "worthy" life, and win the approval of the congregation's native council. All that, before the seeker could be baptized and received into church, so that sometimes the preparation time extended up to two years. Ernest E. Miller, who visited Africa en route from India in 1937, declared approvingly that the Africa missionaries' "task will not be to persuade people to become members of the visible Church but to check their eagerness until they clearly understand the breadth and the depth and the full meaning of becoming a follower of Jesus Christ."[27]

Such a view, and the pains taken to prepare believers before baptism, certainly expressed the ancient Mennonite concern for the faithful church.

Similarly, Mennonite Church missionaries in the first half-century of their movement tried to plant disciplined churches. If members in India did not measure up to the church's standards, M. C. Lehman assured *Gospel Herald* readers in 1918, the church imposed sanctions— not only for infractions such as smoking, but for sins such as quarreling as well. John Friesen has recounted that even after the Indian church shortened its initial time of indoctrination, its discipline was so strong that many young people held back for years from joining, so as to be free of the church's sanctions. African churches, despite the care taken before baptism, suffered many excommunications in the early years. In Argentina there was apparently a kind of crisis of discipline, even a purge, in the mid-to-latter 1920s.[28]

The Argentine church's standards for faithfulness were not entirely legalistic, for its conference programs included topics such as the responsibility of members to give each other moral and other support, and the group did not take a rigid stance on the military service question. But, as retired missionary Nelson Litwiller has recalled, Mennonites in Argentina did at first try to be quite strict in matters of attire and behavior. In 1929, after wrestling with quesions such as the cutting of women's hair, Hershey reported that a time of testing had come, and "automatically some withdrew while others had to be expelled"—eleven expelled in 1928, in fact, out of membership of some 250.[29] By World War II, however, any "legalism" in the Argentine church seems to have receded considerably.

But overall in the first fifty years of their mission movement, Mennonite Church people had tried to transplant a fairly rigorous church discipline. It was another way of working for a faithful church.

The concern for faithfulness was surely admirable. Yet much of the discipline would now seem less like mere enforcement of North American Mennonite peculiarities, or like missionary paternalism, had Mennonite Church missionaries been able to communicate more clearly a unity of obedience and the way people experience God's saving grace.[30] In their quickening, Mennonites had borrowed heavily from theologies that did not emphasize very much the role of the disciplined, obedient, fellowshiping new community of believers as a means of grace and salvation. So Mennonite Church people went into the mission movement with various perceptions of what church meant—and without fully grasping the evangelical implications of their own tradition's understanding of church. They retained strongly the ideal of a faithful church. But they did not connect that concept intimately with their understanding of basic salvation, or of the essence of the gospel.

* * *

If that was true of how mission-minded Mennonites experienced and thought about church, it was even more poignantly true in the case of nonresistance and peace. How Mennonite Church missionaries handled that part of the "all things" is a sharp etching of how Protestant influence affected their concepts of gospel.

"I think," declared J. D. Graber in a study paper in 1950, "it is fair to say that Mennonite foreign missionaries in general have given comparatively little attention to the doctrine of nonresistance in their missionary efforts." Graber—who of course knew whereof he spoke since he had long been a missionary to India and was now the board overseas secretary—offered three reasons. First the missionary movement was well underway before the American peace movement became strong about the time of World War I. Second, until recently war had not threatened the fields where Mennonites were working.[31]

Then, Graber's third reason: "a lack of appreciation of the centrality of the peace message in the Gospel." "After all," said the secretary, "nonresistance is not a salvation doctrine"—or so at least "modern fundamentalism" taught. So nonresistance seemed to be "a matter on which Christians may differ." Missionaries, Graber observed, "have been so busy trying to get people to accept Christ as Savior and Lord," and so preoccupied with "the problems of everyday practical Christian living," that few "got as far as nonresistance in their teaching." Until "fundamental problems of faith, integrity, purity of life, unselfishness, service, etc." were solved, "there was simply no time nor inclination to get on with nonresistance."[32]

In fact, Graber continued, when missionaries read in their church papers of conferences on nonresistance and of a burgeoning peace movement at home, they "were often honestly skeptical and wondered wherein the heart of the Gospel lies." "This," thought the astute Graber, "is really a most fundamental question"; and until missionaries saw "that nonresistance is much more than a cultural aspect of Mennonite life...much more than merely an attitude toward war on which Christianity may differ to no consequence," they could hardly "take much time out for its promotion." But—if nonresistance was "primarily a question of Christian love," and if it "represents the true, the only Christian way of life," a way "none other than the way of the cross," then Graber was confident that missionaries would "bring it into the scope of their doctrinal and practical teaching. What," challenged he, "can be done to give our missionaries this point of view?"[33]

Some concept of peace, at least of individual "peace with God," has of course been part of virtually every Christian missionary's message. Moreover, missionaries have rather often spoken out against tribes' and nations' violence and militarism, and thus—as mission historian R. Pierce Beaver has recounted at book length—have been "envoys of peace." Yet too seldom have proclaimers of gospel perceived peace in humans' outer relationships to be part and parcel of the salvation message. At worst, "Christian" missionaries have uttered statements such as one did in 1858 regarding China: that to civilize the Chinese would require a "Society for the Diffusion of Cannon Balls."[34]

Others in the modern missionary movement have argued, on the other hand, that for pacifying peoples, missions were cheaper than armies. That is an argument of pragmatism, of course, not one of gospel principle. In 1912 an important World Missionary Conference Continuation Committee meeting did rest the case more on principle, for those present spoke of the "intimate connexion between missions and the peace movement." Yet they suggested that pacifism might be the framework still of extending Western influence, only by other means, for they spoke also of "the responsibilities of the civilized nations of the West towards the less civilized East." Against that backdrop a 1906 statement of Daniel Kauffman was quite enlightened. "When your patriotism rises to a point" where you want an army to destroy the Chinese government "because of the outrages upon our missionaries there," he advised *Gospel Witness* readers ("our" apparently meaning "American"), "then think of how you would look upon" an African army coming over "to do the same thing for our government because of so many negroes being lynched in this country."[35]

Yet even Kauffman had not quite gotten to the heart of the question. Jesus, Paul, and others in the New Testament had spoken of peace out of the Hebrew concept of *shalom*—total well-being, as a community, for the people of God. The *shalom* concept was broader than peace as release from the weight of sin's guilt, the Reformers' emphasis; than personal intimacy with Jesus, Pietism's emphasis; than inner tranquility following the turmoil of a conversion experience, American revivalism's emphasis; or yet than the formalized anti-militarism into which Mennonites both before and after the quickening had fallen. *Shalom* was a holistic concept, covering everything from a personal experience of God's love and blessing to political peace and economic justice.[36] Whether "gospel" did not refer to this total understanding of what God offers His children, was the heart of the question.

Late-nineteenth and early-twentieth century Mennonites still had within their own traditions the wherewithal to come close to that faith—that is, if they had not narrowed their peace teachings to a few quick check-offs regarding not going to war and not suing at law, or fragmented their thought to fit the two-track formula. They retained, reinforced by Pietism in Europe and revivalism in America, an original Anabaptist emphasis on personal relation to Jesus. In rejecting war and lawsuits, even if too formalistically, they retained some idea that God's peace covered political and not only inner, "spiritual" matters. At least the pre-quickened among them emphasized humility, which at its best translated into egalitarianism and some concern for social justice. They retained a strong sense of being God's people in community. In fact they had a term to cover the holistic vision: not, to be sure, "*shalom*" but "the gospel of peace."[37]

The quickening and the forces surrounding it had seriously eroded some of these elements and destroyed the wholeness of the vision. Yet Mennonites as they went forth in mission retained some of the "gospel of peace" idea. M. S. Steiner in the wake of the Spanish-American War wanted "messengers of the gospel of the Prince of Peace" to go where "the war method of humanitarianism" had only brought new suffering. A decade later, in 1908, his friend C. K. Hostetler advocated mission work in the U.S. South because the region needed "some settlements of non-resistant people to teach the Gospel in a practical way." In 1912 Peter (P. R.) Lantz, city missionary in Canton, Ohio, reasoned that Mennonites' "love of peace and order as taught by the Prince of Peace" gave his church a grand opportunity to rescue "lost souls in the cities teaching them the ALL THINGS." During World War I, M. C. Lehman spoke of nonresistant Christianity's having the answer to the problems of a Europe that was piling dead men six feet deep.[38]

So Mennonite Church missionaries might have gone forth with the integrated, holistic "gospel of peace" idea at the center of their message. Generally, however, they did not.

From the quickening until at least World War II their home church was not integrating it salvation and peace messages very well. Out of the throes of World War I the Mennonite Church's general conference evolved a Peace Problems Committee. In 1925 the mission board turned down a request from the committee for assistance in handling the committee's funds. The board's reasoning was logical—that it did not want to confuse organizational lines.[39] Nevertheless in its refusal it lost an opportunity to draw the denomination's peace leadership closer to its mission effort. In 1926 and 1927 the board did reconstitute an earlier war-relief agency into a Relief Committee. On the other hand, in 1927 a request to a dozen church leaders to suggest topics for annual mission board meeting brought many proposals ranging from "Orthodoxy and Evangelism" through "The Missionary on Furlough" but scarcely one that had even remotely suggested the peace concern.[40]

Allen H. Erb of La Junta did suggest "Non-resistance as Related to Missionary Endeavor," but program planners did not include the topic. And late in life Erb himself could not recall making the suggestion, indicating that probably even he did not think long on the matter. Ten years later a 1937 position statement on military service that the Peace Problems Committee prepared and the church's general conference adopted did assert that "we believe His Gospel to be a Gospel of Peace, requiring us as His disciples to be at peace with all men."[41] But that did not exactly tie peace with salvation or the missionary message. Only about World War II and after did writers such as Guy F. Hershberger and younger persons clearly abandon two trackism, and present New Testament pacifism more as central to the basic gospel.[42]

If the sending church was separating its peace convictions from its basic salvation message, small wonder that missionaries scarcely knew where to fit nonresistance with the Good News. Missionaries could on occasion rejoice at cases such as that in 1942 of a new believer, a grandmother convinced through mission effort in Lancaster, Pennsylvania. The grandmother was amazed to learn that "these things were in the Bible" and decided that she would pray for troublemakers in her neighborhood rather than call the police.[43]

But in the early World War II years home missionaries often seemed to emphasize troubles they were having because of their nonresistance more than they spoke of nonresistance as the message the world especially needed. In 1942 Marcus Lind of the Portland, Oregon mission wrote privately of "difficulties arising from the unpopularity of our Mennonite attitude toward war," noting that "some of our converts, who don't have the Mennonite background, are gradually yielding the point" on the war issue. The following year C. Warren Long, mission superintendent in Peoria, offered an enigmatic list of problems wartime had brought: "parents in the shop, children on the streets"; "nudism"; "families of service men in congregation"; "the high school militarism"; "Local Defense movements"; "Black Foremen"; "young men of draft age whom boards reject"; and, "the regimentation of men and women too." In the end Long advised that "there must be a positive approach and testimony."[44] By that, however, if other Mennonites' attitudes are a guide, he probably meant doing something in the vein of relief and service that would relieve Mennonites of a negative, "slacker" image,[45] more than he was calling for the integrated "gospel of peace" message.

For Mennonites in India also, World War II was problematic. By then there was a long tradition for the pattern that Graber has recalled, of teaching nonresistance only after and apart from the initial call to follow Christ. Ernest E. Miller, out of his service in India from 1921 to 1937, thought late in his life that the first generation of Indian Mennonites seemingly had shown stronger convictions on nonresistance than had the generation coming to maturity in World War II times. By all accounts economics worked against the convictions: army and police forces offered attractive jobs to young Indian men educated in the mission schools.[46] One suspects—although to prove the point would require much further study—that mission efforts had unleashed a thirst for raising one's place in society so powerful as almost to overwhelm the religious message that missionaries wanted to communicate. Another force, no doubt, was the politicizing effect of the Gandhi-led independence movement in the interwar years. Although nonviolent, the movement implanted a spirit of nationalism that must have helped undermine the outward nonpoliticism of Mennonite pacifism. Finally, there was the force of Mennonites' constant interaction with Protestants of other missions, treating them as true followers of Jesus whether or not pacifist.[47]

By way of formal policy, the rules and discipline of the Mennonite Church in India, from its organization in 1912, listed nonresistance as a "restriction" and forbade suing at law or "taking up carnal weapons and engaging in warfare."[48] In World War I, in the absence of a draft, the India church did not officially speak out on nonresistance. It did contribute 500 rupees to a fund for wounded soldiers, "to show," missionaries explained to the church in North America, "that we were patriotic in a Christian sense" and willing to give all possible help to the government "to whom we owe the possibility of our mission work."[49] Here was the pattern that Mennonites had often followed elsewhere: reducing the nonresistant message from a total one against the world's violent methods to a lesser one of personal nonparticipation in military affairs, coupled with gesture of positive contribution.

In 1935 the Mennonite Church in India made police and military service a test of membership, and throughout the 1930s its leaders gave some increased attention to nonresistance.[50] Partly, it would appear, this new attention grew out of need to respond to the nonviolent teachings of Gandhi. (At first, in the 1920s, at least the missionaries had largely viewed Gandhi as a rebel against legitimate government, but by the 1930s they understood his nationalism and appreciated his nonviolent stance somewhat more.) Partly also, the increased attention seems to have risen out of communication with the church in North America, where the Peace Problems Committee and others were promoting peace education.[51] In any case, when World War II came, the India church formally excommunicated young men who entered the armed forces, even when (as was common) they chose noncombatant service as cooks, drivers, medics, and other support personnel.[52]

Many Indian men entered, nevertheless. And the missionaries did not interpret such action as outright rejection of Christ. Instead, in 1942 they asked North American Mennonites to pray that such young men "may realize that they are not in the will of God, and that they may not lose their Christian experience." And the India Mennonite Church, far from assuming that those whom they loosed on earth were loosed in heaven, gave some young men letters attesting to their good standing on all matters except the military one. That was to help them enter the fellowship with other denominations.[53]

From one point of view, of course, the letters stated the matter honestly. But they also highlighted how much the Mennonite Church in India operated on the two-track premise. And later developments highlighted even more poignantly how the ethical track could shrivel away, once its connection to the salvation track got severed. For in 1952, in the course of reorganizing to become more indigenous, the India Church dropped the prohibition of police and military service as a test of membership. Some parts of the church continued it, and since 1952 at least some Indian church leaders have gotten new appreciation for the place of peace in the gospel message.[54] Yet if prohibitions against police and military service make a fair, rule-of-thumb test, it would seem that fifty-three years of Mennonite Church missionaries' and national church leaders' efforts in India did not plant very firmly the centrality of the whole peace ethic in God's salvation.

In World War II Africa as in India the money, the chance to learn trades, and other economic attractions of military service seemed to overwhelm any peace convictions in new believers. Negotiating with Tanganyika's British rulers, Eastern Board missionaries won exemption for conscientious objectors and advised African members to claim it. But apparently not one did. Only later, under the guidance of non-Mennonites in the East Africa Revival, did African Mennonites begin seriously to consider (and practice) nonresistance. Perhaps that should not have been surprising. In 1937, at least one Mennonite missionary in Africa had forthrightly, under the obvious influence of the premillennialism popular among Fundamentalists, repudiated any vision of peace larger than the individual one. "War rumors again remind us of the necessity of pressing on more vigorously in the conquest of souls," missionary John Leatherman had asserted. "Getting sidetracked on peace testimony and solving of social ills in a time when the kingdoms of this world are preparing to line up against the kingdoms of our Lord and of His Christ is a crime against the God of heaven." Continued Leatherman: "We have a Gospel which brings peace to the individual by the cleansing of his heart and remission of his sins, and if a man thinks that too narrow, we have nothing else for him or for the world."[55]

Leatherman's was an extreme statement for a Mennonite, and did not really reflect the Lancastrians' whole approach. The Eastern Board was busy with various relief and charitable efforts, and its magazine, *Missionary Messenger*, occasionally ran pieces expressing a larger peace vision. Orie O. Miller and others with a broader concept of peace were active and influential in it. In 1931, J. Paul Sauder, the *Messenger's* associate editor, had combined the larger vision with realism and observed that if Mennonites could not stop war, at least their message could stop new Christians from killing one another. Or in 1939 Africa missionaries John (Jr.) and Ruth Mosemann at least hinted at an understanding of sin and lostness that went beyond only the personal; for they suggested that the African might have a right to consider "his sin small in comparison to the Christian (?) nations' unholy slaughter."[56]

Yet Leatherman's language fit Mennonite-Fundamentalist views on peace that bishop John Mosemann (Sr.) and other strong voices, especially of the Eastern Board's constituency, had been expressing. Publication of Leatherman's views in the *Messenger* brought no outcry, nor any suggestion of repudiation. Small wonder, then, that in Africa the missionaries hardly communicated a message in which salvation and the broad vision of peace were integrated and inseparable.[57]

Nor in Argentina did that *shalom*-like message come through. From the outset of work there, Mennonite Church missionaries and their home board did not quite know what to do with their nonresistance, and found it posing problems. Through World War II and beyond they dealt with the problems mainly by sticking to the two-track formula and giving the "salvation" track clear priority.

As early as 1913, when he reported on his investigative trip to the southern continent, J. W. Shank observed that Argentina had "rigid military laws" that made it "very difficult" for Argentine citizens and even foreigners to escape military service. In 1917, fresh on the field, Hershey pointed out in the *Gospel Herald* that nonresistance was a new doctrine for the Argentine government, and any Protestant group would certainly find it hard to win legal concessions on such an issue; but, Hershey hastened to add, even in the face of persecution "it is better to obey God than man." A Baptist missionary warned Hershey further in 1919 that even if some Argentine official orally promised Mennonites military exemption, other officials would hardly feel bound to the promise.[58]

In 1919, of course, neither did the United States clearly exempt religious objectors from military service. So perhaps it was natural that when S. C. Yoder and Samuel Musselman visited Argentina in 1919 and 1920 they allowed the mission to proceed despite the military problem. Upon his return home Yoder ran into some criticism for buying property in "a country where one of the vital and fundemental [sic] principles of our faith can not be practiced." But, Yoder reflected, "we hope that the time may come soon when we may be exempt from military service in the Argentine as well as in the U.S."[59] Yoder gave no grounds for his hope. And apparently the board examined the question no more deeply.

Also in the early missionaries' attitude on the question, there was a softness. Statements of Shank and Hershey dealing with nonresistance on their missionary-candidate questionnaires were sound enough. But in 1920 Shank published a small book defining the task of a missionary to South America in language that was entirely Protestant; so he made no point of teaching the peace ethic. Meantime, in 1918, some of Hershey's relatives in North America left the Mennonite Church for the Reformed. Hershey urged them to be sure that their new church was sound on such matters as justification, baptism, predestination, and activism in mission. But despite the World War I context, he mentioned not a word on nonresistance![60]

Throughout the 1920s and 1930s, the missionaries and the church surely transmitted the message of nonresistance and peace to some degree. The *20 Lecciones* that they printed for instructing new Christians presented love of one's enemy as a positive virtue and included nonresistance—albeit as usual in the negativist category of *restricciones*. In 1922 Shank inserted in an early issue of the tract-like Mennonite paper *El Camino Verdadero* (*The True Way*) an editorial presenting Christian love as the cure for the world's ills. He also ran an item about some Japanese women who, under Christian influence, had petitioned for peace. In 1924 a Mennonite "fundamentals conference" in Argentina included, along with topics such as "The Plan of Salvation" and "The Victorious Life," one on "The Message of Love for the World of Today." The Bible School that the missionaries began in the late 1920s for training pastors and other Christian workers became a vehicle, of course, for teaching the doctrine of nonresistance, among other matters. Another vehicle was weekly Bible Study or Christian Endeavor meetings in the congregations.[61]

In the early 1930s peace concerns in the Argentine church took an upsurge. The new Bible Training School may have been one cause, but apparently another was political events. In 1932 a new conservative dictator, Agustín P. Justo, took power in the country with a call for an end to all clamor "that may kindle or perpetuate hate, and incite to violence." Moreover, it was a time of war between Argentina's neighbors Bolivia and Paraguay, and of the beginning of the Spanish Civil War. Whatever the stimuli, in 1932 a third-year student of the Bible school, Carlos Barbosa, wrote a piece that got translated and printed in the North American Mennonite *Christian Monitor* as "War: From the Social, Moral, and Religious Point of View." Barbosa even brought the ideas of peace and salvation somewhat together, for he argued at one point that through war "we have denied the work of reconciliation made by Christ which should bring us joy and peace." In 1932 also, Argentine Mennonites began a church periodical, *La Voz Menonita* (*The Mennonite Voice*), and for a regular motto on its masthead put Christ's enjoinder from Matthew 5:39: "Resist not evil: but whosoever shall smite thee on thy right cheek, turn to him the other also." Young people in the Argentine church put on a spate of programs on peace, with orations, essays, and posters. Peace was a notable topic at Argentine Mennonite Church conferences in 1933 and 1934. The 1934 conference created a Peace Committee that communicated with its counterpart in the Mennonite Church in North America and helped to undergird the young people's efforts.[62]

"To hear the young native ministers discuss, in such a forceful and practical way, themes pertaining to peace and war, our attitude toward the Government, Nonresistance, Nonconformity, and Consecration," wrote Hershey in 1934, "was to us missionaries most inspiring and very encouraging indeed." Nor was it just talk and theory that encouraged them. In 1924, when in North America on furlough, Hershey included among his stories for the home churches an account of a revolver-toting young man in Pehuajó who, upon becoming converted, had ceased to carry his weapon. In later years another missionary, William Hallman, remembered that when someone had pushed one of the Mennonite Sunday school boys into some mud, the lad had asked to be pushed in on the other side also. Missionaries and other church leaders in Argentina were communicating something about peace.[63]

Culminating peace thinking in the Argentine Mennonite Church up to and through the World War II period were two writings that surely deserve prominent place among Mennonite writings on peace. In 1940, in an obscure, mimeographed periodical designed to reach Argentine Mennonite leaders, missionary Elvin Snyder published a substantive, sixteen-page article on church and state. Up-to-date in his reading, Snyder commented on the thought of European theologian Karl Barth, and specifically rejected the idea on the one hand that the social and political impact of the gospel could come only through the calling of individuals, or on the other that the Christian was obliged to offer military service to his nation if the nation were, to use Barth's language, a "just state." From the venerable Mennonite stance that in such matters one must understand the Old Testament in light of the New, he also refuted, head-on, positions of "Militarist-Fundamentalists" (as he called them) who explained away nonresistant passages in the New Testament and defended war from the Old.[64]

Snyder upheld the idea Anabaptists and Mennonites had long emphasized of distinct realms of church and world. Without denying a God-ordained place for worldly government, he was sure that sometimes it was necessary to follow a loyalty higher than one's loyalty to the state. Yet, very much anticipating a position that would come to fruition in North American Mennonite writings and official positions only from about mid-1950s onward, he suggested that as states extended their activities into education, welfare, and the like, Christians would find it less and less possible, or even desirable, to avoid roles in the state's affairs. Whatever the church's separation from the state, he concluded, Christians should nevertheless work to bring Christian ideals to bear in critique of national policies—should be "today's prophetic and apostolic voice" in public affairs.[65]

In 1948 an Argentine Mennonite pastor, Feliciano Gorjón, published a 150-page book evolving out of a series of peace lectures that he had given at a Mennonite youth retreat. With a title that meant "Church and State: Toward a Christian Philosophy of Their Relationship," Gorjón's was an able treatise, well-researched and well-stated. If flawed at all it was flawed only slightly by a few near-harangues against the Catholic Church and possibly by too much effort to find a position compatible with Argentine patriotism. Its main thrusts were much like those of Snyder. At some length, Gorjón appealed to the Anabaptist position vis-à-vis the state. And he gave further evidence that Argentine Mennonites had not let Fundamentalistic or other Protestant influences prevent them from applying peace to social questions. Indeed, Gorjón was at least as inclined to cite Protestants with "social gospel" slant as he was to quote Fundamentalists. He applauded concern for social justice, even when he recognized that communists also had some such concern. Perhaps Gorjón strongest point was to see nonresistance in positive terms, not in the old *"restricciones"* category. For Jesus, nonresistance meant more than simply not resisting, Gorjón declared: it meant that the nature of the Kingdom of God was to forgive, love, bless, and do good. Nonresistance was not a matter of weakness or indifference. It was the proclamation of the truth and love and peace and power of Christ.[66]

With the Snyder and the Gorjón writings, the Argentine missionaries and church made two highly worthwhile contributions to Mennonite peace literature. Meantime in 1943 they reproduced a major work on Anabaptism by publishing *Menno Simons' Life and Writings*, edited by Harold S. Bender and John Horsch, in Spanish translation. In *La Voz Menonita*, their most substantial journal, they further translated two articles that were key to the North American Mennonite Church's understanding of how nonresistance was based in scripture—*Mennonite Quarterly Review* articles by Guy F. Hershberger that would become core chapters in his landmark book, *War, Peace, and Nonresistance.*[67]

Yet somewhere between the high level of such notable writings, and the admirable way some Argentines were applying nonresistance in their personal lives, there was a practical gap. When in 1924 a young member whom Hershey had counted on to become a trained Christian worker found himself called up for military training, with no apparent way to escape,[68] the missionaries did not make it an occasion for soul-searching or policy review. And the peace emphasis in the early 1930s remained largely a movement of the young people. Middle-aged church members, observed Snyder in 1933 and 1934, were still under patriotic influences from the public school system and national history books. And so they had "a sort of a repulsive feeling when one talks about the Higher Patriotism," as if "it is all right to preach 'Peace in

Christ' but that has nothing to do with national defence, or offence either."[69]

Ironically, a critic might raise the same objection to Snyder's article of six years later. Both his and Gorjón's pieces, despite their many merits, were loudly silent on specifics about how to respond to Argentina's draft laws. For when the question was the very practical (and very difficult) one of military service, Mennonite Church missionaries and the Mennonite Church in Argentina were still quite able, in World War II times, to separate peace from gospel.

In 1938 J. W. Shank wrote a troubled letter to board secretary Yoder. The Shanks' son Pablo would soon be eighteen, the first missionary son born in Argentina to reach military age. Pablo had several choices: put on the uniform and apply for a stint of record-keeping in a local military office; as a student, attend military training camp in summers; do nothing until twenty, and hope then to draw a lucky number in the military draft lottery; or go to North America for college, refuse to return if drafted, and thus forego the privilege ever to return to the land of his childhood. Pablo was uncertain, but inclined to do service in the local record office. He was "quite shocked" when his father told him "that I did not see how I could bear to see him wearing the uniform and be occupied in making plans in the war system."[70]

Why was the son of an articulate and thoughtful Mennonite Church missionary shocked at his father's position, after seventeen years of rearing? The fact was, as Shank reported, the whole group of missionaries was uncertain. Argentine members had been taking military training, though many had escaped through good luck in the lottery or by not passing physical examinations. Missionaries with growing sons felt much as Shank did, yet the group was not ready to "commit themselves to a finality decision." All the missionaries could do, Shank reported, "was to encourage the boys to be an example for Christ." (Pablo himself went to the U.S. for college, but after a time of personal unsettlement, actually served with the U.S. armed forces.)[71]

"Be an example for Christ." But that answer, of course, still begged the issue: What had been Christ's example, and the essence of His message? Perhaps response to the military system in Argentina does not provide the best test for examining that issue. Argentine missionaries and others have raised at least two words of caution. The first is to remember that Argentina, unlike the U.S. and Canada, had gone a century without actually engaging in foreign war, so that a stint with the military seemed harmless there, as compared with North America. The second warning is that criticisms of the Argentine Mennonite Church for its response to the draft, criticisms which have flowed southward from North America rather frequently, all too often assume the possibility of North American models of alternative service. Indeed they may be another species of wanting missionaries to impose North American solutions on other people's problems. For the last warning the missionaries have even gotten some support from that uncompromising North American Mennonite peace writer, John Howard Yoder. Latin solutions to problems such as this one often take unofficial forms rather than the formal legal ones of Anglo-America, Yoder has pointed out; so it is difficult to judge from North America exactly when a satisfactory Argentine solution may exist. After all, alternative service in North America is also a species of accommodation with military systems.[72]

The words of caution themselves beg further questions, of course, but surely they are to the point, sobering to anyone looking from a distance at Argentine Mennonite responses. Moreover, the Argentine Mennonites, as they faced the hard questions, were a first-generation church. As such, they were discerning afresh the way to go, and so they were faithful in a way that fellow-Mennonites elsewhere hardly are, if those fellow-Mennonites have settled into formulas, such as alternative service, without continual discernment and seeking of God's will. Shank in his troubled letter at least had a proper concern that Argentines themselves develop convictions for a solution, rather than having missionaries violate the meaning of church by imposing the answer. "A real solution...," he wrote, "should satisfy our native Christians as well as the missionaries."[73]

Yet from wherever one stands in the thicket of questions, surely the policies of Mennonites in Argentina, and the words they used to defend the policies, constantly raise that central question of "What does the Gospel really proclaim?"

As World War II arrived Argentina increased her military activity, even though in the end she did not formally enter the war. In that heated situation Mennonites operated, somewhat uncomfortably, from a formula that Hershey articulated at the Argentine church's conference in 1940: keep out of politics except to vote, do military service if government requires it, but keep yourself clean and do not kill or destroy in any way contrary to the Bible. When a young brother was drafted, "all that we can do and have been doing," Hershey thought, was to pray with him that he might remain faithful, keep up correspondence with him, send

7
HELPING GOSPEL TAKE ROOT

Shapers of the Protestant missionary movement have said over and over that missionaries have not truly planted the gospel until there is a church that is self-supporting, self-propagating, and self-governing. That formula appeared about mid-nineteenth century, particularly in writings of two outstanding mission thinkers and administrators, Rufus Anderson of the (predominantly Congregational) American Board of Commissioners for Foreign Missions and Henry Venn of the (British, Anglican) Church Missionary Society. Early in the twentieth century three-selfism evolved into an even more inclusive concept: indigenization. "Indigenization" embraced more because it dealt not so much with structure and activity as with relating gospel to culture. Its central idea was to make the Christian faith truly "at home with"—in some sense "native to"—peoples newly accepting it.

These concepts became conventional wisdom, to the point that before World War II Protestant missionary thinkers seldom questioned them. Instead they mainly refined them. Probably the most influential refiner was an Anglican, Roland Allen, author of various books, especially *Missionary Methods: St. Paul's or Ours?*, first published in 1912. To a degree Allen did question three-selfism. Venn had written of the new church being the edifice, and mission structure only scaffolding to be dismantled in due time. Allen, by contrast, emphasized the way the

New Testament's Paul had planted congregations directly and then moved on. Thus Allen challenged all mission structure, especially its proliferation of programs and institutions that might be humanitarian but did not necessarily produce churches.[1] In an uneasy synthesis, Allen's use of St. Paul as model became further conventional wisdom for the Protestant mission movement.

In other refinements, an International Missionary Conference at Jerusalem in 1928 fostered the language of being "church-centric" rather than mission-oriented, and of "older" and "younger" churches rather than the supposedly more condescending terminology of "mother" and "daughter" churches. About the same time "devolution" became another bit of jargon, meaning the transfer of responsibilities from missions to new churches. Missionaries and mission theorists wrestled with questions of how to achieve devolution. As the new church assumed responsibility should there be a clean structural separation from the mission, to make it easier to dismantle the mission or to move it on? Or should mission and new church structures intertwine to reflect an ideal of "cooperation," as missionaries in the 1930s were more and more saying, especially at a landmark missionary conference in 1938 at Madras in India?[2]

Some of the questions were quite troublesome. Mission thinkers, even when they accepted the three-self formula, often argued that to achieve it required time, time especially to train leaders. But some objected, as one mission commentator put it in 1913, that much of the concern about leadership training came from lack of "confidence in the power of any but a white race to maintain the Christian standard of morals."[3] Another question was to what extent missionaries should expect new churches, as products of *three-selfism* or of indigenization, to resemble the "mother" or "older" churches—and whether missions should hold off "devolution" until they did. A late-nineteenth century German mission thinker, Gustav Warneck, had argued that the aim was a *Volkskirche* (people's church) so attuned to the culture in Asia or Africa or wherever that it would be very different from the sending church.[4] Such an idea, and other talk of separate new churches and indigenization, reflected Westerners' habits of thinking in terms of nation, national boundaries, national cultures, and state churches.

By World War II Western missionaries were beginning to lose confidence in the idea that Christianity could really fuse with culture anywhere. For they were becoming impressed that their own nations might be profoundly anti-Christian. Expressing such doubts in 1940, a him tracts, and encourage him to testify for Christ daily. To show that his formula worked, Hershey publicly praised one young Argentine Mennonite who was doing military service. The young man's superiors had lavished praise upon him for exemplary conduct, Hershey reported happily, and had awarded him with a prestigious certificate. Moreover the youth had kept up his devotions, and had not smoked or drunk. Some fellow-soldiers had ridiculed him and nicknamed him "pastor," but most had liked him.[74]

After all, Hershey argued by way of defense, the missionaries were foreigners. To tell young men to refuse military training on scriptural grounds "would offend the government greatly"; and that in turn would risk "being asked to discontinue our mission work." His words of course suggested trade-off of formal nonresistance for mission. It was a logic that the home board had long since accepted. At the mission's very beginning, Shank had put the question: "Would Christ expect us to withhold the Gospel from a country because its laws required military service?" In 1940, as World War II came on, secretary Yoder revisited Argentina. Before his going the board, apparently prodded by the Peace Problems Committee, directed Yoder to consult with the missionaries on the military service question. Yoder returned to North America reporting a "very wholesome and healthy attitude." The missionaries, he said, had taught nonresistance, and with other nonresistant Christians had formed a committee to study the military service issue. But the missionaries were foreigners, he reasoned, and the question was "very delicate."[75]

Implicit in Yoder's account was the two-trackism that left uncertain how an ethical matter such as pacifism relates with the gospel. Should the mission have *wanted* to exist, and was it truly proclaiming Jesus, if it had to mute its peace testimony? The board, like everyone else, left the main question hanging. With his explanation, Yoder wrote back to Argentina, the board "all appeared to be satisfied."[76] In short the uncertainty about connection between nonresistance and gospel rested with the home church at least as much as with the missionaries.

* * *

The Great Commission's language of teaching "all things" held great potential for the missioners of the Mennonite church. It intrigued them, and they sensed that it could be the cord for keeping many of Mennonites' distinctive concepts of Christian ethics and life tied into the missionary task. Had they used that phrase more like earlier Mennonites had used the phrases "nonresistant gospel" or "gospel of peace," they might have communicated more of a seamless, holistic understanding of the biblical message and of the nature of God's salvation. Such understanding would have been more akin to biblical *shalom*. They did use the "all things" phrase, and use it often. In it they found courage to teach some of the more external distinctives such as the footwashing rite and dress codes—although how vigorously they did so depended also on how direct the scriptural command, how culturally adaptable a practice was, and how much the observance disrupted new members' lives. In it they found reinforcement also for teaching such historic doctrines as those of faithful and disciplined church, and of nonresistance and peace. Mennonite Church people in mission taught these distinctives, earnestly, often struggling mightily to translate and apply them in the new cultures and contexts. Yet their understanding of the basic gospel message did not quite include them, even though Jesus had made the teaching of " all things" part of the Great Commission itself. To quite an extent gospel and salvation remained one matter, obedience and the "all things" another.

time of course when the *Volkskirche* idea had taken a very bad turn in Germany itself, mission historian Kenneth Scott Latourette cast doubt on the very idea of indigenization. After all, he argued, "Christianity, if it is not hopelessly denatured, never becomes fully at home in any culture." A Christianity "true to its genius" instead "creates a tension." As had the prophets of old, Christianity put forward goals far beyond those that any people or society had achieved.[5]

Logically speaking, in light of their history and beliefs, Mennonites should have been among the first modern missionaries to voice Latourette's kind of doubt. But before World War II scarcely anyone in the Mennonite Church's mission movement was examining conventional missionary wisdom that carefully. Few had the theological or the secular education that might have helped them do so. The one or two who had the training, for instance J. D. Graber, were at that time too busy with the doing to be quite that reflective. Although Mennonite mission commentators did use the word "indigenization" from time to time, they scarcely seemed to perceive that it was a cultural concept more than a procedural and structural one. They were not prepared to deal with its deepest meanings either in the anthropological sense or in theological terms. Instead they treated it as meaning hardly more than the three-self formula.[6] That three-self credo they repeated profusely, borrowing happily and uncritically from the Protestant missionary movement.

Mennonite Church missionaries did not embrace all three elements of the credo equally, however. It was a time when paternalism toward other ethnic or national peoples still seemed like kindness, and when the Mennonite Church in North America was centralizing authority. So they found it much easier to speak of self-support and self-propagation than of self-governance.

* * *

The very first Mennonite Church mission manual, published in 1899 just as the first foreign misisonaries were going to India, declared that "the raising up of self-supporting and self-extending churches" was always the ideal; when native helpers "become able, they should be allowed to bear responsibility," and "foreign teaching, pastoral care, and supervision be gradually withdrawn."[7] By referring to self-support first, to self-propagation second, and to self-government only indirectly, the manual set the tone for Mennonite missionaries' statements for the next forty-five years.

Self-support. For some years many Mennonites, unused to paying preachers or church officials at home, thought of missionary support as did one L. O. King of Hesston, Kansas, in 1917. Commenting on city missionaries, he asked why they did "not do something toward their own support when our ministers must support themselves." Such sentiment was strong, and an undercurrent of it was so harsh that it often made mission people defensive. Yet its advocates could also be sober and constructive. Were not Mennonites getting caught up too much in what was sometimes "manufactured enthusiasm" for foreign work, with its expensive voyages to distant lands, asked Solomon (S. B.) Wenger of Iowa in 1907. Should they not rather be satisfied with less glamorous work in country areas at home? Mennonites already had nuclei of members in many home-field areas, and in the long run mission activity that built up these weak nuclear churches would create a better base even for the foreign work. And at home the missioners could probably support themselves.[8]

Missionaries themselves and their mission-advocate allies often fed such hopes for cheaper, self-supported work. Early appeals for starting a mission in the Argentine, especially for funds to buy a farm there, rested heavily on the self-support idea. Once he got to Argentina the entrepreneurial Hershey wrote back expansively that Mennonites, "being a rural people ... could, thru investing in Argentina's rich soil as well as in operating some simple industries, make the present mission activities self-supporting, and make possible the opening of new and aggressive work." Fifteen years later when he helped develop Spanish-language work in Texas, Hershey again used the self-support argument. Yet by then the Argentina missionaries had long since found that even partial self-support had another side. In 1922 Hershey argued for a farm and industries, but in the same breath asked the home board to send more money so he could quit holding English classes because they consumed too much time. In 1932 J. W. Shank wrote publicly that a missionary could earn money in Argentina, but at the cost of less time for his mission work. Besides, Shank added, to mix mission with business could easily damage the mission effort. On the other hand, if a missionary did not support himself, how could he set an example for Argentines who became Christian workers?[9] Such were the dilemmas.

Elsewhere also, while they sometimes fed the enthusiasm in the sending church for self-support, missionaries and others often found themselves giving warning. Mennonites in India outdid other denominations' missionaries in frugality, declared J. A. Ressler in 1905, yet anyone who visited their mission for two weeks would easily see that missionaries in their part of India could not support themselves. Even if foreign workers could earn their own livings, George Lapp asked *Gospel Herald* readers in 1913, would that not be "disastrous to the [home church's] spirituality and interest in evangelism?" In 1932 J. N. Kaufman warned that self-support could work in India only if the board sent people already independently wealthy (which, although Kaufman did not say it, would surely have produced what some might consider another disaster: missionaries with the outlook only of the well-to-do). Meantime on the home field, a critic of developments at the Lima, Ohio mission objected in 1923 to an old streetcar that some self-support-minded person had turned into a chicken coop. The thing was ugly, thought the critic, it wasted mission time and money, and in all it was a "monument of folly."[10]

Ever the church statesman, Daniel Kauffman put the missionary self-support issue from both sides. To have Christian workers be as self-reliant as possible was good, he suggested in a 1923 book. It kept them in touch with common folks' problems. It helped keep their bodies strong (knowing Mennonites, Kauffman assumed manual labor). Paul in the New Testament had supported himself. And it helped the missionaries remember "the value of a dollar," which was sorely necessary for people who handled others' money. Yet people at home should not slacken their support, argued Kauffman. To keep a missionary on the field cost a certain amount whether or not he had time for much mission work, so why not support him enough so that he could work well? Twice as much money for missions, if "judiciously invested," might quadruple results.[11]

The ideal of missionary self-support never died. It continued on the foreign field and often at home to be more the ideal than the reality, although particularly in rural work at home Mennonite church people often more or less achieved it.[12] Surely the greater fact, however, was that the mission movement produced sentiment in the church to pay Christian workers, or at least to give them living allowances. Before it had missions, the Mennonite Church had no church professionals and had supported its ministers only on an irregular, mutual-aid basis, if at all. Missions helped move the church away from that pattern. The ideal of self-support stayed alive, but a counter-ideal of adequate backing for special classes of Christian workers, plus difficulties achieving the self-support ideal, moved the Mennonite Church toward salaries, careers, and professionalism.[13] And that meant profound change in

Mennonites' understanding of what the church was and how it ought to function.

That change in perception of the home church, on the other hand, by no means undercut another self-support idea: that the new churches that missions were planting should cut themselves off as quickly as possible from North American money, and work from their own resources.

When Mennonite missionaries and commentators advocated that idea, they sometimes did so at least in part out of concern for the new churches' spiritual growth.[14] The idea was that indigenous giving and financial independence were sources of such growth, and at the same time evidence of it. There was probably some of that concern, despite some grumbling, in remarks of secretary Yoder in 1922. Welcoming a plan of the Kansas City mission to stimulate local giving, Yoder asserted that people in at least one other mission "have become church beggars and are sitting down and kicking the rest of us."[15] But if Yoder's concern was for new believers' Christian maturity, his words and those of quite a few others surely reflected also an Anglo-American bias toward self-help as a great virtue and against dependency as moral failure.[16] In fact, concern primarily for new churches' Christian growth was all too rare.

Statements that new churches should become self-supporting usually reflected attitudes and conditions in the North American church more than any attempt carefully to evaluate the circumstances of the new churches. When Eastern Board missionaries began schools in Africa in the 1930s they insisted that Africans pay toward African teachers' support; and they limited North American money for education to the point that apparently they rather interfered with quality of education.[17] That probably reflected Lancaster County Mennonites' attitudes about education at least as much as it did assessment of what Africans needed. A decade earlier the same attitudes had clearly underlain those assertions that the missionaries in India were pursuing strategies too oriented to schools and not designed enough for producing a self-supporting and self-propagating church. And they had worked against a Bible training school in Argentina. Argentina missionaries had better meet Bible school expenses from local sources, board treasurer Vernon Reiff advised in reply to their proposal in 1927. Said he: The board could hardly find support for education in India, despite all the illiteracy there; so surely the South America mission could not expect much money for education.[18] Reiff must have written with easterners' criticisms in mind. And in the next decade, efforts of the Argentina missionaries to build their Bible school at least partly on self-support turned out to be almost pathetic.

Even stronger than one region's distrust of education was a more general hope, especially in depression years, that new churches' self-support would relieve the home board and church from financial pressures. Calling in 1933 for worshipers at the Los Angeles mission to become a regularly-organized, self-sustaining congregation, Yoder reasoned that "our contributions have decreased so tremendously... that we are not able to furnish our missionaries with the support that we once did." And in fact already in 1931 a board-induced cut in foreign mission budgets had moved Argentina missionaries to try, in J. W. Shank's words, to get "our native people to see the necessity of them shouldering some of these responsiblities."[19]

Specifically, the Argentina group got their mission and the Argentine church to create a *Junta*, or Board, of Evangelization and Finances. Then in 1933, "after discussing the financial world crisis," the mission's governing council engineered a further plan by which the Argentine church pledged to reduce its use of North American funds by 5 percent of the 1933 amount each year, and to increase its own giving accordingly. Thus the church was supposed to become self-supporting in twenty years, while the mission was to have the money to open new work.[20] Meantime in India, in 1931, missionaries and church somewhat similarly created an Evangelistic Board, or *Samaj*. In part, the *Samaj* grew out of efforts since the late 1920s to transfer more responsibility to Indians. But it too became a reality only when the home board cut overseas budgets. And at least some missionaries thought that one of its main purposes was to stimulate more giving in India.[21] Together the *Junta*, the 20-year plan, and the *Samaj* illustrated this fact: For stimulating real, practical steps toward the self-support ideal, nothing served like financial crisis in the North American church.

Throughout the first fifty years of Mennonite Church mission, missionaries could claim some growth in new churches' giving. As early as 1905 superintendent A. Hershey Leaman could report from the Chicago Home Mission that the "little congregation of about 33 of us" was meeting its own congregational expenses. India workers very early convinced even orphans and lepers to give—if necessary by skipping meals—for projects that appealed to missionaries: the British and Foreign Bible Society, a tract and book society, relief for famished Indians, and at least in 1907 aid also for famine-sufferers in China. By 1916-1917 the India church opened a home mission on its own resources, with a partially supported Indian in charge. And by the early 1940s Indian Mennonites were paying, in addition to various other church and home mission expenses, about half the support for five Indian pastors.[22] Argentina missionaries at first hesitated to teach giving for fear of appearing as mercenary as they considered the Catholic Church to be. But by the late 1920s they were reporting steady year-by-year increases in Argentines' giving for church building funds and other congregational expenses, the orphanage and the printery, and more. In the 1930s depression hit Argentina as it did North America, but Argentines' giving by no means dropped off entirely. As for Africa, the work in Tanganyika was still too new in the early 1940s to measure great progress in giving. Yet there too the people were helping pay for their own church buildings and the like.[23]

The Eastern Board's missionaries in Africa approached self-support somewhat differently from the Mennonite Church's other foreign workers, especially India ones. Their strategy at least at first was more to keep the church, its buildings, and its programs scaled down to be in keeping with the African's economic level.[24] The India missionaries had taken the rather opposite approach that self-support would require first building up the church's economic base. That philosophy had drawn from various sources: work ethic in the Mennonite communities from which missionaries had come, other missions' examples, that affinity for Negro leader Booker T. Washington's manual education philosophy, and less fear of humanitarian work as opposed to "direct" evangelism.

So in 1906 the India missionaries launched the quasi-feudal enterprise, the purchase and operation of the village Balodgahan; in 1915 Charles L. Shank went to India specifically to help teach trades; and in the early 1920s M. C. Lehman studied at Hampton Institute. "If we believe that honest work has benefited our Church in America," argued missionary A. C. Brunk in 1923, "then should we not give the same kind of training to those who constitute our Mennonite Church in India, so that they may pass it along their children?" "It is very difficult to build up a church that will be self-propagating and self-supporting out of people that are half-starved and half-clothed, a class of paupers," observed C. D. Esch in 1920. Yes, agreed fellow-India-missionary George Lapp in 1933, "I thank God that we put our Christian community on a business basis right from the beginning and made rural economic welfare our interest." Now "our Indian Christians own property and are in a position to maintain a self-supporting Church," at least to a degree.[25]

The India mission's strategy, in a country where economic role and social caste or subgrouping went hand-in-hand, apparently did much to make new Christians a visible and viable community.[26] At another time the India missionaries might even have seen their economics as contributing substantially to *shalom*, and thus to salvation. As the case was, by the 1930s they seem to have emphasized such efforts somewhat less. Apparently they lessened that emphasis largely because they imbibed new philosophies from the larger mission movement: the idea of scaling activities down in preparation for eventually withdrawing the mission "scaffold"; and the mass-movement concept of evangelism. And they seem to have done so partly also out of sober realization that economic and other humanitarian activities, by building up expensive programs, could actually work against the self-support goal. By 1935 the perceptive J. D. Graber, observing how difficult it would be for the Indian church to support mission-created institutions in any foreseeable future, decided that "the idea of gradually turning the financial responsibility of our work over to the Indian church is a vain dream."[27]

The fact was, both in India and in Argentina, that by 1935 the structures created for self-support were failing badly. In that year the Argentine church was to enter the third stage of its 20-year plan, and pay 15 percent. But in fact, the depression-ridden congregations in the previous year had failed even to pay that year's 10 percent. Shank, treasurer of the *Junta*, reported that more than one pastor was trying to pay his congregation's shortfall from his own pocket. By 1939 both the *Junta* and the 20-year plan had entirely broken down.[28] By mid-1935 meantime, missionaries decided to help the several Argentine pastors get projects started to support themsleves and their families, and finally got the home board to send down part of that original $20,000 farm fund to invest in that purpose. Pastor Albano Luayza began a grocery; Pablo Cavadore, a small truck farm; and a third, Santiago Battaglia, a business arrangement with his brother.[29]

But ¡*que disastre*!—what disaster! Luayza was soon letting people have food when they could not pay, and then finding it impossible to collect on the bills. The mission's executive committee decided that the pastors were neglecting church work, and that their Sunday schools were beginning to decline. By 1938 the missionaries reversed their advice and promised to help the pastors withdraw honorably from their projects.[30] One, Battaglia, refused to quit and in 1940—whether partly because of the economic fiasco or entirely for other reasons—left the Mennonites. Inquiries revealed that similar attempts by other denominations' missions had turned out just as badly. Still the self-support idea did not die. In 1942 Hershey wrote that the pastors' projects had lost money, but had given the mission valuable experience. Unquenchable, Hershey said that the missionaries still hoped "that some farming project or other legitimate business might be worked out for the good of the mission."[31]

In India, the *Samaj* lasted for only six years, in fact almost expired after three. Instead of stimulating Indians' support for evangelism, wrote missionary S. Jay Hostetler in 1935, the *Samaj* seemed almost to reduce their financial contributions. Evangelists and Bible women working under it received better pay than that received by most church members and therefore members did not feel like contributing, Hostetler explained. And the Indians' contribution was still so small compared to the North American that Indians had difficulty seeing theirs as important. According to J. D. Graber that imbalance between local and North American contributions even made Indians reluctant to voice opinions. The *Samaj* had taught the ideal of evangelism and had given experience to Indian church leaders who served on it, Graber wrote by way of epitaph when the organization died. But he said that the seeming insignificance of Indian monies had made Indians "reticent in taking too active a part in the decisions." So Indian representation on the *Samaj*, compared to missionaries, "became largely nominal."[32]

In some home missions, especially the city ones, self-support was hardly more successful. "Sometimes we feel that our city missions cost us too much for the returns that we get from them," wrote secretary Yoder privately in 1931. The main benefit, Yoder thought, was perhaps to keep Mennonites who migrated to the city from being lost to the church. Even with such Mennonites participating, "putting the missions on a self-supporting basis ... is a problem" that the board had not "worked out satisfactorily." And city people, "not accustomed to having their ministers work for their living," lost respect for ministers who did. About two years after Yoder's discouraged remarks, eight of ten city mission superintendents claimed that their congregations were underwriting significant portions of congregational expense. The claims, however, ranged from the Chicago Home Mission's statement that it was paying virtually all the expenses to others' accounts of paying perhaps only for coal and Sunday school supplies. Six of the ten superintendents declared flatly that there was no prospect of their missions becoming more self-supporting in a foreseeable time. And, why should city missions be self-supporting? asked Chicago superintendent Levi Hartzler, in effect, in 1936. "Personally I do not see how a Mission church with only a few members that can really give very much can be expected to support three and four workers and a Mission home besides the regular expenses of running the church when our country churches do not even support their one or two ministers."[33]

Not all the quest for self-support was failure. By 1941, for instance, even in a city, the mission in Peoria worked out a plan for congregational self-support, and a model agreement whereby the board would turn the church property over to the congregation when the congregation really fulfilled the plan. In India also, by World War II congregations had made enough progress financing their own church buildings that the board decided to turn over the properties as quickly as legal arrangements would allow. [34] And missionaries' reports of new believers' giving on the various fields were more than mere fluff.

Yet Hartzler, by asking whether mission congregations *should* have to support themselves, had raised worthwhile questions about the self-support ideal. For better or for worse the mission movement had stimulated professionalization of church work. The professionalizing, Protestant models the Mennonites followed of course implied allowances and salaries. But, paradoxically, Mennonites also seized upon the self-support ideal, quite uncritically. Sometimes they saw it as fitting their tradition of unsalaried ministers. More often they perceived it as a way to lighten the financial burdens of Mennonites and the board at home. Seldom did they, especially the homeside officials, consider very carefully the financial problems that people in the new churches were having. Almost never did anyone ask how biblical principles of justice and wealth-sharing might apply. Nor did they examine whether, in light of Mennonites' historic refusal to identify church with nation, it was logical to speak of the church in a particular nation as a natural unit for self-support. Did not the Mennonite perception of church ignore international lines? Finally, nobody much asked whether there could be a different way of mission, other than Protestant models and language.[35] "Self-support," borrowed from conventional Protestant missionary wisdom, was just too easy a slogan.

* * *

"Self-propagation" was much the same: an idea so appealing, a slogan so commonsensical, that it seems to have blocked more than stimulated attempts to discern further how best to communicate gospel, to evangelize, to build church and kingdom. Arriving in India in 1899 Ressler and the Pages quickly assumed that having "native Christians ... preach and teach to their countrymen" was "the only effectual way."[36] Only rarely in the next forty-five years did a Mennonite Church missionary or commentator question that idea.

The idea was a handy tool as well as a slogan. For instance, it was a tool for occupying territory, almost imperialistically. The India mission had better "push out and utilize the native talent which we have trained," thought George Lapp in 1914; otherwise neighboring missions would "come in and build their work in our district." Similar advice passed from secretary Yoder to Argentina missionaries a few years later. Or the self-propagation idea was an economic tool, once again to take money pressure off the home board and church. In 1927 the Argentina mission wanted more workers from the North. Financial conditions were not good in the U.S., replied Yoder. "I hope you will be able to use some of your native product."[37]

As early as 1876 Virginia Mennonites had begun to use the "native product," for they had ordained a local man for a West Virginia congregation. The case, if anyone remembered it, did not bode well. For the man, one John Baker, apparently feeling overwhelmed when the lot and ordination fell on him, had quit the Mennonite Church at once. But by about 1910 some four or five West Virginians had become ministers or deacons. In city missions, by 1921 field-worker Allgyer could report that some stations were getting by with fewer missionaries than formerly because members were getting involved in the work. By the latter 1920s one Maurice O'Connell, drawn to the Mennonite church through the mission at Ft. Wayne, Indiana, had become a revivalist and an outstanding superintendent at Lima, Ohio. O'Connell also served on the board's City Missions Committee and was so soundly Mennonite that it was his church that Allgyer described gleefully in 1933 as having "not a hat in the bunch." In the 1930s Simon Del Bosque, a longtime, Spanish-speaking member of a Mennonite congregation in Texas, was very helpful in getting the Mennonite Church started doing Spanish-language work in his state. A Mennonite missionary to Blacks in Harrisonburg, Virginia felt "very fortunate" in 1940 that several "colored members" from Washington, D.C., and Lancaster, Pennsylvania, were teaching in his mission's vacation Bible school.[38] Et cetera. Thus, on the home field, there was some progress toward the self-propagation ideal.

On foreign fields, at least in India and in Argentina, missionaries of the Mennonite Church rapidly and systematically engaged nationals as evangelists, Bible women, colporteurs or distributors of literature, orphanage workers, teachers, nurses, or whatever. The Africa mission, whether out of greater concern for a pure, orthodox gospel or for other reasons, was not so quick to send out "native" evangelists; instead, it waited until it had given some interested Africans a Bible-centered teacher training, and then established them in rudimentary village "out-schools" as teacher-evangelists.[39] Argentina missionaries, working among people with more education than was common in India or in East Africa, were especially quick to involve nationals. By the end of 1919 Shank could write that of the first baptismal class of seven, three were helping in the Sunday school. Argentines were soon doing many different church and outreach tasks, sometimes even taking the initiative to open work at new locations. One young man, a Ford mechanic whose work moved him from town to town, reputedly began a Sunday school wherever he went.[40] Named Carlos Cavadore, he and others of his family were among the first to become part of the Mennonites' new church. At least one of his brothers and three of his sisters were for years among the most faithful of the church's workers.

Such workers remained mostly in subordinate roles. But by 1913 India missionaries ordained two to be deacons, by 1920 all of the officers of the India church's Sunday school conference and the assistant moderator of its church conference were Indians, and in 1931 came the first installation of an Indian as a pastor. By 1939, of ten congregations in India, five had Indian pastors.[41]

Giving such responsibility to nationals caused missionaries some unease and crises of confidence. Even a well-prepared and very loyal national was not quite in the inner circle with the missionaries. Hardly had the Hersheys and the Shanks opened their first place of worship in Argentina when Albano Luayza, at that time a worker for a nearby Christian and Missionary Alliance mission, asked to join the Mennonite team. After some time, and pretty thorough negotiation and examination, the missionaries and the home board accepted him with the status of "Native Missionary." In 1924 Hershey ordained him, and he went on to make a stable and respected contribution as evangelist, pastor, and editor. Yet his allowance remained somewhat lower than the level for North Americans.[42] And in 1927 the perspicacious Yoder noticed that the Luayza name was not appearing on major mission committees. What, Yoder asked, was the matter? Replied Hershey: "We employ him and use his judgment a great deal, when dealing with the local problems," and he was "on a number of minor committees." But, Hershey continued, the mission had not put Luayza on any committee handling monies from the home church and board.[43]

Sometimes missionaries had cause for their unease. On one field in the 1920s a young man left a bank position to work with the mission; later the missionaries learned he had borrowed money under false pretenses. Or a few years later a new pastor on a certain field was found to have been hiding an illicit sex involvement even as he was ordained (a kind of sin not absolutely unknown, unfortunately, among Mennonite Church missionaries themselves). But most of the unease and lack of confidence did not arise from such flagrant lapses. Most grew out of the subculture surrounding mission.

Given the mission methods and structures that Mennonites so easily borrowed, missionaries found themselves in roles that made them something other than just Christians winning and fellowshiping with brothers and sisters. So they tended to see a gap between themselves and nationals. It was not just the inevitable horizontal gap between people of different cultures, but also a vertical one. Missionaries often described it paternalistically as reflecting their own greater experience in the faith.

Actually the gap was more complex even than difference in Christian maturity. Missionaries were very often in an employer, or at least an employer-like, role. Illustrating some of the dilemmas of that role were questions of what to pay national workers, and of missionary living standards compared to those of the national workers—questions that have been perennial problems for the missionary movement generally. To say that missionaries should have lived absolutely at the level of the people among whom they worked is probably too simple, unless they were supposed to cut all ties with the homeland for retirement, for educating their children, etc.[44] On the other hand, nationals have felt hurt, for instance as they have grown up seeing missionaries living in what have seemed to them large houses and general affluence. At least a bishop in the India Mennonite church, Obadiah P. Lal, has recalled such hurt, even as he expressed very deep appreciation more generally for missionaries. Lal also has concluded that the missionaries kept the salary of his father, a Christian worker for the mission, too low. And regarding Argentina, Nelson Litwiller, in retirement, has said ruefully that the gap that missionaries maintained between their own and Argentine workers' pay was inexcusable. On the field Litwiller argued at least once, in 1926, that "we must treat our native brethren like ourselves." But Mennonite missionary attitudes all too frequently tended instead toward what J. A. Ressler said as early as 1900, putting it more boldly than most. At the particular time, Ressler did not want to let a certain Indian hospital assistant support himself with fees. That, he said, "would spoil almost any native of India as he would feel independent of the mission and would not behave himself so well."[45]

In the first fifty years of formal Mennonite Church mission, nobody worked out satisfactory solutions. The employer-like role put missionaries in a dilemma. To pay national workers too little could bring embarrassing questions about missionaries' high living standards, and maybe even investigation by government. But to pay too much could also bring problems. An Argentine school official once advised the Mennonite missionaries that if they paid their workers too little, Argentines would accuse them of exploiting; but that if they paid too much, the charge would be that they were trying to win converts with foreign money.[46] So the various missions of the Mennonite Church operated without finding real answers. One way, if nationals asked for more pay, was to put the burden on the national church. At least a pay request from national workers was another stimulus for beginning the *Junta* in Argentina in 1931. Another way was confrontation. In 1941 elders of the budding Mennonite Church in East Africa wanted more North American money particularly for school teachers. But the missionaries replied with a "patient but firm NO," and missionary bishop Elam Stauffer, firmly committed to national church self-support as a goal, hoped the "no" would mean "the death struggle of this issue." Yet another, the way of the India church about 1940, was to let North American money help support national pastors, but to hope piously to find an arrangement soon that would be "more according to the church's economic abilities, and which she could continue in the eventuality of the Mission ceasing to exist."[47] Still another way, of course, was that one of letting the mission pay nationals less than missionaries got, and then feeling guilty about it in retirement. Paradoxical as that way was, it surely was better than seeing no moral issue at all. But of course none of the ways was a real answer. Was it simply a conundrum, impossible to solve?

The dilemma of the employer role went beyond questions of pay. Like most employers, the missionaries were entrepreneurs of a sort, quick to initiate and push forward toward preconceived goals. Without that spirit the early ones in particular could hardly have stepped out of their Mennonite communities and become missionaries. But imbued with that spirit they, like many employers, were not always well-prepared to understand why persons in employee or employee-like roles were less likely to enjoy the entrepreneur's risk-taking and scurrying about.

In their employer role missionaries sometimes sounded pleased with their workers, as in 1929 when William Lauver reported that Argentine Bible Readers under the direction of María Cavadore had made 1,000 visits in one year, with 35 people hearing the gospel story each week. But often they sounded the disgruntled, good-help-is-hard-to-come-by tone. J. A. Ressler complained in 1904 of how "these natives have very little concern for the work. It is the salary they are after." In 1935 Litwiller expressed disappointment in national workers, complaining that they seemed to expect money from North America just because missionaries got it. A missionary in Africa lamented in 1942 that Africans "engaged in the work of propagating are tempted to be hirelings rather than true shepherds," content to "do just what the European wants them to do and no more."[48] The missionary seemed not to perceive how roles in the mission subculture might have fostered that attitude.

The missionaries were in the role of teacher, as well as of entrepreneur and employer. And the teacher role strengthened an apparent feeling that they had a right to scrutinize and judge, sometimes rather bluntly. The missionaries themselves tended to see their teaching function in hopeful, sometimes glowing terms. Throughout Protestant missions, leadership training has seemed to be the great key to the self-sustaining and self-propagating church.[49] Despite their own traditions of untrained ministry, Mennonite missioners have, almost to a person, agreed with that premise. The premise very much underlay India missionaries' defense of their schools in the late 1920s and early 1930s. "It is the policy of the India Mission to develop a self supporting and propagating church as fast as possible," wrote M. C. and Lydia Lehman in 1932. And, they added flatly, "the problem becomes largely one of training a leadership with the requisite religious experience, character and ability."[50]

Meantime Argentina missionaries argued strenuously for their Bible training school. "One of the most rapid ways of evangelizing this country is through the natives themselves," their logic ran. It was much cheaper to support a national than a missionary, and besides, if Mennonites had no school other denominations would attract away their most promising youth.⁵¹ In the 1930s in Africa, Eastern Board missionaries were most cautious about education beyond the rudiments if it seemed at all secular. Yet scarcely two years after beginning their work they began a Bible-centered school to train schoolteachers—then in 1938, when a deputation from the home church visited, recast it to be more clearly a Bible training school.⁵²

Thus, leadership training being conventional missionary wisdom, each foreign field in due time got its Bible training school: India in 1908, Argentina in 1926 after a false start in 1923, and Tanganyika that school in 1936-1938. Such schools, the rhetoric ran, would provide the leadership for the self-propagating church.

Practice did not always rise to meet the soaring hopes. The Bible school in India was a reasonable success. In the 1920s, nevertheless, it ran only six months each year rather than the nine originally envisaged; actually closed down in 1929 when its principal, George Lapp, was absent on furlough; had trouble attracting the best students; and never developed into the college-level seminary that some missionaries hoped for. In Argentina the Bible training school operated as a part-time effort of those who staffed it, recessed for a year in 1933 when the Litwillers were in North America, and had to struggle constantly because of meager budget. In a country where university education was available and respected it continued to accept students with only elementary schooling, and never developed into the institution of higher learning that particularly Litwiller, its main principal, thought it should become. The school in East Africa, still young of course as World War II came on, was a small operation of six or seven students.⁵³

Despite their anemia the training schools surely benefited the new churches greatly. And the efforts missionaries made to establish them with limited resources were often next to heroic. But schools had that one further problem: They formalized missionaries' role as teacher, putting them in a socially superior position within the church. In 1943, after several years on the Argéntina field, a young missionary thought his older fellow-missionaries tended to treat national pastors as if the pastors were still their Bible school students.⁵⁴

Of course missionaries at times spoke highly of nationals' accomplishments, as a well-pleased teacher speaks of bright students. But at other times they gave out bad grades. In 1913 when missionaries first began to ordain Indians, C. D. Esch spoke of trouble finding men "that have the stability and conviction necessary to help in the work as they ought." Or in 1938 J. W. Shank commented that when Argentines went into Christian work from humble backgrounds their new white-collar status tended to make them pretentious and unhappy with their incomes. Often such statements were routine parts of published mission reports, even though their tone was one that missionaries would hardly have used publicly against, say, their missionary colleagues.[55]

Missionaries were of course human, in very human situations, so that often they were just giving vent to very normal frustrations. And being idealistic themselves, they judged by high standards. But much of their comment surely arose also out of the roles in which the conventional ways of doing mission cast them. Much as they wanted to fellowship with the new Christians just as brother and sister, and much as they surely often did, the missionary roles seemed a license to demand of new Christians an almost entrepreneurial kind of drive or to pass judgment as a teacher grades a student. From the vantage point of a second-generation missionary reared in India, John Friesen has commented that one of the hardest of accomplishments was for a missionary to see "Indians in their own right." Like other missionaries, Friesen also could point out weaknesses in Indians as church leaders. But he recognized that in his criticisms he, still essentially a North American, did not look at matters quite as Indians did.[56]

Such were some key roles that missionaries assumed as on the one hand they employed new Christians, and on the other hand schooled them, in order to create self-propagating churches. They were roles that tended to extend the vertical gap, rather than to put missionaries and new Christians side-by-side. Maybe the roles were implicit in the carrying out of the Great Commission, and inescapable. Or perhaps they were so only within the kinds of mission methods and structures that the Mennonite Church had borrowed. In any case the "self-propagation" phrase, bound up as it was with Protestant concepts of what evangelism consisted of, did not help very much. Like the self-support slogan it was a bromide that probably blocked more than it encouraged fresh approach.

* * *

If self-support and self-propagation were easy slogans, self-government was not. Ex-missionary Ressler might write flatly in 1923 that "the ultimate aim of any mission should be to disband." Or ten years later J. W. Shank might remark that "a native church sponsored and controlled by natives must be established." Yet it was common for such commentators to mention self-support and self-propagation without saying very much about self-government. Or they insisted that self-support had to come first.[57] Or they spoke of self-governance with a note of fear.

Missionaries were of the opinion that many of the new believers themselves did not feel ready for self-government and so preferred that missionaries decide and control. But by the World War II era, and in some cases as early as the 1920s, new believers or congregations were asking for more voice. In a 1943 article Argentine pastor Feliciano Gorjón, although conceding that self-support had to come first, thought that the Argentine Mennonite Church should "soon be able to organize and govern herself in harmony with her local necessities and idiosyncrasies." In response, missionary Lewis Weber made clear how friendly missionaries could be to the first two "self" formulas, and yet how unfriendly to the third. "All of us," Weber commented, had long been hoping for the Argentine church's financial independence, and now Argentines were agreeing. "But we fear sometimes that they confuse self-support and self-propagation with independent self-government."[58]

In church (as contrasted to mission) affairs, there was gradual movement toward more voice for nationals. In India, about 1910, congregations organized councils called *panchayats* to help missionaries in practical matters such as discipline. Resembling traditional village governments, the *panchayats* were quite indigenous. In 1912 missionaries formed a church organization separate from the mission by creating the India Mennonite Conference—with a constitution that resulted in a majority of delegates being Indian. By the late 1930s missionaries were beginning to receive their ordinations from the Indian church rather than more or less forcing that church to accept North American ordinations. Meantime congregations took more responsibility for Sunday schools, young people's programs, cottage meetings, etc., and for managing church properties.[59]

In Argentina a church structure separate from the mission emerged even more rapidly, the Argentina Mennonite Conference beginning in 1923. At the first of its 1923 sessions Hershey was moderator. But Luayza and one Bartolomé González moderated other sessions already that year, and an Argentine woman, Felisa Cavadore, shared with missionary D. Parke Lantz the office of secretary. In 1923 also, the oldest congregation, Pehuajó, elected Argentines to new offices of secretary and treasurer, putting in their hands congregational business that Hershey, as pastor, had been doing. Congregations gained voice even in discipline: At least in 1932 when the strong-willed Hershey, as bishop, wanted to put an erring brother on probation, he reluctantly yielded to congregational sentiment to restore the person fully.[60]

In East Africa before World War II, Eastern Board missionaries, despite a strong commitment to three-selfism, did not produce a church structure clearly distinct from mission. They did consult with Africans quite early on some important decisions, and by 1938 more or less formalized the process by having councils made up of Africans elected by congregations. In mid-1937 they also began an annual "Native Bible Conference" somewhat distinct from the mission's "European" conference, although missionaries spoke also at the "native" sessions. Talk of ordaining Africans began in the late 1930s. As visiting Lancaster Conference officials put it in 1938, those running the mission even had faith that "out of the African Church in due time it will be possible to ordain a native bishop." But ordination talk did not produce the reality until the 1950s and 1960s.[61] Apparently various considerations caused the Eastern Board missionaries to delay independent church structures. One was that as they de-emphasized institutional programs in favor of church-planting, they made little distinction between mission structures and church. Another may have been Lancasterians' exceptional concern about safeguarding the new church's purity and orthodoxy. A less happy one—one from which the missionaries on the whole deeply repented after the first decade[62]—was perhaps that they at first operated very much with the "dark continent" stereotype of their field, more or less equated "black" with "ignorant," and had an especially strong sense of themselves being civilized and capable and of the Africans not being so, at least not yet.[63]

For home missions, the ideal that missionaries, board officials, and other commentators suggested fairly often was that new believers should eventually organize themselves under the church's district conferences. "Our missions are not primarily of the rescue mission type," wrote Eastern Board president Henry Garber in 1938 of his agency's work. "Our aim in establishing a mission is that it may develop into a regularly organized congregation." Nevertheless, Eastern Mennonite Seminary teacher Linden Wenger, in a 1955 study of the Mennonite Church's rural missions, has suggested strongly that the church's missioners did not do nearly enough to create strong, indigenous congregations. Indeed he made the point that while district mission board constitutions invariably set forth goals of organizing missions and charitable institutions, none set forth directly the purpose of establishing congregations that would soon be independent of the missions. Wenger seems to have been correct at least in saying that the move toward independence was often slow in coming. "A number of our mission stations are not young," Garber admitted in 1938. "Will we always care for them as little children?"[64]

There was some progress.[65] For instance when the general board opened Spanish-language outreach in Texas in the late 1930s and wanted missionary Amsa Kauffman ordained to lead it, the board and the Missouri-Kansas district conference observed at least the formality of letting the brand-new congregation at Normanna vote for the ordination. On the other hand, a separate Spanish-language conference that T. K. Hershey wanted from the beginning did not develop. The Spanish-language congregations did hold such a conference in 1940, but it did not become an ongoing organization. Instead, like new gatherings of Christians in many another home mission, the congregations eventually joined the regular district conference of their area.[66]

Much of the discussion about control of new congregations on the home field was not really about a voice for new believers themselves. To be sure in 1918 the board did provide that such congregations might appoint trustees to care for their church buildings—but only if they were paying the buildings' costs. It also provided that a mission congregation might have a representative on the mission's local board (usually made up of old-line Mennonites of the area who had taken initiative or interest in the work)—but it kept that representation to one member on a board of at least five.[67] Discussion about governance of home mission congregations turned on whether the general board should have charge, or whether the authority should be a district conference or its board. And Hershey's recommendation for a separate conference in Texas was probably less to give new believers control than to allow missionaries some freedom from the sending church—freedom of a kind Hershey was used to, in distant Argentina.

In Argentina, perhaps most revealing was a reluctance on the part of missionaries to let bishop authority fall into Argentine hands. In the 1920s and 1930s some missionaries wanted pastors and not only the bishop to be able to baptize and give communion. Hershey, sole bishop in Argentina until 1934, opposed the change on grounds that while the plan might be suitable for pastors who were missionaries, it was not suitable for inexperienced native ones. In 1933 and 1934 the mission moved to ordain a second bishop. Thereupon missionaries held a "frank discussion" among themselves and decided that only North Americans could be candidates, reasoning that the Argentine pastors (apparently including Luayza) lacked experience and did not meet biblical requirements. Only in the late 1940s did an Argentine move into a bishop-like office, that of Area Superintendent.[68]

Meantime in India the church conference very early served as forum for Indians to present an Indian point of view; and more and more it shared in church control.[69] Yet the conference was hardly an indigenous institution. Apparently it was so different from anything in Indian life that there was no suitable Hindi word for the institution, so that through the years its name has been an English one, transliterated into Hindi as *Kanfarens* or *Kanfrens*. North Americans wrote its rules and discipline. Even Joseph S. Shoemaker and J. S. Hartzler, visiting in India in 1910 as representatives of the home board, helped. (Its other authors were missionaries M. C. Lapp and P. A. Friesen.) And, according to Lapp, most Indians who attended the first sessions of the conference did so "out of curiosity." Lapp did think that the Indians who participated showed "greater interest and intelligence ... than we had expected." But by such comments missionaries quite clearly meant that Indians had agreed with missionaries' judgment.[70]

At the congregational level also, where Indians were even more deeply involved, patterns of church life reflected much North American transplanting. Moreover, although an Indian was Assistant Moderator of the conference by 1920 none became its highest official until 1951. As for bishop authority, an Indian pastor named John Haider was a candidate in 1939, but the final choice was by lot, and the lot fell to a missionary, J. D. Graber. So the highest church office also remained in North American hands.[71]

In mission (as contrasted to church) affairs, developments intended ostensibly to foster indigenous control were often ambiguous, at best. Home missions that the India church began in 1916-1917 are perhaps exceptions. But a "Committee on Transfer of Work to Indian Hands" in the late 1920s and the *Samaj* of the 1930s were not.

The Transfer of Work Committee was so important that in a rare move the home board eventually printed and circulated 2,000 copies of its report. Formed by the mission in 1927, the committee sent representatives to places where other denominations were at work in India to study application of the three-self formula. It did involve Indians. Committee members took Indian church leaders with them in their travels. After the committee reported, the mission created a new one—a continuation committee—and to that body, with three missionary members, it appointed three Indians as well. At the same time the mission made place for two Indian members each on its Evangelistic, Educational, and Medical Committees, which were important permanent committees. But the important Transfer of Work Committee itself consisted only of missionaries J. N. Kaufman, George Lapp, and Ernest E. Miller.[72]

Although in their report they were by no means reactionary, Kaufman, Lapp, and Miller expressed scant sympathy for some noisy reformers on the larger Indian scene who were demanding more Indian control of churches. Those voices, they were sure, did not speak for rank-and-file Indian Christians. And they thought Mennonite Indians were especially unready to take control, for, the three men said, "our mission is young and we do not have, as yet, a trained and developed leadership." The three were sure that Indian Mennonite leaders agreed. Moreover they argued (from the missionary view of church) that "the primary function of the Indian church is aggressive evangelism"; so, said they, Christians in India should be occupied with evangelism, not with "authority" or "control of money."[73]

In some sense the committee's arguments were no doubt very "true," but only from a certain perspective. To say that the more insistent voices did not speak for the masses, for instance, totally ignored that in social movements the most forward leaders may speak sentiments latent but present in the majority. The point that Indians were not ready to be leaders overlooked missionaries' own surprise from time to time at how ready they seemed to be. It also ignored the question of whether anyone ever gets ready to lead except by leading, and it ignored the idea that the Holy Spirit might supply the leadership gifts. Finally, although on the whole enlightened, the report was words only of missionaries, or at most of Indians selected and quoted by missionaries. Lack of any direct Indian voice severely compromised it.

To co-opt Indians on the continuation and the three mission committees was equally ambiguous. Since missionaries had a strong voice in church conference and on the committees, and those bodies appointed or selected the Indians co-opted,[74] missionaries did much of the choosing. And Kaufman wrote privately in 1928 that missionaries knew all along that the home board had to give permission before such committees could "adopt measures involving the transfer of money to Indian hands."[75] The *Samaj*, which grew partly out of the continuation committee, was also ambiguous as a vehicle for transferring control. Its membership was an equal number of (a) missionaries appointed by the mission and (b) congregational representatives appointed by conference. Again, since missionaries had a strong voice in the conference they had a much larger voice than did Indians in the *Samaj*'s membership. Moreover the new body did not, for instance, own property. By its own rules, any houses it furnished workers were to be property of the mission. Actually the designers never even claimed that the *Samaj* would bring self-governance. Rather, they saw it as an interim step, more in the vein of mission/church "cooperation."[76]

Created to oversee the evangelistic outreach of both mission and church, the *Samaj* did send out some new gospel teams made up of four Indians to one missionary, and apparently helped move some Indians into positions of oversight and responsibility. But it hardly fulfilled hopes such as Miller expressed in 1932. In 1932 Miller wrote exuberantly that the *Samaj* was "quite a step in advance in co-operation," and would go "a long ways to dispel the critical attitude [*sic*] of many of our Indian leaders that the Missionaries want to run everything." But a year later he wrote of many rank and file Indians' continuing to distrust missionaries, refusing for instance to believe there was really a depression in America and suspecting missionaries of holding back funds for their own use.[77] At the end of 1936, of course, the *Samaj* expired. Officially the India conference said that congregations would now take more responsibility for evangelism (an arrangement perhaps more in keeping with Mennonite understandings of church than was a special board). But in 1937 the India mission officially advised its home board that it, the mission, had "again assumed the complete control of the evangelistic work."[78]

As an experiment toward self-government, the *Junta* in Argentina was equally if not more ambiguous. As it began in 1931 missionary William Lauver described it as a plan "to make the Natives more directly responsible for the carrying on of the work," especially evangelism, and "a forward step" that should "mean much in uniting more fully the efforts of the Native and Foreign workers." Nelson Litwiller described it in terms of the three-self formula. And its demise at the end of the 1930s did not destroy all effort for self-government. In its wake there continued a "Pastor's Meeting" of all ordained men in the church, North American and Argentine, that dealt not just with internal church matters but also, alongside the mission, with some planning of evangelism, etc. Yet even at the outset the *Junta* consisted of three missionaries to only two Argentines. And the mission kept control of all funds that came from North America.[79]

Years later Litwiller's perception would be that most missionaries had not been ready to "play a lesser role and trust the Argentines to administer." The *Junta*, he would say, was a "sop handed out to make the Argentines feel they had tremendous responsibility."[80] Probably there was more idealism in the experiment than those words by themselves suggest. Yet as a vehicle for moving toward self-government, the *Junta* failed.

While the *Samaj* and the *Junta* were folding, there was some progress toward self-government elsewhere—for instance, in ownership of property, at least of church buildings. Even that was unhurried. In India, where eventually there was the most progress, the negotiations stretched from an early suggestion about 1931 until well into the 1940s. As in so many cases, the home board at first made its decision in response to conditions at home more than to needs on the field. For the board's executive committee at first held back on grounds that critics were charging Goshen College, the India mission, and other institutions with going their own ways, away from the church—and that signing away properties would inflame such talk. By the end of the 1930s the board was ready to consider the question, and in 1941 it authorized transfer. But even then, the question got tangled for some years in legal snarls surrounding World War II and pressures for India's independence.[81] As for movement on other fields, the main motion was on the home front, where the board accepted that agreement with the Peoria mission in 1941 as a model for home missions.[82]

Whatever movement there was in transfer of property, in ordaining more indigenous leaders, in congregational affairs, or wherever, by World War II pressures were building for more self-government. In Africa in 1941 came that confrontation over schoolteachers' pay. In Argentina in 1938 a Bible school student protested enough to disturb mission tranquility by calling for student living allowances and for more pay for evangelistic work. In 1942 another Argentine wrote to the board in North America asking about policies for paying national workers, and charged a missionary with "racial and political" prejudices, with lying, and with too much money-making on the side. Far more serious was that case of pastor Santiago Battaglia, who left the Mennonites early in 1940. Not only was there the matter of his business involvement. He also refused to relinquish a pastorate in the town of Trenque Lauquen when Hershey returned from a furlough and the Argentine church assigned the missionary to be the congregation's pastor in combination with supervising the mission's printery, which was also in the town. Battaglia managed to take most of the Trenque Lauquen congregation with him, and eventually to the Baptists.[83] Yet in Argentina as well as in Africa such cases continued to be separate, scattered incidents.

In India, by contrast, matters came to something of a head. It happened at a specially called church conference in 1939. Pressures had been building for some time. Ernest Miller had of course written early in the 1930s of that rank-and-file suspicion of missionaries, and of Indian church leaders' belief that "the Missionaries want to run everything." As the 1930s continued, matters became very complicated, especially since Indian discontent got entangled with differences in approach and personality among missionaries themselves. Finally at that 1939 conference several missionaries, by one account, "were cornered by a group of Indian men and had to hear a lot of anti-mission sentiment and history till a rather late hour." Later in the conference, the crisis itself dissipated. At the urging of a wise lay leader and teacher, Reginald (R.N.K.) Biswas, the conference at a crucial moment suspended business and turned to extended prayer. That brought a sense of spiritual cleansing and restored the broken fellowship.[84]

Yet the underlying issues remained. Several weeks earlier, at regular conference sessions, delegates had officially requested the mission to restore the practice of putting Indians on major mission committees. (That practice, like the *Samaj*, had not lasted.) This time they wanted to have Indians on the important Managing Committee. To some missionaries it was all rather frightening, for they believed that their Indian brothers had "a strong determination to dictate regarding Mission policies," or that "the political spirit of India has come into the church." J. D. Graber, increasingly the mission's leader, was more philosophical. Political nationalism was having its effect, he agreed. But he also thought "the Church has grown in stature. The son," he said, "is becoming of age."[85]

To help decide the issues, Graber wanted the home board to send two persons to India for at least six months.[86] But the home board never acted. So after nearly a year the mission took upon itself the task of replying to the conference, and mainly said "no." The New Testament's Paul, the "model missionary," it reasoned, had always been an "ambassador of the sending church"; and likewise in modern times, church and mission should not be amalgamated, for the two were fundamentally different institutions.[87] Graber personally admitted that this was opposite from ideas in fashion at the recent World Missionary Conference at

Madras.[88] The larger mission movement was now calling for structures that emphasized mission/church "cooperation."

The mission did go on to say it would transfer to the Indian church those "tasks that are her peculiar ministry, but which the Mission has been performing for the welfare of the Church." The mission's theory was that its own tasks were primarily proclamation and church-founding, while the church—although she too had the task of proclaiming gospel—was the body to deal with local problems. Those problems might be spiritual ones, but they also included social and economic.[89] The mission, in other words, was speaking not only to questions of self-government. It was also commenting on that old question of institutional work, saying such work was not really among a mission's main responsibilities.

Although the India conference never formally accepted the mission's position, the mission gradually gave local boards or councils greater voice, for instance in operating schools.[90] In the early 1940s missionaries thought antagonism between them and Indians had died down, yielding, as one put it, to "a spirit of love and mutual consideration."[91] In fact, however, fundamental issues of self-governance were still present and still unresolved as the first era of Mennonite Church mission ended.

They remained unresolved also in Argentina. By 1943 missionaries there were suggesting that their mission needed a new constitution for a "transition period" of giving Argentines more responsibility.[92] There matters stood, in the World War II era. In Africa, meantime, events were taking shape quite differently. There, by the early 1940s, an interdenominational movement of church invigoration, the East Africa Revival, was reaching the new Mennonite congregations and the missionaries. That movement shaped events—generally in the direction of greater African autonomy but by a different route—more rapidly than missionaries and homeside officials, with all their deliberate commitment to the three-self formula, could respond.[93]

So as World War II closed the first era of Mennonite Church missions, the overall situation was that issues of self-governance and self-determination for new churches were very, very near the surface but not yet really dealt with. Missionaries had long talked as if they, the missionaries, would be the judges of when new churches' leaders would have sufficient experience and maturity to accept control. They had dealt with self-governance questions unhurriedly, either by not even invoking the third part of the three-self formula or by making clear that self-governance came last. Yet from time to time they had also invoked ideals such as working "not as rulers but as servants loving one another."[94] And by the late 1930s they were becoming generally aware, at least in their heads, that nationalism was abroad in the world and that mission dominance could not last. While one part of their beings surely represented the very normal reluctance to give up power, another part did not think their power should last. By World War II times at least some Mennonite mission people were ready to look at new patterns. But almost all self-governance questions still lay unresolved, and often unfaced.

* * *

By World War II, Mennonite Church missionaries had never really gotten to the idea of indigenization. They had very readily taken up the three-self formula, but actually shunned its third element.

The self-support and self-propagation phrases fell easily from their tongues, while the self-governance idea did not really catch on. Self-support and self-propagation both seemed to promise missions that would cost the home church less, or perhaps still better, would let the home church take its missionaries and money and move on to new fields. Self-propagation, moreover, fit the way mission people viewed church; for with the perspective that had led them personally into the mission movement in the first place, they often viewed it as a propagation agency, more than seeing the full-orbed vision of exemplifying the Kingdom of God or *shalom*. So the first two elements of three-selfism fit some trends in the Mennonite Church and its mission movement. Self-government, by contrast, ran mainly counter to the home church's current developments—especially to its trends of guarding orthodoxy and of centralizing power. And of course the Western world at large was only beginning even to think of giving up power over other peoples. Nonconformed as they might think they were, the Mennonite Church and its missionaries were Western.

The three-self formula, particularly the self-support and self-propagation parts of it, served Mennonites as easy slogans rather than stimulators of fresh thought. Mennonite Church missioners invoked the formula earnestly and sincerely. Had they not taken it up quite so quickly, however, they might have questioned some assumptions behind the slogans. For instance, they might have asked whether churches were really to be defined by national borders. And instead of agreeing so fully with the formula's underlying emphasis on self-reliance, they might have asked more often whether the underlying ideal for Christians was not mutuality and sharing across the world's dividing lines. In the end, from some strains of their own history and church life, they might even have offered a rather different vision of what truly fellowshiping, mutually supporting, gospel-embodying new churches could be.

8
GOSPEL AT HOME (I)

Communicating gospel at home is seldom dramatic, and even where Mennonite Church people have gone at it self-consciously as "outreach," most of them have been fairly ordinary folk operating by conventional wisdoms. Surely that is good: ordinary folks should communicate gospel. At the outset of their mission movement, had ordinary Mennonites done so, instead of a few representatives marching so much to Protestant mission drumbeats, they might have gone forth with a testimony more their own.

But when hundreds of ordinary folks do a task, they hardly leave tidy records. At least the data about Mennonite Church outreach at home is scattered and incomplete. From 1860 to 1960 Mennonite Church people began such work of some form or another—preaching, organized missions, outpost Sunday schools or vacation Bible schools or tent meetings, cottage visitation, or whatever—in some 587 or more (surely more) places in North America, and it has been possible to make statistics and graphs on the 587 identified.[1] But statistics even from systematic sources can be deceptive, and those from such a noncentralized people's movement especially so. So, whether results appear in a graph's lines, a table's numbers, or an interpreter's conclusions, nobody should take them to be highly exact.

Besides that, the interpreter has often had to make unclear judg-

Gospel at Home

ments. Did work at Nearby Station *really* begin as outreach, for instance, or as a place to which swarming Mennonites from an overpopulated and perhaps bickering congregation could recluster? At best the statistics on those 587 places can indicate only general patterns. They are more suggestive than certain.

Starting New Places of Work, and Their Fates

Rates at which Mennonite Church people began new places of work seem to have followed something of the course suggested in Exhibit 8-1. If the statistics were by decades rather than by 5-year

Exhibit 8-1: Rates of Starting New Places of Work on Home Field (Ave. per 5 years), 1861-1960

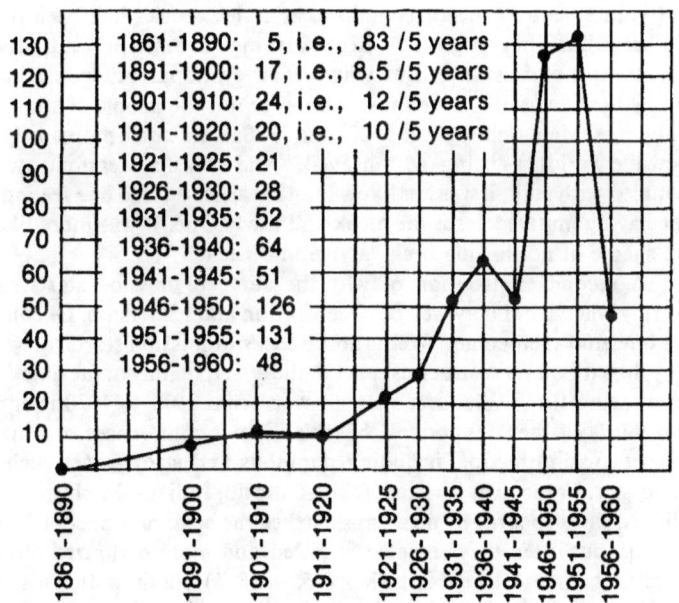

periods, they would show roughly a doubling of new starts each ten years from 1910 to about 1950, then a leveling off.

Perhaps the actual rate of beginnings rose faster earlier and did not decline quite so sharply in the late 1950s. A major source of data was mission newsletters put out by district conferences or their boards, and many of them did not begin until about the 1930s. Another source was conference histories, and some of them went to print well before the 1960 cutoff date. So data were probably most complete for the 1940s and early 1950s, and that fact may have exaggerated the rise and fall of the curve. Yet at least the rising portion of the curve seems to agree with findings of two other studies, one published in 1954 by Temple University sociologist John Hostetler and another completed in 1955 by Eastern Mennonite Seminary teacher Linden Wenger.[2] So up to its peak, at least, it is probably fairly correct. And the picture of drop-off of mission starts in the latter 1950s confirms what is a generally held impression among Mennonite mission board officials. Why the curve?

By the late 1920s and the 1930s, people nurtured on the assumptions and mood of the quickening were in almost full control of congregations and church. Religiously, Sunday schools and revival meetings and young people's meetings and missionaries' stories had been their mother-milk. They might still hear warnings against pride or study lessons on nonresistance. But where their grandparents would have thought the "worldly" were those who were not the people of humility and peace, Mennonites of the 1920s and 1930s were much more likely to view the worldly as being the "unsaved." And now if a Mennonite were troubled with guilt, it was less likely than in earlier days to be a feeling of not having imitated Jesus the meek and lowly One. It was more likely the shame of not having been "active in outreach."

A second explanation of why the curve of mission starts rose sharply when it did may well be organization and leadership. Of course the question then comes: Were those *causes* of mission starts, or were they, like the starts themselves, part of the *effect,* mainly of the quickening bearing fruit? Whatever that answer, from 1911 to 1920 roughly two-thirds of the Mennonite Church's district conferences organized district mission boards, including populous and strong ones such as Lancaster, Franconia, Virginia, Ohio, Ontario, Indiana-Michigan, and Illinois. Those boards by no means marked the beginning of conference activity, but often they signaled renewed and more organized effort. Small wonder, as later exhibits (8-5, 8-6, and 8-7) will show, that district conference efforts began a sharp rise from that decade onward. Congregational efforts began to rise a bit later. Perhaps the district boards had something to do with that also, it taking the boards a bit more time to educate congregations to work than to start work directly. In any case, district organization and leadership very probably related closely to the upturn in total mission starts. Probably it was both effect of other influences stimulating new starts, and a further cause.

Gospel at Home

Finally, by the 1930s an ideal of every-congregation-an-outpost had begun to grow. And there was among Mennonite Church people a new willingness to work in rural areas, as against some earlier notions that mission meant going to towns and cities. Since some of the rural areas to which they went were thinly populated, 587 places of work did not mean contact with masses of people. Yet willingness to go where people were widely scattered probably indicated greater, not less, zeal for mission.

As for why mission starts apparently began to drop off in the 1950s, who can do more than speculate? Maybe the efforts of Mennonite Church people were approaching a kind of maturity, with obvious places of work occupied and as many going as sending churches thought they could manage. Perhaps an economic tightening after boom days in World War II and Korean War times dampened Mennonites' activism. Or maybe Mennonite Church people, who were rapidly becoming more like other North Americans in dress and style of life, no longer sensed they had a message. Maybe they no longer wanted to confront neighbors with gospel because they wanted to mix with them in community life and profession and business, and anyhow, were finding their neighbors not so very much more "lost" than they were themselves. Or were changes theological as much as sociological? Generations had passed, and the quickening had faded from memory and emotion. So, perhaps Mennonites no longer found its throbbing evangelicalism and activism exciting; perhaps they no longer felt they must do "active work" to prove that they were more "spiritual" then those formalistic pre-quickened Mennonites. Or maybe the acid kind of evangelical zeal introduced later by some Fundamentalists had soured quite a few on all evangelical activism.

By the latter 1950s was "Anabaptist vision" theology undermining zeal for "mission outreach"? In the short run, at least, Mennonite Church people may have found its understandings of salvation more complex than the quickening's theology, and therefore harder to communicate in a "missionary" way. Moreover, Harold S. Bender's most classic statement of the "Anabaptist vision," an address he gave in 1943 and that was published several times in the mid-1940s and afterward, was hardly a missionary piece. In it he emphasized Anabaptists' discipleship, their eithics, and their concept of church, but in that very basic statement he said little about their effectiveness as missioners.[3] By the latter 1940s and the 1950s preoccupation among church leaders and thinkers with refining what Anabaptists had stood for may have turned the Mennonite Church again toward being more ingroup-minded, more intent on purifying gospel than on preaching it.

Of course if that were true, it did not necessarily mean less concern for people's salvation. A concern for salvation is hardly to Christians' credit if what they then proclaim is far different from Jesus' Gospel. And again, maybe the ways the Anabaptist-vision-minded tried to communicate gospel were just not so likely to show up in "mission" statistics. In the 1950s a Mennonite sociologist who was inclined toward "Anabaptist vision" ideas was searching for historical cases of Mennonites' witnessing and winning others spontaneously without organized "mission," and admitted that he could not find records of very many. But, declared he, "that is the way to do mission work, even though it does frustrate a research student."[4] Mennonites' new concern for learning from the Anabaptists may really have meant a fuller-orbed understanding of salvation, nearer to *shalom* than to "plan of salvation" language, and hence hard to capture in mission data. If so, the *shalom*-minded might say that in the long-run pursuers of Anabaptist vision were strengthening Mennonite Church mission.

Finally, that latter-1950s decline in new starts may have been due at least in part to another fact: post-World War II expansion of the Mennonite Central Committee's program, and other such relief-and-service endeavors—especially Mennonite Voluntary Service under one agency or another, which provided Mennonite youth a very attractive new channel for activism, adventure, and expression of faith. A pessimist might conclude that post-World War II Mennonites more than ever set "evangelism" and relief-and-service into an unnecessary and unscriptural competition. An optimist might just say that in relief-and-service Mennonites were indeed spreading gospel, and were being evangelical, even if their efforts were not the kind that showed up in statistics of "mission" work.

Whatever such speculation, in the whole period from 1860 to 1960 a fair percentage of new starts resulted in congregations, as the first set of data in Exhibit 8-2 shows. To be sure, probably 20 percent and perhaps nearly 30 percent of the new starts did not begin anything that continued in an organized way. Many others, perhaps 30 percent, produced missions or congregations that as late as the early 1970s still depended on sponsorship or sizable help from the group or agency that had begun them. But some 40 percent or more seem to have produced new congregations that were fully or at least to a large extent independent.

Gospel at Home

Exhibit 8-2: Outcomes of New Starts

	Number (out of 587)	Percentage of 587	Percentage of the 516 on which exist data on outcome
A. Became independent (by 1974) and continued			
1. Within 10 years of starting	61	12	10
2. 10-20 years after starting	72	14	12
3. After 20 years	64	12	11
4. Became independent, date unknown	30	6	5
Total	227	44	39
B. Remained a going concern, but dependent on sponsoring agency either as a mission or as an organized congregation	168	33	29
C. Died or discontinued			
1. After having become independent	6	1	1
2. Without becoming independent	94	18	16
Total	100	19	17
D. Consolidated with another	14	3	2
E. Turned over to another denomination	5	1	1
F. Became interdenominational	2	0	0
Subtotal	516		88
No data on outcome	71		12
TOTAL	587		

A Grass-roots Movement

For Mennonite Church people, home mission activity was not on the one hand something highly orchestrated from a central board, nor on the other very much a matter of individuals free-lancing on their own, faith-mission fashion. The great bulk of activity (at least the activity identified in the sources used) was by congregations, or by district conference or other regional boards. The amount of congregational effort was especially remarkable. In the 1930s and 1940s a slogan of "every congregation an outpost" prodded that effort along.[5]

As was fitting for grass-roots activity, quite a few of the new starts apparently grew out of fairly natural contacts, rather than contrived ones. At least Exhibit 8-3 suggests that conclusion. Figures for A and B in Exhibit 8-3 seem to represent natural contacts for the most part, those for C and D contrived ones. The numbers are none too reliable. With 246, or 42 percent of the cases yielding no data on beginning stimuli, all other figures are highly suspect. Moreover, the researcher had to make especially difficult judgments to categorize in this case, and quite possibly the people who reported new work often were not conscious or entirely candid about motives that lay behind it. Nevertheless, the data suggest tentatively that starting from natural contacts was about as frequent as starting from more deliberate ones.

Among the most deliberate of contacts were some made by college students. With data far more complete and reliable than that of Exhibit 8-3, Exhibit 8-4 indicates what agencies began how many places of work, with college students beginning at least 19. Actually the home mission outreaches of students in the Mennonite Church's three colleges—Goshen in Indiana, Hesston in Kansas, and Eastern Mennonite in Virginia—were only a fraction of the students' total mission activity. If the India mission in the 1920s was "Goshenized," for instance, virtually every missionary who went to Africa under the Eastern Board in the 1930s and early 1940s was a graduate of Eastern Mennonite. Elkhart Institute, Goshen College's predecessor which began in 1894, had a Young People's Christian Association by 1898 and one of the organization's first acts was to pledge support for an orphan in India. The first wedding of two Elkhart Institute students was that of Mary M. Yoder and Jacob Burkhard, who of course soon went to India, where he became the first Mennonite Church missionary to die on the field. Especially in the first two decades of the twentieth century, Goshen students avidly attended interdenominational conferences of the Student Volunteer Movement and other such organizations. Less interdenominationally thereafter, they continued vigorous programs of mission studies, annual mission offering drives, a Foreign Volunteer Band, and the like, right up to and through World War II. At Hesston

Exhibit 8–3: Stimuli for Beginning Work

	Number (out of 587)	Percentage of the 341 on which exist data on stimuli	Percentage of 587
A. Response to particular need or situation seemingly without missioners having searched it out; in some cases, includes requests that Mennonites begin work; in some cases Mennonites had moved to area for other reasons than evangelism, then taken up work.	137	40	2
B. To provide a church for Mennonites in the area as well as to evangelize.	44	13	7
C. Mission-minded Mennonite Church people deliberately seeking out a location, surveying to find area needing mission, and/or moving into the area primarily for mission purpose.	155	45	26
D. Branch work because of racial friction in a mission already going—usually for Blacks rejected by Whites.	5*	1	1
Subtotal	**341**		**58**
No data on stimuli for beginning	246		42
TOTAL	587		

*From general evidence, this number appears to be too small, probably because sources did not point openly to this stimulus.

Exhibit 8-4: Agency or Group Initiating New Work

	Number	Percentage of the 561	Percentage of the 587
A. Individual or small group of ordinary church members, acting on their own account	67	12	11
B. Colonizing Mennonites either acting on own or backed by congregation or board	13	2	2
C. Congregation or congregational representatives	204	36	35
D. Local board or cluster of congregations, district conference, or district conference board	217	39	37
E. Mennonite Board of Missions and Charities (general board)	28	5	5
F. College student group or organization	19	3	3
G. I-W, or CPS (i.e., persons doing alternative to military service), Voluntary Service, student or teacher (on non-Mennonite campuses), or other groups situated more or less temporarily at a location for purposes not specifically "evangelistic"	5	1	1
H. Inter-Mennonite (Members and/or agencies of the Mennonite Church acting in cooperation with those of other Mennonite branches)	2	0	0
I. Non-Mennonites	6	1	1
Subtotal	561		96
No data on originating group	26		4
TOTAL	587		

and Eastern Mennonite much the same was true—although apparently there was much less of that turn-of-the-century kind of interdenominationalism.[6] Those schools began later (1909 and 1917 respectively), partly to guard Mennonites from some of the influences from other denominations.

So quite naturally when the upsurge came in the Mennonite Church's home mission activities in the late 1920s, 1930s, and 1940s, the students of the colleges provided a part in it. Already they had been contributing something to home missions by sending gospel teams, etc. Then about 1930 Goshen students began Sunday school outreach in two poorer neighborhoods in the town of Goshen, and in the 1930s and 1940s they did the same in several places on the outskirts of the nearby, larger town of Elkhart. Also, in 1944, they helped conduct a survey and a vacation Bible school at a Chicago housing project, effort that eventually grew into a mission for Blacks. In the mid-1930s Eastern Mennonite students began services in two locations in Harrisonburg, the city where the college is located, and soon they were doing the same in other nearby Shenandoah Valley towns or rural mountain areas. In the 1940s their "Y" sent a number of student teams westward into Kentucky to make surveys, hold gospel meetings, conduct vacation Bible schools, and do other work, helping to extend Virginia Conference outreach into that state. Also from the Virginia college various gospel teams went to towns in West Virginia, Tennessee, etc., distributed tracts in numerous places, held jail services or furnished Sunday school teachers to mountain congregations and missions within driving distance of Harrisonburg, and the like. Meantime, in Kansas, the Hesston "Y" helped begin work at least as far away as Wichita, more than thirty miles from the campus.[7]

In many of the cases conference or district boards soon stepped in and took some of the responsibility, gave direction, and appointed workers more permanent than students. By the 1970s, of the nineteen or more missions that students had actually begun, four had died out; one had become a social service center operated more or less by various branches of Mennonites in cooperation; one was still a mission; and thirteen had become independent congregations. At least some of those congregations were thriving. But among the thriving ones were some that, being in or near communities with many old-line Mennonites, were not especially missionary in character. Often such congregations were made up mainly of people from Mennonite or Amish families. Nonetheless, the college students had done their part.

A more "natural" kind of contact than those that college students established, perhaps, were those from Mennonites who colonized. But the cases of outright colonization in a way that deliberately or unintentionally led to mission outreach might appear from the data in Exhibit 8-4 to have been surprisingly few. After all, Anabaptists and Mennonites had a long history of uprooting and moving to new places, as groups. Maybe the researcher recorded so few cases because of the way he did the classifying. By no means, for instance, did he count every case to be one of colonization if only a family or two—as happened quite often—established themselves as a nucleus in some new place at least partly to do mission. Even if more families eventually followed and built up a colony, he did not necessarily consider colonization to have been the way that the outreach had started. So perhaps the low numbers of mission-by-colonization reflect only the researcher's way of interpreting.

On the other hand, except perhaps in earlier Anabaptist days, Mennonites had not often moved as groups for the purpose of proclaiming gospel to others, at least not to proclaim in the modern missionary sense. Rather, they had moved for the sake of their group's own lives.[8] So perhaps to find very little outreach by colonization is not surprising at all.

In any case, taking both the "natural" and the more contrived contacts together, quite clearly the big bulge of Mennonite Church home mission starts came not from scattered efforts of college students and colonizers, nor from those of other individuals and small groups going out unofficially in faith-mission fashion. On the other hand, neither did they come very often via centralized direction, from the denominational mission board. Instead, as Exhibit 8-4 makes clear, by far the greatest numbers of new home-field starts by Mennonite Church people from 1860 to 1960 were either by congregations and their representatives or by district conferences or other regional boards or bodies.

That pattern appears all the more striking if considered through time, as in Exhibits 8-5, 8-6, and 8-7. The raw numbers (not percentages) of Exhibit 8-5 suggest that all the groups except colonizers and non-Mennonites helped create that spurt in new starts by the 1930s and 1940s. Efforts by unofficial persons or groups were fairly significant. But of course, as Exhibit 8-6 makes even more clear, congregations and area boards set off the really steep increases. In 8-6, lines C and D indicate further that area boards mobilized a bit sooner than did the congregations and that their efforts did not peak quite so soon. Were the area boards the more stable, and congregations a bit more fickle?

Exhibit 8-5: Originating Agency or Group by Time (ave. number per 5 years; percentages are of all the new starts made in the time period)

Originating Agency or Group (see Ex. 8-4)	1861-1890 (%)	1891-1900 (%)	1901-1910 (%)	1911-1920 (%)	1921-1925 (%)	1926-1930 (%)	1931-1935 (%)	1936-1940 (%)	1941-1945 (%)	1946-1950 (%)	1951-1955 (%)	1956-1960 (%)
A-Unoffic.	—	1(12)	1.5(13)	1 (10)	2(10)	6(21)	8(15)	7(11)	7(14)	13(10)	9 (7)	8(17)
B-Coloniz.	—	—	1 (8)	1 (10)	1 (5)	1 (4)	1 (2)	—	2 (4)	—	1 (1)	3 (6)
C-Congreg.	.33(40)	1(12)	2.5(21)	2.5(25)	1 (5)	5(18)	16(31)	27(42)	17(33)	56(44)	51(39)	17(35)
D-District board, etc.	.5 (60)	6(71)	5.5(46)	4.5(45)	11(52)	13(46)	21(40)	17(27)	15(29)	41(33)	52(40)	12(25)
E-MBMC	—	—	1.5(13)	—	2(10)	1 (4)	2 (4)	1 (2)	6(12)	3 (2)	5 (4)	5(10)
F-College	—	—	—	—	—	2 (7)	—	5 (8)	3 (6)	5 (4)	1 (1)	3 (6)
G-Temporary	—	—	—	—	—	—	—	—	1 (2)	1 (1)	2 (2)	1 (2)
H-Inter-Mennonite	—	—	—	—	—	—	—	—	—	2 (2)	—	—
I-Non Menno.	—	—	—	.5 (5)	—	1 (4)	1 (2)	1 (2)	—	1 (1)	1 (1)	—

Exhibit 8-6: Originating Agency or Group by Time, Graphed (Raw numbers)

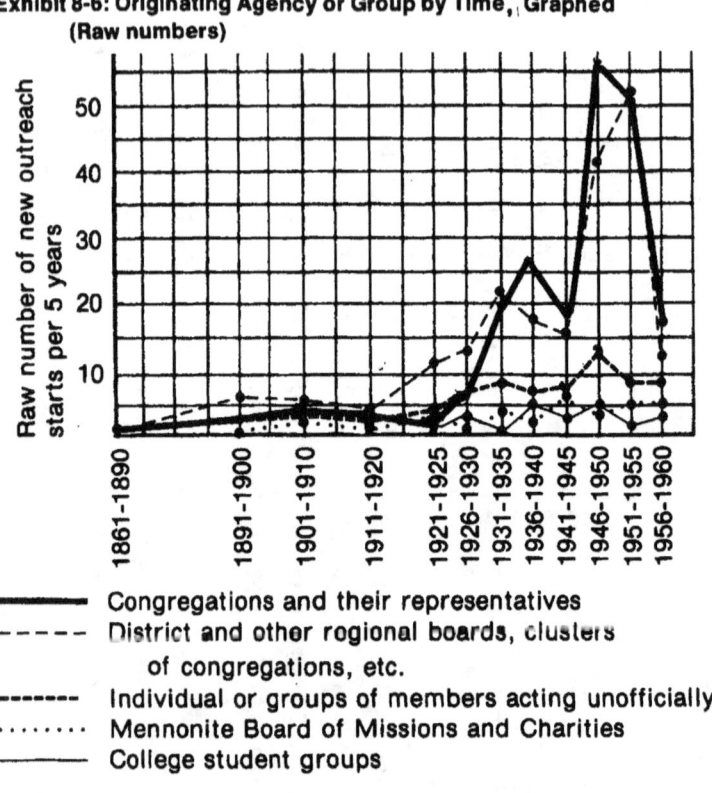

——— Congregations and their representatives
- - - - - District and other regional boards, clusters of congregations, etc.
------- Individual or groups of members acting unofficially
········ Mennonite Board of Missions and Charities
——— College student groups

Perhaps some centralization was a balance wheel.

A graph showing *percentages*, as does Exhibit 8-7, makes much more clear how congregational zeal rose compared to that of other groups. Fluctuations in lines A and E are not very important since they reflect fewer cases, but their generally level patterns show that church members acting unofficially and the general board continued to do their shares. Yet those shares remained fairly low. As for the larger shares, the drop in line D (area boards' percentages) does not really reflect a general lessening of effort by the area boards. Area boards were not lessening their efforts, at least not before 1955-1960. Instead, the line's downward slope results from the sharp rise in the congregations' line, C. Line C dominates the graph. The overwhelming change was the sharp rise in congregational efforts.

Gospel at Home

Exhibit 8-7 : Originating Agency or Group by Time, Graphed (Percentages)

Percentages of all starts made in a given time period for which there is data on origin.

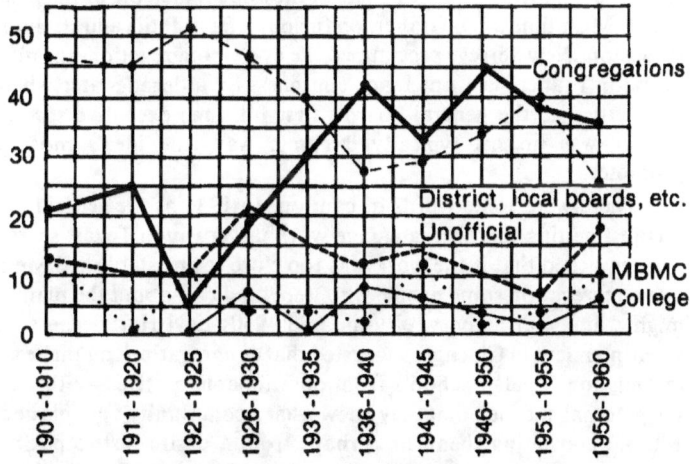

Helping that change, or at least capturing its mood, was that slogan, "every congregation an outpost."

The slogan began to take hold about the early 1930s, but its idea was not exactly new. In 1905, for instance, the Indiana-Michigan district conference asked itself, "What should the church do in the way of establishing mission stations in connection with our home church?" And it gave the answer, "Each congregation having available workers [should] appoint a committee of mission-filled members to find locations and conduct services there, and put forth all efforts to establish mission stations and congregations."[9] Nor was the idea merely talk. About that same year a congregation at Palmyra, Missouri began services at a nearby country crossroads known as Pea Ridge. Pea Ridge then became the first place John (J. R.) Shank preached regularly, to begin his long career as a rural missionary in Missouri and Arkansas. Later, by 1931, it assisted the Palmyra congregation to start a work in nearby Hannibal.[10]

Slogan and activity grew together. In 1933 J. Paul Sauder, prominent home missionary and mission editor for the Lancaster Conference, spoke of a "bus-load of happy children and adults" at a former mission station, and of one bishop district where members in "out-station" congregations outnumbered "members of the home base approximately two to one." "Has your congregation founded out-stations..." up to that ratio? he asked listeners at the annual meeting of the general board. Meantime J. D. Graber, on furlough from India and studying at Princeton, New Jersey, proclaimed the every-congregation-an-outpost theme in Franconia Conference churches. By a decade later when he took office as the general board's first full-time executive secretary, Graber was, in his typically dynamic way, the idea's most avid promoter.[11]

There were some words of caution. In 1936 as the general board was just getting Spanish-language work underway in Texas, secretary Yoder warned that if the work was too close to an established Mennonite congregation some people who were "radical" about the plain coat might "limit our activity." By the mid-1950s Levi Hartzler, erstwhile superintendent in Chicago, suggested that congregations might be starting mission Sunday schools from questionable motives—either from the paternalistic idea that they knew what a community's people needed without consulting them, or perhaps from a desire just to put home congregation members to work to get experience. Eventually even Graber raised some mild question about his slogan, especially the word "out-post." As someone had said, he told *Gospel Herald* readers in 1951, "you have never seen a post that grew." And as for "out," he suggested that congregations sometimes seemed to want missions out and away too far—because they feared that new Christians from non-Mennonite backgrounds might bring a "different cultural and religious climate" into the church.[12]

Of course congregational outreach was not only a Mennonite Church phenomenon. Rather it has been, wrote a British mission commentator in 1965, a "peculiarly American phenomenon."[13] Still, while it lasted, that upsurge in congregational effort was the most remarkable feature of the Mennonite Church's mission effort at home.

Child Evangelism?

Alongside that remarkable feature was another: an overwhelming tendency to lead with programs for children. Even with allowances for some imprecision, the data in Exhibit 8-8 show it. To be sure Sunday schools, which account for the largest numbers in that table, could include classes for adults. But when Mennonite Church missioners

Exhibit 8-8: Program Used Predominantly to Begin Work

	Number (out of 587)	% of 504	% of 587
A. Sunday School			
1. With fairly regular preaching, etc., also	100	20	17
2. With very little support program	187	37	32
Total Sunday School	**287**	**57**	**49**
B. Summer Bible School	110	22	19
C. Benevolence (incl. rescue missions, some V.S.)	11	2	2
D. "Evangelism" (street meetings, evangelistic meetings, tract distribution, etc., sometimes soon followed with Sunday school and preaching)	53	11	9
E. Preaching, little else	22	4	4
F. Other	21	4	4
Subtotal	**504**		**86**
No data on what program predominated at outset	83		14
TOTAL	587		

wrote and spoke they made clear that outreach Sunday schools attracted, and were expected to attract, mainly children. Moreover, outreaching Mennonites began to use vacation Bible schools somewhat later than Sunday schools as lead programs. But when they did, the Bible schools seemed to substitute for Sunday schools, suggesting again how much the Mennonites had been aiming Sunday schools at children. The curves of Exhibit 8-9 demonstrate that pattern.

In Exhibit 8-9 once again, movement in the lines near the bottom of the graph (lines representing benevolence, "evangelism," and preaching services as lead programs) are not very significant since each line represents few cases. More important is the fact that the lines remain near the bottom, and that their cases did remain few. As for the lines at the top of the graph, representing starts with child-programs, their

Exhibit 8-9: Beginning Program by Time, Graphed (Percentages*).

* Percentages of total known outreach starts in the time period.

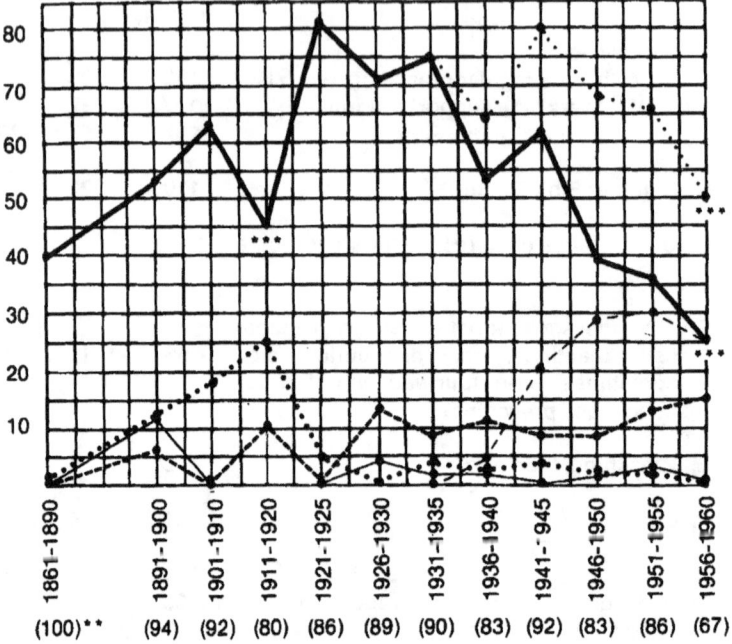

	1861-1890	1891-1900	1901-1910	1911-1920	1921-1925	1926-1930	1931-1935	1936-1940	1941-1945	1946-1950	1951-1955	1956-1960
	(100)**	(94)	(92)	(80)	(86)	(89)	(90)	(83)	(92)	(83)	(86)	(67)

A	——	Starts primarily via Sunday schools
B	----	Via vacation Bible schools
A&B	······	Combined data on the two major child-programs
C	——	Via benevolence—rescue mission, voluntary service, etc.
D	------	Via "evangelism"—street meetings, cottage meetings, etc.
E	······	Via preaching, little else

** Numbers in this line show percentages—cases on which data exists as to beginning program as percentage of total known cases in this time period.

*** Drop-off probably exaggerated by low percentage of cases on which data as to beginning program exists.

peaks and their valleys might not seem quite so sharp if the data were of consistent quality, especially if information existed on the same percentage of cases in all time periods. But the data problems are not large enough to cast real doubt on the main conclusion: Overwhelmingly, Mennonite Church people began their new outreach efforts with programs appealing to children.

Were those Mennonites therefore caught up in a mentality and a strategy of child evangelism? Answer: Yes, but....

Yes, Mennonite Church people very often did start by working with children, and they spoke rather often of converting the little ones. But—although they adopted the vacation Bible school pattern when other denominations did—curves of their child-appeal activities do not seem to have followed closely an upsurge that occurred in child-evangelism organizations among certain evangelical Protestants. Moreover, if Mennonite Church missioners did borrow child-evangelism assumptions, they applied them gently. And by World War II, just as a new magazine entitled *Child Evangelism* appeared on the Protestant mission scene, at least a few leading Mennonite Church people were beginning to question the child-evangelism approach.

In the 1920s, 1930s, and 1940s, people in certain Protestant circles stepped up efforts to convert children. The strategy was by no means new, of course. For a century or more many revivalists had appealed specifically to the little ones, so much so that they had drawn objection for instance from one of the leading theologians of nineteenth-century America, the Congregationalist Horace Bushnell.[14] And concern for bringing children to conversion had been strong in the Sunday school movement. Yet in the second quarter of the twentieth century or thereabouts a number of new child-evangelism organizations appeared. For example, from 1918 to 1937 a worker for the American Sunday School Union evolved an evangelism-oriented Bible memory program for children, eventually called the Rural Bible Crusade; others in the 1930s formed a "Christian Service Brigade" to win and train boys and in 1939 added what soon became the Pioneer Girls; in 1939 also, another organization appeared, sponsoring "Key to Life Clubs" that appealed to children in junior high; and in 1945 child-evangelists began a "Children for Christ Movement." Most notable of all, about 1923 a Californian named J. Irvin Overholtzer began work which since 1937 has been organized as the International Child Evangelism Fellowship. Meanwhile, from about the second decade of the century onward, various denominations began to use a technique begun in New York City in the 1890s, vacation Bible schools—perhaps less strictly geared to child evangelism, and more to general teaching and nurture.[15]

Exhibit 8-9 clearly suggests that Mennonite Church people soon copied the vacation Bible school technique, but that they were not necessarily riding on the upsurge in child evangelism. A vacation Bible school curve appears on the Mennonites' graph about a decade after the movement got underway among Protestants. But as for relationship to those new child-evangelism organizations, or to any trend the new organizations represented, the case was different. Mennonite Church people's use of child programs to lead off in new outreach actually reached its peak, percentagewise, before organizations such as the Child Evangelism Fellowship really began to flourish. At least that is true of the cases that appear among those 587 missions.

And from the beginning, if Mennonite Church missioners did work at child evangelism, they did so quite gently. On the whole they thought children were essentially good so that the task was to save them from corrupting influences more than from depraved natures within. In 1896 a Chicago Home Mission worker declared that children were by nature often "very kind-hearted," although when ignorant "of all that is pure and noble" they were all too likely to get the idea that "to be bad is to be popular." Two decades later A. M. Eash, superintendent of the Twenty-Sixth Street Mission in Chicago, was still repeating almost the same words. "Boys," wrote he, "are not naturally bad; they are largely what their environment and heritage have made them," and they acted in ways that seemed horrible only "because someone has suggested those particular bad things to them and no one made a more wholesome and attractive" suggestion.[16] With such ideas, the Mennonite Church's mission workers did not generally assume that they had on their hands depraved little sinners, who had to confess their sins immediately to escape judgment and damnation. At least they did not carry that assumption very far.

Instead, their ideas were more to bring children under Christian influences, to sow the Word in them, and to *nurture* them to the point of conversion. Along with their Sunday school missions, Lancaster Conference Mennonites (and others) were quick to join "Fresh-Air" programs and other methods that Protestant missionaries and philanthropists had developed in the nineteenth century for getting children out of the city for shorter or longer periods, and into country homes.[17] Here was the environment-and-nurture approach in purest form. But it appeared elsewhere, too. The Sunday school worker prepared the way for the evangelist's harvest, reasoned A. M. Eash at annual mission board meeting in 1915. The superintendent of the orphans' home in Ohio, Laban Swartzentruber, declared in 1932 that daily Bible instruction, moral training, prayers, and the like were all for the purpose that "one by one the boys and girls be adopted into the great family of God, through the blood of Christ."[18]

Yet ultimately, even if gently, conversion was the goal. "Prime object of SS to save souls," jotted J. A. Ressler in his diary in 1894, as the first point of a talk he had given. The Sunday school was no longer merely the "nursery of the church," for it had become an active, soul-saving institution, agreed a recent mission superintendent at Ft. Wayne, John (J. F.) Bressler, in 1905, pointing to the American Sunday School Union for models. Orphans' homes evoked similar logic, with those who spoke for orphanages emphasizing how many of their young charges were accepting Christ. So did vacation Bible schools, when they came into fashion. Promoting them, Paul Mininger, son of the Kansas City superintendent, argued in 1932 that "youthful conversions" might not be as "dramatic or sensational" as adult ones, but "they are certainly to be preferred." Yes, agreed a *Gospel Herald* editorial in 1941, a child converted meant a whole lifetime for God. "Through the home, Sunday School, Summer Bible School and church service, let us win children for Christ."[19]

The age at which the child might make the choice for Christ got lower in Mennonite minds—despite the believers-baptism principle that Anabaptists and Mennonites had so long embraced, which said that to follow Jesus required personal commitment, entered into responsibly. In the early 1890s evangelist Coffman had suggested a goal of children being in the church by age 16. Ten or fifteen years later mission-minded Mennonites seemed to put the goal somewhere about age 10 or 12. In 1928 Clayton (C. F.) Yake, editor of the Mennonite Church's youth paper, wanted Sunday schools to work for conversions in the Junior Department, arguing that "careful and systematic investigation" showed that people converted at "from nine to twelve years of age" showed a "much larger percentage" remaining faithful to the church than those converted at any other age. A decade after that J. Paul Sauder of the Lancaster Conference, in a child evangelism issue of his conference's missionary paper, was careful not to fix an age but suggested that children began to respond to the Spirit at about 8.[20]

Most extremely the *Gospel Herald* printed an article in 1941 telling of a number of persons converted by age 7, and even of two mothers who were convinced that their sons had been "definitely converted at 3." The author said he did not know just how early conversions could happen, but that "I stand in awe before the inmates of the nursery." He and his examples were not Mennonite. But the person who submitted the article was. He was J.D. Mininger, superintendent of mission and children's home at Kansas city, member of the general mission board, and surely his church's outstanding city missionary until his death that year.[21]

The age for conversion was dropping. Meanwhile a rather different idea was common: that the child-programs were really means to get to adults. "One of the easiest and quickest ways to reach the parents' hearts is by way of their child," field worker Allgyer was sure in 1915. At least, hoped one of the Eastern Board's missionaries at Tampa, Florida, in 1937, if the parents did not come to the mission "we believe these little ones will drop something along the way as they sing the songs and tell the stories they learn here." Such hopes were not all vain. A Detroit mother, Lydia Burton, has told in late life how she began attending the Mennonite mission in the 1930s partly because her children had begun there some four or five years earlier—though also because country Mennonites shared garden produce with her in those depression years, after her husband died. Much the same happened in the late 1930s in the Spanish-speaking Ventura family of Chicago, which has since furnished the Mennonite Church with a minister and other Christian workers.[22]

If Mennonite missionaries used children to reach adults, did they exploit children for their own purposes, as Protestant missionaries have been charged with doing?[23] Mennonite Church people would hardly have recognized the question, for they were sure that along the way they were giving children that which has the greatest of value. In 1942 Los Angeles mission superintendent Glenn Whitaker gave small boys a nickel each, if each brought a second boy along to handicraft classes. He conceded that some folks might accuse him of buying the boys. But, the superintendent reasoned, "we had the two boys for a nickel," and "personally I would be glad to buy all the boys we can at two for a nickel." It was a bargain, "if only a few of these are won for the Lord Jesus Christ."[24]

The two-for-a-nickel approach was not really typical. Mennonite child evangelism was much more complex than that. A 1933 editorial in the Lancaster Conference's *Missionary Messenger* told of some 1,000 children attending the Lancasterians' mission Sunday schools, and used the idea that the faith was a heritage—a heritage for all children, not only children of Mennonites.[25] At least for the author of that article, child evangelism was apparently a way for Lancasterians to share with

Exhibit 8-10: Outcomes of Work Begun with Different Programs
            (Percentages,* by 1974)

Begun Predominantly with	% that became Independent congregations and continued.	Additional % that were going concerns although still dependent to a significant extent on initiating group or agency	Total % going concerns**	% that died out or discontinued, a few after becoming independent
A. Sunday School (287 cases)	45%	21%	66%	18%
B. Vacation Bible school (110 cases)	31%***	46%***	77%***	11%***
C. Benevolence (11 cases)****	9%	64%	73%	9%
D. "Evangelism" (53 cases)	34%	34%	68%	17%
E. Preaching**** (22 cases)	45%	9%	54%	27%

*i.e., % of the number known to have been begun by that program, i.e., of 287, of 110, of 11, etc.

**Percentage figures in this column simply represent additions of those of the previous two columns.

***Difference in results of vacation Bible school and those of Sunday schools are probably a reflection mainly that vacation Bible school programs were much more recent in 1974, on the average.

****Number of cases surely too few to allow the percentages that follow to be very significant.

others a deep sense of rootedness. Perhaps the author had glimpsed a little of the vision of *shalom*. In any case, the Mennonite Church's child evangelism was not simpleminded exploitation of children, nor did simple slogans about converting the little ones dominate it.

By the 1940s and certainly in the post-World-War II years, a few in the Mennonite Church began to question child-evangelism assumptions. Had such people had the statistics compiled before them, the results of beginning with child-programs might have looked reasonably good. For the child programs were scoring fairly well if the test was what percentages of different beginning programs produced independent congregations, or at least going concerns. Exhibit 8-10 summarizes that data. Actually the figures on independent congregations and other going concerns may give too much impression of mission success. What Mennonite Church member older than 40 does not, in 1979, remember firsthand at least one place of worship that began as "outreach" but became a congregation whose rolls are filled almost entirely with old-line Mennonite or Amish family names?[26] No doubt the "success" categories in Exhibit 8-10 include quite a few of those. And the "died out" percentages are probably low. Eighty-three of the 587 cases did not yield data as to outcome, and very likely most of the 83 were cases that died out. Yet, even after allowances for data error, child-programs seem to have planted congregations in percentages that compared well with those of other beginnings. In absolute numbers, of course, they planted far more.

Nonetheless, Mennonite Church people began to question the assumptions. In street meetings, reported Philadelphia workers in 1944, "we avoid speaking to the children since we are after the adults"— "except to invite them to the children's meeting inside." And in 1942 Alta Mae Erb, a Mennonite writer on mission, child nurture, and other topics, used the idea of believers baptism to warn against pressing children into professing conversion. If a child showed evidence of understanding the decision she did not want to say the person was too young, she told *Gospel Herald* readers; but "the action must be based on the child's desire," not that of the parents or the Christian workers. Yes, there were dangers in child conversions, agreed her husband, church leader and future *Gospel Herald* editor Paul Erb, in the same issue. "When we try to test for the sincerity and understanding of the child's religious experience we may be satisfied with mere verbalism." Or another danger, thought Erb, was to "expect of the child a stereotyped adult experience of religious conversion."[27]

In 1945 Nelson Kauffman, outstanding churchwide evangelist and home missionary at Hannibal, Missouri, asked whether Protestant missions had not emphasized Sunday school, vacation Bible school, and lately child evangelism too much, until church seemed to be something mainly for children and women. He backed his point with a statement about Anabaptists, although not the best one. Anabaptism had been a man's movement, he said (ignoring the many Anabaptist women who had made the pages of the *Martyrs Mirror*, or otherwise stood out). Later other Mennonite thought-leaders—most notably Paul Lederach, who was a city missioner, bishop, and director of Christian-education curricula at the Mennonite Publishing House—used the believers-baptism principle far more systematically to question child evangelism or its methods. Others raised questions about results. In his 1955 study of the Mennonite Church's rural missions Linden Wenger, although by no means entirely critical of Sunday schools and vacation Bible schools as mission activities, concluded that so much appeal to children had interfered with building indigenous congregations and leadership. And in 1964, in a book chapter reflecting about Lancaster Conference mission history, which ever since "Mennonite Sunday School Mission" days had rested heavily on child-programs, a Lancasterian named H. Raymond Charles made the point that too often "mission" congregations were really transplants of old-line Mennonites looking for something more "spiritual." Mennonite mission effort, as Charles observed it, had brought "only a token response in adult conversions."[28]

"We had heard the statement, 'Get the child and then you will have his parents,' " Charles went on to reflect, and "we almost accepted this as truth." But "after a generation of this approach...we began looking at this strategy in light of apostolic and early church practices and found it wanting." Yes, agreed no less a participant in the Lancasterians' home-mission history than J. Paul Sauder. "Factually we have not been able to persuade adults. First-century Christianity was an approach to adults." It had meant an "ingathering of households....This we must do, or learn how to do. ..."[29]

Such comments were surely to the point. In their child-programs Mennonite Church people were neither harsh nor terribly simplistic. Yet when they began to reflect upon the programs, the programs did not completely fit what Mennonites said they believed about becoming followers of Jesus.

Jew, Gentile, Brown, Black, White

Mennonite outreach at home, even with the post-World War II years to 1960 included, was overwhelmingly mission to Whites. The percentage of missions appealing primarily to Blacks, for instance, was

Exhibit 8-11: Ethnic Groups to Which Missions Appealed in Their Early Days

	Number	% of the 524 on which data exists	% of 587
A. White			
1. White only, in some cases due to artificial segregation	412	79	70
2. White, with a few non-Whites, etc.	21	4	4
Total White	433	83	74
B. Black	31	6	5
C. Black and White,			
1. Integrated	9	2	2
2. Segregated and/or clearly approached with different methods	2	0	0
D. Brown (usually Spanish-language)			
1. Mission or work primarily to reach Browns	23	4	4
2. Integrated with White, but usually bilingual services	5	1	1
E. Red (Indian)			
1. Primarily for Reds	4	1	1
2. Connected to work with Whites but separated	1	0	0
F. Jewish			
1. Primarily for Jews	11	2	2
2. Connected to work with Gentiles, usually separated	3	1	1
G. Mix of Black, Brown, and White	1	0	0
H. French-speaking Canadian	1	0	0
Subtotal	524		89
No data on ethnicity	63		11
TOTAL	587		

less than Blacks' percentage in the North American population. That was understandable, considering the degree to which Mennonite Church people were northern and rural. The more they reached out via "natural" rather than contrived contacts, the more White their missions would be. Exhibit 8-11 shows the 1860-1960 pattern in some detail; Exhibit 8-12 summarizes it through time. Exhibit 8-13 shows what beginning programs Mennonites used in appeals to different ethnic groups, and Exhibit 8-14 tries to test what kinds of programs predominated after work with the different groups had developed.

In sum, the tables show some differences in work among the various ethnic groups, but seem more often to show that differences in approach or result was not very great. Exhibit 8-11 suggests what overwhelmingly large percentage of their efforts Mennonite church people aimed at Whites. Exhibit 8-12 indicates that beginnings of outreach to White Gentiles averaged somewhat earlier than those for other groups. But when it came to types of programs used as beginnings, as shown in 8-13, any difference among the groups appears insignificant—except a notable use of adult "evangelism" rather than child-programs to appeal to Jews. Nor—again except in the case of Jewish evangelism—were there great group-to-group differences in programs developed out of the different ethnic beginnings (Exhibit 8-14). Because of the many cases for which there was no data on developed program (189 cases, or 32 percent of the 587), Exhibit 8-14 tells nothing very precisely. But it does indicate that witness to Jews did not develop into the usual Sunday schools and congregations. And it does say, negatively, that the data thus far do not show significant differences in programs for the different ethnic groups.

Neither do graphs, as in Exhibit 8-15, show great differences among the groups in terms of how many of the beginning eventually produced independent congregations or other going congregations and missions. For integrated cases, and really for Jewish work and for appeals to Browns, raw numbers are so small that the exhibit's information is scarcely significant. The graph does seem to show that appeal to Whites produced independent congregations in greater percentages than appeal to Blacks, but even that data might not be very good. Since missions to Blacks began later on the average than missions to Whites, one might expect a smaller proportion to have developed into independent congregations by the mid-1970s. Moreover, compared with missions to Blacks, those to Whites were surely more likely to become congregations mainly of old-line Mennonites, which of course would

Exhibit 8-12: Ethnicity by Time

		1861-1890 (%)*	1891-1900 (%)	1901-1910 (%)	1911-1920 (%)	1921-1925 (%)	1926-1930 (%)
A-1.	White only (412 cases)	5 (1)	12 (3)	17 (4)	18 (4)	18 (4)	21 (5)
B.	Black (31 cases)	—	1 (3)	—	—	—	1 (3)
D-1.	Brown (23 cases)	—	—	—	—	1 (4)	2 (9)
E.	Red (5 cases)	—	—	—	—	—	—
F.	Jewish (14 cases)	—	—	—	—	—	—

		1931-1935 (%)	1936-1940 (%)	1941-1945 (%)	1946-1950 (%)	1951-1955 (%)	1956-1960 (%)
A-1.	White only (412 cases)	41 (10)	42 (10)	39 (9)	89 (21)	81 (20)	32 (8)
B.	Black (31 cases)	2 (6)	4 (13)	2 (6)	7 (23)	13 (42)	1 (3)
D-1.	Brown (23 cases)	1 (4)	5 (22)	2 (9)	3 (13)	2 (9)	7 (30)
E.	Red (5 cases)	—	—	—	1 (20)**	2 (40)	2 (40)
F.	Jewish (14 cases)	—	4 (29)	—	3 (21)	7 (50)	—

*i.e., % of known cases directed to that ethnicity, (i.e. of 412, 31, 23, 4, etc.)
**This is the case of work connected with a mission to whites (E-2).

Gospel at Home 251

Exhibit 8-13: Beginning Program by Ethnicity

	Sunday school Number (%)	Vacation Bible school Number (%)	Benev- olence Number (%)	"Evang." Number (%)	Preaching Number (%)
A-1. White (412 cases)	226 (55)	83 (20)	2 (0)	31 (8)	16 (4)
B. Black (31 cases)	12 (39)	11 (35)	1 (3)	2 (6)	— —
D-1. Brown (23 cases)	11 (48)	— —	— —	2 (9)	3 (13)
F. Jewish (14 cases)	— —	— —	1 (7)	8 (57)	— —

hardly make them "successful" as mission.

The sources of information did not make it possible to distinguish well, except in cases of witness of Jews, between various groups of Whites. The idea of going to *foreign* peoples in the cities was strong in the early days of Mennonite Church mission. Even in rural work, the Lancasterians, for instance, often went to mining settlements or other communities with numerous Italians, Poles, Hungarians, or other immigrant poeples. Generally however immigrant groups were too much on the move, and ethnic neighborhoods too much in change, for the mission to identify with a particular group or groups.[30] Gradually, moreover, immigrants got more assimilated and meantime Mennonites shifted more to rural settings, so mission became less a matter of work with "foreigners." For such reasons, the data hardly allow statistical breakdown of the categories for Whites.

And in any case, where the sources do allow statistics for different groups, the differences in methods of work or in results seem not to be very significant —except in that one case, the case of Jewish evangelism.

What of Mennonite attitudes toward those ethnic minorities, especially toward Blacks and Browns? Answer: Mennonite Church people pretty much continued the kind of uplift ideas that took them to the Welsh Mountain in the 1890s, except that less and less did they speak of

Exhibit 8-14: Developed Program by Ethnicity

Ethnicity	No.	Mainly Sunday School % of all cases*	% of cases with data**	Normal church program No. %* %**	Mainly benevolence No. %* %**	No developed program No. %* %**	No data No. %*
All groups (587 cases; data on 398)	54	(9)	(13)	270 (46) (68)	9 (2) (2)	23 (4) (5)	189 (32)
A-1. White (412 cases; data on 294)	48	(12)	(16)	215 (52) (73)	1 (0) (0)	16 (4) (5)	118 (40)
B. Black (31 cases; data on 26)	1	(3)	(4)	20 (65) (77)	— —	2 (6) (8)	5 (16)
D-1. Brown (23 cases; data on 14)	2	(9)	(14)	10 (43) (71)	— —	1 (4) (7)	9 (39)
E. Jewish*** (14 cases; data on 9)	—	—	—	— —	1 (7) (11)	1 (7) (11)	5 (36)

*% of all known cases where the beginning appeal was to this ethnic group.
**% of known cases where the beginning appeal was to this ethnic group, and where data existed as to what program predominated after the work had developed.
***In the seven cases of Jewish work not included in the table, developed program consisted heavily of cottage meetings, personal visitation, etc., with club work or someting similar prominent in several cases.

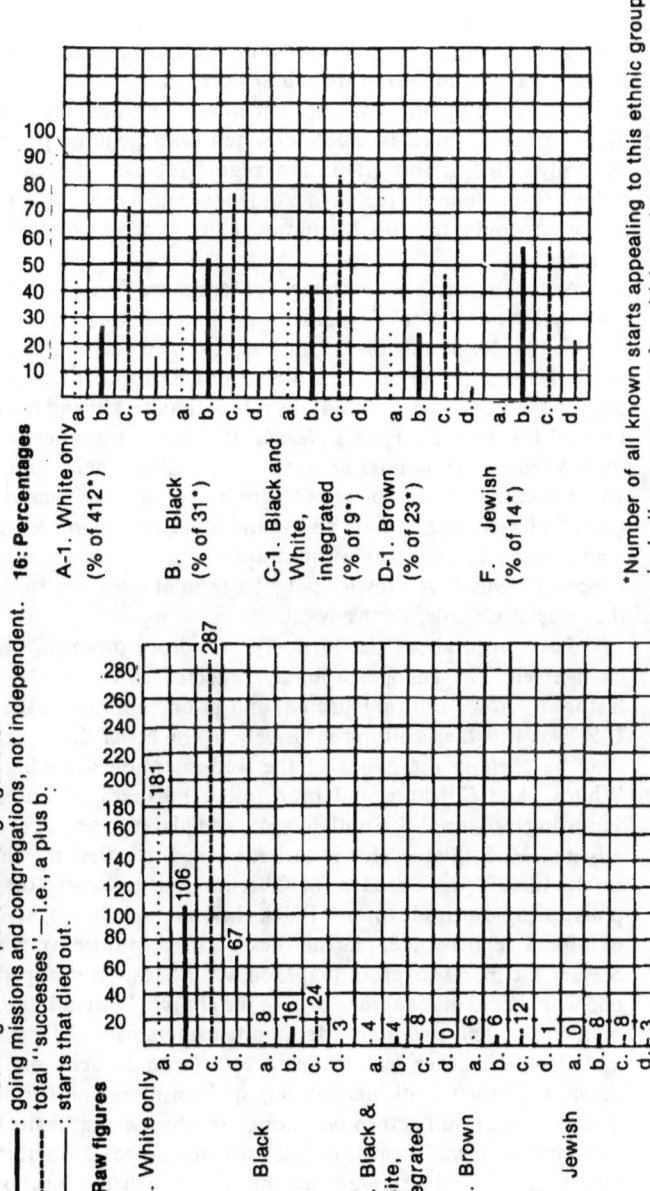

Exhibits 8-15 and 8-16: Outcomes, Compared by Ethnicity

producing good citizens and more and more they spoke of souls to be saved. The Mennonites at their best occasionally broke through with some genuine empathy. Even at their worst their missioners still looked upon minority folks as God's children with genuine potential, not hatefully as a Ku Klux Klansman might. Yet overall Mennonite attitudes left very much to repent of. And in the end it more or less fell to the minority peoples to bring Mennonite Church people toward the point of repentance.

As the twentieth century began, Mennonite Church leaders echoed very well the attitudes of philanthropic-minded northerners, Quakers, and the like. Regarding Blacks, they were somewhat judgmental against the South and its race relations. Regarding Red Indians, they called for programs to help and civilize Reds rather than to kill and exploit them. In 1889 for instance, Funk's *Herald of Truth* got itself crosswise with some Virginia Mennonites because of generalizations an editorial made about southerners' treatment of Negroes—a situation from which evangelist Coffman, as associate editor and a native Virginian, tried rather ambiguously to extract it without approving racism outright. And in the early 1890s J. A. Ressler taught a term at a leading Indian school that was at Carlisle, Pennsylvania.[31]

Then from about the turn of the century onward, a noticeable change fell. The change probably reflected two facts. (1) As every historian knows, both intellectual and public opinion in the northern U.S. was just then shifting massively to the belief that race relations were best left in the hands of the well-intentioned among southern Whites. And (2) more and more often northern Mennonites were venturing into the U.S. South to scout out places to settle or perhaps do mission. M. S. Steiner, for instance, seemed to reflect the change that befell. In 1891, as a student at Oberlin College (where the northern philanthropic attitude toward Blacks had a long history), Steiner wrote of a Black fellow-student as the "best spirited soul I have met yet." To Steiner the man was proof that God was no respecter of persons, and one who would make a fine "Bro. in the church." But in 1896, reporting on a trip he and two other Mennonite leaders named Joseph Smoker and Peter Unzicker had made in the South to seek out places to colonize, Steiner (with his fellows) spoke a more southern language. The three were still perceptive enough to observe that if the Black had lost courage, it was because of "all work and no pay." But they wrote of "the 'nigger' "; and they suggested that most northern objections against the South "exist more in the mind than in reality."[32]

Not surprisingly, then, in the first half of the twentieth century, when missioners and others in the Mennonite Church alluded to race, their words fell across a wide range. At one end of the range the language was extremely careless. At the other, it occasionally showed some understanding of what non-Whites were up against.

Even the careless utterances were not quite of the Ku Klux Klan variety, for virtually never did Mennonite Church people who were connected with mission try deliberately or self-consciously even to be derogatory, much less really hateful. But the carelessness could be awful. In 1908 C. K. Hostetler, interested in southern colonization partly for purposes of mission, listed "Negroes everywhere" as one of the problems, and lumped them with flies and mosquitoes, hot summers, yellow fever, typhoid, and malaria. Or in 1927 the Lancasterians' *Missionary Messenger* printed a story from a Protestant mission journal about a poor African woman married to a "big, black, burly, brutish" man—as if blackness and brutishness went together. In 1927 also, at annual mission board meeting, a home missionary from Colorado unthinkingly spoke from westerners' particular prejudices. Wanting to make a case for taking gospel to everyone, he pictured a burning house and said firemen would not let desperate people caught in it perish—even if they were three gamblers, "toughs," "sinners of the lowest type," "scum of the earth." In the dramatic picture, the Mennonite made the three toughs "a Jap, a Negro, and an Indian." And the carelessness went beyond a slip of the tongue; for whoever prepared the mission boards' published report did not bother to edit out the terrible slurs.[33]

Such utterances, even if unconscious, were downright insensitive, irresponsible, and inexcusable. But they were at one extreme of the range, not typical. At the other extreme, Mennonites now and then gave some glimpse of what minority peoples faced. Writing of Welsh Mountain Blacks, Jacob Mellinger in 1901 observed that "they have many discouragements which we do not have." In 1920 one E. D. Hess of Masontown, Pennsylvania observed in the *Gospel Herald* that Mennonites who saw the unconverted as " 'Hunkies' and 'Dagoes' and 'Niggers' " were "not spiritually qualified to work among them." Or in 1926, *Missionary Messenger* editors printed from a non-Mennonite journal a Black woman's laments about having to stand in subway trains when men gave seats to White women, about prejudice interfering with her children's education, about storekeepers' impudence toward Blacks, about Whites' teaching history with no Black heroes, about an Africa pictured as full of savage Blacks but philanthropic-minded Europeans, and about how she, a schoolteacher, had to stoop to intellectual dishonesty if she wanted a position in her native Philadelphia.[34]

These were only glimpses toward understanding. Mellinger buried his insight among phrases that breathed of Whites' cultural superiority and of uplift. Hess, like many another Mennonite, wanted to replace the slurs with a view of people as lost sheep or lost souls. If that meant seeing persons not completely, but only as candidates for mission, it too was a stereotyping, even if it was better-intentioned than the "Dago" and "Nigger" varieties. The editors borrowed the laments of the Black schoolteacher from a non-Mennonite source; apparently they had neither formed their own statement nor found a Mennonite who could state the Blacks' case clearly. Still, a few Mennonites were reflecting some understanding of what minority peoples faced.[35]

Most Mennonite utterances fell somewhere more midrange. Like many other well-meaning Americans in North and South, Mennonites were quite enthused about Negro leader Booker T. Washington—who of course in the 1890s had forged the so-called "Great Compromise" that called for manual education and other economic opportunities for Negroes without asking immediately for social and political equality. As for Indians and Mexicans, the Carlisle Indian School where J. A. Ressler taught operated from a philosophy of education much like that of Hampton Institute, the school from which Washington had formed most of his ideas. And reflecting much the same philosophy, in 1920 one J. A. Hilty, a Mennonite who had lived at Phoenix, Arizona, treated *Christian Monitor* readers to a series of articles on the Southwest's "Mexicans." Hilty presented the Mexican-Americans as generally indolent and yet, if given opportunity, ambitious to rise. He thought that the Christians among them (by which he apparently meant the few Protestants) were especially ambitious. Hilty's two minds about the "Mexicans" reflected many Mennonite Church missioners' attitudes toward non-Whites. And like most missioners' and others' utterances, his words fell between those two ends of that scale.[36]

And really, Mennonite Church people often used about the same words for subgroups of Whites. Their language reflected not just color-consciousness but ethnic attitudes more generally. In 1897 lay leader Jonathan K. Hartzler visited New York City and some non-Mennonite city missions, then wrote in the *Herald of Truth* of scenes such as one "full of dark-skinned men and bonnetless women, speaking not a word of English, only rough, gutteral Italian." Chicago Superintendent Leaman felt discouraged in 1907 at seeing the "foreign element crowding out the better class of people in the vicinity of the Home Mission." Soon thereafter the Youngstown mission was working to teach foreigners "the habits, customs and language of the American people." In the 1930s board secretary Yoder had some strong private doubts when the daughter of a missionary couple intended to marry an Argentine who had come to the U.S. It might have been better, the secretary thought, for the couple to return and work in Argentina "where there is not the discrimination against mixed marriages that there is here."[37]

In that case Yoder was thinking in racial terms. But race was not necessarily the key factor. Mildly, Yoder had some of the same doubt when a son of other missionaries married a girl from Portland, Oregon, who, Yoder understood, was "a member of the Mennonite church, but has no Mennonite background." Southern mountain Whites could hardly have been "racially" suspect, yet Mennonite evangelists or mission workers on occasion spoke of them or their cultures unflatteringly. On the other hand, not every reference to subgroups of Whites was unflattering. For instance at annual mission board meeting in 1917, Leaman of Chicago also emphasized the inventions and the hard work that Bohemians or Poles or others had contributed to America.[38]

Mennonite mission people did think in the racist categories of the times, as when in 1924 Yoder referred to southern mountaineers as "7,000,000 people of the purest Anglo Saxon blood."[39] But the language for White groups was not so very different from that for non-Whites. It too ranged from the careless put-down to at least limited understanding. Mennonites were responding to ethnicity, not only to color.

The Mennonites were in North America, and more than they knew they were North Americans; so where color was an issue, they resorted to segregation. In 1922 Lancaster Conference people opened a mission in Reading, Pennsylvania, predominantly for Whites, then in 1938 added a separate one for Blacks. Soon after the one for Blacks opened, Noah Good, superintendent in Reading, publicly summed up his racial perceptions. Probably his words expressed about as well as one statement could what Mennonite Church missionaries on the eve of World War II generally thought about Blacks and about segregation. Good's main point was to challenge Mennonites to evangelize among Blacks. The Negro, he reasoned, "desires a simple way of living just as we as a plain church do." So by "our way of living a simple life" Mennonites were "uniquely adapted to reach them."[40]

Along the way, Good delivered a sweeping put-down. "It is generally conceded," he declared, that Negroes were "not superior as a race, intellectually." In that, unfortunately, Good accepted as true what the North American public and even some scientists widely believed at the time. Much more deliberately and very extensively, however, he tried to make the Blacks' case. To the put-down he immediately added that "it is surprising that the American Negro is not worse, after the 250 years of training we gave him."[41]

Good made Whites' exploitation of Blacks a very major theme of his article. He began it: "The history of the Negro in the United States is one of the severest indictments against the white man's sense of justice." At mid-point he declared that "the white man's treatment of the Negro, and [of] the Indian are two great shames." He denounced southern-style laws to keep Blacks from voting, etc., warned against the "nigger" label, and said Negroes knew there were "many 'niggers' among the white race." In conclusion Good called on his fellow Mennonites to "love the Negroes because Christ loved us, and because they have a soul which Christ died to save."[42]

Nevertheless, the superintendent firmly defended segregation. Although "Christians in the North" rejected the southern " 'keep his place' attitudes," he averred since more Blacks had come North "we now see that it is necessary for the Negro and the white man to live separate lives." So it was clear "that there must be some form of segregation, and that promiscuous mixing is not healthy." "Shall we invite the Negro to our regular church services in our country churches, in our city missions?" Good asked rhetorically. "You know very well what would happen in the South if we were so careless as that, and the same thing is fast coming in the North. ...There is a difference, and we must provide separate places of worship in most places."[43]

At times, Good and others who spoke for Mennonite Church mission seemed to suggest that segregation was something Mennonites accepted only because forced to. "The race problem," thought Eastern Board secretary Mellinger in 1931, "is one that must be dealt with cautiously or much harm may result." In some Mennonite missions, Mellinger continued, Whites and "colored" mingled "while in others the reverse is true." Where there was race feeling, he asked, "shall the colored children be barred from coming?"[44] (Apparently nobody thought of barring intolerant Whites.)

Mellinger was convinced that at the Eastern Board's Tampa, Florida mission, for one place, "if one colored child should be admitted to our Sunday school...the next Sunday you would not find a single white person there." He was certain also that such mixing would in fact alienate Blacks from the mission as well. Virginia Conference and district board officials followed similar logic when, in 1936 and 1937, the "Y" at Eastern Mennonite School began work among both Blacks and Whites in the town of Harrisonburg. At first the workers held separate services at the same location, but later separated the locations. Conference and district board officials approved, and indeed went even farther. In 1940 they declared that "in view of the general attitude of society in the south toward the intermingling of the two races," and of the need for "a practical working policy" to promote "the best interests of both black and white," Mennonites, as "a matter of expedience" had better "make some distinction to meet existing conditions." So the officials established as policy that a Black congregation should be "under a separate but auxiliary organization." Mission workers and congregation members might observe ordinances when meeting together, but "ordinances of footwashing and the kiss of charity should be practiced in each racial group" (in other words, separately). And "individual cups should be used in the communion service."[45]

Whatever the degree to which Mennonite missioners felt segregation to be something forced upon them, apparently everyone involved up through World War II assumed that they should bow to it for the sake of continuing their missions. If Argentina missionaries to some extent traded away testimony against militarism for the privilege of doing mission, home missionaries were even less inclined to say that gospel, to be gospel, had to speak against American race patterns. Some did deplore a need to segregate. When in 1934 it seemed necessary to open separate work for Mexicans in Chicago, Edwin Weaver, serving there before leaving as missionary to India, blamed the attitudes of people living around the Chicago Home Mission, especially foreigners. And P. A. Friesen and J. W. and Emma Shank, temporarily working in Chicago while on furlough from India and Argentina, felt that "there is so much race prejudice....It seems awful to us foreign missionaries...."[46]

Yet all concerned agreed that it was better to have a separate work. Moreover Friesen, unlike Weaver, blamed the situation mainly on country Mennonites who had moved to the city and become part of the Home Mission congregation (and there is some evidence to support his view).[47] The fact was, Mennonites more often saw segregation as a positive good than as something forced upon them, certainly more often as a positive good than as a failure to speak gospel. Many of Noah Good's other points were surely in that vein. Or in 1926 Selina Jennings of Concord, Tennessee, in an annual meeting address that represented the board's Rural Missions Committee report, quoted an Episcopalian source calling for accepting Blacks as "in reality brothers in Christ" without assimilating them racially, and another source asserting that "race feeling and discrimination are not southern but human characteristics." Of course that latter point was true enough. But to Selina Jennings it all meant that separate work for Negroes was "the natural, normal, the legal, the legitimate method of procedure in the south." She considered "shiftlessness and indolence" to be "racially innate" and thought that not to separate the work would bring failure. Nor did her words seem to trouble board members, board officials, or anyone else at annual board meeting.[48] In social attitudes Mennonite Church people were too much North Americans to question segregation of races.

All of that did not mean that the Mennonite Church's missioners were constantly preoccupied with ethnicism or race. Many, obviously, established warm confidence among various peoples. In 1914, a time when city mission meant primarily working with various ethnic groups, a committee of city missionaries introduced an account of city mission efforts by saying that if they were too candid about city people's feelings and experiences they would betray their people and tread on "sacred and forbidden ground."[49] The Eastern Board segregated its work for Blacks in the city of Lancaster in the 1930s, but workers there wanted quarters large enough so they could actually live among the people. Most of the time workers' reports from the Lancaster mission to Blacks showed no particular consciousness of color, or of working with people any different from other poor folks.[50] And it would seem that mission contacts did gradually teach Mennonites some greater empathy with minority peoples and their situations—however slowly and inadequately the Mennonites learned.

What it cost the "missioned" to be teachers of the Mennonites in that way, who can say? Compared to a U.S. nation that could not even pass a nationwide anti-lynching law, Mennonite mission people, with attitudes more or less like those of Noah Good, were perhaps fairly "enlightened." Yet there would come the day when the minority folks would witness forthrightly to Mennonites. In 1962, for instance, Vincent and Rosemarie Harding, Black Mennonites from Atlanta, would point out to an old-line Mennonite community that its people boycotted merchants who sold liquor, but resented boycotts for racial justice. Or earlier, about 1950, an Indian at Cass Lake, Minnesota, would stop Mennonite mission workers short. The workers had decided, without consulting the Indians, to try to avoid frictions between Indians and local Whites by constructing a separate building for Indian services. The one in charge got funds from Pennsylvania and began to build. But an Indian spokesman soon informed him that if Indians were not good enough for the Whites' church, they would not attend any Mennonite service. The building was never built.[51]

As usual where humans are involved, the case was not clear-cut. For at about the same time, also in Minnesota, another Indian testified that "the Mennonite people treat an Indian just like one of them. When I am in the church or when I visit with them, I feel like we are one big family," whereas "some churches think you are not good enough to be with them."[52] At best, mission-minded people of the Mennonite Church did establish empathy with minority people. Moreover, on the whole, they were fairly enlightened for their times and even at worst were not downright hateful. Yet some of them uttered cutting, irresponsible, inexcusable racial slurs. And so long as segregation was firmly a part of North American culture, almost none had asked whether the gospel and its love ethic ought not remove such a dividing wall. In the end courageous minority people such as that Cass Lake Indian or the Hardings had to bear much of the burden of bringing Mennonites to apply gospel and break down the walls.

So whatever empathy missioners and others in the Mennonite Church occasionally established among minority peoples, they also had much to repent of. They eventually did begin to repent of racism and segregation. But by that time enlightened North American opinion was also beginning to repent. And those who repent only when cultural forces call them to repent do not necessarily speak the gospel.

* * *

Or should no one expect a church's missioners to break very sharply with cultural patterns around them for the sake of the gospel, when those missioners are pretty much the ordinary folks of the church?

The outreach efforts of the Mennonite Church on the home field did involve many quite ordinary church members, especially by the 1930s and 1940s. At least the fact that so much of the initiative came from congregations, or at least was no more centralized than district conference or other area boards, suggests that. So also does the movement for "every congregation an outpost." The grass-roots pattern probably had its weaknesses. Not only did it perhaps mean slowness to recognize denial of gospel in a pattern such as segregation, it may have helped Mennonites fall into that easy habit of gearing up their evangelism to children. Child evangelism by Mennonite Church people may have been gentle, yet the question that eventually got raised, of whether it really fit with Mennonites' historic understandings of Christian commitment, was pertinent.

Actually, however, who can say that Mennonite Church "outposts" would have been less racially segregated, or less child-oriented, had home mission efforts of the Mennonite Church been more professionalized? And surely, almost any Christian group would say that getting its ordinary people involved in proclaiming gospel is a value in itself. Moreover, one reason that ordinary Mennonites got involved is that, by about 1930, Mennonite Church people saw their home mission field as lying more and more among rural folks.

9
Gospel at Home (II): The Rural Gospel

From the time in the late nineteenth century when Mennonite Church people began to do mission work, they set some strange patterns with regard to going or not going to rural areas. By that time Virginia Mennonites had of course begun to preach to rural mountain people without calling their effort "mission." Then the middle generation of quickened pretty much neglected the Andrew Crooks and instead let their youngsters begin mission in Chicago. Other youngsters, the Lancaster progressives, let themselves be checked more by church authority, and did begin more rurally. Thereafter, when it came to going to rural places as contrasted to going to cities (meaning, for statistical purposes here, urban centers with 100,000 or more people) or to towns (smaller cities that were more than merely shopping centers for rural people), the patterns continued to vary rather strangely.

A graph showing mission starts in rural areas, through time, looks familiar enough when done from raw numbers, as in Exhibit 9-2; for it more or less follows the line for total home mission starts. But a graph of percentages, as in Exhibit 9-3, shows rural mission starts rising and falling oddly. The two graphs of course reflect the data in Exhibit 9-1.

The early segments of the graphs in 9-2 and 9-3, up to 1900-1910, are hardly a mystery. As quickened Mennonites copied Protestant mission, home mission seemed to them more and more to mean city work. But in

Exhibit 9-1: Type of Community by Time (raw numbers are ave. number per 5 years; percentages are of all missions known to have begun in the time period)

	1861-90 (%)	1891-1900 (%)	1901-10 (%)	1911-20 (%)	1921-25 (%)	1926-30 (%)	1931-35 (%)	1936-40 (%)	1941-45 (%)	1946-50 (%)	1951-55 (%)	1956-60 (%)	TOTALS of 587 %*
A. Rural, rural village, rural town	6 (100)	11 (69)	7 (29)	13 (57)	10 (53)	9 (33)	29 (57)	37 (60)	36 (69)	83 (66)	74 (56)	24 (49)	339 (58*)
B. Town, more than just a rural center	---	3 (19)	10 (42)	7 (30)	5 (26)	15 (56)	15 (29)	17 (27)	12 (23)	24 (19)	30 (23)	12 (24)	150 (26*)
C. City, or city suburb or fringe (city of 100,000 or more)	---	2 (13)	6 (25)	2 (9)	3 (16)	1 (4)	4 (8)	3 (5)	4 (8)	11 (9)	22 (17)	13 (27)	71 (12*)
D. Mining camps, migrant camps, etc.	---	---	---	---	---	---	2 (7)	1 (2)	---	---	1 (1)	2 (2)	---	6 (1*)
No data	---	---	1 (4)	1 (4)	1 (5)	---	2 (4)	5 (8)	---	6 (5)	5 (4)	---	21 (4*)
													587

*Before adding to derive totals, multiply raw figures in 1861-1890 by 6 (to cover 6 five-year periods), and those between 1891 and 1920 by 2.

Exhibit 9-2: Kind of Community by Time (Raw numbers*), Graphed

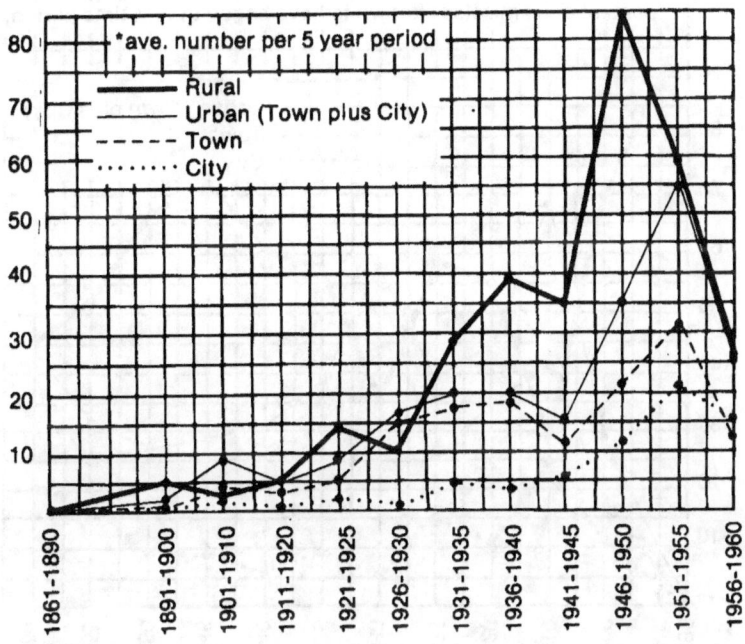

practice towns were more convenient. The lines for the time between 1910 and 1930 are more baffling. No doubt the upsurge in rural work's percentage (Exhibit 9-3), until it clearly reached first place, came largely because the first flush of Mennonite Church enthusiasm for city work was passing. The Youngstown story would surely suggest that inference, as would some persistent problems elsewhere, for instance in Chicago.[1] Perhaps World War I interfered with city and town missions more than with rural, although Mennonites' nonresistance apparently repelled some country folks also.[2] The strange fluctuation about 1926-1930, when town mission starts moved temporarily back into first place, remains the largest puzzle. Perhaps that change was mainly accidental. It could well have been, since missions then were still relatively few and therefore the raw numbers in the data so small as to be easily able to fluctuate widely, percentagewise. Or perhaps some problem in quality has made the data inconsistent. Whatever the cause or causes of that

Exhibit 9-3: Kind of Community by Time (Percentages*), Graphed

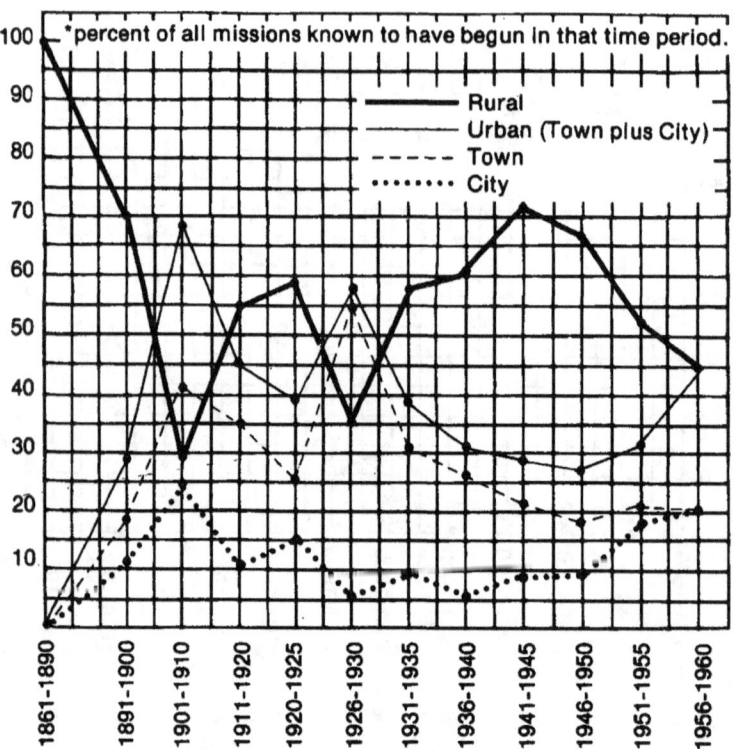

1926-1930 fluctuation, however, the longer-term pattern is clear. After about 1930 rural mission beginnings moved into a strong first place—even well above all urban starts, town and city combined.[3]

* * *

The period of increase in rural starts from about 1910 into the 1920s, a time of more modest rise and yet almost a doubling from decade to decade, occurred just when there was in the U.S. at large a well-defined movement to renew and reassert the values of country life. That national movement seemed to evoke from Mennonite Church people new arguments for rural mission, ranging from we-are-after-all-a-rural-people to rural work being an expression of manhood. In the end those arguments fell more or less into three patterns.

In 1908 U.S. President Theodore Roosevelt sponsored a White House Conference on Country Life and followed it with a Commission that in 1909 published what in some circles became a much-heralded report.[4] Very soon, mainline Protestant denominations and interdenominational organizations (the informally established church in the U.S.?) echoed the Commission's sounds. And almost immediately Mennonites also began to resonate, despite their long-held idea that church was a people quite distinct from nation. Already before 1908 a few Mennonite Church voices had been calling for more emphasis on rural mission. Now the sound sharply increased.

Just why churches and particularly the Mennonite Church needed government to help tell them where to do mission work, defies all explanation. But in 1910 the northern Presbyterians, as a denomination, created a "Department of Church and Country Life" with one Rev. Warren H. Wilson as its head. Wilson (who had actually begun actively to promote country church renewal a bit before Roosevelt's public moves) went on to become probably the strongest leader, nationwide, of the rural church movement. Meanwhile an influential, interdenominational Home Missions Council of North America made some mission surveys in rural states, then in 1912 created a Committee on Rural Fields to promote such missions. By 1913 the Federal Council of Churches of Christ in America created a similar committee. Northern Methodists established a Department of Rural Work in 1916, Congregationalists a similar body in 1919, Episcopalians likewise in 1924, southern Presbyterians in 1925. ...And so forth.[5]

Mennonite Church people who echoed the country life movement and its related rural-mission ideas did so mainly in a home magazine that their church published, the *Christian Monitor*. In 1909 the *Monitor* ran a quick summary of the country life commission's report. By late 1912 both it and the *Gospel Herald* devoted issues especially to rural mission, the *Monitor* repeating that strategy from time to time thereafter.[6] One writer in that 1912 *Monitor* number, Goshen College student Crissie Yoder (later, married to Charles Shank, a missionary to India), quoted extensively from a 1911 book by Rev. Wilson. And another, one J. J. Fisher of Iowa, clearly borrowed from it, even using one of its illustrations, without acknowledgment. In the *Gospel Herald* issue Mabel Silcock, a Mennonite Church member of Tuleta, Texas, observed that "some of the larger denominations...are turning their attention to the country." Yes, agreed a *Monitor* editorial in a rural-missions issue in 1914. "No religious movement in America today is more significant and hopeful than the revival of interest in the rural Church."[7]

Mabel Silcock went on to imply that especially Mennonites should take up the cause, for the centuries had made ruralness "a part of their being." That was a point Mennonite Church people repeated often. Mennonites were 98 percent rural, insisted Indiana-Michigan bishop and district board secretary Jacob (J. K.) Bixler in 1916, citing census figures; so rural work was their natural calling. Usually the argument came in that simple, straightforward version, but especially the editors of the *Monitor* sometimes varied it. Actually Mennonites were becoming less isolated in their rural areas, declared editor H. Frank Reist in 1919, and so they had better help build up the countryside's spiritual resources. Then the country would be more able to hold back bad influences from the city. Or in 1921 a new editor, Vernon Smucker, declared that the church could be a strong base for foreign mission only if it built itself up in rural areas at home.[8]

In 1910, with the country life movement aborning, the Young Men's Christian Association began a magazine called *Rural Manhood*. And sure enough, Mennonites also took up that theme. Some speakers or writers in the Mennonite Church were arguing that rural work did not require brilliance or advanced education. But in 1916 *Monitor* editor Reist publicly objected, and deplored any suggestion that rural work required anything less than "the most talented young Christian manhood." (Like mission advocates so often did, Reist seemed to ignore the fact that women were a strong part of both the general and the Mennonite missionary movements.) Shortly after World War I India missionary George Lapp, temporarily in North America and serving as president of Goshen College, spoke in similar tone. Young Mennonite men were ready for rural work, he said; they had stood up bravely as conscientious objectors in wartime, and now they were willing to go to remote corners and "die on the great battlefield of Christian service."[9]

Between those two poles—Mennonites as a humble rural folk and Mennonites as ready to do red-blooded battle—lay various other arguments. Some Mennonites played still more tunes using that old theme of the badness of cities and city living. Some, borrowing especially heavily from the larger country life and rural church movements, and sounding almost social-gospelish, called for rural reconstruction (what by the 1970s would go by the name "community development"). Or some argued economy and effectiveness. Religious studies or Mennonite

The Rural Gospel

experience showed, the assertions ran, that rural people responded to gospel more readily, and backslid less, than did city folks. Besides, in rural districts missionaries could at least keep gardens, and maybe could support themselves almost entirely.[10] To that last idea, however, still others dissented, and called for the Mennonite Church to bring as much system and support to rural as to city work.[11] Clearly these wanted to make rural effort into systematic, organized *mission,* rather than something growing just out of natural and informal contacts. And in 1919 the general mission board, in keeping with what Protestant denominations were doing, created a Committee on Rural Missions and Evangelizing.[12]

Gradually the various lines of reasoning fell more or less into three patterns.

The first actually meant less reasoning. By the mid-1920s Mennonite Church people seemed to offer less and less analysis for why they should go into rural work, and instead just asserted the idea as an axiom that was natural, obvious, and self-evident. So by the latter 1920s, and for a quarter-century or so thereafter, rural-gospelism was for Mennonite Church people a matter of conventional wisdom.

Second, urban evils that had once been calls to city mission now became enemies of city work and reasons to stay in open country. In 1906 Ft. Wayne, Indiana mission superintendent B. B. King had, typically, reminded fellow-Mennonites that cities abounded with vice, liquor, billiards, card-playing, dancing, and prostitution. But he also reminded them that where sin abounded, grace abounded much more.[13] Now, to serve the rural gospel, the logic flowed the other way. Not only did the city drag too many converts back to sin, but those who remained faithful did so only in spite of, not because of, city environments. Mennonites could teach the simple life more easily in rural areas. Moreover, ran some arguments, city missions had the unfortunate effect of encouraging Mennonites themselves to move cityward, and urban congregations tended to cause the church more trouble. By contrast, more active rural work would make the city seem less attractive to Mennonite youth.[14]

The country was "more desirable for our children," board president C. Z. Yoder argued in 1912, referring apparently to the children of home missionaries themselves. That argument, of course, like so much of the Mennonite mission movement, showed Mennonites responding to their own needs more than to needs of others. But in others the view was larger. City and country now depended upon and influenced each other, declared the *Monitor* in 1919. So a good strategy even for taking the gospel to the city was to evangelize rural folks before they moved there. Then, they could be the influence the evil city needed.[15]

So the logic changed its course, and formed a second new pattern. Where mission advocates had earlier called upon Mennonites to challenge city sin head-on, now they were much more likely to make the city's evils a chief reason for staying and working in rural places.

* * *

A third shift in pattern got to the very question of what Mennonites considered gospel to be.

The larger rural church movement got underway just as Fundamentalism was making a social emphasis less and less respectable in some Protestant circles, and just before Fundamentalism's deep inroads among Mennonites. The country life commission's report, Rev. Wilson's writings, and much of that rural church movement, as they called the churches in broad social and economic terms to take up the task of rural reconstruction, breathed heavily of the Social Gospel. Thus they often treated church much less as new communities of God's people than as a network of local community centers, as an institution to help give the nation its social fabric, and in general, as the U.S. version of established religion. Occasionally even a Mennonite sounded as if the unit for salvation was indeed the community or the nation, as an out-and-out Social Gospeller might imply, rather than the individual. "It behooves the Mennonite Church, as a rural people [,] to save the country community for Jesus Christ," declared one William Weaver of Goshen, Indiana, in a 1914 issue of the *Monitor*. Asserted an Ontario minister, Lewis (L. J.) Burkholder, as late as 1921: "The *rural population must be increased* and a *strong religious life be established"* in order "to save the North American nations from moral decay."[16]

Actually, however, those in the Mennonite Church who echoed the rural church movement stayed within the framework of a socially conscious evangelicalism. No one or at least virtually no one preached the Social Gospel, in the sense of making salvation a matter *primarily* of social reform. Indeed, the Mennonite voices sometimes made their rural emphasis into an escape from having to face a set of problems that Protestant Social Gospellers were eagerly attacking: the problems that industrialism was creating in cities. Time and again Mennonites declared that in rural work they would not have to deal (as field-worker Allgyer put it at annual board meeting in 1915) with "life insurance agencies, labor unions, Sunday and night work, theatres, picture shows, saloons, and other evils."[17]

Yet for rural areas, the same Mennonites wanted to work at a fairly broad range of problems, including economic and social ones. Even as he wanted to escape questions such as labor unions, Allgyer in that 1915 address called for men to go into backward rural places as self-supporting farmer-ministers who could give broad community leadership: "consecrated young men, born of the Spirit, men with push, who are able to develop agricultural, educational and religious interests in the neglected communities." Another spokesman, writing as "A Layman" in the *Monitor* of 1912, thought that the ideal rural missionary needed to study scientific agriculture more than theology—to be a practical example to his community, and to make farming "a *part of* and not *apart* from his mission work." William Weaver, in his 1914 piece, went on to say that "a community-serving Church will not only save every man in the community as far as possible but it will also save the *whole* man." By that Weaver meant that it would "be interested in the man's physical and intellectual as well as spiritual welfare," and would "care for the sick, the poor and [the] needy."[18]

So however baffled they were at social and economic problems of cities, quite a few rural-work advocates in the Mennonite Church of the 'teens were eager to attack social and economic problems in rural areas. As Weaver's "save every man" phrase implied, in the end they still saw basic salvation in individual terms. But if they did not look ultimately to a new social order for humans' deliverance, they at least thought it was the business of Christians to work at specific social and economic problems, and to provide a broad range of services. That added up to a socially conscious evangelicalism, of a kind that, before the Social Gospel movement and then Fundamentalism, had thrived in America without any sense of contradiction.[19] Mennonite Church people had borrowed that socially-conscious kind, in their quickening.

By 1920 of course, in some Protestant circles, Fundamentalists were making such social and economic emphases more suspect—partly, at least some analyses would say, due to some Social Gospellers' excesses.[20] With that development, the tone of Mennonite rural-mission talk changed perceptibly. A round-table discussion at annual board meeting in 1919, for instance, still emphasized that the rural missionary should be a good farmer, but now he was not to lose "himself in the soil; he should be a good soul winner."[21]

Hardly anyone could have reflected the change better than did bishop Bixler, the Indiana-Michigan district board secretary, who by then had become perhaps the most avid promoter of Mennonites' working in rural areas. In the mid-'teens he could write very much in the style of the larger rural church movement, declaring that Mennonites needed "to have our leaders able to instruct in crop culture as well as in the Gospel of Christ"—or that "the future of the rural church depends on her interest in rural development." To be sure, he also spoke of house-to-house evangelism in the countryside, not just social and economic work. And he warned against using the Sunday pulpit for lectures on "farming, dairying, or marketing." But the warnings were his of-course-we-must-remember-also kind of statement more than being his main point—until about 1920, when he shifted.[22]

In an Indiana-Michigan district paper he edited and called the *Rural Evangel,* Bixler still wrote approvingly in 1920 about what the Commission on Country Life had said on some matters back in 1909, and he still conceded that "the Church performs a social function." In 1924 he still spoke of the church, for rural areas, needing a "program of service." In 1925 he might still cite a sociological survey to make a point, and comment that "the rural Church problem is vitally associated with the agricultural and economic conditions of the community." But his main point was changing. In that 1925 case, he used the sociological data not to say that social and economic needs called for response in themselves, but to show how they hurt the church. For he made the point that depressed rural conditions were forcing strong people to move away, robbing the church of potential leaders. Already in 1920 he had noted "with regret" that "surveys of rural conditions" tended to "treat the Church from a sociological viewpoint only."[23]

Or in 1924, when he called for a "program of service," he set up a test rejecting all activities that did not somehow "aid the Church to function as a soul-saving and recruiting station." To be a "strong rural church," Bixler now emphasized, (1) meant to teach "not only the ordinances and restrictions...but the groundwork of the Christian Faith," and "the Bible as a whole and as it is." (2) It meant having a strong passion for souls, teaching strongly on mission, and having evangelistic outreach. That kind of reaching out to the "outcasts" of the community (as he put it in 1925) was clearly what Bixler now meant by a "program of service." (3) The strong rural church provided activities of a kind that led not to worldliness but to sacrifice, and to sharing others' "needs and burdens." And (4) the healthy rural church exercised discipline that led "violators to see their error" and to repent.[24]

By no means had Bixler completely repudiated his earlier rural reconstructionism, and his new formulas had some social vision. But the emphasis had shifted. And that shift was part of a larger one in the Mennonite Church. More important than Bixler's district paper, in churchwide influence, was the *Monitor*. In 1923 the *Monitor* got a new person to sit in the chair in which the rural-reconstruction-minded Frank Reist had recently sat, and the new editor had a much more strictly soul-saving view of evangelism. He was the popular, premillennialist, Fundamentalistic Mennonite revivalist Clayton F. Derstine.

Thereafter, except for what still appeared in articles mainly by Bixler, the *Monitor* communicated virtually nothing of the rural-reconstruction vision.[25] That vision would not appear prominently in the Mennonite Church until a decade and more later, when Guy F. Hershberger and others put forward a set of ideas for revitalizing Mennonite community. Hershberger outlined those ideas as early as 1939, and expressed them especially in some church committee reports during the early 1940s. But he and others managed to spread them more widely only after they formed a Mennonite Community Association in 1946, which from 1947 to 1953 published a magazine with the title *The Mennonite Community*. Until the early 1960s the Association spread ideas (not always just rural ones) through means such as conferences on various social and economic questions.[26] As a look back at Exhibits 9-2 and 9-3 will show, that movement's more public activity got going just when Mennonite Church people were bringing their rural outreach starts to that high, post-World War II peak.

Did the Mennonite Community movement and its new rural reconstructionism somehow create that peak? Probably not. Although those in the movement sometimes connected their ideas with mission,[27] they were less inclined to start from the standard ideas of mission than the earlier rural reconstructionists had been. Moreover, the rural mission curve had been moving upward well before the community movement was really underway. In fact it began to drop off just as the movement was really going public. Probably both developments—that peak in rural mission starts, and the community movement—were products of still other influences. Perhaps an influence on both was groundwork that the earlier rural reconstructionists had laid. Even stronger, no doubt, were urban forces pushing in on Mennonite Church people. Apparently Mennonite Church people were becoming more and more self-conscious about ruralness because of that push, and were responding in various ways—a main one being rural missions, and another the

Mennonite Community movement. Not that growing urbanism exactly determined the responses. Surely Mennonites' faith and theological understandings deeply influenced *how* they responded.

In the end, in any case, Mennonite Church people were not quite willing to call rural reconstructionism "mission." In earlier days they had done so, for on Welsh Mountain and elsewhere they had spoken of "industrial mission." They had almost done so also when rural-reconstruction talk was running high. But after about 1920 and at least until those rural mission starts had passed their peak, their idea of the nature of gospel did not quite allow for that. The retreat from rural reconstructionism, then, formed a third pattern in the logic of Mennonite rural mission.

* * *

Exhibit 9-4: Comparison of Movements, Rural Mission Starts with Selected Phenomena...(rates per 5 year period): Raw Figures Adjusted to Make Each Curve Peak at Same Height as Peak in Rural Mission Starts Curve, Thus Emphasizing Similarities or Differences in Slope and Shape

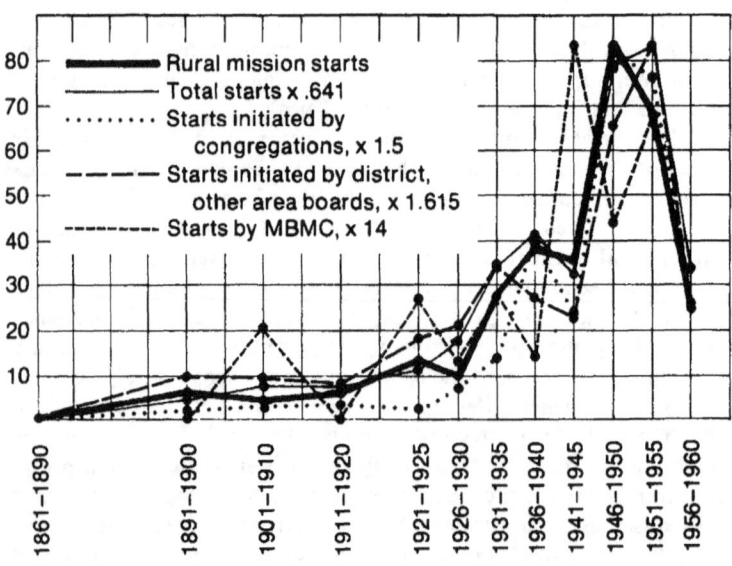

The Rural Gospel

If the sharp rise in rural outreach starts began while rural reconstructionism was in a lull, was the rise then due to that more Fundamentalist-style narrowing and sharpening of the focus of rural mission? Was it a result of making mission a more "spiritual" or "soul-saving" ministry, without the social and economic burden? Perhaps. The data hardly prove any answer, either yes or no. They do show very clearly, however, two other points. (1) The curve of rural mission starts and that for starts by congregational initiative were very alike in shape and timing, especially in the heyday when both reached their peaks. And (2) the rural-mission-starts curve was far less similar to the pattern of starts by the general board. The curve for local and district board initiative was somewhat like the rural mission curve, but not nearly as much so as was the curve for congregational initiative. The evidence is especially clear when graphed with certain adjustments, to make each curve peak at the same level on the graph, as has been done in Exhibit 9-4.

If one assumes that Fundamentalism got its foothold in the Mennonite Church about 1920, surely the curves of Exhibit 9-4 do not show that the Fundamentalists' more narrow and sharply focused "spiritual" concept of mission took Mennonites to rural areas more than to other places. After 1920 total mission starts turned upward sooner than did rural ones. Rural ones in fact took that slight dip in the latter 1920s, a fairly sharp dip if expressed as percentage of total starts as in Exhibit 9-3.

Did the more "spiritual" approach nevertheless eventually stimulate rural mission starts along with others? In other words, was a more Fundamentalist style nevertheless responsible for the sharp increases in the 1930s and the 1940s? Again, it may have been, but the curves offer no proof. Although 1920 is a convenient date for marking its coming, Fundamentalism did not take hold suddenly enough for firm conclusions. Moreover for the 'teens and the 1920s, when the new emphases were taking root, the lines move too erratically to prove much of anything. If the new emphases were responsible for the sharp rise in rural activity, their influence apparently came only after a time of settling into place.

More probably the explanations for the rural curve's rise are otherwise, and more or less the same as those for total mission starts. Specific discussion of rural mission no doubt added some height to the rural mission curve, yet the pillars that held it up were surely the more general influences. Those were first of all the effect of people fully nurtured on the quickening coming to maturity and inheriting control. Some of those people had turned to Fundamentalism, of course, but the quickening itself had built upon a broader kind of evangelicalism of which Mennonite Fundamentalism then became only a part. Something was bearing fruit in the 1930s and 1940s, but most probably it was an evangelicalism broader than only Fundamentalism—in the rural curve as in the others. And along with that evangelicalism were those other ingredients: organization and leadership reflected especially in the formation, between 1911 and 1920, of many district boards; and, a bit later on, the every-congregation-an-outpost formula. Very probably these, more than Fundamentalism's trimming of social and economic work from mission, explain the rise of the rural work curve.[28]

Mennonite Fundamentalism simply did not have clear enough character and sharp enough limits for anyone to indicate precisely how it affected rural or any other mission starts—especially not for anyone to distinguish its influence from that of the more general evangelicalism that Mennonites had earlier imbibed. On a specific issue such as rural reconstructionism it could have a clearer effect. For as Mennonites shaped that issue, the debate was between two versions of evangelicalism, one that had more room for social consciousness and one that had less. But where the two kinds of evangelicalism agreed, as on the larger question of whether there should be rural missions, the special character of Fundamentalism was hardly distinct enough to allow judgments about its particular role.

Much clearer than Fundamentalism's influence were those other two facts: of some definite relationship between rural-work curve and congregational effort, and of very little connection between it and general board effort.

The rural-work and the congregational-initiative curves did not move together absolutely. As Exhibit 9-4 makes clear, the two curves show decidedly different movement in the 1920s, and somewhat different in the 1930s and during World War II. Yet after 1930 their movements were always in the same directions, at least; and during those final, peak post-World War II years, their shapes were so alike as to be almost uncanny. Indeed, a quick glance might suggest that congregational activity accomplished that final great rise and then decline in rural mission starts, and did so almost singlehandedly.

But...might the relationship have run mainly in the other direction—that is, with the idea of rural mission moving congregations to action? Or both ways, interacting? And does the similarity of the two

The Rural Gospel

curves really tell why, percentagewise, rural starts dropped sharply after 1946-1950 while starts in urban places (town plus city) rose percentagewise, and for a while even in raw numbers? Urban starts increased compared to rural, to the point that back in Exhibit 9-3 rural and urban percentage lines actually cross in 1956-1960. After all, by the 1950s a much higher percentage of North Americans lived in urban areas than in the early days of Mennonite Church mission. And Mennonites themselves were becoming more a town and city people so that presumably many even of their "natural" contacts were urban ones.

Yet the rural and the congregational-initiative curves apparently followed each other more closely than they followed anything else in the data. If various influences caused both of them to drop after 1946-1950, those influences must have worked the same way on both of them, or else on one via the other. One way or another, after about 1930 and especially after World War II, there must have been some very close relationship between congregational initiative and rural starts.

On the other hand, there was very little relationship between rural starts and starts initiated by the general board.

The Mennonite Board of Missions and Charities and its officials were generally reluctant to take initiative on the home field, believing—whether out of a legitimate kind of church politics or more from principle—that within the geographical areas of district conferences and their district boards, they should tread lightly.[29] Yet that was not the whole story, for of course in Texas they did work out accommodations that let them start work for Spanish-speaking people.[30] Moreover for the southern highlands, the region stretching from the Ozarks through the Appalachians, the board and its officials felt free at least to think about beginning new outreach.

As Bixler, the *Monitor*, and others were leaving the rural reconstruction approach, board secretary Yoder and others held onto it, for the southern highlands, a bit longer. In the 1920s Yoder wrote to people in various Protestant denominations or in interdenominational organizations for information about what the highlands needed, and his correspondents generally fit the rural-reconstructionist pattern. Those Episcopal and other sources that Selina Jennings quoted in the mid-1920s on behalf of the board's Rural Missions Committee were more or less rural reconstuction also. The strongest proposal that Yoder and others considered for the highlands in the 1920s was to take up educational work, either establishing a Mennonite school somewhere or at least sending teachers for public ones. Also, there were suggestions for medical work, and Yoder wrote generally of the challenge of the region's poverty.[31]

Meantime, of course, board people and others also considered more "direct" evangelism. Particularly in the Ozarks where that outstanding rural missionary J. R. Shank was working, Mennonites living in or near highland areas did gospel touring and the like. As Rural Missions Committee chairman, Yoder himself emphasized direct evangelism, saying by 1928 that personally he thought any effort in the highlands should be mainly for "spreading the Gospel," and that "whatever else is done must be contributory to that end in a very direct and positive way." Shank, also a committee member, agreed. For some time he had been skeptical of other denominations' organizing their work too highly, and had counseled that the rural missionary had to be flexible and work with small bands of believers. "I too feel that the main effort should be ... evangelization," he advisd Yoder in 1928. "... You will often find that schools do not appeal to the people ... in these sections."[32]

J. L. Stauffer, thoroughly Mennonite-Fundamentalist teacher at Eastern Mennonite School in Virginia and third member of the committee, was even more emphatic. He was willing to acquaint himself with other denominations' "various institutional efforts," he advised Yoder, also in 1928. But he understood that various denominations were "retrenching." So in the highlands, Mennonites had better be pretty slow about taking the institutional path. "There is one line of work that I know is safe," Stauffer advised: Station two workers at a place and let them "give their time wholly to evangelism."[33]

As matters turned out, the general board did almost nothing of substance in the highlands. In 1929 and 1930 field-worker Allgyer finally, after almost a decade of talk, took two tours of Appalachian areas. On them he did not hesitate to consult missionaries who were running industrial schools and the like, yet apparently his main idea was to find a location for starting a Sunday school and eventually a church. But he and others (two Mennonites of the region accompanied him in his travels) found virtually no place they considered promising for the board to sponsor work.[34] So deep was the inaction that an official board resolution of 1933 noted "with regret" that the years had brought only "spasmodic interest in and support of rural missions," while at the same time the Rural Missions Committee said lamely that "we have nothing definite to report." The next year the committee professed faith that there was work to do in mountain districts, but said it was waiting for

The Rural Gospel 279

authority to make further investigation. In 1935 it did not bother to report.[35]

That is about where matters continued through the 1930s, and as late as 1943 the general board's involvement in the southern highlands was still mainly to discuss and to authorize more survey.[36] No doubt the Great Depression and lack of money held board officials back. But even before the Great Depression, the rural reconstructionism underlying some of Yoder's and others' interest in the southern highlands had fallen more or less from the Mennonite Church's favor. Also, the jurisdictional problem could be very real. For instance, in 1932, regarding work near the Mennonite congregation at Concord, Tennessee, board treasurer Vernon Reiff felt that Virginia Conference officials were at odds with the board's efforts to help.[37] Whether or not Reiff's feelings were justified, they were strong enough to suggest that, more than board officials were usually willing to say aloud, jurisdictional friction helped make the board afraid to act in the highlands region.

The story of Spanish-language work and its beginnings in Texas is of course happier.

Even there, the board moved slowly. Mennonites here and there proposed such work from at least 1892, when Reuben (R. J.) Heatwole suggested it to *Herald of Truth* readers. In 1920 Allgyer and D. H. Bender took a southern tour for the board, visiting Upland in Louisiana; San Antonio, Brownsville, and El Paso in Texas; Phoenix and Yuma in Arizona; and San Diego in California. In the usual fashion, along the way they consulted missionaries already there for other denominations. Upon return they concluded that Mennonites should open work in Phoenix, but also mentioned smaller towns in Texas; and in 1921 board secretary J. S. Shoemaker said informally that the board wanted to "open work on the borders of Mexico as soon as workers are available." In 1921 also, the board's executive committee encouraged/one William Nunemaker of La Junta, Colorado to move to Phoenix, find employment, learn Spanish, and watch further for the proper place and time to open work. But 1921-1922 brought a downturn in the U.S. economy, and the committee soon advised Nunemaker that "we can not crowd the opening of the work among the Mexicans in view of all the other demands on the Board."[38]

Thereafter not much happened until 1936. Then the board sent T. K. Hershey to scout out possibilities, and with him a home missionary from Canton, Ohio named William G. Detweiler, soon much better known for pioneering Mennonite Church outreach by radio, but at the

Exhibit 9-5: Types of Communities to Which the Different Initiating Groups Tended to Go

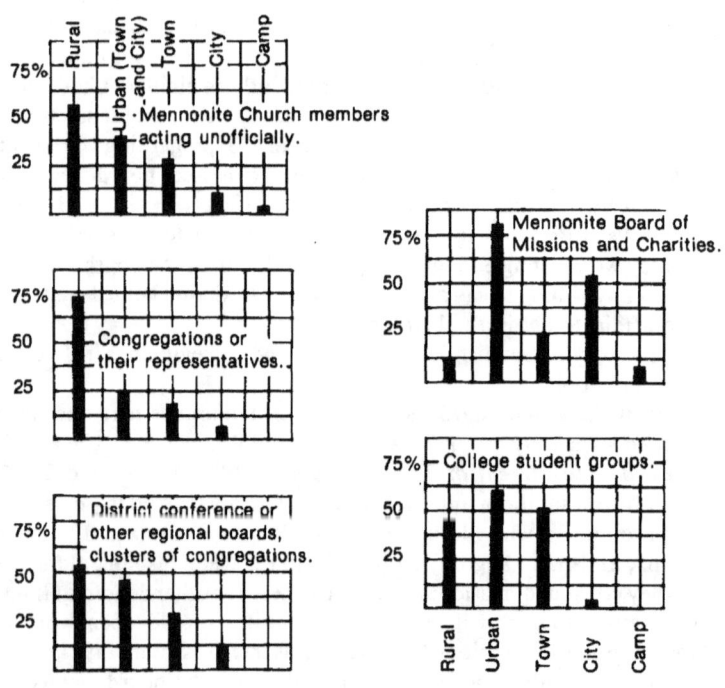

time strongly inclined to learn Spanish and go to work in the Southwest. The board was still concerned with economy in 1936, but now reasoned another way. Now the idea was that there were many qualified young people in the Mennonite Church who wanted to do mission work, but the board could not afford to send them abroad; and work among Mexican-Americans could be a substitute.[39] So it had Hershey open the work, and soon of course sent Amsa and Nona Kauffman to take charge. All concerned worked out the plans whereby a bishop of the Missouri-Kansas conference ordained Amsa Kauffman and baptized new members, without the new congregations having to observe some of the

Mennonite distinctives in exactly the way that the conference required elsewhere.[40]

Clearly the board was able to proceed as it did in Texas because the established Mennonites of the region recognized Mexican-Americans as being a distinctly different people, for practical purposes a "foreign" field. Also, Hershey's forceful go-ahead style, a style that the unpaid, conciliatory secretary Yoder and the rest of the board rather lacked, helped make the difference. In any case, the Spanish-language work in Texas became the major case of board initiative to open rural missions on a home field. But the case was about as exceptional as it was outstanding.

Another set of graphs, those of Exhibit 9-5, make still more clear the close relation of rural work with congregational initiative, and how different was the case especially of the general board. And maps in Exhibit 9-6 show how the Mennonite Church's home missions—urban, camp, and rural—spread geographically. However they started, Mennonite home missions dotted more and more states and provinces, often because of rural outreach.

Not all the rural effort brought success, at least not by ordinary human calculations. Given some tendency on the part of Mennonites to turn nearby mission congregations into congregations made up largely of people from old-line Mennonite families, one might guess that rural missions produced independent congregations in a higher percentage of cases than did urban ones. Yet, as Exhibit 9-7 shows, the percentage of such "success" in rural missions was slightly lower than the percentage for all known mission starts. Although city missions succeeded far less often, town missions appear to have been somewhat more "successful" than rural, if measured by percentages of cases resulting in independent congregations.

In the Ozarks, for instance, despite the stature and the hard work of J. R. Shank, numbers of congregations established and of people attracted permanently into the Mennonite fellowship were in the long run quite low. By the 1970s there were only a half-dozen congregations, totaling only about 100 members. Of course, the opening of the Bagnell Dam in 1930 and the way it dislocated people are part of the explanation and soften the appearance of failure. But matters such as Mennonites' unpopularity in wartime, perhaps overly stiff application of some Mennonite distinctives, and surely general economic and social conditions of the region each played some part.[41]

Not only in the Ozarks but more generally, the number of rural

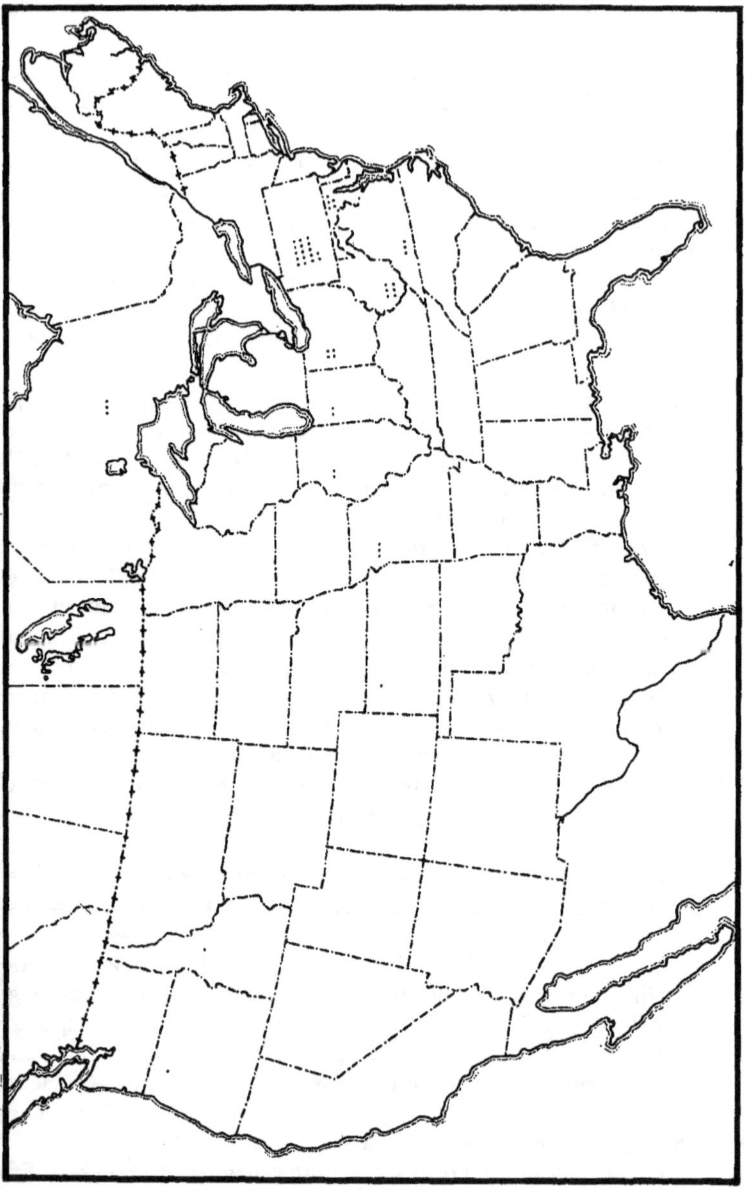

Exhibit 9-6a: Geographical Distribution. New Starts in States and Provinces by 1910.
(Each dot represents one mission begun.)

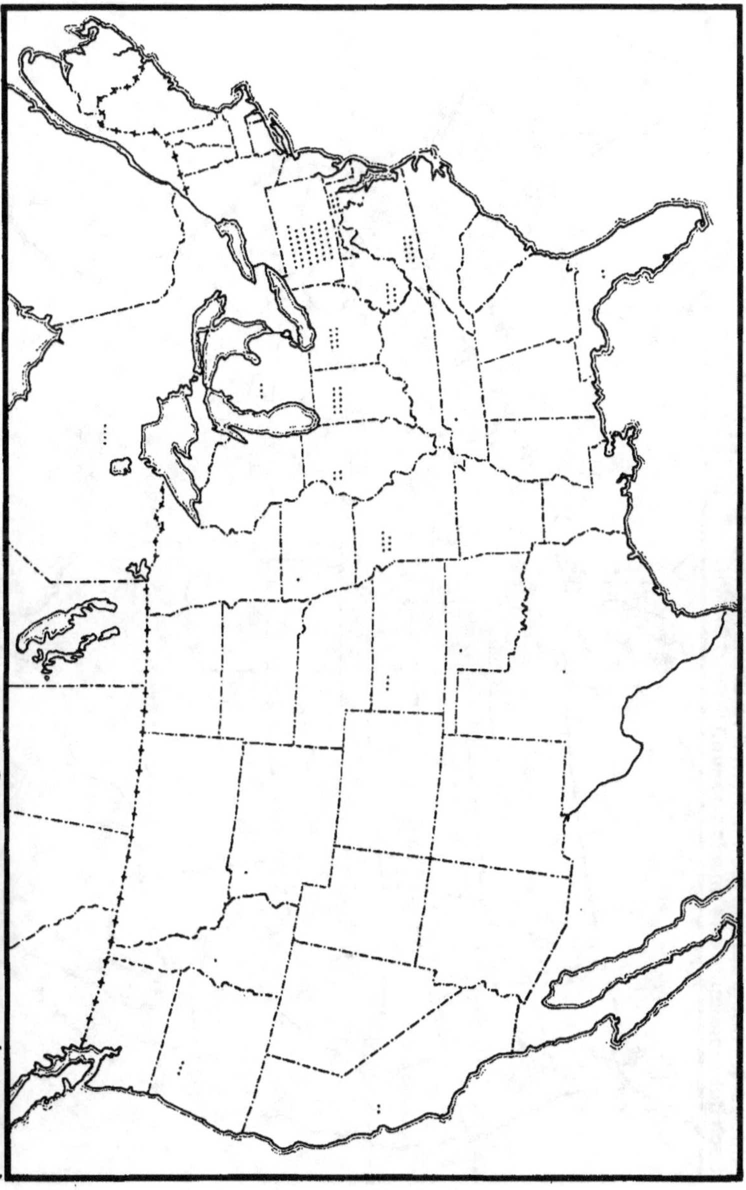

Exhibit 9-6b: Geographical Distribution. New Starts in States and Provinces by 1930. (Each dot represents one mission begun.)

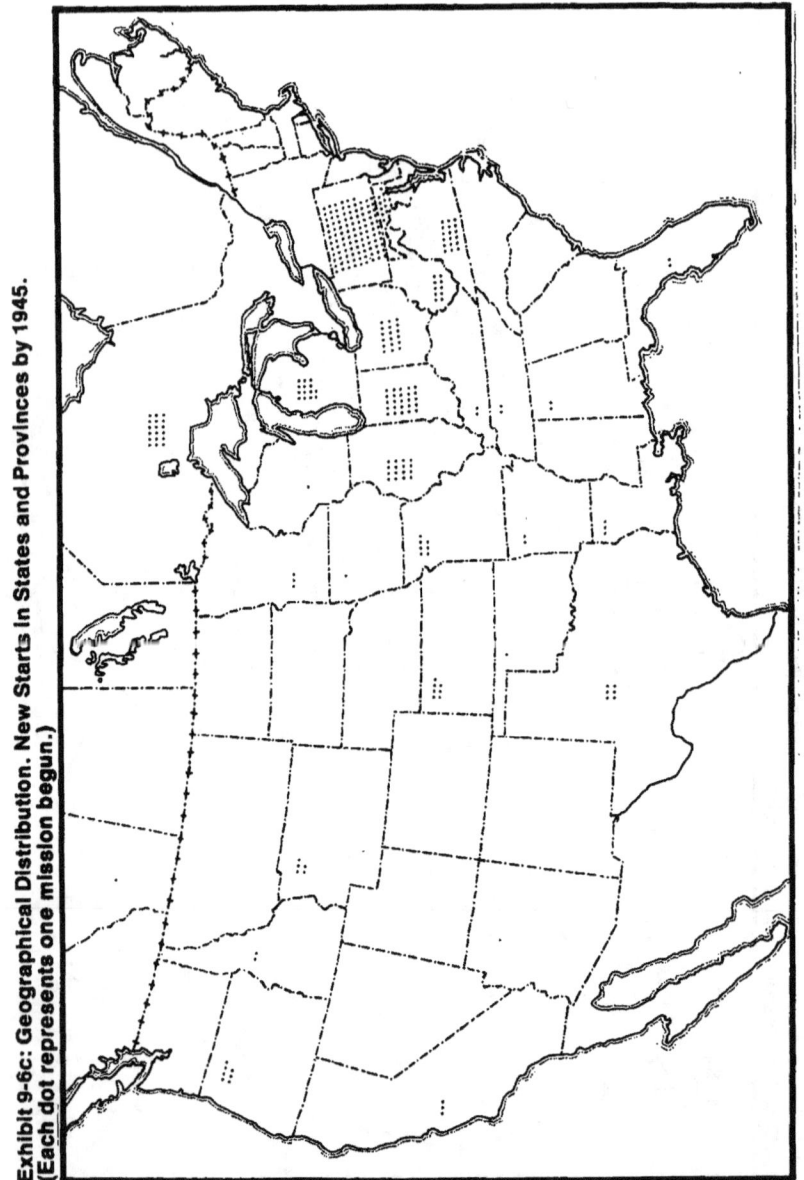

Exhibit 9-6c: Geographical Distribution. New Starts in States and Provinces by 1945. (Each dot represents one mission begun.)

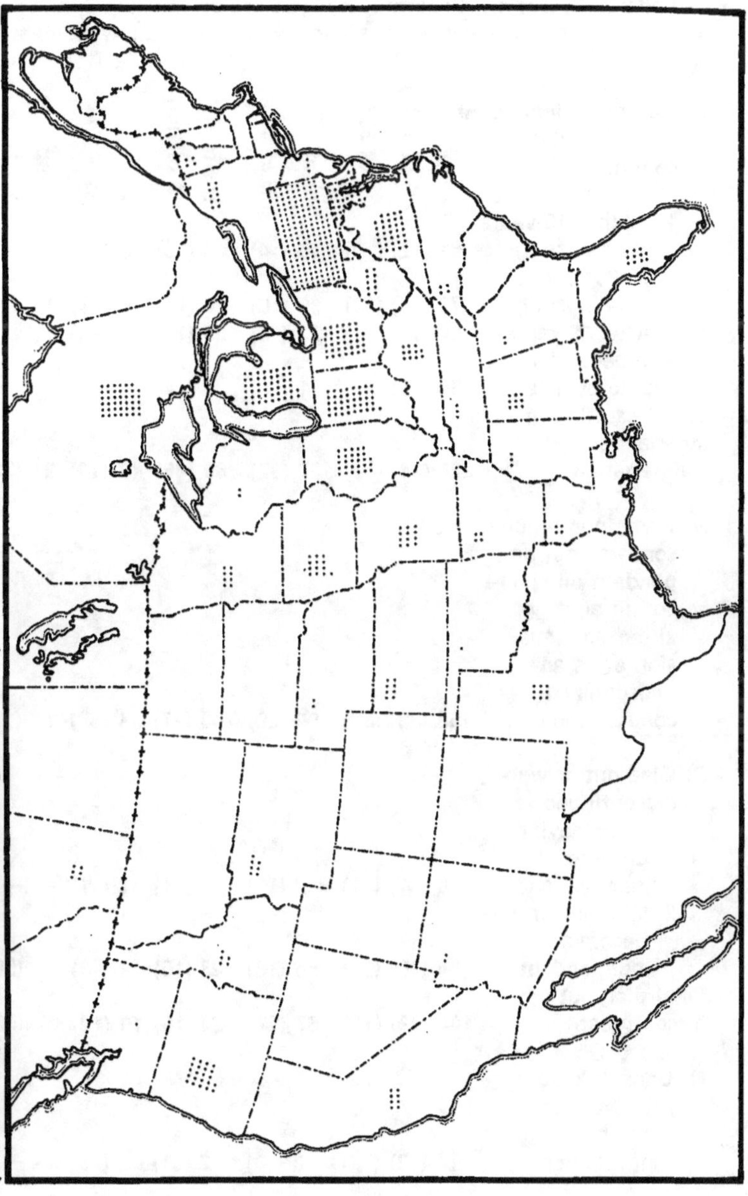

The Rural Gospel 285

Exhibit 9-6d: Geographical Distribution. New Starts in States and Provinces by 1960.
(Each dot represents one mission begun.)

Exhibit 9-7: Outcomes, Compared by Type of Community
(Percentages are of all know starts in the type of community indicated).

	Total (% of 516*)	(% of 587)	Rural (% of 339)	Town (% of 150)	City (% of 71)	Camp (% of 6)
A. Became independent (by 1974) and continued						
1. Within 10 years after starting	61 (12)	(10)	46 (14)	8 (5)	3 (4)	— —
2. 10-20 years after starting	72 (14)	(12)	33 (10)	26 (17)	5 (7)	1 (17)
3. After 20 years	64 (12)	(11)	27 (8)	29 (19)	4 (6)	1 (17)
4. Independent at unknown date	30 (6)	(5)	21 (6)	6 (4)	1 —	—
Total resulting in independent congregations	**227 (44)**	**(39)**	**127 (37)**	**69 (46)**	**13 (18)**	**2 (33)**
B. Remained a going concern, but dependent on sponsoring agency either as a mission or as an unorganized congregation	168 (33)	(29)	89 (29)	40 (27)	34 (48)	1 (17)
C. Died out or were discontinued						
1. After having become independent	6 (1)	(1)	2 (1)	1 (1)	1 (1)	— —
2. Without first becoming independent	94 (18)	(16)	55 (16)	23 (15)	9 (13)	3 (50)
Total died out or discontinued	**100 (19)**	**(17)**	**57 (17)**	**24 (16)**	**10 (14)**	**3 (50)**
D. Consolidated with another mission, or congregation	14 (3)	(2)	9 (3)	2 (1)	2 (3)	— —

E. Turned over to
another
denomination   5 (1) (1) — —   3 (2) 1 (1) — —

F. Became inter-
denominational   2 (0) (0) 2 (1) — —   — —   — —

Subtotals   516 *   (88) 284 (84) 138 (92) 60 (85) 6 (100)

No data   71 (12) (12)   55 (16)   12 (8) 11 (15) — —

TOTALS   587   339   150   71   6

*516 is the number on which data exist as to outcome, in the total sample of 587.

mission starts looks quite a lot more impressive than do the visible results that followed. Linden Wenger made that point in his 1955 study,[42] and some explanations that he wove into his discussions are that—

> Especially from about 1930 onward, Mennonites went into rural work with what was probably a fundamental misconception: that in rural areas they would face fewer problems and fewer evils than in cities.
> Once there, thinking that they did not have to compete with the city's social attractions and entertainment, they often did not develop a set of programs adequate to attract and hold people.
> Much use of lay people working only part-time probably meant less visible effect per worker than in city missions, which were more likely to have full-time staff.
> Mennonite Church people very often went to sparsely populated, marginal districts, and generally to poor folks. So they planted in soil too thin for large, thriving congregations.
> When people in such places did hear gospel preached, a side effect often seemed to be a motivation to move out to places that appeared less impoverished economically, culturally, and otherwise.
> Where Mennonite Church people tried to bring some help to depressed rural areas, by starting small businesses, improving agriculture, teaching school, and the like, the forces depressing the regions were simply much larger than the Mennonite efforts, perhaps than Mennonite Church people's resources.
> Sometimes Mennonites were content to stop with only charity work.
> A number of Mennonite characteristics probably played a

part. For instance, Mennonite Church people have been a close-knit group who have made "outsiders" feel uncomfortable; and as a small, minority group, they have probably never expected large numbers and therefore have not really worked to draw them.

Because of various distinctive Mennonite teachings, people whom those Mennonites have led to initial commitments have often joined some other church; and although often discouraged by this, the Mennonites have accepted it as (in Wenger's words) "the offense of the cross as Mennonites understand it."[43]

If the Lord sees not as humans see, surely Wenger's less-than-optimistic explanations did not necessarily add up to failure. And even by human understandings, if Mennonites proceeded naively at times, if they were reluctant to proliferate programs, if they were a close-knit group—well, such ways were hardly sins in themselves. Moreover to take gospel to poor people in out-of-the-way places, without real hope of grand, status-conferring results, surely fit some central themes of the Bible. As for sticking to their distinctives, the greater problem of course was that Mennonites often taught the distinctives without being sure how they fit with gospel. Of course to be faithful by their own lights Mennonite Church people should have been (and indeed often were, sometimes willy-nilly, sometimes cautiously) constantly discerning and seeking to find out whether God wanted them to reevaluate some rules and practices. According to their own faith they should have been asking whether through their mission experiences the Holy Spirit was not bringing them, as a body, to some new understandings of scripture. But during that process, if they were preaching gospel and cross as they understood them, should they have preached less? To do so could hardly have been Christian mission.

Linden Wenger by no means suggested that the Mennonite Church's rural outreach failed, in any overall or ultimate sense. He also saw successes in it, even beyond the obvious ones of people to whom Mennonites did communicate gospel and congregations they planted. For instance he suggested that many of the old-line congregations, taking on outreach work, gained new understandings of the congregation as teaching agency, as school for Christian living, and as working unit of the larger church.[44]

Of course an established Mennonite congregation's need for new understandings and roles could hardly be, in itself, good reason for its people to impose themselves on others. But by those congregations' holy writ, their Lord had commanded His disciples to go and had Himself sent missioners out two by two; the person who lost his or her soul lost more than the world; and the Master had said He counted as righteousness even the cup of water given in His name. Persons who treat lightly such words of scripture, or who come with assumptions that Mennonite Church people would hardly have understood, might easily find the rural mission efforts of these missioners, and of the earnest congregations and agencies who backed them, to have been failures. But those who accept the writ as holy, and who try to think with the mind of Jesus, can hardly judge such oft-humble efforts to have failed in any ultimate sense.

* * *

Success or failure, Mennonite Church people had at least for a few decades found their way, by a meandering road, back to rural work. Youngstown-style disillusionment with city mission surely helped guide them to it. A nation's rediscovery of values in country life made the road temporarily respectable and thus, even for Mennonites more passable. Rural sociology and some vapors of the Social Gospel were part of the fuel, although as time passed, rural mission advocates switched to an evangelicalism blended more from Fundamentalism. For most on the journey, local initiative was the motor. On what parts of the road the Spirit of God led the way, historians' sources do not tell. In some ways, no doubt, by the time Mennonite Church people got back to rural missions there was less and less reason to be there, since all the while they themselves were thinking and living in more and more urban ways. Yet the rural-mission road was, at least for the time being, a natural one for Mennonite Church people to travel.

At last, mission-minded Mennonites had heard the pleas of Andrew and Mary Crook. But was their message the one the Crooks thought they had heard? Was it the Gospel of Peace?

CHAPTER NOTES

KEY TO SYMBOLS

AMC: Archives of the Mennonite Church, on the campus of Goshen College, Goshen, Ind.

CM: *Christian Monitor*. Mennonite Church magazine for the home, published 1909-1953.

Funk papers: Letters, diaries, article manuscripts, and other papers of John F. Funk; deposited in AMC.

GH: *Gospel Herald.* Organ of the Mennonite Church, published since 1908.

HT: *Herald of Truth.* Publication of John F. Funk's Mennonite Publishing Company, 1864-1908; for most of its life quasi-official, leading organ of the Mennonite Church.

MBMC: Mennonite Board of Missions and Charities (now Mennonite Board of Missions), Elkhart, Ind.

MBMC *Annual Reports.* Published record of the MBMC's annual meetings and leading business sessions.

MBMC minutes: Typed minutes of the MBMC and its leading committees; deposited in MBMC papers, AMC.

MBMC papers: Correspondence, records, minutes, and other materials of the MBMC; deposited in AMC.

MHL: Mennonite Historical Library, Goshen College, Goshen, Ind.

MM: *Missionary Messenger*. Organ of the (Lancaster Conference of the Mennonite Church) Eastern Mennonite Board of Missions and Charities, published since 1924.

MQR: *The Mennonite Quarterly Review.* Scholarly journal devoted to Anabaptist and Mennonite studies, published since 1927.

Steiner diary: Unpublished diary of Menno S. Steiner, in Steiner papers, AMC.

Steiner papers: Letters, diaries, and other material left by Menno S. Steiner; deposited in AMC.

NOTES

Chapter 1. New Drumbeats

1. Sidney Rooy, *The Theology of Mission in the Puritan Tradition* (Grand Rapids, 1965), 156-241
2. A. J. Lewis, *Zinzendorf, the Ecumenical Pioneer: A Study in the Moravian Contribution to Christian Mission and Unity* (Philadelphia, 1962), 11-80, esp. 15, 21-23, 59, 74-80. See also John R. Weinlick, *Count Zinzendorf* (New York & Nashville, 1954); and Edward Langton, *History of the Moravian Church: The Story of the First International Protestant Church* (London, 1965).
3. Kenneth Scott Latourette, *A History of Christianity* (New York, 1953), 1018-1024.
4. *Ibid.*, 1024-1040; Lewis, *Zinzendorf*, 12, 17, 73-74, 125-126; Wade Barclay, *History of Methodist Missions* (New York, 1949), I, 15-41, 104 ff.
5. Barclay, *History of Methodist Missions*, I, 28.
6. For the U.S. story, see esp. Alice Felt Tyler, *Freedom's Ferment* (Minneapolis, 1944); and Timothy L. Smith, *Revivalism and Social Reform* (New York & Nashville, 1957).
7. Kenneth Scott Latourette, *A History of the Expansion of Christianity* (London, 1944), IV, 66-69, quote on p. 68; Max Warren, *The Missionary Movement from Britain in Modern History* (London, 1965), 21-22; Stephen Neill, *Christian Missions* (Grand Rapids, 1964), 262-263; Max Warren, *Social History and Christian Mission* (London, 1967), 81; Ruth Rouse, "William Carey's Pleasing Dream," *International Review of Missions*, 38 (Apr., 1949), 181-192.
8. Warren, *Social History*, 37-38, 40, 51, 55-57, 60-63.
9. *Ibid.*, 60-62, 70-74, quote on p. 62; R. Pierce Beaver, *Envoys of Peace: The Peace Movement in Christian World Mission* (Grand Rapids, 1964), 24-25, 31-32.
10. Quoted in Neill, *Christian Missions*, 315.
11. Johannes van den Berg, *Constrained by Jesus' Love: An Inquiry into the Motives of the Missionary Awakening in Great Britain in the Period between 1698 and 1815* (Kampen, 1956), 147-149, 153-155; Keith R. Bridston, *Mission Myth and Reality* (New York, 1965), 21-30, 35-36.
12. Van den Berg, *Constrained by Jesus' Love*, 147-153, 155-159.
13. *Ibid.*, 159-165. See also R. Pierce Beaver, "Missionary Motivation Through Three Centuries," in Jerald C. Brauer, ed., *Reinterpretation in American Church History* (Chicago and London, 1968), 113-152.
14. R. Pierce Beaver, *All Loves Excelling: American Protestant Women in World Mission* (Grand Rapids, 1968); Warren, *Social History*, 85-103, 108.
15. Peter Beyerhaus, "The Three Selves Formula: Is It Built on Biblical Foundations?" *International Review of Missions*, 53 (Oct., 1964), 393-407; verse quoted in Constance Padwick, "Children and Missionary Societies in Great Britain," *International Review of Missions*, 6 (Oct., 1964), 570; Warren, *Social History*, 67, 81.
16. In this book, Mennonite Church with upper-case "C" refers to only one Mennonite branch—that with its general mission board at Elkhart, Ind. (the Mennonite Board of Missions, formerly Mennonite Board of Missions and Charities), its publishing house at Scottdale, Pa., and colleges at Goshen, Ind., Hesston, Kan., and Harrisonburg, Va. It is the branch whose missions are the subject of the book. How to designate the different Mennonite groups precisely without interrupting one's prose is always a problem. Some writers, especially writers from other Mennonite branches, have used the term "(Old) Mennonites." But because that label tends to confuse them with Old Order groups, Mennonite Church people themselves generally prefer the designation used here. Some-

times writers add the parenthesis (MC) to distinguish the group from the General Conference (GC), the Mennonite Brethren (MB), and smaller Mennonite bodies, but that method also interferes with flow of language.

17. For an introduction to the Anabaptist movement, see esp. Walter Klaassen, *Anabaptism: Neither Catholic nor Protestant* (Waterloo, Ont., 1973), and/or J[ohn] C. Wenger, *Our Christ-Centered Faith: a Brief Summary of New Testament Teaching* (Scottdale, Pa., 1973); for an implicit but strong rejection of the neither-Catholic-nor-Protestant thesis, see Harold S. Bender, "The Response of our Anabaptist Fathers to the World's Challenge," *MQR*, 36 (July, 1962), 196-207; to examine the question of the Mennonite forebears' relation to other Anabaptists, a good starting place is James M. Stayer, Werner O. Packull, and Klaus Deppermann, "From Monogenesis to Polygenesis: The Historical Discussion of Anabaptist Origins," *MQR*, 49 (Apr., 1975), 83-121.

18. Van den Berg, *Constrained by Jesus' Love* (note 11), 4-12; Franklin H. Littell, *The Anabaptist View of the Church: A Study in the Origins of Sectarian Protestantism* (Boston, 1958; republished in 1964 under somewhat different title), 114-117; John Howard Yoder, "Reformation and Missions: A Literature Review," *Occasional Bulletin from the Missionary Research Library*, 22 (June, 1971), 1-9.

19. See esp. Littell, *Anabaptist View of Church.*

20. On relation of the *corpus christianum* concept to mission, see esp. van den Berg, *Constrained by Jesus' Love* (note 11), 146, 167, 170-172, 190-192, 212.

21. See esp. writings of Littell: *Anabaptist View of Church*, ch. 4; "An Anabaptist Theology of Missions," *MQR*, 31 (Jan., 1947), 5-17; "Protestantism and the Great Commission," *Southwestern Journal of Theology*, 2 (Oct., 1959), 28-33. See also Robert Friedmann, "The Oldest Church Discipline of the Anabaptists," *MQR*, 29 (Apr., 1955), 162; and J[ohn] C. Wenger, "The Doctrinal Position of the Swiss Brethren as Revealed in Their Polemical Tracts," *MQR*, 24 (Jan., 1950), 65-72. See also note 5.

22. Christian Hege and Harold S. Bender, "Martyrs' Synod," *Mennonite Encyclopedia*, IV, 529-531; Litte, "Anabaptist Theology of Missions," 16.

23. Myron S. Augsburger, "Conversion in Anabaptist Thought," *MQR*, 36 (July, 1962), 248; Harold S. Bender, "Walking in the Resurrection," *MQR*, 25 (Apr., 1961), 96-110; Stayer, etc., "From Monogenesis" (note 17), 91; Robert Friedmann, "Anabaptism and Protestantism," *MQR*, 24 (Jan., 1950), 12-24; Gordon D. Kaufman, "Some Theological Emphases of the Early Swiss Anabaptists," *MQR*, 25 (Apr., 1951), 91-99; Erland Waltner, "The Anabaptist Conception of the Church," *MQR*, 25 (Jan., 1951), 10.

24. John Howard Yoder, "The Hermeneutics of the Anabaptists," *MQR*, 41 (Oct., 1967), 292.

25. Harold S. Bender, "The Anabaptist Theology of Discipleship," *MQR*, 24 (Jan., 1950), 25-32. For a classic formulation of Anabaptists' essential beliefs, see Harold S. Bender, "The Anabaptist Vision," *MQR*, 18 (Apr., 1944), 67-88; Wenger, "Doctrinal Position of Swiss Anabaptists," 65-72; and Friedmann, "Anabaptism and Protestantism," 12-24.

26. Roland H. Bainton, "The Anabaptist Contribution to History," in Guy F. Hershberger, ed., *The Recovery of the Anabaptist Vision* (Scottdale, Pa., 1957), 320-321; Cornelius J. Dyck, "Early Anabaptist *Sendungsbewusstsein*," unpublished paper in its author's possession, Associated Mennonite Biblical Seminaries, Elkhart, Ind.; Littell, "Anabaptist Theology of Missions" (note 21), 15-16; Robert Friedmann, "Moravia," *Mennonite Encyclopedia*, III, 749.

27. Leo Shelbert, "Eighteenth-Century Migration of Swiss Mennonites to America," *MQR*, 42 (July, 1968), 164, n. 2; Yoder, "Reformation and Missions" (note 18), 6; conversation with John Howard Yoder, at Elkhart, Ind., Dec. 15, 1973.

28. Quoted in Dyck, "Early Anabaptist *Sendungsbewusstsein*," 25-26.

29 Wolfgang Schäufele, "The Missionary Vision and Activity of the Anabaptist Laity," *MQR*, 36 (Apr., 1962), 99-115; Menno as quoted in Bender, "Response of

Anabaptist Fathers" (note 17), 205-206. For further study of Anabaptists as missioners, see esp. Dyck, "Early Anabaptist *Sendungsbewusstsein*"; Schäufele, *Das missionarische Bewusstsein und Wirken der Täufer* (Neukirchen, 1966); Wilhelm Wiswedel, "Die alten Täufergemeinden und ihr missionarisches Wirken," *Archiv für Reformationsgeschichte* (1943), 183-200, and (1948) 115-132; and John Howard Yoder, *Täufertum und Reformation im Gespräch* (Zürich, 1968).

30. Dordrecht Confession, as presented and printed in J[ohn] C. Wenger, *The Doctrines of the Mennonites* (Scottdale, Pa., 1950), 75-85.

31. Leo Schelbert, "Swiss Immigration to America: The Swiss Mennonites" (Columbia University PhD dissertation, 1966), 139-141. For a full study of Pietism's impact see Robert Friedmann, *Mennonite Piety Through the Centuries: Its Genius and Its Literature* (Goshen, Ind., 1949).

32. "Martyrs Mirror," *Mennonite Encyclopedia*, III, 527-529.

33. Guy F. Hershberger, "The Founding of the Mennonite Central Committee" (unpublished ms. in possession of it author at Glendale, Ariz.), 20-30; Schelbert, "Swiss Immigration . . . Mennonites," 139-141; Dyck, "Early Anabaptist *Sendungsbewusstsein*" (note 26) esp. pp. 3-4, 39.

34. For additional material on Mennonitism in America in the 18th and 19th centuries, see J[ohn] C. Wenger, *The Mennonite Church in America* (Scottdale, Pa., 1966), 43-143; and Theron F. Schlabach, "Mennonites, Revivalism, Modernity, 1683-1850," in *Church History*, 48 (Dec. 1979). John Ruth's *'Twas Seeding Time: A Mennonite View of the American Revolution* (Scottdale, Pa., and Kitchener, Ont., 1976), although not written as a scholarly work, is reliable and highly informative as well as most readable.

As for Amish Mennonites, the historical relation of Amish to Mennonites is complex. The two groups separated in Europe, in 1693. Their stories of coming and settling in North America and relating to American culture are quite parallel, with much interaction between the two groups. With their authority dispersed in somewhat less centralized fashion among local congregations and bishops, the Amish have varied perhaps even more than Mennonites in practices and rates of acculturation; and coming in different waves of migration has added to that variation. Most of them cooperated more and more closely with Mennonites in the latter 19th and early 20th centuries until over the years 1916 to 1959 they merged into or otherwise affiliated with the Mennonite Church. Some, meantime, found their way into Mennonite groups even more acculturated to American revivalistic Protestantism than the Mennonite Church. Only a minority continued as Amish, to become the Old Order Amish of today.

35. J. Weber to Martin Möllinger, Sept. 20, 1823, trans. and printed in *Mennonite Research Journal*, 13 (July, 1972), 26-27; Samuel F. Pannabecker, "Missions, Foreign Mennonite," *Mennonite Encyclopedia*, III, 713; Melvin Gingerich, "North American Mennonite Overseas Outreach in Perspective, 1890-1965," *MQR*, 39 (Oct., 1965) 262-263.

36. M. Möllinger to "Beloved Brother-in-law and Sister Weber," Oct. 2, 1821, trans. and printed in *Mennonite Research Journal*, 12 (July, 1971), 26.

37. The "Russian" Mennonites came to North America already fragmented into a number of groups. The main body, which immediately began some mission activity in America, gradually grafted into the General Conference Mennonite branch. Another major group, not nearly as large but very zealous for missions, continued as the Mennonite Brethren Church. There were smaller groups, some interested in mission and some not.

38. Cornelius J. Dyck, ed., *Introduction to Mennonite History* (Scottdale, Pa., 1967), 193, 197; Edmund G. Kaufman, *The Development of the Missionary and Philanthropic Interest among the Mennonites of North America* (Berne, Ind., 1931). 60-109, 135-142, 152; Gingerich, "North American Mennonite Overseas," 262-263; Samuel F. Pannabecker, *Open Doors: The History of the General Conference Mennonite Church* (Newton, Kan., 1975), 44-50, 278, 301-309. For a provocative account of the early work among

Red Indians in America, see an unpublished paper by James C. Juhnke, "General Conference Mennonite Missions to the American Indians in the Late 19th Century" (1977; copies extant at Bethel College, North Newton, Kan., and in MHL). See also Juhnke, *A People of Mission: A History of General Conference Mennonite Overseas Missions* (Newton, Kan., 1979).

39. Samuel F. Pannabecker, "The Development of the General Conference of the Mennonite Church of North America" (Yale University PhD dissertation, 1944), 75-179; Pannabecker, *Open Doors*, 32, 54-60. See also Leland Harder, "The Oberholtzer Division: 'Reformation' or 'Secularization'?" *MQR*, 37 (Oct., 1963), 310-331, 342.

40. "Hershey, Eusebius," *Mennonite Encyclopedia*, II, 715; Kaufman, *Development*, 70-71, 259-260; Gingerich, "North American Mennonite Overseas," 264. *HT*: 27 (Nov. 15, 1980), 246-347; 28 (July 1, 1891), 203-204.

41. Gingerich, "North American Mennonite Overseas" (note 35), 265; John A. Lapp, *The Mennonite Church in India, 1897-1962* (Scottdale, Pa, 1972), 27. *HT*: 34 (Aug. 1, 1897), 229; 34 (May 15, 1897), 154; 33 (Dec. 15, 1896), 374-375; 34 (Nov. 1, 1897), 329.

42. Lewis J. Burkholder, *A Brief History of the Mennonites in Ontario . . .* (Toronto, 1935), 277-315; Linden M. Wenger, "A Study of Rural Missions in the Mennonite Church" (Union Theological Seminary [Richmond, Va.] ThM thesis, 1955), 100, 59.

43. Harry A. Brunk, *History of Mennonites in Virginia, 1727-1900* (i.e., Vol. I; Staunton, Va. 1959), 11, 82-83, 83-89, 101-102, 110-143, 274, quotation on p. 128; "Funk, Joseph," *Mennonite Encyclopedia*, II, 423.

44. *HT*, 34 (July 15, 1897), 209-210; Brunk, *History of Mennonites in Virginia*, I, 286-289, 317, 361-364.

45. Virginia Mennonite Conference *Minutes* (Oct. 5, 6, 1883), 21; (Oct. 3, 4, 1884), 24; (Oct. 2, 3, 1891), 37; (Oct. 4, 1901), 61. Brunk, *History of Mennonites in Virginia*, I, 295, 175-183, 192, 336.

46. John. M. Brenneman, *Christianity and War: A Sermon Setting Forth the Suffering of Christians*; John F. Funk, *Warfare: Its Evils, Our Duty* (both Chicago, 1863, and available in MHL).

47. For biographies of Funk, see entry by John A. Hostetler in *Mennonite Encyclopedia*, II, 421-423; Helen Kolb Gates *et al*, *Bless the Lord O My Soul* (Scottdale, Pa., 1964); and, Aaron C. Kolb, "John F. Funk, 1835-1930: An Appreciation," *MQR*, 6 (July and Oct., 1932), 144-155, 250-263. It would seem that Funk's debt to Moody has been much exaggerated—see *HT*, 13 (Dec., 1876), 201-203, and note that his direct relationship to Moody had apparently been sporadic. Note also that in 1876 it did not seem to occur to Funk to claim that he was much indebted to Moody. Distortion has probably come from a statement, claiming Moody's influence on him and through him on the Mennonite Church, that he made on the occasion of his 92nd birthday, in 1927. But by that time, Moody's fame and the passing of so many years may well have colored his recollections. Interestingly, even in a similar autobiographical statement on the occasion of his 90th birthday he commented on his days in Chicago with no mention of Moody. See pamphlets, *An Address by John F. Funk On the Occasion of the Ninety-Second Anniversary of His Birth, at the Mennonite Church, Elkhart, Ind., April 6, 1927*, and *Sermon Preached by John F. Funk at the Mennonite Church, Elkhart, Ind., Sunday, April 5, 1925, Celebrating His Ninetieth Birthday, April, 6, 1925* (copy of each extant in MHL).

48. For a history of Mennonite Church publishing, see John A. Hostetler, *God Uses Ink: The Heritage and Mission of the Mennonite Publishing House After Fifty Years* (Scottdale, Pa., 1958); for a photograph of some of the young men Funk attracted to Elkhart, see *Mennonite Historical Bulletin*, 22 (July, 1961), 1.

49. Harold S. Bender, *Mennonite Sunday School Centennial, 1840-1940: An Appreciation of Our Sunday Schools* (Scottdale, Pa., 1940), reprinted as ch. 10 of Wenger, *Mennonite Church in America* (note 34); Paul M. Lederach, "History of Religious

Education in the Mennonite Church" (Southwestern Baptist Theological Seminary DRE thesis, 1949), ch. 4.

50. "Proceedings of the Mennonite Sunday School Conference...[Oct. 5-8, 1892]," *HT*, 29: (Nov. 1, 15, 1892), 326-327, 340-342; (Dec. 1, 1892), 356-357. A. Kolb to M. Steiner, Dec. 4, 1894; J. Smucker to Steiner, Nov. 17, 1892; Steiner papers.

51. For discussions of whether the 1872 meetings were really the first revival meetings in the Mennonite Church, and of Funk's attitude, see two unpublished papers: Marion G. Bontrager, "The Birth of Evangelism in the Mennonite Church and the Traveling Evangelist West of the Mississippi River 1864-1895" (copy in MHL); and especially Bernard Bowman, "John F. Funk and the Revival Movement" (copy in AMC). For primary sources on Funk's attitude toward revivalism as expressed at camp meetings, see *HT*, 16 (Nov., 1879), 215; 18 (Sept., 1881), 155-156; and 26 (Sept. 1, 1889), 265. For further sources on the beginning of revivalism in the Mennonite Church, see *HT*, 16 (Dec., 1879), 224-225; *HT*, 43 (Mar. 22, 1906), 89-90; Harold S. Bender, "Nineteenth-Century Protestant Revivalism and Its Effect on the Mennonite Church" (unpublished paper, from internal evidence apparently written in late 1940s, copy in AMC); Bender, "Outside Influences on the Mennonite Church," *Mennonite Educational and Cultural Conference Proceedings*, 9 (1953), 33-41; and Sem Sutter, "John S. Coffman, Mennonite Evangelist (1848-1899)" (University of Chicago term paper, 1974, copy in AMC).

52. For biographies and other sources on Coffman, see Menno S. Steiner, *John S. Coffman* (Spring Grove, Pa., 1903); Barbara Coffman's somewhat fictionalized *His Name Was John* (Scottdale, Pa., 1964); Barbara Coffman, ed., "Extracts from J. S. Coffman's Diaries," *MQR*, 28 (July, 1949), 147-160; and his papers and diaries and Sem Sutter's paper (note 51) in AMC.

53. Brunk, *History of Mennonites in Virginia* (note 43), I, 199-203; Sutter, "John S. Coffman," 3; J. Coffman to J. Funk, Mar. 10, 1879, Funk papers; "Coffman, John S.," *Mennonite Encyclopedia*, I, 633-634; *HT*, 36 (Aug. 1, 1899), 225.

54. *HT*, 24 (Oct. 15, 1887) 314-315; Paul M. Miller, "The History of Revival Meetings in the Mennonite Church" (unpublished paper, copy in MHL); Sutter, "John S. Coffman," 9, 11; J. Brubacher to J. Funk, Nov. 8, 1893, Funk papers; Brunk, *History of Mennonites in Virginia* (note 43), I, 194-196. J. Coffman to M. Steiner, July 11, 1894, and Nov. 17, 19, 23, 1896; J. Heatwole to Steiner, Mar. 20, 1900, Steiner papers.

55. J. Brenneman to P. Nissley, Mar. 10, 1865, copy in Peter Nissley papers, AMC.

56. *Ibid.*

57. *HT*, 2 (Apr., 1865), 30-31.

58. *Ibid.*, 31.

59. *HT*, 2 (Sept., 1865), 68-69.

60. *HT*, 13 (Mar., 1876) 36-37; 19 (Dec. 15, 1882), 379; 3 (Mar., 1866), 17; 3 (May, 1866), 38-39; 3 (June, 1866), 45-46. Note Brenneman's failure to develop the mission theme in an article such as his "How the World Lieth in Wickedness," *HT*, 8 (Aug., 1871), 115-116.

61. Reprinted in *HT*, 3 (June, 1966), 51.

62. *HT*, 15 (Apr., 1878), 71.

63. *HT*, 6 (Mar., 1869), 41;6 (Apr., 1869), 49-50; 6 (May, 1869), 65-66.

64. *HT*, 9 (Jan., 1872), 6-7.

65. *HT*, 3 (Oct., 1866), 78; 19 (June 1, 1882), 163.

66. *HT*, 29 (Apr. 15, 1892), 114-116.

67. *HT*, 25 (Mar. 1, 1888), 65-67; J. Funk, draft of letter, from internal evidence intended for Jacob N. Brubacher, *ca.* Apr., 1890, box 14, Funk papers. Contemporaries themselves recognized the confusion in terminology: see editorial footnote, *HT*, 17 (July, 1880), 129, col. 3. For a general history of traveling Mennonite Church evangelists west of the Mississippi River, see Bontrager paper (note 51).

68. Indiana-Michigan Mennonite Conference *Minutes* (Oct. 14, 1864), 9; Virginia

Mennonite Conference *Minutes* (Sept. 27, 28, 1867), 9. *HT*, 18 (Nov., 1881), 193-194; 1864-1880, *passim;* 27 (Nov. 1, 1890), 323-324. For a good example of the dynamics at work, see J. Kreider to J. Funk, May 26, 1893, Funk papers.

69. Bontrager paper (note 51), 42-46.
70. One John O. Smith even proposed furnishing the minister with a hired man or a farm: *HT*, 20 (Dec. 15, 1883), 371. *HT*, 18 (Nov., 1881), 193.
71. John S. Coffman diary, June 23, 1880, AMC.
72. *Ibid.*
73. Documents printed in *GH*, 45 (Mar. 4, 1952), 230-233; *HT*, 20 (Apr. 1, 1883), 105.
74. "Mission Fund" reports in *HT* during the 1880s; documents printed in *GH*, 45 (Mar. 4, 1952), 231-232.
75. Report of Jan. 20, 1892, meeting, in "Mennonite Evangelizing Committee Annual Meeting Report" folder, IV-1, MBMC papers; *HT*, 29 (Feb. 1, 1892), 42-44; documents printed in *GH*, 45 (Mar. 4, 1952), 254.
76. *HT*, 28 (Jan. 15, 1891), 18-19; 28 (Apr. 15, 1891), 121. J. Brubacher to J. Funk, Apr. 8, 1892, and Oct. 7, 1894; W. Graybill to Funk, Apr. 21, 1893, Funk papers.
77. *HT*, 23 (Jan. 15, 1886), 25; J. Brenneman to P. Nissley, Nov. 28, 1867, Peter Nissley papers, AMC. *HT*, 18 (Mar., 1881), 44-45; 19 (May 1, 1882), 138. J. Coffman to J. Funk, Feb. 28, 1887, Funk papers; *HT*, 27 (Nov. 15, 1890), 348; G. Brunk to J. Funk, Sept. 27, 1899, Funk papers; *HT*, 41 (June 30, 1904), 211.
78. *HT*, 36 (June 15, 1899), 188-189; 39 (Oct. 15, 1902), 308.
79. *HT*, 30 (Mar. 1, 1893), 77.
80. *HT*, 37 (Apr. 15, 1900), 124.
81. *HT*, 33 (Aug. 1, 1896), 227-228; 37 (Sept. 15, 1900), 275-276.
82. *HT*, 23 (Feb. 1, 1886), 33-36; 25 (Mar. 1, 1888), 65-67; 26 (Mar. 1, 15, 1889), 65-67, 81-82; 24 (Feb. 15, 1887), 49-51; etc.
83. See, for example, *HT*, 26 (Mar. 1, 15, 1889), 67, 81-82; *HT*, 27 (Sept. 1, 1890), 265; and M. Steiner to J. Funk, Nov. 23, 1891, and S. Herner to Funk, Mar. 22, 1892, Funk papers.
84. For examples, see *HT*, 22 (May 15, 1885), 152; 22 (July 15, 1885), 216; 26 (Nov. 1, 1889), 333-334; 29 (Aug. 1, 1892), 235. Juhnke paper (note 38).
85. For this sentence I have compared a lot of Mennonite evidence with van den Berg, *Constrained by Jesus' Love* (note 11), 164-177.
86. For an example of the earlier caution, see *HT*, 10 (June 15, 1882) 178-179; for Coffman's statement, see *HT*, 29 (Mar. 1, 15, 1892), 86.
87. Coffman to Funk, Mar. 10, 13, 1879, Funk papers.
88. *Ibid.,* Steiner to Funk, Mar. 1, 1889; Mar., 1890, *passim;* Aug. 19, 1890, Funk papers.
89. Coffman to Steiner, July 11, 1894; Bender to Steiner, May 6, 1893; Hershey to Steiner, Nov. 24, 1894, Steiner papers.
90. Gates, *Bless the Lord* (note 47), 73.
91. Guy F. Hershberger has stated a rather different view in "Historical Background to the Formation of the Mennonite Central Committee," *MQR*, 44 (July, 1970), 218-219. Wrote he: "While this new vision owes much to the general religious awakening in America it owes its unique character to the fact that Funk's work was consciously and deliberately built upon the foundation of the sixteenth-century fathers. It was in fact an introduction to the Anabaptist vision. . . ." Insofar as the Mennonite quickening had a "unique" character, Hershberger was no doubt at least partly correct (although Mennonite traditions built up after the sixteenth century were probably even stronger influences than was memory of the Anabaptists). But the story of the Mennonite "awakening" breathes much of the contemporary revivalism of Dwight L. Moody, etc., and seems very much like the more general "awakening" in Anglo-American Protestantism a century

earlier that produced the modern Protestant missionary movement, and that Kenneth Scott Latourette, for instance, described in his *History of Christianity* (note 3), 1018-1021. Therefore John Howard Yoder has written (at pp. 291-292 of his article cited in note 24) that "in terms of theological and ethical substance ... it could be effectively argued that modern American Mennonites have about them more that has been derived from John Wesley or Dwight L. Moody than from Conrad Grebel, Pilgram Marpeck, or Menno." In a recent manuscript as yet unpublished, "Christian Living is Christian Family and Christian Community" (copy in my possession), pp. 16-17, Hershberger revised his earlier view.

92. J. A. Ressler diaries, 1892-1899, *passim*, AMC: conversion experience at May 19-21, 1893, synod reference in memoranda section of 1899. Taped interview with Erb, Oct. 12, 1974, at Hesston, Kan., tape in AMC. Erb thought that his first acquaintance with the story of the Swiss Brethren came from an address by Harold S. Bender at sessions of the Mennonite Church's general conference at Eureka, Ill., which would put the date at 1925, a year in which Mennonites were celebrating the 400th anniversary of the Swiss Brethren's beginnings. The published report of those sessions records no such address, but conversations with Elizabeth (Mrs. H. S.) Bender (by telephone, Jan. 10, 1975), and others make it plausible that Bender, having returned from study in Europe a year earlier, told the story in discussion or in an unofficial session at Eureka. Even M. S. Steiner's papers impress me with how little real exploration there was in the late 1880s and early 1890s of the meaning of Mennonites' faith. Everything was activity, not search for basics.

93. *HT*, 28 (Dec. 1, 1891), 358-359; J. Coffman to M. Steiner, Apr. 5 (marked and filed 1899, but from internal evidence 1895); Steiner papers. *HT*, 33 (Mar. 15, 1896), 81.

94. See, for example, *HT*, 22 (Aug. 15, 1885), 248-249.

95. M. Vincent to J. Funk, Jan. 31, 1887, Funk papers; Hershey to Steiner, Nov. 24, 1894, Steiner papers. J. A. Ressler diary, AMC: Jan. 9, 11, 12, 14, 18; Feb. 21; Mar. 1, 11; May 5; Sept. 23; Oct. 1; Dec. 30, 1894; Feb. 2, 1896. See also *HT*, 33 (Feb. 1, 1896), 43; D. Bender to G. Bender, Mar. 15, 1894, G. L. and Elsie (Kolb) Bender papers, AMC; J. Braun to J. Funk, Nov. 1, 1888, Funk papers; and A. Ebersole to M. Steiner, Oct. 22, 1893, Steiner papers.

96. W. Coy to J. Funk, May 5, 1887, Funk papers; Paul Erb, *South Central Frontiers: A History of the South Central Mennonite Conference* (Scottdale, Pa., 1974), 185 and *passim*; "Members of the Mechanics Grove Sunday School During the Term of 1887" (document in box 4, T. K. Hershey papers, AMC).

97. [Abraham Blosser] to J. Funk, "Letters to editor regarding S. S.," box 67, Funk papers— quoted also in Bender, *Mennonite Sunday School*, 29-30; in Wenger reprint of Bender, 157-158; and in Lederach thesis, 99-100 (note 49). For more on the opposition Blosser represented, see the following and documents accompanying it, file IMS 5, Menno Simons Historical Library, Eastern Mennonite College, Harrisonburg, Va.: [Abraham Blosser,] "Exposition on Sunday schools Between John F. Funk Editor of the Herald of Truth of Elkhart Indianna [sic] And The Antisundayschool Mennonites of Virginia" (handwritten booklet, from internal evidence ca. 1871, extensively reprinted in Brunk, *History of Mennonites in Virginia* [note 43], I, 199-203, and therein attributed to Blosser). For further evidence of Blosser's authorship of the documents, see Blosser to J. Funk, Jan. 15, 1872, Funk papers.

98. P. Nissley to J. Funk, Aug. 22, 1863, box 6, Funk papers.

99. Sources cited in note 97. Conservatives may have been reflecting influence from other denominations somewhat like the quickened were, for there were Sunday school opponents in other denominations—see T. Scott Miyakawa, *Protestants and Pioneers: Individualism and Conformity on the American Frontier* (Chicago and London, 1964), 104-109. Indeed, among the Baptists, an especially strong anti-mission movement existed also, based partly on reaction but seemingly quite a bit also on rejection of the kind of institutional rationalization implied in ch. 3 of this study—see Miyakawa's ch. 11, and

esp. B. H. Carroll, Jr., *The Genesis of American Anti-Missionism* (Louisville, 1902).

100. *HT*, 27 (Dec. 15, 1890), 378; 28 (June 1, July 15, Sept. 15, Nov. 1, 1891), 171, 218, 284-285, 333; 27 (Jan. 15, 1890), 20-21. Erb, *South Central Frontiers*, 185; *HT*, 30 (June 15, 1893), 196; J. Blosser to M. Steiner, Aug. 8, 1892, Steiner papers.

101. See especially Sydney Ahlstrom, *A Religious History of the American People* (New Haven, 1972), 742; Perry Miller, *The Life of the Mind in America from the Revolution to the Civil War* (New York, 1965), ch. 2; and Robert T. Handy, *A Christian America: Protestant Hopes and Historical Realities* (New York, 1971), 95, and for excellent additional background, 27-154.

102. Coffman to M. Steiner, Mar. 3, 1894, Steiner papers.

103. *HT*, 32 (Nov. 1, 1895), 331; 35 (Mar. 1, 1898), 65-66. Miyakawa has suggested that this activism represented a popularization of the aristocratic Calvinist ideal of calling, but that it was strong also among nineteenth-century Methodists. A Methodist in the 1860s summarized the ideal as "Work! work! work! this world is no place for rest." See Miyakawa, *Protestants and Pioneers*, 215-218.

104. Van den Berg, *Constrained by Jesus' Love* (note 11), 179-180.

105. J. Brenneman to P. Nissley, Aug. 17, 1864, Peter Nissley papers, AMC. For a good example of such a non-Mennonite piece, see *HT*, 19 (June 15, 1882), 188.

106. *HT*, 9 (Feb., 1872), 23; 19 (July 15, 1882), 211.

107. A. Kolb to M. Steiner, Dec. 4, 1894, Steiner papers; *HT*, 30 (Dec. 1, 1893), 370; MBMC minutes, ann. bd. mtg., May 18-20, 1915, p. 266. J. Smucker to Steiner, Nov. 17, 1892; Steiner diary, Oct. 5-7, 1893; S. Werner to S. Ebersole, May 19, 1894; Steiner papers. Harry F. Weber, *Centennial History of the Mennoites of Illinois, 1829-1929* (Goshen, Ind., 1931), 273; Weber is probably wrong in saying that the decision to open the Home Mission was made at the 1893 conference, for according to Ebersole's conference speech the decision had already been made.

108. Ebersole to M. Steiner, Aug. 6, 1892, Steiner papers; *HT*, 29 (Dec. 15, 1892), 370-372; 30 (Dec. 1, 1893), 370-371.

109. *HT*, 29 (Dec. 1, 1892) 356 357; 31 (May 1, 1894), 140, 31 (Oct. 15, 1894), 318. Daniel Shenk wrestled with the question of whether the new activities were leading to "worldliness"—see *HT*, 30 (Oct. 1, 1893), 299-301; and Shenk to J. Funk, July 23, 1889, Funk papers. For an editorial on the question, see *HT*, 31 (Aug. 1, 1894), 226-227; for comments by Daniel Kauffman, see his letter to S. D. Guengerich, Aug. 21, 1896, I-2, box 3, AMC; for a grass-roots voice, see *HT*, 29 (June 1, 1892), 162.

110. *HT*, 2 (Sept., 1865), 69; 29 (Apr. 1, 1892), 99. Regarding Steiner, see "Memorandum of M. S. Steiner's notes and comments gathered during travels..." (notebook dated Mar. 21, 1891, box 18, Steiner papers), and *HT*, 28 (May 15, 1891), 147; 28 (Dec. 1, 1891), 358-359; 35 (Aug. 15, 1898), 242. M. Wenger to Steiner, Feb. 20, 1898, Steiner papers.

111. Compare, for instance, "The Mennonites," in the Mennonite Publishing Company's *Family Almanac for ... 1886*, n. p., and Funk's "A Discourse," *HT*, 25 (Mar. 1, 1888), 65-66, with the following: *HT*, 37 (Mar. 15, 1900), 82, and 38 (Jan. 15, 1901), 18, and "Population of the Earth," *Family Almanac for... 1906*, n. p. A more thorough study of how Funk handled religious census reports might be fruitful on this point.

112. *HT*, 28 (Feb. 1, 1891), 35; 35 (Apr. 1, 1898), 97.

113. Despite accusation to the contrary against Steiner, as in D. Shenk to J. Funk, July 23, 1889, Funk papers. On Coffman, see *HT*, 23 (Dec. 1, 1886), 362.

114. Sem Sutter, "John S. Coffman" (note 51), 11-13; Berkey to M. Steiner, Nov. 21, 1893, Oct. 14, 1895, Steiner papers; *HT*, 32 (Oct. 15, 1895), 306-307.

115. Though not for all—see *HT*, 31 (June 1, 1894), 171-172; 31 (Feb. 1, 15, 1894), 36-37, 51-52; 34 (Feb. 1, 1897), 36. For a perception of how the process of laying out that different track was developing but in 1898 was not yet complete, see esp. John S. Coffman, comp., *Outlines and Notes Used at the Bible Conference Held at Johnstown, Pennsylva-*

nia. .. [Dec. 27, 1897—Jan. 7,1898] (Elkhart, Ind., 1898).
  116. For notable examples, see *HT*, 26 (Jan. 1, 1899), 8; 29 (Mar. 15, 1892); 30 (June 15, 1893), 185-186.
  117. J. Smith to M. Steiner, Aug. 14, 1899, Steiner papers. The formula got transmitted to the mission field—see *20 Lecciones Biblicas* (Trenque Lauquen, Argentina, n.d.; copy available in MHL). For the evolution of the formula, compare Daniel Kauffman's following three books: *Manual of Bible Doctrines* ... (Elkhart, Ind., 1898), title page and 11-14, 205-207; *Bible Doctrines* ... (Scottdale, Pa., 1914), 181-278, 457-469, 535-549; and *Doctrines of the Bible* ... (Scottdale, Pa., 1928), 237-310, 505-516.
  118. G. Bender to M. Steiner, July 14, n.y. (filed 1894, a plausible dating), Steiner papers; *HT*, 32 (Feb. 15, Mar. 1, 1895), 60-61, 67-68.
  119. *HT*, 32 (Feb. 15, 1895), 60.
  120. Implicitly saying that classical Anabaptism and Mennonitism does not divide its religious convictions the way the two-track formula does, Franklin H. Littell has commented that the "classical Anabaptist-Mennonite testimony" has not been that either of Fundamentalism, or of pietism, or of orthodoxy, but of "'Integral' Christianity, which presumes faithfulness in both intellectual and ethical areas"— see Littell, *The Free Church* (Boston, 1957), xii.

Chapter 2. Whose Mission?

  1. *HT*, 35 (Sept. 1, 1898), 265; 25 (June 1, May 1, 1888), 162, 138.
  2. *HT*, 23 (Feb. 1, 1886), 33-36; 25 (Mar. 1, 1888), 65-67; 18 (Dec., 1881) 211-213. *GH*: (July 10, 1913), 239. *HT*, 25 (Feb. 15, 1888), 62; Crook article, 27 (Jan. 15, 1890), 26; 21 (Oct. 15, 1884), 314-315; 28 (Jan. 1, 1891), 12, 18-19; 25 (Nov. 1, 1888), 330. A. Crook to J. Funk, Apr. 15, May 27, 1894, box 21, Funk papers. *HT*, 27 (Dec. 15, 1890), 371.
  3. *HT*, 19 (Aug. 15, 1882), 248; 23 (Dec. 15, 1886), 379; Shenk article, 18 (Dec., 1881), 212-213.
  4. *HT*, 29 (Dec. 1, 1889), 362-363; 27 (June 15, 1890), 187-188.
  5. *HT*, 21 (July 15, 1884), 217; S. Ebersole to "Dear Friend," Dec. 30, 1890, Steiner papers.
  6. M. Steiner to J. Coffman, Apr. 1, 1895, box 9, Coffman papers, AMC.
  7. "Indiana District Conference," *HT*, 28 (Apr. 15, 1891), 122-123.
  8. *HT*, 28 (June 15, July 1, 1891), 178-179, 199, 206; 29 (May 1, 1892), 131.
  9. J. Blosser to M. Steiner, Mar. 4, 1894, Steiner papers; Steiner to J. Coffman, May 1, Aug. 8, 1894, box 9, Coffman papers, AMC. S. Coffman to Steiner, Dec. 10, 1894, Apr. 27, 1895, Steiner papers; Steiner to J. Funk, Aug. 9, 1894, box 21, Funk papers; J. Shenk to Steiner, Aug. 22, 1894, Steiner papers.
  10. *HT*, 29 (Oct. 1, 1892), 292; 28 (June 15, 1891), 178-179; 29 (Aug. 15, Dec. 15, 1892), 246-247, 370-372; see also D.J. Johns sermon at 31 (Feb. 1, 15, 1894), 52.
  11. *HT*, 29 (June 15, 1891), 178-179; 29 (Aug. 15, Dec. 15, 1892), 246-247, 370-372, 377. Page to M. Steiner, Jan. 10, 1893, Steiner papers; *HT*, 30 (Feb. 15, 1893), 67-68; M. S. Steiner diary, Aug. 21, 1893. *HT*, 30 Sept. 15, 1893), 292-293.
  12. *HT*, 30 (Dec. 1, 1893), 370-371, 361. M. S. Steiner diary, Oct. 6, and Nov. 6, 12, 13, and 17, 1893.
  13. M. S. Steiner diary, Nov. 19, Dec. 3, 1893, Jan. 21, 1894. *HT*, 30 (Dec. 1, 15, 1893), 361, 385-386. S. Ebersole to Steiner, Dec. 13, 1893, Steiner papers.
  14. D. Yoder to M. Steiner, Nov. 18, 1893; E. Gehman to Steiner, Jan. 14, 1894; A. Baughman to Steiner, Jan. 23, 1894; Steiner papers.
  15. E. Eicher to M. Steiner, Dec. 21, 1894; J. S. Hartzler to Steiner, Jan. 26, 1894; C. Yoder to Steiner, Dec. 11, 1893; C. M. Brackbill to Steiner, Jan. 27, 1894; 1894, *passim*; Steiner papers.
  16. S. Coffman to M. Steiner, Nov. 27, 1894, Steiner papers.
  17. Coffman to M. Steiner, Mar. 27, 1894, Steiner papers.

18. Coffman to M. Steiner, Oct. 17, 1893, Steiner papers.
19. J. K. Brubaker to J. Funk, July 27, 1894, box 21, Funk papers. Coffman to M. Steiner, Mar. 3, 1894; H. Charles to Steiner, Apr. 3, 1894; Steiner papers.
20. George [G. L. Bender?] to M. Steiner, Apr. 6, 1893, Steiner papers. Steiner papers, 1894-1895, *passim,* especially: E. Berkey and S. Coffman to Steiner, Nov. 3, 1894; J. Coffman to Steiner, Oct. 30, Nov. 16, 1894; S. Coffman to Steiner, Sept. 18, Nov. 12, Dec. 10, 1894; S. Ebersole to Steiner, Aug. 22, Nov. 1, Dec. 6, Dec. 15, Dec. 19, 1894; A. Zook to Steiner, Nov. 24, 1894; E. Berkey to Steiner, Mar. 26, July 3, 1895; and J. Funk to E. Berkey, Mar. 20, 1894, F-H 1894 folder.
21. In addition to other references cited hereafter, see D. Bender to G. Bender, Mar. 15, 1894, G. L. and Elsie (Kolb) Bender papers, AMC.
22. Coffman to M. Steiner, Mar. 3, 1894, Oct. 17, 1893, Mar. 16, 1894, Steiner papers.
23. J. Blosser to M. Steiner, Mar. 4, 1894, Steiner papers; Steiner to J. Coffman, May 1, Aug. 8, 1894, box 9, Coffman papers, AMC. S. Coffman to Steiner, Dec. 10, 1894, Apr. 27, 1895, Steiner papers; Steiner to J. Funk, Aug. 9, 1894, box 21, Funk papers; J. Shenk to Steiner, Aug. 22, 1894, Steiner papers.
24. Shenk to J. Coffman, Feb. 24, 1894, box 3, Coffman papers, AMC. For possible source of her "Methodism" charge, see R. Heatwole to M. Steiner, Mar. 17, 1894, Steiner papers.
25. MBMC *Annual Report* (1933), 87-91; M. S. Steiner diary, Mar. 3, Apr. 15, 29, Aug. 2, 1894; C. Yoder to Steiner, Dec. 11, 1893, Steiner papers.
26. Brubaker to G. Bender, July 20, 1894; D. Bender to G. Bender, Sept. 4, Oct. 24, 1894; G. L. and Elsie (Kolb) Bender papers, AMC. A. Zook to M. Steiner, Aug. 22, 1894, Steiner papers. *HT*, 33 (Dec. 1, 1896), 364; 31 (Nov. 1, 1894), 324-325. Brubaker to Funk, July 27, 1894, box 21, Funk papers.
27. Brubaker to J. Funk, July 27, 1894, box 21, Funk papers; J. Coffman to M. Steiner, July 11, 1894, Steiner papers; J. N. Brubacher to Funk, Dec. 4, 1894, box 22, Funk papers.
28. *HT*, 31 (Aug. 1, 1894), 227-228; I. Eby to J. Funk, Oct. 11, 1894, box 22, Funk papers.
29. J. N. Brubacher to J. Funk, Nov. 8, 1893, box 20; J. K. Brubaker to Funk, June 15, 1895, box 22; draft of letter, Funk to J. K. Brubaker, Aug. 6, 1895, box 23; J. K. Brubaker to Funk, Aug. 9, 1895, box 23; Funk papers.
30. *HT*, "Indiana Amish Conference Report," 31 (May 1, 1894), 140; "Missouri Conference Report," 31 (Oct. 15, 1894), 315; "Southwestern Pennsylvania Conference Report," 31 (Nov, 15, 1894), 346; "Illinois Conference Report," 31 (June 15, 1894), 189.
31. J. Horsch to M. Steiner, Dec. 2, 1893; J. Funk to Steiner, Jan. 5, 1893 [from internal evidence 1894]; Steiner papers.
32. *HT*, 31 (Feb. 1, 1894), 43.
33. J. Coffman to M. Steiner, Mar. 3, 1894, Steiner papers; M. S. Steiner diary, Apr. 15, 16, 1894; Illinois charter, Apr. 23, 1894, IV-3, AMC.
34. A. Zook to M. Steiner, Mar. 31, 1895, Steiner papers; Steiner to Coffman, Apr. 1, 1895, box 9, Coffman papers, AMC. Coffman to Steiner, Apr. 2, 1895; S. Coffman to Steiner, Apr. 8, 1895; J. Coffman to Steiner, Apr. 5, 1899 [*sic*; from internal evidence actually 1895]; Steiner papers. *HT*, 32 (Apr. 15, 1895), 116-117; John F. Funk diary, Apr. 21, 1895, Funk papers.
35. *HT*, 32 (July 15, 1895), 210.
36. *HT*, 32 (Aug. 1, 1895), 226; 33 (May 1, 1896), 138. Draft of J. F. Funk to J. K. Brubaker, Aug. 6, 1895; Funk diary, Mar. 17, 1896; Funk papers.
37. S. Coffman to M. Steiner, June 13, 1895; J. Coffman to Steiner, July 11 and Nov. 4, 1895; A. B. Kolb to Steiner, July 15, 1895; Steiner papers. Charter, "Mennonite Evangelizing and Benevolent Board," issued by the State of Indiana on Mar. 20, 1896,

IV-4-1, AMC. *HT,* 33 (Aug. 15, 1896), 242-243; Articles of Incorporation of the Mennonite Evangelizing and Benevolent Board, IV-4-1, AMC. *HT,* 33 (Oct. 15, 1896), 311; 33 (Sept. 15, 1896), 273. "Copy and Certificate of Amendments," July 9, 1903, IV-5; M. Steiner to G. Bender, May 4, 1897, IV-4-2; AMC. *HT,* 33 (Aug. 15, Oct. 15, 1896), 243-244, 311.

38. M. Steiner to J. Funk, Mar. 18, 1894, box 21, Funk papers. S. Ebersole to Steiner, Dec. 13, 1893; Mrs. J. Eigsti to Steiner, Jan. 8, 1894; J. Gingrich to Steiner, Feb. 3, 1894; J. Horsch to Steiner, Mar. 9, 1894; S. Coffman to Steiner, Aug. 22, 1894; Steiner papers. S. Ebersole to "Dear Friends in Jesus Christ," Aug. 24, 1894, box 21, Funk papers. W. Page to "Suffering Humanity," Aug., 1894; S. Ebersole to Steiner, Dec. 13, 1893; Steiner papers. M. S. Steiner diary, Dec. 4, 20, 1893, Aug. 7, 1894. *HT,* 32 (Aug. 1, 1895), 226.

39. *HT,* 32 (Aug. 1, 1895), 226.

40. S. Coffman to M. Steiner, Aug. 22, Nov. 27, 1894, Steiner papers; Steiner to J. Funk, Aug. 9, 1894, box 21, Funk papers; Steiner diary, Sept. 4, 8, 1894; J. Coffman to Funk, Sept. 3, 1894, box 22, Funk papers.

41. J. Funk to M. Steiner, Aug. 11, 1894; S. Coffman to Steiner, Jan. 28, 1895; E. Berkey to Steiner, Jan. 28, 1895; S. Coffman to Steiner, Apr. 8, 11, 25, 1895; Steiner papers. Funk diary, Apr. 21, 1895, Funk papers; Emma Oyer, *What God Hath Wrought in a Half Century at the Mennonite Home Mission* (Elkhart, Ind., 1949), 37-38.

42. See John Howard Yoder, *As You Go* (Scottdale, Pa., 1961).

43. *HT,* 33 (Aug. 15, 1896), 243-244; Oyer, *What God Hath Wrought,* 10-16, 30-41; Harry F. Weber, *Centennial History of Illinois Mennonites, 1829-1929* (Goshen, Ind., 1931), 613-614.

44. A. Leaman to J. Funk, Dec. 8, 1898, Jan. 9, 1899, box 25, Funk papers.

45. *Mennonite Yearbook and Directory* (1920), 44.

46. M. Steiner to J. Coffman, May 1, 1894, box 9, Coffman papers; *HT,* 34 (May 1, 1897), 137; E. Berkey to Coffman, Jan. 6, 1896, box 3, Coffman papers, AMC. Lina Zook diary, Sept. 3, 1897; Zook to A. B. Kolb, June 2, 1898, box 2; J. A. Ressler and Lina R. Zook papers, AMC. S. Kurtz to Steiner, Sept. 19, 1898, Steiner papers.

47. C. Shoemaker to M. Steiner, Dec. 20, 1894, Steiner papers.

48. D. Bender to M. Steiner, Feb. 4, 1895, Steiner papers.

49. See, for example, J. A. Ressler diary, 1890-1895, *passim,* esp. Feb.-Apr., 1893, AMC; or *HT,* 35 (Mar. 1, 1898), 66.

50. J[ohn] C. Wenger, *Separated Unto God* (Scottdale, Pa., 1951), 252; H. S. Bender, "Voting," *Mennonite Encyclopedia,*IV, 860; *GH,* 5 (Oct. 3, 1912), 428-429; J. Brenneman to P. Nissley, Jan. 9, 1866, Peter Nissley papers, AMC; J. F. Funk diary, Nov. 2, 1880, box 3, Funk papers; J. A. Ressler diary, Feb. 20, 1894, AMC; J. C. Wenger conversation with Elihu Clemmer, as recounted by Wenger to author, Feb. 10, 1975.

51. See for example, J. Kenagy to J. Funk, box 7; Elias Martin article, Oct. 7, 1894, box 22; Funk papers. G. Bender to M. Steiner, July 15, 1898, Steiner papers; *HT,* 32 (Feb. 15, 1895), 59-60.

52. See: *HT,* 30 (Feb. 1, 1893), 45-46; J. Coffman to M. Steiner, Mar. 20, 1894, Steiner papers.

53. *HT,* 32 (Apr. 15, 1895), 117-118.

54. C. M. Brackbill to M. Steiner, Sept. 24, 1894, A. and K. Metzler to Steiner, Jan. 20, 1895; George [Bender] to Steiner, May 6, 1893; Steiner papers. J. Paul Sauder, "The Movement Begins," in Paul Kraybill, *Called to Be Sent* (Scottdale, Pa., 1964), 35; C. M. Brackbill to Steiner, Jan. 27, 1894, Steiner papers.

55. *MM,* 22 (June, 1945), back cover; J. A. Ressler diary, Sept. 12, 1894; John Mellinger, in *MM,* 22 (June, 1945), 6.

56. J. A. Ressler diary, 1894, *passim,* AMC, especially: Sept. 23, 26, 27, 29; Oct. 1, 13, 22, 27; and Dec. 6, 14, 16. Mellinger (note 55); A. and K. Metzler to M. Steiner, Jan.

20, 1895, Steiner papers.
57. J. Coffman to M. Steiner, July 11, 1894, Steiner papers; J. N. Brubacher to J. Funk, Nov. 8, 1893, box 20, Funk papers; C. M. Brackbill to Steiner, Feb. 20, Mar. 3, 1894, Steiner papers.
58. A. and K. Metzler to M. Steiner, Jan. 20, 1895, Steiner papers; Sauder, "The Movement Begins," 32.
59. A. and K. Metzler to M. Steiner, Jan. 20, 1895, Steiner papers; J. A. Ressler diary, Jan. 13, 1895, AMC.
60. Sauder (note 54), 35; A. and K. Metzler to M. Steiner, Jan. 20, 1895, Steiner papers.
61. *HT*, 32 (Feb. 15, 1895), 49.
62. Unsigned ms. marked "For the Herald," box 95, Funk papers.
63. *Ibid.*
64. J. Coffman to M. Steiner, July 11, 1894, Steiner papers.
65. A. Metzler to M. Steiner, Apr. 30, 1895; H. Charles to Steiner, May 1, 1895; Steiner papers. J. A. Ressler diary, Apr. 6, 1895, AMC—because of the nature of this source, I have corrected misspellings, etc.
66. J. A. Ressler diary, as in note 65.
67. J. A. Ressler diary, Sept. 12, 1894, AMC. H. Charles to M. Steiner, May 1, 1895; A. Metzler to Steiner, Apr. 30, 1895; Steiner papers. Sauder (note 54), 37.
68. Quoted by Amos Ressler, *GH*, 10 (Sept. 6, 1917), 433-434.
69. Mellinger (note 55). Sauder (note 54), 37.
70. Mellinger (note 55), 5-8. *HT*, 33 (Sept. 1, 1896), 266; 34 (Aug. 15, 1897), 250; 34 (May 1, 1897), 139; 35 (July 1, 1898), 203.
71. Sauder (note 54), 32.
72. *GH*, 10 (Sept. 6, 1917), 433-434.
73. Quotations in Sauder (note 54), 35-37.
74. Sauder (note 54), 36, 39; *HT*, 34 (May 1, 1897), 138-139; Jonas S. Hartzler and Daniel Kauffman, *Mennonite Church History* (Scottdale, Pa., 1905), 352; Mellinger (note 55), 7.
75. J. A. Ressler diary, July 23, 1896, AMC. Sauder (note 54), 38.
76. Sauder (note 54), 43; Mellinger (note 55), 7.
77. *HT*, 35 (Mar. 15, 1898), 91-92; 32 (Feb. 15, 1895), 60.
78. *HT*, 35 (July 1, 1898), 199.
79. *Ibid.*
80. *HT*, 35 (July 1, 1898), 193.
81. *HT*, 29 (Apr. 1, 1892), 99.
82. *HT*, 35 (Mar. 1, 1898), 74-75; 35 (Sept. 1, 1898), 266; Wenger article, 36 (Apr. 15, 1899), 119. Hartzler and Kauffman (note 74), 351.
83. For examples, see *HT*, 35 (Mar. 1, 1898), 65, 91-92; 36 (Mar. 1, 1899), 71. Wenger in *HT*, 36 (Apr. 15, 1899), 119; 36 (July 15, 1899), 219-220.
84. "Report of Joint Meeting of Mission Board," May 22, 1906, IV-6-2, AMC; Ira D. Landis, *The Missionary Movement Among Lancaster Mennonites* (Scottdale, Pa., 1938), 86.
85. *HT*, 36 (Oct. 1, 1899), 295; 34 (Aug. 15, 1897), 250.
86. MBMC *Annual Report* (1926), 139-140; N. Mack to M. Steiner, Jan. 16, 1905, Steiner papers; MBMC Minutes, Sept., 1918, AMC.
87. Landis, 86-88; MBMC *Annual Report* (1926), 138-140; John H. Mellinger, in *MM*, 2 (Apr. 15, 1925), 1; Alta Mae Erb, *Studies in Mennonite City Missions* (Scottdale, Pa., 1936), 66.
88. MBMC *Annual Report* (1926), 138-140; J. Paul Graybill, Ira D. Landis, and J. Paul Sauder, *Noah H. Mack* (Scottdale, Pa., 1952), 19; *Gospel Witness*, 3 (May 1, 1907), 72; MBMC *Annual Report* (1926), 138-140.

89. J. A. Ressler in *Gospel Witness*, 1 (July 5, 1905), 111-112; *HT*, 43 (Nov. 29, 1906), 451; G. L. Bender in *GH*, 1 (June 20, 1908), 186; M. C. Lapp in *GH*, 1 (Aug. 22, 1908), 331.
90. Groff to Chicago Home Mission workers, Dec. 22, 1894; A. Zook to M. Steiner, Mar. 31, 1895; C. Hostetler to Steiner, Jan. 2, 1896; Steiner papers.
91. John A. Lapp, *The Mennonite Church in India 1897-1962* (Scottdale, Pa., 1972), 28-30. G. Bender to H. Dirks, Apr. 1, 1897, box 2, IV-4, MBMC papers; *HT*, 34 (Oct. 15, 1897), 305; C. Hostetler, *HT*, 35 (Nov. 15, 1898), 345-346.
92. E.g., *HT*, 33 (Feb. 15, Apr. 15, May 1, 1896), 49, 113, 143; J. Guengerich to Mennonite Publishing Company, Mar. 2, 1897, Mennonite Evangelizing and Benevolent Board corr., MBMC papers. *HT*, 29 (Apr. 15 and May 15, 1892), 125, 150; Lapp, *Mennonite Church in India*, 30.
93. On Lambert's fall from favor, see, e.g., M. Lapp to G. Bender, Mar. 25, 1909; G. Lapp to G. Bender, Aug. 20, 1913; J. Bixler and A. Christophel to MBMC exec. comm. (Kauffman folder), n.d. (attached to letter of May 1, 1924); IV-7-1, MBMC papers. Lapp, *Mennonite Church in India*, 27-35; George L. Lambert, *Around the Globe and Through Bible Lands* (Elkhart, Ind., 1896).
94. Lapp, *The Mennonite Church in India*, 28, 30, 34; Lambert, *HT*, 34 (Aug. 1, Nov. 1, 1897), 227-228, 323; "Famine and Famine Relief," clipping from *The Bombay Guardian*, 3 (June 19, 1897), pp. 1-2, VII-1-2.1, AMC; *HT*, 34 (Dec. 1, 15, 1897), 353, 369, 371; George L. Lambert, *India: The Horror-Stricken Empire* (Elkhart, Ind., 1898).
95. J. D. Graber, taped interview with John S. Miller, Jan. 31, 1973, AMC.
96. Lapp, *Mennonite Church in India*, 29; Guy F. Hershberger, "Historical Background to the Formation of the Mennonite Central Committee," *MQR*, 44 (July, 1970), 223-224; Hershberger, "Home and Foreign Relief Commission," *Mennonite Encyclopedia*, II, 797.
97. Shelly to D. Jansen, June 18, 1898, box 25, John F. Funk papers. *HT*, 35 (May 15, 1898), 145; Bender to M. Steiner, May 25, 1898, Steiner papers; *HT*, 35 (Sept. 1, 1898), 257.
98. Hershberger (note 96), both articles. C. Hostetler to M. Steiner, Feb. 5, 1901; J. Bare to Steiner, Mar. 16, 1901; J. Ressler to Steiner and Hostetler, Feb. 24, 1905; G. Bender to Steiner, Apr. 3, 1906; Steiner papers.
99. Lambert in *HT*, 34 (Sept. 15, Oct. 15, 1897), 282, 307-308; *HT*, 34 (Dec. 1, 1897), 353-354. Hostetler to M. Steiner, Dec. 7, 1898; Kauffman to Steiner, May 3, 1898; Steiner papers.
100. J. Funk to G. Lambert, Aug. 31, 1897, VII-1-2.1, AMC. Loucks to Funk, Jan. 18, 31, 1898, box 24; Loucks to Funk, July 5, 27, 1898, box 25; Funk papers. J. A. Ressler diary, Jan. 18, 31, Feb. 21, 23, Mar. 2, Oct. 21, Nov. 5, 1898, AMC; *HT*, 35 (Aug. 1, 1898), 226; *Building on the Rock* (Scottdale, Pa., 1926), 13-14; Southwestern Pennsylvania Conference *Report* (1898), 47.
101. Lapp, *Mennonite Church in India* (note 91), 39.
102. J. A. Ressler diary, Nov. 1-4, 1898, and 1898, *passim*, AMC; Lapp, *Mennonite Church in India* (note 91), 39; *Building on the Rock*, 15-17.
103. J. Ressler to M. Steiner, Aug. 28, 1905, Steiner papers.

Chapter 3. The Urge to Make Institutions

1. One could assemble a vast bibliography on this organizational revolution. For samples, see Carl G. Gustavson, *The Institutional Drive* (Athens, Ohio, 1966); and Jerry Israel, ed., *Building the Organizational Society: Essays in Associated Activities in Modern America* (New York and London, 1972).
2. Indiana-Michigan Mennonite Conference *Minutes* (Ind. conf.): (1873), 18-19; (1881), 31; (1882), 31-32. B. Kauffman, D. Seekman, and H. Herr to J. Funk, June 17, 1879, box 8, Funk papers. Virginia Mennonite Conference *Minutes:* (1887), 30; (1895), 45; (1903), 66; (1911), 103.

3. *HT*, 18 (Apr., 1881), 65-66; 19 (June 1, 1882), 164; 29 (Mar. 15, 1892), 86.
4. *HT*, 32 (Nov. 1, 1895), 325; 35 (June 1, 1898), 161. Loucks to M. Steiner, July 31, 1906, Steiner papers; Ressler diary, Oct. 14, 1897, AMC; *HT*, 35 (Dec. 1, 1898), 357.
5. J. Hartzler to M. Steiner, Apr. 15, 1896; C. Hostetler to Steiner, Dec. 2, 1897; J. Ressler to Steiner, Aug. 28, 1905; Steiner papers.
6. For instance, in *HT*, 41 (Aug. 18, 1904), 271; 41 (Nov. 3, 1904), 358.
7. *HT*, 18 (Apr., 1881), 66.
8. *HT*, 28 (Dec. 1, 1891), 358-359.
9. *HT*, 26 (Feb. 15, 1889), 52; Zook to J. Funk, Mar. 5, 1889, Mar., 1899 [*sic*] folder, box 26, Funk papers.
10. See note 8; M. S. Steiner in *HT*, 29 (Oct. 15, 1892), 313.
11. Southwestern Pennsylvania Conference *Report* (1893), 35; A Kolb to M. Steiner, Dec. 4, 1894, Steiner papers; *HT*, 32 (Sept. 15, 1895), 282-284; Alta Mae Erb, *Our Home Missions* (Scottdale, Pa., 1920), 146-147; E. Hartman to Steiner, Mar. 30, 1896, Steiner papers; Hartman to G. Bender, Apr. 13, 1896, IV-4, MBMC papers. *HT*, 33 (June 1, 1896), 167; 33 (June 15, 1896), 182.
12. *HT*, 33 (Dec. 1, 1896), 356; 33 (Aug. 15, 1896), 243-244.
13. *HT*, 34 (Oct. 15, 1897), 307; 35 (May 1, 1898), 138-139. D. Garber to M. Steiner, Nov. 28, 1898, Steiner papers.
14. *HT*, 34 (Oct. 15, 1897), 305-306; 35 (Feb. 1, 1898), 35.
15. G. Bender to M. Steiner, May 16, June 17, July 15, 20, 1898; D. Kauffman to Steiner, Aug. 24, 1898; Steiner papers. *HT*, 36 (June 15, 1899), 187.
16. *HT*, 34 (Dec. 1, 1897), 364.
17. *HT*, 35 (Feb. 1, 1898), 35; Bender to J. Shoemaker, Mar. 19, 1898, IV-4, MBMC papers; Bender to M. Steiner, May 16, 21, 1898, Jan. 13, 29, 1899, M. S. Steiner papers.
18. *Gospel Witness*, 1 (June 7, 1905), 78-79; John Mellinger to M. Steiner, May 7, July 2, Aug. 6, 1905, Steiner papers.
19. *HT*, 34 (Dec. 1, 1897), 364.
20. *HT*, 28 (Dec. 1, 1891), 358; M. S. Steiner diary, Mar. 5-7, 1895.
21. Young People's Paper Association to Steiner, Jan. 18, 1895. M. S. Steiner diary, 1895: Jan. 23, 24; Jan. 25 - Feb. 17, *passim*; Feb. 18, 19, 20; Mar. 14. J. Funk to Steiner, Mar. 22, Apr. 4, 18, 1895; G. Bender to Steiner, Feb. 4, Mar. 2, 7, 1895: Steiner papers.
22. "Articles of Incorporation of the Mennonite Board of Charitable Homes" (printed copy), May 23, 1899; "Copy and Certificate of Amendments" (legal document), July 9, 1903; IV-5, MBMC papers. J. Bressler to Steiner, Jan. 4, 1904; N. Blosser to Steiner, Jan. 18, 1904; G. Bender to Steiner, Dec. 22, 1904; J. Ressler to Steiner, Aug. 28, 1905; John Mellinger to Steiner, Oct. 8, 1905; Steiner papers.
23. *HT*, 41 (Aug. 18, 1904), 271.
24. *HT*, 41 (Sept. 8, 1904), 290.
25. *HT*, 42 (July 6, Aug. 17, 1905), 214, 262.
26. *HT*, 42 (July 20, 1905), 225-227; (Ressler at) 41 (Nov. 10, 1904), 362-363.
27. *Gospel Witness*: Guengerich, 1 (Nov. 1, 1905), 245; Hostetler, 1 (Oct. 4, 1905), 215.
28. *Ibid.* (both articles).
29. Mellinger to M. Steiner, Aug. 6, 1905; Mack to Steiner, Sept. 27, 1906; Kauffman to Steiner, Apr. 27, 1905; Steiner papers.
30. Kauffman to M. Steiner, July 19, Oct. 11, 1905, Steiner papers.
31. C.K. Hostetler in *Gospel Witness*, 1 (Dec. 6, 1905), 309; MBMC minutes, I, pp. 1-26; M. S. Steiner and J. S. Shoemaker in *Gospel Witness*, 2 (Apr. 18, 1906), 44. C. Z. Yoder to Steiner, Mar. 24, 1906; Shoemaker to Steiner, Apr. 12, 1906; Steiner papers.
32. MBMC minutes, I, 5-6, 9, 13, 16, 26; MBMC minutes, II, 192, 301; Mennonite [Church] General Conference *Proceedings* (Nov. 13-14, 1907), 117. A. Kolb to G. Bender

(treas. corr., 1914 folder), Apr. 13, 18, 1914; D. Bender to G. Bender (treas. corr., Kansas), July 31, 1914; J. Shoemaker to G. Bender (treas. corr., Illinois), June 13, 1915; D. Weaver to G. Bender (treas. corr., 1915), Oct. 26, 1915; MBMC papers.
33. Steiner in *GH*, 2 (Mar. 10, 1910), 789-790.
34. MBMC minutes, I, 15, 24.
35. Note 33.
36. *HT*, 38 (Jan. 15, 1901), 23.
37. *HT*, 36 (Nov. 15, 1899), 343.
38. *Ibid.*
39. *HT*, 37 (Feb. 1, 1900), 39.
40. *HT*, 37: (Feb. 15, 1900), 54; (Apr. 1, 1900), 102-103; (Nov. 1, 1900), 335; (Mar. 15, 1900), 87; (Oct. 15, 1900), 311.
41. J. A. Ressler diary, Dec. 10, 24, 1899, AMC; *Building on the Rock* (Scottdale, Pa., 1926), 41; John A. Lapp, *The Mennonite Church in India 1897-1962* (Scottdale, Pa., 1972), 166; *Gospel Witness*, 1 (June 28, July 5, 1905), 103, 111; Kaufman in *GH*, 4 (Mar. 21, 1912), 808-809.
42. *HT*, 43 (May 24, 1906), 184; Lapp, *Mennonite Church in India*, 140.
43. *Gospel Witness*, 1 (Sept. 20, 1905), 199; *GH*, 1 (Apr. 4, 1908), 11; *HT*, 43 (May 24, 1906), 184. *GH*, 1 (July 4, 1908), 218-219; 1 (Aug. 8, 1908), 298-299; 4 (Apr. 20, 1911), 37, 46; 4 (Sept. 14, 1911), 372-373.
44. *Gospel Witness*, 2 (Oct. 31, 1906), 484; (Oct.-Nov., 1906), *passim*. G. Lapp to M. Steiner, Sept. 4, 1907, Dec. 8, 1909; M. Lapp to Steiner, Nov. 20, 1907; J. Shoemaker to Steiner, Sept. 23, Oct. 10, 1907, Aug. 21, 1909; John Mellinger to Steiner, July 29, 1909; G. Bender to Steiner, Apr. 27, 1910; J. Stauffer to Steiner, Apr. 29, 1910; J. Kaufman to Steiner, Jan. 20, 1909; Steiner papers. *GH*, 4 (Sept. 14, 1911), 372-373.
45. MBMC minutes, ann. bd. mtg., May 21-22, 1907, p. 50; *Gospel Witness*, 2 (Nov. 21, 1906), 540; (Dec. 19, 1906), 604-605. C. Hostetler to M. Steiner, Nov. 21, 1906; J. Ressler to Steiner, Jan. 9, 1907; Steiner papers. C. Esch to G. Bender, June 17, 1914, IV-7-1, MBMC papers.
46. *Gospel Witness*, 2 (Nov. 21, 1906), 538; G. Lapp to G. Bender, Nov. 12, 1908, IV-7-1, MBMC papers. M. Lapp to M. Steiner, Nov. 2, 1909, Steiner papers; Kaufman in *GH*, 1 (Apr. 4, 1908), 11.
47. Hartzler to mission and exec. committees, Nov. 24, 1917, treas. corr., MBMC papers.
48. Corporation charter for Benevolent Organization of Mennonites, Apr. 23, 1894, IV-1-2, AMC. *HT*, 30 (Feb. 15, 1893), 67; (Brunk, at) 41 (Jan. 14, 1904), 20.
49. *HT*, 43 (Feb. 22, 1906), 61; Mennonite [Church] General Conference, *Proceedings* (1905), 113; D. Kauffman to M. Steiner, Feb. 11, 1905, Steiner papers; MBMC minutes, May 23, 1906, p. 11.
50. *Gospel Witness*, 2 (Feb. 6, 1907), 715; D. Weaver to G. Bender, July 24, 1916, treas. corr., MBMC papers.
51. *Gospel Witness*, 2 (Apr. 18, 1906), 45; C. Hostetler to Steiner, 1906, *passim*, Steiner papers.
52. MBMC minutes, exec. comm. mtg., Nov. 12, 1907, |p. 52½. *Gospel Witness*, 2 (July 4, 1906), 217; Metzler at (Aug. 22, 1906), 331.
53. G. Bender to D. Weaver, Jan. 8, 1914; Weaver to Bender, Jan. 12, 1914; treas. corr., MBMC papers.
54. B. Gingrich to M. Steiner, July 21, 1907, Steiner papers; Metzler (note 52).
55. Allen H. Erb, *Privileged to Serve* (Elkhart, Ind., 1975), chs. 4-5; MBMC minutes, joint exec. and mission committees, June 26-27, 1919, pp. 91-92.
56. G. Bender to D. Bender, June 14, 1919, box 5, G. L. and Elsie (Kolb) Bender papers, AMC.
57. MBMC minutes, joint exec. and mission committees, Oct. 14, 1919, pp. 104-105.

58. MBMC minutes, joint exec. and mission committees, June 16, 1939, p. 3. V. Reiff to A. Erb (sec.-treas. folder), Dec. 21, 1932; Reiff to C. Esch, Sept. 14, 1928; S. Gamber to S. Yoder, Feb. 23, 1934, IV-7-1, MBMC papers. On the evangelism question, see ch. 4.

59. Kansas-Nebraska Mennonite Conference *Record*: Oct. 10 [*sic*, but must be 19]-21, 1911, p. 167; Oct. 17-19, 1912, p. 175. MBMC minutes, ann. bd. mtg., May 20-22, 1912.

60. S. Yoder to V. Reiff, Jan. 4, 1933, IV-8-10; Yoder to exec. and mission committees, Feb. 18, 1933, IV-7-1; MBMC papers. Selena Gamber Shank, taped interview with John S. Miller, Nov. 15, 1972, AMC; MBMC *Annual Report* (1940), 9.

61. MBMC minutes, exec. comm. mtgs.: Dec. 5, 1924, p. 11; Mar. 18, 1925, pp. 19-20.

62. Erb in *GH*, 18 (Feb. 4, 11, 18, Mar. 4, 11, 25, 1926), 930, 949, 965, 1015, 1029, 1038, 1062, 1065; V. Reiff to J. Shoemaker, July 20, 1926, treas. corr. Illinois, MBMC papers; treas. reports in MBMC *Annual Report* (1926-1929), *passim*, esp. 1928, pp. 44-45.

63. See ch. 4.

64. King to Yoder (La Junta folder), May 27, 1924, IV-7-1, MBMC papers.

65. Lehman "To Whom itmay [*sic*] concern," Aug. 7, 1915, Youngstown Mennonite Mission early records (hereafter cited as YMM records) III-35-29, AMC.

66. Tobias K. Hershey, *I'd Do It Again* (Elkhart, Ind., 1961), 27-28.

67. Hershey, *I'd Do It Again*, 14.

68. *GH*, 4 (Oct. 12, 1911), 441; MBMC minutes, exec. comm. mtg., Jan. 18, 1912; documents in box 1, YMM records (note 65), including J. I. Byler, *The Mennonite Mission Settlement, Youngstown, Ohio, January 1914 to December 1915* (printed booklet), 3.

69. Byler, *Mennonite Mission Settlement*, 4-6; T. K. Hershey "To whom it may concern," Jan. 25, 1912; Civic Committee of the Youngstown Chamber of Commerce to Mennonite Gospel Mission, Feb. 23, 1912; J. Hanson to Mrs. Westlake, Feb. 29, 1912; box 1, YMM records (note 65).

70. For material on the Charity Organization movement see for example Kathleen Woodroofe, *From Charity to Social Work in England and the United States* (London, 1962), ch. 2-4; or Theron F. Schlabach, "Rationality and Social Welfare: Public Discussion of Poverty and Social Insurance in the United States, 1875-1935" (unpublished research report to the Social Security Administration, 1969; copies in author's possession and in various U.S. Government libraries), ch. 1.

71. *HT*, 20 (Nov. 15, 1883), 338-339; 22 (Dec. 15, 1885), 375; (Byers, at) 40 (Feb. 12, 1903), 50-51, 53-54. A. M., handwritten note, attached to G. Bender to M. Steiner, May 12, 1894, Steiner papers. Coffman in *HT*, 21 (July 1, 1884), 200; 31 (July 15, 1894), 213-215, quote on 215.

72. *HT*, 36 (July 1, 1899), 202.

73. Hansen to Westlake (note 69); Byler, *Mennonite Mission Settlement* (note 68), 3; *Report of the Mennonite Mission, Youngstown, Ohio, 1917* (copy extant in box 10, Hershey papers, AMC), 3.

74. Byler, *Mennonite Mission Settlement* (note 68), 15, 19, and *passim*.

75. J. Shoemaker to G. Bender, June 22, 1915, treas. corr. Illinois, MBMC papers.

76. Undated, unsigned note on G. L. Bender's letterhead, from internal evidence sometime after June, 1916, Youngstown folder; C. Yoder to Bender, Sept. 18, 1916; treas. corr., Ohio; MBMC papers. L. Mumaw to Bender, Sept. 21, Oct. 7, and Nov. 6, 1916, IV-7-1, MBMC papers.

77. MBMC minutes: exec. comm. mtg., May 18, 1915, p. 263; joint exec. and mission committees, Aug. 10, 1915, p. 299; ann. bd. mtg., May 22-24, 1916, pp. 327-329.

78. Youngstown Mission *Minutes*, Oct. 30, 1914, box 2, YMM records (note 65). Weaver to Bender (1915 folder), June 23, July 10, 1915, treas. corr.; C. Hostetler to Bender

(Youngstown folder), Nov. 12, 1918, treas. corr., Ohio; MBMC papers.
79. Hostetler to G. Bender (Youngstown folder), Apr. 17, 1918, treas. corr. Ohio, MBMC papers.
80. Hostetler to Bender (note 78).
81. Youngstown Mission *Minutes*, Apr. 8, 1918, box 2, YMM records (note 65). Yoder to Hershey, Apr. 12, 1918; Hershey to A. Steiner, Sept. 5, 1918; box 3, Hershey papers, AMC. Yoder to G. Bender, Sept. 18, 1916, Apr. 8, 1918, treas. corr. Ohio, MBMC papers; *CM*, 6 (Jan., 1914), 415; Byler, *Mennonite Mission Settlement* (note 68), 3. Youngstown Mission *Reports*: (n.d.—from internal evidence ca. Jan., 1914), 3; (1917-1918), 7, 8; box 1, YMM records (note 65).
82. C. Hostetler to V. Reiff (Youngstown folder), Sept. 14, 1921, treas. corr. Ohio, MBMC papers; MBMC minutes, superintendents with bd. committees, June 4-6, 1919, p. 57; Hostetler in *The Christian Exponent*, 1 (Mar. 28, 1924), 102-103.
83. MBMC minutes, ann. bd. mtgs.: May 18-20, 1915, p. 283; May 22-24, 1916, p. 328; May 20-22, 1918, p. 29. MBMC minutes, exec. comm. mtg., Oct. 25, 1921.
84. MBMC minutes: exec. comm. mtg., May 18, 1915, p. 263; ann. bd. mtg., May 22-24, 1916, pp. 328-329.
85. *HT*, 43 (Mar. 22, 1906), 93-94; *Gospel Witness*, 2 (Apr. 25, 1906), 59-60.
86. *HT*, 42 (Jan. 12, 1905), 12-13; 42 (May 11, 1905), 150; 43 (Mar. 22, 1906). *Gospel Witness*, 2 (Dec. 12, 1906), 590.

Chapter 4. The Pure Gospel: Orthodoxy and Evangelism...and Benevolence?

1. D. Bender to G. Bender, June 29, 1893, G. L. and Elsie (Kolb) Bender papers, AMC; *HT*, 36 (June 15, 1899), 189. G. Bender to M. Steiner, May 21, 1898; D. Kauffman to Steiner, June 17, 1901; Steiner papers. *HT*, 40 (Oct. 29, 1903), 346; Allen and Melinda Erb, taped interview with Theron F. Schlabach, Oct. 12, 1974, AMC; Allen H. Erb, *Privileged to Serve* (Elkhart, Ind., 1975), 23-27, 30-31; Paul Erb, *South Central Frontiers* (Scottdale, Pa., and Kitchener, Ont., 1974), 188, 229-230, 242-245. Kauffman to J. Coffman, Dec. 9, 1895, box 5, Coffman papers; Coffman diary, Jan. 11, Apr. 29, 1896; AMC. Kauffman to Steiner, Oct. 20, 1899, Nov. 3, 1903, Steiner papers.
2. Kauffman to Steiner, Nov. 3, 1903, June 29, 1908, Steiner papers.
3. *HT*, 35 (Aug. 1, 1898), 226-227.
4. Daniel Kauffman, *Manual of Bible Doctrines* (Elkhart, Ind., 1898); Kauffman, *Bible Doctrine* (Scottdale, Pa., 1914); Kauffman, *Doctrines of the Bible* (Scottdale, 1928).
5. For strong evidence that for instance young people applying to Mennonite Board of Missions and Charities accepted Kauffman's books as definitive, see MBMC Mission Committee corr., MBMC papers, 1907-1920, *passim*.
6. See John A. Hostetler, *God Uses Ink: The Heritage and Mission of the Mennonite Publishing House After Fifty Years* (Scottdale, Pa., 1958), 72-76, 79-85. P. Erb, "Kauffman, Daniel," *Mennonite Encyclopedia*, III, 157.
7. See C. Norman Kraus, *Dispensationalism in America* (Richmond, Va., 1958).
8. See Ernest R. Sandeen, *The Roots of Fundamentalism: British and American Millenarianism, 1800-1930* (Chicago, 1970), 167-172.
9. *Ibid.*, ch. 5.
10. A few further main sources on Fundamentalism are Stewart G. Cole, *The History of Fundamentalism* (New York, 1931); Norman F. Furniss, *The Fundamentalist Controversy, 1918-1931* (New Haven, 1954); Willard B. Gatewood, Jr., ed., *Controversy in the Twenties: Fundamentalism, Modernism, and Evolution* (Nashville, 1968); James Barr, *Fundamentalism* (London, 1977).
11. See Timothy L. Smith, *Revivalism and Social Reform: American Protestantism on the Eve of the Civil War* (Nashville, 1957).
12. Ressler diary, Oct. 30, 1892; Coffman diary, Aug. 15-17, 1893; AMC. Coffman,

"The Spirit of Progress: A Lecture" (delivered at opening of first school bldg. of Elkhart Institute, Feb. 11, 1896, printed as tract; copy extant at MHL), 19.

13. For a fuller discussion of how Fundamentalist influence changed Mennonite understanding of biblical inspiration, see C. Norman Kraus, "American Mennonites and the Bible, 1750-1950," *MQR*, 41 (Oct., 1967), 309-329.

14. Albrecht Schiffler, John Durr, E. M. Hartman, D. J. Johns, and Daniel Kauffman, in *HT*, 33 (May 15, 1896), 147; *HT*, 34 (Apr. 15, 1897), 116.

15. Kraus, "American Mennonites and the Bible," 321-322.

16. See *HT*, 32 (July 1, 1895), 194; *HT*, 35 (Apr. 1, 1898), 98; and J. Horsch to M. Steiner, May 1, 1897, Steiner papers. Steiner, *HT*, 34 (May 1, 1897), 130-131; *Gospel Witness*, 1 (Jan. 17, 1906), 373.

17. *GH*, 1 (June 20, 1908), 178-179; Horsch to Steiner (note 16); D. Kauffman to M. Steiner, June 29, 1908, Steiner papers.

18. See especially John Horsch, *Modern Religious Liberalism: The Destructiveness and Irrationality of the New Theology* (Scottdale, Pa., 1920); Horsch, *The Social Gospel* (Scottdale, 1920); Horsch, *The Modernist View of Missions* (Scottdale, 1920); and Horsch, *The Mennonite Church and Modernism* (Scottdale, 1924).

19. *GH*: 12 (Nov. 27, 1919), 654-655; 14 (Nov. 10, 1921), 627. Guy F. Hershberger, in *An Evening to Honor Sanford Calvin Yoder* (Goshen, Ind., 1974), 26-27.

20. *GH*, 14 (Nov. 10, 1921), 627.

21. See Kauffman to J. Kratz, Dec. 21, 1935, Eastern Pennsylvania Mennonite Historical Library (EPMHL), Christopher Dock High School, Lansdale, Pa.; Kauffman to J. Smith, G. Brunk, and A. Wenger, Dec. 17, 1918, Kauffman papers, AMC.

22. Daniel Kauffman, *The Conservative Viewpoint* (Scottdale, Pa., 1918); Horsch, *Mennonite Church and Modernism*, 65-70; Kauffman in *GH*, 16 (Feb. 28, 1924), 959-960; S. Yoder to J. Kaufman (India Mission Secretary folder), Aug. 29, 1931, box 6, inactive files, AMC.

23. For Kauffman's Fundamentalist language in the early years of *Gospel Herald*, see for example *GH*, 2 (Feb. 17, 1910), 738, and *GH*, 5 (Apr. 11, 1912), 17, 19; see also note 25. Daniel Kauffman, *The Mennonite Church and Current Issues* (Scottdale, Pa., 1923), 19; "Fundamentalism," in Kauffman, ed., *Mennonite Cyclopedic Dictionary* (Scottdale, Pa., 1937), 116. Kauffman did use the "verbal and plenary" formula privately as early as 1920; see Kauffman to J. E. Hartzler, Nov. 10, 1920, Kauffman papers, AMC.

24. Daniel Kauffman, *Fifty Years in the Mennonite Church, 1890-1940* (Scottdale, Pa., 1941), 69-70.

25. *GH*, 3 (July 21, 28, Aug. 4, 1910), 251, 266-267, 283 (quotes on pp. 267, 283); *GH*, 3 (Aug. 11, 18, 25, Sept. 1, 8, 15, 1910), 292, 302, 307, 317, 323, 340-341, 355, 366, 370-371 (quote on p. 323).

26. The classic "Anabaptist Vision" statement is of course Harold S. Bender's "The Anabaptist Vision," *Church History*, 13 (Mar., 1944), 3-24; reprinted with minor changes in *MQR*, 18 (Apr., 1944), 67-88; in Guy F. Hershberger, ed., *The Recovery of the Anabaptist Vision: A Sixtieth-Anniversary Tribute to Harold S. Bender* (Scottdale, Pa., 1957), 29-54; and in J[ohn] C. Wenger, *The Mennonite Church in America* (Scottdale, 1966), 315-328. The essay has also been reprinted as a pamphlet, several times as an offset reprint of the *MQR* version, and later in a smaller and more attractive format (Scottdale, 1971).

For Bender's view of scripture see his *Biblical Inspiration and Revelation* (Scottdale, 1959). Rodney Sawatsky, in "The Influence of Fundamentalism on Mennonite Nonresistance" (University of Minnesota MA thesis, 1973), and in "History and Ideology: American Mennonite Identity Definition Through History" (Princeton University PhD dissertation, 1977), chs. 6-8, has seen Bender and his school also as quite Fundamentalist. I must disagree with the main thrust of that argument and would see Bender more as merely conservative (see C. Norman Kraus, ch. 5, in J. R. Burkholder and Calvin

Redekop, eds., *Kingdom, Cross, and Community* [Scottdale, 1976]; but I would concede that at the outset Bender was very near to Fundamentalism, as for instance in *GH*, 18 (Jan. 21, 1926), 885-887.

27. Kansas-Nebraska Mennonite Conference *Record* (1911), 168; J. Mosemann in *GH*, 14 (Sept. 1, 1921), 436.

28. MBMC minutes, exec. comm. mtg., May 26, 1913, p. 156. For Hartzler's view of scripture see: D. Kauffman to Hartzler (note 23); Hartzler to Kauffman, Nov. 13, 1920, Kauffman papers, AMC; and Kraus, "American Mennonites and the Bible" (note 13), 320-322.

29. MBMC minutes, ann. bd. mtg., May 26-28, 1913, pp. 178-179.

30. MBMC minutes, ann. bd. mtg., May 20-22, 1918, pp. 31-34.

31. For an example of how much emphasis even moderates were putting upon correct propositional belief by the mid-1920s, see H. R. Schertz in MBMC *Annual Report* (1926), 11-12.

32. MBMC minutes: joint exec. and mission committees, Mar. 14, 1913, p. 153; exec. comm. mtg., Oct. 29, 1913, p. 190; special comm. mtgs. May 22 and May (June?) 25, 1914, pp. 196, 251; South American Special Comm. mtg., Aug. 26, 1916, pp. 348-349; exec. comm. mtg., Oct. 26, 1916, pp. 351-352; joint exec. and mission committees, May 16 and 17, 1917, pp. 361-362. Mennonite [Church] General Conference *Proceedings* (1913), 156.

33. J. Shank to S. Yoder, Jan. 13, Sept. 27, 1923, and June 18, 1924; Yoder to Shank, Oct. 6, 1923, Apr. 23, 1924, and Jan. 6, 1925; J. Heatwole to Yoder, Mar. 4, 1924; Yoder to Heatwole, Mar. 11, 1924; Yoder to D. Lapp, Apr. 23, 1924; Yoder to T. Hershey, Apr. 23, 1924; Shank folder, IV-7-1, MBMC papers.

34. William E. Hocking, ed., *Rethinking Missions: A Laymen's Inquiry After One Hundred Years, by the Commission of Appraisal* (New York, 1932); S. Yoder to J. Graber, Feb. 28, 1933, IV-7-1, MBMC papers. MBMC *Annual Report* (1933): Graber, 61-62; H. F. Garber, 102-107; 118-119.

35. See note 12; *HT*, 36 (June 15, 1899), 183; Yoder, *GH*, 9 (Dec. 7, 1916), 652.

36. Horsch, *Modernist View of Missions* (note 18), 8-9; Erb, in MBMC *Annual Report* (1927), 52-53.

37. J. Harnish to S. Yoder, Aug. 6, 1921; Earl Miller to Yoder, Feb. 7, 1929; C. W. Long to Yoder, June 20, 1930; Peoria Mission folder, IV-7-1, MBMC papers.

38. Coffman, in MBMC *Annual Report* (1927), 31, 33-34.

39. B. King to S. Yoder, May 27, 1924; A. Erb to Yoder, Jan. 10, 1926; La Junta folder, IV-7-1, MBMC papers. V. Reiff to Yoder, May 26, 1924, box 22, IV-8-10, MBMC papers.

40. D. Bender to G. Bender, Apr. 15, 1914, treas. corr. Kansas, MBMC papers; *GH*, 17 (Aug. 21, 1924), 418-419; Allen H. Erb, in taped interview with Theron F. Schlabach, Oct. 12, 1974, AMC; Mennonite [Church] General Conference *Report* (1921), 9; *GH*, 15 (May 4, 1922), 106; Erb, in MBMC *Annual Report* (1925), 55.

41. Allen Erb, "The Mennonite Church and Hospital Work," *MQR*, 1 (Jan., 1927), 28-33 (quote on p. 32); Erb, in MBMC *Annual Report* (1931), 86.

42. A. Erb, in MBMC *Annual Report* (1926), 80; *GH*, 15 (May 4, 1922), 106; Erb, in MBMC minutes, ann. bd. mtg., May 22-24, 1932, p. 433; Erb, in MBMC *Annual Report* (1925), 54, 56.

43. P. Erb, *South Central Frontiers* (note 1), 414-420, 453; Linden M. Wenger, "A Study of Rural Missions in the Mennonite Church" (Union Theological Seminary [Richmond, Va.] ThM thesis, 1955), 199-204.

44. Gamber to S. Yoder, Feb. 23, 1934, IV-7-1, MBMC papers; *GH*, 33 (Oct. 3, 1940), 578.

45. Committee report, Apr. 12, 1925, La Junta folder, IV-7-1, MBMC papers.

46. See "Mental hospitals 1936" and "Wauseon Hospital 1939-40" folders, *passim*, IV-7-1, MBMC papers. In 1952 Lancaster Conference Mennonites began Philhaven

Hospital (a mental institution) at Lebanon, Pennsylvania. Mennonite Church agencies assumed administration of hospitals in Lebanon, Oregon (1948), and Greensburg, Kansas (1950).

47. See Peter J. Klassen, "Mutual Aid Among the Anabaptists: Doctrine and Practice," *MQR*, 37 (Apr., 1963), 78-95; Donald F. Durnbaugh, ed., *Every Need Supplied: Mutual Aid and Christian Community in the Free Churches, 1525-1675* (Philadelphia, 1974), 21-52, 69-90. John C. Wenger, ed., and Leonard Verduin, trans., *The Complete Writings of Menno Simons* (Scottdale, Pa., 1956), 633, 94, 558.

48. Gerhard Hein, "Palatinate," *The Mennonite Encyclopedia*, IV, 110; J. Martin of Switzerland to D. Gehman in America, n.d., and related papers, Apr. 19, 1754, and following, Bowmansville-Reading papers, Lancaster Mennonite Conference Historical Society Archives, Lancaster, Pa.; Alms Book of the Franconia Mennonite Congregation (near Souderton, Pa.), trans. by Raymond Hollenbach (copy extant in EPMHL—see note 21), Nov. 3, 1768, Dec. 30, 1771, June 4, 1773.

49. I. Pemberton, handwritten document, June 7, 1760, copy in Commissioners for Indian Affairs papers, Gratz collection, Historical Society of Pennsylvania, Philadelphia; "A Short and Sincere Declaration," Nov. 7, 1775, reprinted in John C. Wenger, *History of the Mennonites of the Franconia Conference*, Appendix IV.

50. See Guy F. Hershberger, "Historical Background to the Formation of the Mennonite Central Committee," *MQR*, 44 (July, 1970), 213-244, especially 220-221, 223, 231-232, 241-242.

51. *Ibid.*, 231-233, 238-239.

52. MBMC *Annual Reports*: (1926), 75; (1927), 5-14, 96-97.

53. Relief Committee, Women's Sewing Circle Committee, and financial reports, MBMC *Annual Reports* (1927-1944), *passim*.

54. *Ibid.*

55. MBMC *Annual Reports*: (1937), 12; (1938), 14-15; (1939), 9-13, 30, 43-44.

56. Relief Committee and financial reports, MBMC *Annual Reports* (1940-1944), *passim*.

57. John H. Mellinger in *MM*, 11 (Sept., 1934), 18; *MM*, 1924-1940, *passim*. MBMC *Annual Reports*: (1938), 18; (1941), 17; (1943), 23, 29-32; (1944), 11-13; (1953), 112. Guy F. Hershberger, "Is Alternative Service Desirable and Possible?" *MQR*, 9 (Jan., 1935), 20-36.

58. Shank, in MBMC minutes, ann. bd. mtg., May 26-28, 1913, p. 166; on Hershey's orientation see the Youngstown story in ch. 3.

59. See ch. 3.

60. MBMC minutes, ann. bd. mtg., May 20-22, 1918, p. 28.

61. T. Hershey to J. S. Hartzler, Mar. 22, 1920, box 3, Hershey papers, AMC; Hershey to S. Yoder, Aug. 12, 1920, IV-7-1, MBMC papers.

62. "Concerning a Mission Farm for South America," n.d. (signed by the Argentina missionaries, attached to letter of Nov. 30, 1926); T. Hershey to S. Yoder, Feb. 9, 1927, Apr. 1, 1928; "Answers to Kauffman's Questions About the Mission Farm Idea," n.d. (filed at early 1925, but apparently early 1927); Yoder to Hershey, June 10, 1927; Hershey folder, IV-7-1, MBMC papers. Hershey, in J. W. Shank and others, *The Gospel Under the Southern Cross* (Scottdale, Pa., 1943), 160-161.

63. Argentina missionaries to MBMC exec. and mission committees, Mar. 28, 1919, box 3, T. K. and Mae Hershey papers, AMC; T. Hershey, in MBMC minutes, ann. bd. mtg., May 17-20, 1920, p. 154; M. Hershey in *GH*, 13 (July 15, 1920), 309.

64. T. Hershey to S. Yoder and S. Musselman, July 31, 1920; Hershey to Yoder, Aug. 2, 1921; IV-7-1, MBMC papers. *GH*, 14 (July 7, 1921), 282-283; Shank, *Autobiographical Notes on the Life of Josephus Wenger Shank* (Hesston, Kan., 1969), 100-101; Nelson Litwiller, in Shank and others, *Gospel Under Southern Cross*, 131-133; Shank to Yoder, Nov. 21, 1924, IV-7-1, MBMC papers; South America Mennonite Mission

Annual Report (1924), 27-29.
  65. D. P. Lantz to V. Reiff, Apr. 22, Sept. 23, 1925, IV-7-1, MBMC papers; *GH*, 19 (Aug. 12, 1926), 437. Shank and others, *Gospel Under Southern Cross*, 183, 185, 197-199, 201, 153. MBMC *Annual Report* (1939), 127-128; MBMC minutes, VIII, exec. comm. mtg., Apr. 24, 1942.
  66. *GH*, 13 (Aug. 5, 1920), 372-373.
  67. MBMC minutes, ann. bd. mtg., May 17-20, 1920, p. 166; Litwiller, in Shank and others, *Gospel Under Southern Cross*, 149-150.
  68. Argentina missionaries to MBMC exec. and mission committees, Mar. 28, 1919, box 3, T. K. and Mae Hershey papers, AMC; *GH*, 16 (May 3, 1923), 103-104; South America Mennonite Mission *Report* (1923), 9-11.
  69. MBMC minutes, ann. bd. mtg., May 6-8, 1928, p.99.
  70. Argentina missionaries (note 68); *GH*, 18 (Jan. 28, 1926), 901.
  71. Josephus W. Shank, *South America: An Open Door* (Scottdale, Pa., 1920), 93-94; T. Hershey to S. Yoder and V. Reiff, June 6, 1923, IV-7-1, MBMC papers.
  72. T. K. Hershey, ch. 3 in Shank and others, *Gospel Under Southern Cross* (note 62).
  73. Elvin Snyder, ed., in Shank and others, *Gospel Under Southern Cross* (note 62), 174; N. Litwiller to S. Yoder, Apr. 20, 1935, IV-7-1, MBMC papers. MBMC minutes: joint exec. and mission committees, Aug. 20, 1927, p. 40; exec. comm. mtg., Oct. 26, 1927, p. 47; D. D. Miller at ann. bd. mtg., May 19-21, 1929, pp. 164-166.
  74. Tobias K. Hershey, *I'd Do It Again* (Elkhart, Ind., 1961), 89.
  75. *GH*, 1 (Aug. 22, 1908), 331; 4 (Sept. 14, 1911), 372-373; 5 (Nov. 7, 1912), 501; 5 (Dec. 19, 1912), 597.
  76. *CM*, 8 (Dec., 1916), 745; Lehman, "An Explanation Regarding the Article Headed, 'A Foot-ball Game in India,'" attached to Lehman to G. Bender, Apr. 7, 1917, IV-7-1, MBMC papers.
  77. M. C. Lehman, "An Explanation" (note 76); G. Bender to D. Lapp, Feb. 14, 1917, treas. corr. Nebraska, MBMC papers. G. Lapp to Bender, Mar. 29, 1917; Bender to Lehman, June 20, 1917; M. Lapp to Bender, May 2, 1918; M. Lapp to Franconia Conf. ministers and bishops, n.d. (1918); Friesen to V. Reiff, June 30, 1922; IV-7-1, MBMC papers.
  78. G. Bender to G. Lapp, Jan. 25, 1917; Stauffer (signature largely cut out, but quite evidently his) to Bender (M. C. Lehman folder), n.d. (internal evidence suggests 1917, but filed at late 1915 or early 1916); IV-7-1, MBMC papers. Lehman, "Goshen in the East," *The Maple Leaf* (Goshen College yearbook), 1 (1915), 119.
  79. *GH*, 14 (Sept. 1, 1921), 435-436.
  80. See note 34.
  81. For "soul-winning" and "personal Savior" language, see for instance MBMC minutes, ann. bd. mtg., May 20-22, 1918, pp. 10, 39; American Mennonite Mission *Annual Report* (1918-1919), 19; *GH*, 14 (Nov. 17, 1921), 645. For "community" and "Kingdom" language, see for instance J. Kaufman to T. Hershey, Jan. 8, 1920, box 3, Hershey papers, AMC; A. Brunk to V. Reiff, Apr. 3, 1922, IV-7-1, MBMC papers; E. E. Miller to Reiff, July 26, 1923, IV-7-1, MBMC papers; *GH*, 18 (Oct. 1, 1925), 547-548.
  82. Lehman, in MBMC minutes, ann. bd. mtgs.: May 18-20, 1915, p. 269; May 2-6, 1924, p. 319.
  83. M. Lehman to S. Yoder, Nov. 14, 1922, Apr. 11, 1923; Yoder to Lehman, Dec. 23, 1922, Jan. 18, 1923; Lehman to V. Reiff, Dec. 12, 1923; IV-7-1, MBMC papers.
  84. American Mennonite Mission *Annual Report* (1922), 22.
  85. Brunk in American Mennonite Mission *Annual Report* (1918-1919), 34-36.
  86. *Ibid.*, 36-37.
  87. *Ibid.*, 34; American Mennonite Mission *Annual Report* (1918-1919), 43-47; *India Mission News*, 1 (May, 1922), 4.

88. Brunk (note 85), 34.

89. *CM*, 18 (Apr. 1, 1926), 104; V. Reiff to S. Lapp, Aug. 14, 1926, IV-7-1, MBMC papers; India missionaries, *Building on the Rock* (Scottdale, Pa., 1926) (mustaches clearly visible on pp. 22, 41, 65, 67, 84, 122, 138). J. Bixler and A. Christophel to MBMC exec. comm. (Kaufman folder), n.d. (attached to letter of May 1, 1924); A. Brunk to S. Yoder (India Mission Secretary folder), Feb. 5, 1926; Yoder to Brunk (India Mission Sec. folder), Mar. 12, 1926; Brunk to Reiff, June 3, 1926; G. Lapp to Reiff, May 24, 1927; IV-7-1, MBMC papers. *GH*, 19 (May 27, 1926), 177. The title may have been *Modernism in India*; see "Report of Meeting ... July 22, 1929," p. 9, G. Lapp folder, IV-7-1, MBMC papers.

90. J. Stauffer to S. Yoder, Apr. 14, 25, 1927; Yoder to Stauffer, Apr. 20, 1927; India Mission folder. Yoder to A. Brunk, May 14, 1927, India Mission Sec. folder. IV-7-1, MBMC papers.

91. T. Hershey to S. Yoder, June 1, 1927, IV-7-1, MBMC papers; see Stauffer to Yoder, Apr. 25 (note 90).

92. S. Yoder to D. Miller, Mar. 23, 1928, IV-7-1; Yoder to V. Reiff, Apr. 13, 1928, IV-8-10; Yoder to J. Kaufman (India Mission Sec. folder), May 14 Oct. 29, 1928, IV-7-1; MBMC papers. Virginia Mennonite Conference *Minutes*, Aug. 2-3, 1928.

93. Yoder to Reiff (note 92); Kauffman to Yoder, Mar. 19, 1928, IV-7-1, MBMC papers.

94. Yoder to Miller (note 92). Yoder to B. Weaver and N. Mack, May 11, 1928; typewritten questionnaire, n.d., and attached document, "Meeting of Committees: Re India Mission," Nov. 6, 1928; Mack to Yoder, Feb. 27, 1929; John Mellinger to Yoder, July 17, 1929; Eastern Mennonite Board of Missions and Charities (EMBMC) folder, IV-7-1, MBMC papers. "Report of Meeting" (note 89). J. Mosemann to Yoder, Apr. 3, 16, 1929; Yoder to Mosemann, Apr. 13, 1929; Mosemann to Yoder, Mar. 26, 1929, EMBMC folder, IV-7-1, MBMC papers.

95. "Reply of the Mennonite Board of Missions and Charities to the Paper Sent Out by the Board of Bishops of the Lancaster County Conference," May 1-6, 1930, attached to MBMC (S. C. Yoder, sec.) to Board of Bishops of Lancaster County [sic] and MBMC members, May 24, 1930, IV-8-10, MBMC papers; reprinted in MBMC minutes, private bd. mtg., May 3, 1930, pp. 229-233.

96. MBMC minutes, special bd. mtg., May 18, 1929, pp. 156-157; S. Yoder to E. Miller, Mar. 27, 1929, IV-7-1, MBMC papers.

97. Mosemann to Yoder, Apr. 3 (note 94).

98. See John A. Lapp, *The Mennonite Church in India, 1897-1962* (Scottdale, Pa., 1972), pp. 94-98.

99. J. Kaufman to S. Yoder (India Mission Sec. folder), July 18, 1927, IV-7-1, MBMC papers.

100. J. D. Graber, taped interview with John S. Miller, Aug. 22, 1972; E. E. Miller taped interview with J. S. Miller, Nov. 6, 1972; AMC. Kaufman, "The National Christian Council (India)," typewritten document, attached to Kaufman to Yoder (India Mission Sec. folder), Oct. 12, 1933; Graber to Yoder (India Mission Sec. folder), May 12, 1938; G. Lapp to V. Reiff, Aug. 28, 1933; IV-7-1, MBMC papers.

101. MBMC *Annual Report* (1934), 26. Brenneman to S. Yoder, July 17, 1935, Mar. 5, 1936; Yoder to Brenneman, Apr. 17, 1936; box 5, Yoder papers, AMC. Yoder to J. Graber, Apr. 5, June 28, 1938; Graber to Yoder, May 12, 1938; India Mission Sec. folder, IV-7-1, MBMC papers.

102. "Reply" (note 95), p. 4; Miller to S. Yoder, Dec. 17, 1929, IV-7-1, MBMC papers.

103. Burkhard to S. Yoder (Gladys Weaver folder), July 15, 1933; unsigned (Yoder?) to P. Friesen, Feb. 23, 1924; G. Lapp to Yoder, Sept. 1, 1924; IV-7-1, MBMC papers. For evidence of continued support in Lancaster Conf., see, e.g., "Teachers" (with list of donors

sponsoring them), attached to V. Reiff to O. Miller, Dec. 26, 1928; R. Smucker to Reiff, Oct. 6, 1928; G. Lapp to Reiff, June 13, 1929; Yoder to W. Lauver, Jan. 6, 1930; IV-7-1, MBMC papers. Coffman to Yoder (EMBMC folder—see note 94), Mar. 17, 1930, IV-7-1, MBMC papers.

104. M. Kanagy to S. Yoder, Apr. 16, Sept. 30, 1931; Yoder to Kanagy, Apr. 17, 1931; IV-7-1, MBMC papers. Edwin and Irene Weaver, taped interview with John S. Miller, Feb. 8, 1973, AMC.

105. J. Kaufman to S. Yoder, Mar. 4, 1930; Yoder to Kaufman, June 13, 1930; India Mission Sec. folder, IV-7-1, MBMC papers. Yoder to G. Nice and I. Ruth (M. C. Lehman folder), Sept. 12, 1930; Lehman and V. Reiff to "Dear Friend of Education," Nov. 12, 1930; Yoder to E. E. Miller, Oct. 24, 1928; IV-7-1, MBMC papers.

106. Pickett in J. W. Pickett, A. L. Warnshuis, G. H. Singh, and D. A. McGavran, *Church Growth and Group Conversion* (Lucknow, U.P., India, 1936), ch. 6 (quotations from pp. 63 and 61 of 1962 edition).

107. MBMC *Annual Report* (1934), 25-26; George J. Lapp, *The Christian Church and Rural India: A Report on Christian Rural Reconstruction and Welfare Service by the Christian Forces of India and Burma* (Calcutta, 1938).

108. MBMC minutes, special bd. mtg., May 20, 1929, p. 159. S. Yoder to "Dear Fellow-Worker" (India Mission folder), Sept. 11, 1929; Hershey to MBMC (Declaration of Faith ... folder), Oct. 23, 1929; IV-7-1, MBMC papers.

109. For the photo of Hershey see his book *I'd Do It Again* (note 74), between pp. 80 & 81; a 1927 photo in the same location shows him with raincoat buttoned to the chin, perhaps for different reason. E. Shank to S. Yoder (Declaration of Faith ... folder), Oct. 19, 1929, IV-7-1, MBMC papers.

110. Shank to Yoder (note 109); Declaration of Faith ... folder, *passim*, IV-7-1, MBMC papers.

111. J. Kaufman to S. Yoder, Dec. 17, 1930; Yoder to Kaufman, Jan. 13, 1931; India Mission Sec. folder, IV-7-1, MBMC papers. Mellinger in MBMC *Annual Report* (1931), 97-98.

112. MBMC *Annual Report* (1933), 102-103.

113. See ch. 7. See also George R. Anchak, "An Experience in the Paradox of Indigenous Church Building: A History of the Eastern Mennonite Mission in Tanganyika, 1934-1961" (Michigan State University PhD dissertation, 1975), ch. 3; and *MM*, 1934-1940, *passim*, especially H. Lutz and H. Garber in *MM*, 15 (Nov. 27, 1938), 5-7, 14-17. E. W. Stauffer in *GH*, 34 (May 15, 1941), 149; "Reply" (note 95), p. 3.

114. Kaufman to S. Yoder (India Mission Sec. folder), Mar. 28, 1928, IV-7-1, MBMC papers.

115. S. Yoder to J. Graber (India Mission Sec. folder), June 28, 1939, IV-7-1, MBMC papers.

116. Wenger, "Study of Rural Missions" (note 43), 245.

Chapter 5. The Pure Gospel: Teaching the "All Things" (I)

1. J. N. Kaufman and M. C. Lehman in *GH*, 4 (Apr. 20, 1911), 37.

2. *GH*, 4 (Feb. 1, 1912), 702; 14 (June 9, 1921), 197, 204.

3. E. Shank to S.C. and Emma Yoder (J. W. Shank folder), Apr. 10, 1920, IV-7-1, MBMC papers; George Ronald Anchak, "An Experience in the Paradox of Indigenous Church Building: A History of the Eastern Mennonite Mission in Tanganyika, 1934-1961" (Michigan State University PhD dissertation, 1975), 164-165.

4. A. Yoder to General Problems Committee (Chicago Home Mission folder), Dec. 13, 1930, IV-7-1, MBMC papers. Regarding missionary children see, e.g. G. Bender to R. Blosser, May 29, 1918, and Blosser to Bender, June 28, 1918, E. E. Miller folder; C. Esch to V. Reiff, Dec. 17, 1929; Reiff to Lydia Lehman (M. C. Lehman folder), Dec. 2, 16, 1930; IV-7-1, MBMC papers. See also, Mary Good, taped interview with John S. Miller,

Jan. 26, 1973, AMC. N. Litwiller to S. Yoder (South American Mission Secretary folder), July 20, 1943, IV-7-1, MBMC papers.

5. Yoder to S. King, Feb. 7, 1933, S. C. Yoder papers, AMC; Yoder to C. Snyder and H. Shoup (Los Angeles folder), IV-7-1, MBMC papers; Sanford C. Yoder, *The Days of My Years* (Scottdale, Pa., 1959), 143.

6. *GH*, 1 (Mar. 27, 1909), 821; 24 (Oct. 8, 1931), 611.

7. MBMC minutes, ann. bd. mtg., May 25-27, 1914, pp. 228-229, 233.

8. *GH*, 18 (June 18, 1925), 245; *HT*, 42 (Apr. 20, 1905), 126.

9. Tobias K. Hershey, *I'd Do It Again* (Elkhart, Ind., 1961), 74-75; Miller to S. Yoder (Peoria folder), Feb. 7, 1929, IV-7-1, MBMC papers.

10. *HT*, 2 (Oct., 1865), 83; 32 (May 15, 1895), 146.

11. Review of Robert E. Speer, *South American Problems* (New York, 1912), in *International Review of Missions*, 1 (Oct., 1912), 735-737 (quote on p. 737); LeFeber in *CM*, 6 (Jan., 1924), 397; Reist in *Missionary Conference: Addresses Delivered at the First General Missionary Conference ...*, Dec. 24-26, 1917 (copy extant in MHL), 52-61.

12. MBMC minutes, ann. bd. mtg., May 20-22, 1918, p. 15; Lehman in *CM*, 6 (Dec., 1914), 758-759.

13. For confirmation of this evaluation see David W. Shenk, *Mennonite Safari* (Scottdale, Pa., 1974), ch. 7, esp. pp. 105-106.

14. *GH*, 3 (July 14, 1910), 225.

15. *GH*, 15 (Mar. 1, 1923), 949-950; Gingerich (note 8); Noah Good in *MM*, 16 (Apr. 16, 1939), 15.

16. Paul Erb, *South Central Frontiers* (Scottdale, Pa., and Kitchener, Ont., 1974), 131; Harry A. Brunk, *History of Mennonites in Virginia* (Staunton and Verona, Va., 1959, 1972), II, 342; Raber to S. Yoder (Detroit folder), Feb. 24, 1941, IV-7-1, MBMC papers; Allgyer, in MBMC minutes, ann. bd. mtg., June 13-15, 1937, p. 322.

17. *HT*, 34 (Dec. 15, 1897), 374-375; "Answers to Questions Submitted to Workers," n.d., contiguous to A. Eash to I. Detweiler (Chicago Home Mission folder), late 1909, IV-6-4, MBMC papers; *CM*, 6 (Jan., 1914), 399; Kanagy to G. Bender, Mar. 1, 1918, treas. corr. MBMC papers.

18. Edmund G. Kaufman, *The Development of the Missionary and Philanthropic Interest Among the Mennonites of North America* (Berne, Ind., 1931).

19. Horsch in *GH*, 24 (Oct. 29, Nov. 5, 12, 1931), 674-675, 690-691, 706-708.

20. *Ibid.*, 674.

21. Concerning A. M. Eash, see Eash to A. Good, July 5, 1913; J. Shoemaker to Good, July 19, 1913; Shoemaker to G. Bender, June 30, 1919; Shoemaker folder, treas. corr. Illinois, IV-8-11, MBMC papers. See also, V. Reiff to D. Bender, Nov. 19, 1921, treas. corr. Kansas, IV-8-11; Eash to S. Yoder, Feb. 1, 1923, 26th St. Mission folder, IV-7-1; MBMC papers. Mininger, "A Message from Our Kansas City Missions," mimeographed form letter, Nov. 9, 1921, exec. off. corr. IV-7-1, MBMC papers; Weyandt in *CM*, 19 (May, 1927), 145; Lehman in MBMC *Annual Report* (1931), 126.

22. Hershey in *GH*, 14 (July 7, 1921), 274; 20 *Lecciones Bíblicas* (Trenque Lauquen, Argentina, n.d.; copy extant in MHL); Lehman, in MBMC minutes, ann. bd. mtg., May 2-6, 1924, p. 235.

23. "Adopted at the Last Annual Conference," typed document, n.d., contiguous to letter of Apr. 10, 1929; J. Kaufman to S. Yoder, Jan. 7, 1931, Dec. 14, 1933; Yoder to Kaufman, Feb. 27, 1931; India Mission secretary folder, IV-7-1, MBMC papers. "Minutes of the Evangelistic Samaj held at Bethel Church Balodgahan, January 29, 1931," India Mission folder, IV-7-1, MBMC papers; MBMC minutes, ann. bd. mtg., May 26-29, 1934, pp. 95-96; Yoder, "South American Trip 1940," typewritten diary, box 29, S. C. Yoder papers, AMC.

24. MBMC *Annual Report* (1933), 98.

25. *Ibid.*, 99, 100.

26. See ch. 4 at footnote 34.
27. *CM*, 3 (Feb., 1911), 41-42.
28. Ressler in *HT*, e.g.: 36 (June 1, 1899), 167; 37 (Feb. 15, 1900), 58; 37 (Oct. 1, 1900), 299; 37 (Dec. 1, 1900), 357-358; 38 (Jan. 1, 1901), 6; 38 (Mar. 15, 1901), 86.
29. Burkhard in *GH*, 2 (June 10, 1909), 174-175; Graber in *GH*, 21 (Aug. 2, 1928), 394-395. Lehman to S. Yoder, Nov. 14, 1922, Apr. 11, 1923; Yoder to Lehman Dec. 23, 1922, Jan. 18, 1923; IV-7-1, MBMC papers. MBMC minutes, exec. comm. mtgs., June 16, Dec. 20-21, 1923, pp. 189, 205; Martin Clifford Lehman, "The Religious Significance of the Writings of Harishchandra" (Yale University PhD dissertation, 1934).
30. *MM* (1930-1940), *passim*. Magdalena Edelman Nice, taped interview with Theron F. Schlabach, Oct. 24, 1977, AMC; Erb, *South Central Frontiers* (note 16), 62, 110, 129-135, 416-420.
31. MBMC *Annual Report* (1926), 127-128.
32. Hershey to MBMC exec. comm., Mar. 31, 1921, IV-7-1, MBMC papers.
33. See especially Josephus W. Shank, *South America: An Open Door* (Scottdale, Pa., 1920); Shank, *South America: A Report of Observations in Five Nations* (n.p., 1913; copy extant in MHL); Shank, "Central Argentine as a Background for Christian Evangelism" (Bethany Biblical Seminary, Chicago, BD thesis, 1933); Lewis S. Weber, *Argentina from Within* (Scottdale, 1945).
34. MBMC *Annual Reports*: (1929), 66; (1932), 81-82; (1938), 102.
35. Hubert Pellman, *Eastern Mennonite College, 1917-1967: A History* (Harrisonburg, Va., 1967), 76-77; J. C. Wenger, tel. convers. with Theron F. Schlabach, Oct. 13, 1977.
36. MBMC minutes, joint exec. and mission committees, May 18, 1933, p.6; S. Yoder to E. Weaver (Chicago Home Mission folder), Feb. 7, 1935, IV-7-1, MBMC papers.
37. Yoder to N. Litwiller, Nov. 13, 1940, IV-7-1; MBMC papers.
38. J. Kaufman to T. Hershey, Jan. 8, 1920, box 3, Hershey papers, AMC. " Meeting of Committees: Re India Mission," Nov. 6, 1928; John H. Mosemann (Sr.) to S. Yoder and D. Miller, Apr. 16, 1929; Eastern Mennonite Board of Missions and Charities folder, IV-7-1, MBMC papers. MBMC minutes, bd. mtg., May 18, 1929, pp. 156-157.
39. *MM*, 13 (Apr. 26, 1936), 11; Whitaker in *CM*, 34 (June, 1942), 180.
40. S. Yoder to T. Hershey, Sept. 24, 1923; T. and M. Hershey, D. P. and L. Lantz, and W. and F. Lauver to MBMC exec. comm., Nov. 2, 1923; T. K. Hershey folder, IV-7-1, MBMC papers. V. Hallman and S. Gamber to "Dear Brethern [sic]," n.d. (Nov., 1923); Hershey to Yoder, Nov. 19, 1923; Gamber folder, IV-7-1, MBMC papers. A. Kauffman to Yoder, Sept. 8, Nov. 30, 1937; Hershey to Yoder, Sept. 16, 1937; Yoder to Kauffman, Sept. 22, Nov. 15, Dec. 4, 1937; Yoder to Kauffman and E. Hallman, Nov. 15, 1937; Mexican border folder, IV-7-1, MBMC papers.
41. T. K. Hershey and E. V. Snyder, ch. 4 in J. W. Shank and others, *The Gospel Under the Southern Cross* (Scottdale, Pa., 1943), 86.
42. *CM*, 15 (Mar., 1923), 75.
43. *MM*, 4 (Sept. 15, 1927), 4; Kaufman to Hershey (note 38).
44. Indiana-Michigan Mennonite Conference *Minutes* (1875), 23. For the later, more absolute stance on divorce, see, e.g., South American Mennonite Mission *Annual Report* (1924), 37-38; also, C. W. Long to S. Yoder, Sept. 19, 1930, and Yoder to Long, Sept. 22, 1930, Peoria folder, IV-7-1, MBMC papers. On the marriage question in India, see, e.g., Kaufman to Hershey (note 38); and MBMC *Annual Report* (1931), 104. For Africa, see for instance *MM*, 15 (Oct. 16, 1938), 13; *MM*, 15 (Nov. 27, 1938), 4; Noah K. and Muriel T. Mack, "Our Memories" (typewritten memoir, 1971; copy available at Eastern Pennsylvania Mennonite Historical Library, Christopher Dock Mennonite High School, Lansdale, Pa.), 36-38; and MBMC *Annual Report* (1939), 56.
45. A. Kauffman to S. Yoder, Mar. 25, and Apr. 22, 1941, Feb. 2, 1942, and May 10,

1943; Yoder to Kauffman, Mar. 29, 1941; Mexican border folder, IV-7-1, MBMC papers. Amsa and Mona Kauffman, taped interview with John S. Miller, Nov. 30, 1973, AMC; Amsa Kauffman, tel. convers. with Theron F. Schlabach, Dec. 31, 1975.

Chapter 6. The Pure Gospel: Teaching the "All Things" (II)

1. Allgyer in MBMC *Annual Report* (1927), 144. Allgyer, "Occupying Our Home Fields," typescript, n.d., filed at Dec. 30, 1931, IV-7-1; Daniel Kauffman, "Our Standard for Missionaries," typescript, pp. 2-3, treas. corr., Pennsylvania, IV-8-11 (copy retyped and slightly revised by J. L. Stauffer, in Mission Comm. folder, IV-6-1); MBMC papers.

2. Samuel Frederick Coffman, "Extol the Love of Christ" (1925), hymn no. 410 in *The Mennonite Hymnal* (Newton, Kan., and Scottdale, Pa., 1969); Coffman in MBMC *Annual Report* (1927), 25-34, quotes on pp. 31, 33.

3. Bender in MBMC minutes, ann. bd. mtg., May 2-6, 1924, p. 233; Rutt in MBMC *Annual Report* (1936), 159-160.

4. Good in MBMC *Annual Report* (1927), 34-41. quotes on p. 38.

5. Tobias K. Hershey, *Old Time Revival* (Scottdale, Pa., 1937), 36.

6. J. D. Graber, taped interview with John S. Miller and Theron F. Schlabach, Aug. 18, 1972; Graber, taped interview with Miller, Jan. 30, 1973; AMC.

7. Franklin H. Littell, *The Anabaptist View of the Church* (Philadelphia, 1952); Robert Friedmann, *The Theology of Anabaptism* (Scottdale, Pa., 1973). See especially Guy F. Hershberger, *The Way of the Cross in Human Relations* (Scottdale, 1958), 43-56, 194-197; and Hershberger, *War, Peace, and Nonresistance* (Scottdale, 1944), 321.

8. Walter Freytag, "The Meaning and Purpose of the Christian Mission," *International Review of Missions*, 39 (Apr., 1950), 153-161; J. Waskom Pickett, *Christian Mass Movements in India* (New York, Cincinnati, etc., 1933); Donald A. McGavran, *Understanding Church Growth* (Grand Rapids, 1970); Pickett, A. L. Warnshuis, G. H. Singh, and McGavran, *Church Growth and Group Conversion* (Lucknow, U.P., India, 1936).

9. See John Howard Yoder, "Church Growth Issues in Theological Perspective," ch. 2 in Wilbert R. Shenk, ed., *The Challenge of Church Growth* (Scottdale, Pa., 1973), 25-47; Donald McGavran, "Wrong Strategy: The Real Crisis in Mission," *International Review of Missions*, 54 (Oct., 1965), 451-461; McGavran, *Understanding Church Growth*.

10. Yoder, conversation with Theron F. Schlabach, Dec. 15, 1973, at Elkhart, Ind.

11. Steiner to J. Coffman, Dec. 5, 1894, box 9, Coffman papers, AMC; C. Yoder in *CM*, 6 (Jan., 1914), 425; Lapp in MBMC minutes, ann. bd. mtg., May 20-22, 1918, p. 10; Graber in MBMC *Annual Report* (1932), 80-85 (quotes on pp. 84, 85); Miller in MBMC *Annual Report* (1938), 97-106 (quote on p. 101).

12. Miller (note 11).

13. Roland Allen, *Missionary Methods: St. Paul's or Ours? A Study of the Church in the Four Provinces* (London, 1912); MBMC *Annual Report* (1926), 13; J. D. Graber, tel. convers. with Daniel W. Hertzler, Oct. 11, 1917.

14. MBMC *Annual Report* (1939), 16.

15. *MM*, 7 (Aug. 24, 1930), 3-4.

16. Bender in MBMC minutes, ann. bd. mtg., May 25-27, 1914, pp. 244-245; Schertz in MBMC minutes, ann. bd. mtg., May 2-6, 1924, p. 295; Weber in MBMC *Annual Report* (1927), 116; Lutz in MBMC *Annual Report* (1940), 86; S. E. Allgyer in MBMC minutes, ann. bd. mtg., May 2-6, 1924, p. 268.

17. T. K. Hershey in MBMC minutes, ann. bd. mtg., May 2-6, 1924, p. 286. John and Genevieve Yoder Friesen, taped interview with John S. Miller, Feb. 23, 1973; Joe, Natty, and Esther Ventura, taped interview with Miller, Feb. 3, 1973, AMC.

18. S. C. Yoder, "Report of the Mennonite Board of Missions and Charities," Mennonite [Church] General Conference *Report* (1939), 15-18, quote on p. 16; MBMC minutes, joint exec. and mission committees, May 16-17, 1941, pp. 2-3; Brenneman to S. Yoder, May 20, 1936, box 5, Yoder collection, AMC.

19. L. C. Miller in MBMC *Annual Report* (1927), 127; Lutz in *MM*, 15 (Nov. 27, 1938), 3-4. William and Beatrice Hershey Hallman and Mae Hershey, taped interview with John S. Miller, Oct. 26, 1972; Selena Gamber Shank, taped interview with Miller, Nov. 15, 1972, AMC. Graber, 1973 interview (note 6); T. K. Hershey and E. V. Snyder, in J. W. Shank and others, *The Gospel Under the Southern Cross* (Scottdale, Pa., 1943), 82; A. C. Brunk in American Mennonite Mission *Annual Report* (1926), 5. For translations of key Anabaptist and Mennonite works, see below, note 67.

20. Orley Swartzentruber, taped interview with Theron F. Schlabach, May 31, 1977, AMC; Friesen, interview (note 17); Graber, 1973 interview (note 6).

21. T. and M. Hershey and J. and E. Shank to exec. and mission committees, Mar. 28, 1919, box 3, Hershey papers, AMC; Miller in American Mennonite Mission *Annual Report* (1932), 119-122.

22. Derstine in MBMC minutes, ann. bd. mtg., May 17-19, 1921; p. 231; Swartzentruber, interview (note 20).

23. Ressler in *HT*, 35 (Jan. 1, 1898), 12; Kauffman in *Gospel Witness*, 1 (Aug. 23, 1905), 161; S. C. Yoder in MBMC *Annual Report* (1927), 137.

24. *GH*, 15 (Oct. 5, 1922), 530.

25. MBMC *Annual Report* (1924), 18.

26. Graber, both interviews (note 6).

27. Regarding the home field, consult for example Edna and Bertha Mertz, taped interview with John S. Miller, Feb. 19, 1973, AMC. Henry Lutz and Henry Garber in *MM*, 15 (Nov. 27, 1938), 15; David W. Shenk, *Mennonite Safari* (Scottdale, Pa., 1974), 86; Miller in MBMC *Annual Report* (1938), 104.

28. Lehman in *GH*, 11 (July 4, 1918), 250-252; Friesen, interview (note 17); Shenk, *Mennonite Safari*, 86; South American Mennonite Mission *Annual Report* (1926), 3, 7, 9.

29. *Convenciones de las Iglesias Menonitas de la República Argentina* (i.e., Conferences of Argentina Mennonite Churches) reports (1932); Nelson Litwiller, taped interview with John S. Miller, Dec. 28, 1972, AMC; T. K. Hershey in MBMC minutes, ann. bd. mtg., May 19-21, 1929, p. 179.

30. For an excellent case on this point, consult Magdalena Edelman Nice, taped interview with Theron F. Schlabach, Oct. 24, 1977, AMC.

31. Graber, "Nonresistance and Missions," in (mimeographed) "Report of the MCC Peace Section Study Conference held at Winona Lake, Indiana, on November 9-12, 1950," p. 117.

32. *Ibid.*

33. *Ibid.*

34. R. Pierce Beaver, *Envoys of Peace* (Grand Rapids, 1964); 1858 statement quoted in Arthur Schlesinger, Jr., "The Missionary Enterprise and Theories of Imperialism," in John K. Fairbank, ed., *The Missionary Enterprise in China and America* (Cambridge Mass., 1974), 349.

35. Beaver, *Envoys*, 24; Louise Creighton, "The Meeting of the Continuation Committee of the World Missionary Conference ... Sept. 26 to Oct. 2, 1912," *International Review of Missions*, 2 (Jan., 1913), 118-125, quotes on p. 123; see also "Noteworthy Articles," *International Review of Missions*, 3 (Apr., 1914), 359. Kauffman in *Gospel Witness*, 1 (Mar. 14, 1906), 469.

36. See especially C. Norman Kraus, *The Community of the Spirit* (Grand Rapids, 1974), ch. 4; also, Beaver, *Envoys*, ch. 3; James Engle Metzler, "Shalom and Mission" (Associated Mennonite Biblical Seminaries MA thesis, 1977); John Driver, *Community and Commitment* (Scottdale, Pa., 1976); Robert L. Ramseyer, "The Christian Peace Witness and Our Missionary Task: Are Mennonites Evangelical Protestants with a Peace Witness?" (unpublished paper, June, 1976, copy extant in MHL).

37. See ch. 1, and/or Theron F. Schlabach, "Reveille for *Die Stillen im Lande*," *MQR*, 51 (July 1977), 213-226.

38. Steiner in *HT*, 35 (Aug. 15, 1898), 242-243; Hostetler in *GH*, 1 (Dec. 19, 1908), 604-605; Lantz in *CM*, 4 (Apr., 1912), 489-490; Lehman in MBMC minutes, ann. bd. mtg., May 18-20, 1915, p. 269.
39. O. Miller to V. Reiff, Oct. 13, 1925; Reiff to Miller, Oct. 29, 1925; IV-7-1, MBMC papers.
40. See ch. 4, section on relief; J. Shoemaker to V. Reiff, Feb. 9, 1927, treas. corr. Illinois, MBMC papers.
41. Shoemaker to Reiff (note 40); Erb to Theron F. Schlabach, Mar. 4, 1974, in Schlabach's possession; "A Statement of Our Position on Peace, War and Military Service," in Mennonite [Church] General Conference *Report* (1937), 123-126, quote on p. 123.
42. Guy F. Hershberger, "Christian Nonresistance: Its Foundation and Its Outreach," *MQR*, 24 (Apr., 1950), 156-162. Hershberger, "Nonresistance an Integral Part of the Gospel," in *War, Peace, and Nonresistance*, second ed., rev. (Scottdale, Pa., 1953), 58-60. For vivid illustration of the fact that the idea of an integrated gospel message with peace really a part of gospel was just beginning to germinate in the 1940s, compare the 1953 to the first edition of Hershberger's book (Scottdale, 1944), in which there is no section with that title, but only on p. 55 the following. "The principle of nonresistance is an integral part of God's plan for His people...the nonresistant way of life is in accord with the whole tenor of the Gospel." Hershberger, *Way of the Cross* (note 7); John Howard Yoder, "The Place of the Peace Message in Missions" (1960; copy in MHL); Yoder, *As You Go* (Scottdale, 1972); Yoder, *The Original Revolution* (Scottdale, 1972); Yoder, *The Politics of Jesus* (Grand Rapids, 1972); Kraus, *Community of the Spirit* (note 36).
43. *GH*, 35 (Apr. 30, 1942), 100-101.
44. Lind to Raber, July 16, 1942, city mission corr. folder; Nelson Kauffman, mimeographed letter to city workers, July 12, 1943, *City Missions Quarterly Bulletin* folder; IV-16-5, MBMC papers.
45. See James Juhnke, "Mennonites and the Great Compromise," *The Mennonite*, 84 (Sept. 23, 1969), 562-564; Juhnke, "Mennonite Benevolence and Civic Identity: The Post-War Compromise," *Mennonite Life*, 25 (Jan., 1970), 34-37.
46. Ernest E. Miller, taped interview with John S. Miller, Jan. 18, 1973, AMC. On the economic lure away from nonresistance, see for example MBMC *Annual Report* (1942), 68; Friesen, interview (note 17); Graber, 1972 interview (note 6); Graber, "Nonresistance and Missions" (note 31).
47. E. E. Miller, interview (note 46).
48. "Restrictions," section of undated (apparently 1911), unsigned document also containing "Constitution of the Mennonite Conference in India," "Rules and Discipline for the Mennonite Church in India," "Regulations," and "Ordinances," document no. 10, business meetings, reports of committees, IV-17-1, MBMC papers. This document was apparently prepared by board representatives J. S. Shoemaker and J. S. Hartzler and missionaries M. C. Lapp and P. A. Friesen; see American Mennonite Mission *Annual Report* (1910-1911), 21. The mission approved the document, translated it into Hindi, and submitted it to the congregations for approval; this led to the organizational meeting of the Mennonite Conference in India in January 1912—see American Mennonite Mission *Annual Report* (1911-1912), 6, 8. The same "Restrictions" are printed with minor changes as Article 4 of "Rules and Discipline ... " in American Mennonite Mission *Annual Report* (1923-1924), 34-38.
49. Mennonite Church in India Conference *Minutes*, 1914-1919, *passim*, IV-17-17, MBMC papers; John A. Lapp, *The Mennonite Church in India, 1897-1962* (Scottdale, Pa., 1972), 91-92.
50. Mennonite Church in India Conference *Minutes*, Dec. 16, 1935, IV-17-17, MBMC papers; Graber, 1973 interview (note 6).
51. Graber, 1973 interview (note 6).

52. MBMC *Annual Report* (1942), 68.
53. *Ibid.*, Graber, 1972 interview (note 6); Lapp, *Mennonite Church in India*, 92.
54. Lapp, *Mennonite Church in India*, 191, 193; Obadiah P. Lal, taped interview with Theron F. Schlabach, Aug. 21, 1973, AMC; Graber, 1972 interview (note 6).
55. George Ronald Anchak, "An Experience in the Paradox of Indigenous Church Building: A History of the Eastern Mennonite Mission in Tanganyika, 1934-1961" (Michigan State University PhD dissertation, 1975), 171; Shenk, *Mennonite Safari* (note 27), 60; Leatherman in *MM*, 14 (Oct. 17, 1937), 12-13.
56. *MM*, 1924-1940, *passim*; Sauder in *MM*, 8 (Nov. 29, 1931), 4-5; the Mosemanns in *MM*, 16 (Oct. 22, 1939), 13.
57. Theron F. Schlabach, "To Focus a Mennonite Vision," in J. Richard Burkholder and Calvin Redekop, *Kingdom, Cross, and Community* (Scottdale, Pa., 1976), 27-28; Guy F. Hershberger, "Questions Raised Concerning the Work of the Committee on Peace and Social Concerns of the Mennonite Church and Its Predecessors" (mimeographed paper, copy in AMC).
58. Josephus W. Shank, *South America; A Report of Observations in Five Nations* (n.p., 1913, copy extant in MHL), 80; Hershey in *GH*, 10 (Dec. 6, 1917), 650; J. Quarles to Hershey, Sept. 13, 1919, box 3, Hershey papers, AMC.
59. Yoder to Hersheys and Shanks, Mar. 29, 1920, box 3, Hershey papers, AMC.
60. J. W. Shank, replies to questionnaire for mission-work candidates, May 12, 1908, and n.d. (1912?), June 25, 1914, and n.d. (1917?); T. K. Hershey, reply to questionnaire for mission-work candidates, n.d. (1917?); Mission Comm. corr. IV-6-1, MBMC papers. Josephus W. Shank, *South America: An Open Door* (Scottdale, Pa., 1920), T. and M. Hershey to H. and A. Hess, Dec. 6, 1918, box 3, Hershey papers, AMC.
61. *20 Lecciones Bíblicas*; (Trenque Lauquen, Argentina, n.d.; copy in MHL): Shank in *El Camino Verdadero*, 2 (Mar., 1922), copy in South American Mission, misc., folder; D. P. Lantz to V. Reiff, Dec. 3, 1924; IV-7-1, MBMC papers. N. Litwiller in South America Mennonite Mission *Annual Report* (1929), 16-17; Elvin V. Snyder to Theron F. Schlabach, July 26, 1976, in Schlabach's possession.
62. First quote from Hubert Herring, *A History of Latin America*, second ed., rev. (New York, 1961), 670; Snyder to Schlabach (note 61); Barbosa in *CM*, 24 (June 1932), 190; *La Voz Menonita*, 1932-1958, *passim*. MBMC *Annual Report*: (1933), 182-183; (1934), 105-106; (1935), 153-155. Peace Problems Committee minutes, Sept. 21, 1934, AMC.
63. Hershey in MBMC *Annual Report* (1935), 146; MBMC minutes, ann. bd. mtg., May 2-6, 1924, pp. 305-306; William Hallman, Nelson Litwiller, and Elvin Snyder, interview with Theron F. Schlabach, Aug. 25, 1976, notes in Schlabach's possession.
64. Elvin V. Snyder, "La Iglesia Cristiano y el Estado," published in Snyder and J. W. Shank's paper *El Pastoral*, 2 (Nov. and Dec., 1940: copy extant in MHL).
65. *Ibid.* In 1959 Snyder also wrote a paper, unpublished. "Anabaptist Characteristics in Spanish Mennonite Literature" (copy in MHL) in which he classified articles in *La Voz Menonita* to argue statistically that the Argentine Mennonite Church *was* teaching Anabaptist-Mennonite doctrines, perhaps better than the North American church was doing through its *Gospel Herald*. However, a rather thorough examination of how he classified materials, and of the amount of actual space within articles devoted to communicating Mennonite positions on given topics as opposed to what were general Protestant or other positions, leaves me convinced that he did not make the case.
66. Feliciano Gorjón, *La Iglesia y el Estado: Hacia una Filosofía Christiana de las Relaciones Entre la Iglesia y el Estado* (Buenos Aires and Trenque Lauquen, Argentina, 1948).
67. Harold S. Bender and John Horsch, *Menno Simons' Life and Writings* (Scottdale, Pa., 1936), trans. by Carmen Palomeque as *Menno Simons: Su Vida y Escritos* (Trenque Lauquen, Argentina, 1943); Guy F. Hershberger, "Peace and War in the Old

Testament," *MQR*, 17 (Jan., 1943), 5-22, trans. by Elvin V. Snyder as "Paz y Guerra en el Ant. Testamento," *La Voz Menonita*, 12 (July/Aug., 1943), 371-382; Hershberger, "Peace and War in the New Testament," *MQR*, 17 (Apr., 1943), 59-72, trans. by Snyder as "Paz y Guerra en el Nuevo Testamento," *La Voz Menonita*, 12 (Sept./Oct., 1943), 416-425; Hershberger, *War, Peace, and Nonresistance* (note 7).

68. J. Shank to S. Yoder, Nov. 21, 1924, IV-7-1, MBMC papers.

69. Elvin Snyder in MBMC *Annual Reports*: (1934), 105-106; (1935), 153-155 (quote from p. 155).

70. Shank to S. Yoder, Sept. 26, 1938, IV-7-1, MBMC papers.

71. *Ibid.*; Lydia Shank, tel. convers. with Theron F. Schlabach, Mar. 3, 1976.

72. Snyder to Schlabach (note 61); Litwiller, interview (note 63). For criticisms of Argentine Mennonites by North Americans, see for example John W. Miller to John Howard Yoder, July 28, 1954; and compare to Yoder to Miller, Aug. 6, 1954; AMC. For a defense of the Argentine position see Anita Swartzentruber, "The Argentine Mennonite Church, the State, and Military Service" (unpublished paper, 1954; copy in MHL). Communications between Yoder and Theron F. Schlabach, September, 1977.

73. Shank to Yoder (note 70).

74. Argentine conference minutes, 1940, pp. 22-23; Hershey, in Shank and others, *Gospel Under Southern Cross* (note 19), 241-242.

75. T. K. Hershey, in Shank and others, *Gospel Under Southern Cross* (note 19), 241; Shank to Yoder (note 70); MBMC minutes, joint exec. and mission committees, May 3-4, 1940, p. 85; S. C. Yoder, "Report of Trip to Argentina" (from internal evidence 1940), box 29, Yoder papers, AMC.

76. S. Yoder to N. Litwiller, Nov. 13, 1940, IV-7-1, MBMC papers.

Chapter 7. Helping Gospel Take Root

1. Roland Allen, *Missionary Methods: St. Paul's or Ours? A Study of the Church in the Four Provinces* (London, 1912); see also Allen, *Missionary Principles* (London, 1964, and Grand Rapids, 1964). P. Beyerhaus article in *International Review of Mission*, 53 (Oct., 1964), 394-396; J. D. Graber, "Roland Allen on Leadership," n.d. (from internal evidence after 1968), copy in the possession of John H. Yoder, Associated Mennonite Biblical Seminaries, Elkhart, Ind.

2. See *International Review of Missions*: W. Paton article, 17 (Jan., 1928), 5-6; A. M. Chirgwin, 17 (July, 1928), 531-532; A. H. Clark, 18 (Apr., 1929), 199-207; H. A. Van Andel, 24 (July, 1935), 349-357; O. Thomas, 24 (July, 1935), 404-407; W. Freytag, 29 (Apr., 1940), 204-215. J. D. Graber in MBMC *Annual Report* (1940), 17.

3. W. Gascoyne-Cecil in *International Review of Missions*, 2 (Oct., 1913), 730.

4. *International Review of Missions*: P. Beyerhaus article, 53 (Oct., 1964), 395-396; W. Freytag, 39 (Apr., 1950), 155.

5. *International Review of Missions*, 29: John McKay article, (July, 1940), 391-394; Latourette, (Oct., 1940), 429-440 (quotes on p. 431).

6. See especially: a special issue of the Eastern Board's *Missionary Messenger* on indigenization—*MM*, 16 (Nov. 26, 1939); also, *MM*, 16 (Feb. 11, 1940), 16-17.

7. *A Manual on Foreign Missions: Setting Forth the Conditions Incumbent on Those Who Wish to Enter the Service under the Auspices of the Mennonite Evangelizing and Benevolent Board* [MEBB] (Elkhart, Ind., 1899; copy in MEBB papers, AMC), 10.

8. King in *CM*, 9 (May, 1917), 139-140; Wenger in *Gospel Witness*, 2 (Feb. 27, 1907), 762-763.

9. T. K. Hershey in South America Mennonite Mission *Annual Report* (1922) 9; Hershey and W. Detweiler in MBMC *Annual Report* (1936), 16-20; Hershey to S. Yoder, Sept. 9, 1922, IV-7-1, MBMC papers; Shank in MBMC *Annual Report* (1932), 74-80.

10. Ressler in *Gospel Witness*, 1 (July 5, 1905), 111-112; Lapp in *GH*, 5 (Jan. 16, 1913), 661. India mission (Kaufman, sec.), answers to 1932 Study & Revisions Committee

questionnaire, Missionary Questionnaire folder, IV-25-3; H. Mueller to S. Yoder (Lima Mission folder), Dec. 7, 1923, IV-7-1; MBMC papers.

11. Daniel Kauffman, *The Mennonite Church and Current Issues* (Scottdale, Pa., 1923), 103.

12. See Linden Wenger, "A Study of Rural Missions in the Mennonite Church" (ThM thesis, Union Theological Seminary [Richmond, Va.], 1955), 234.

13. To sample how that change was occurring, compare for instance: *HT*, 17 (Nov., 1880), 201-202; C. A. Hartzler in *Missionary Conference: Addresses Delivered at the First General Missionary Conference ... Dec. 24-26, 1917* (copy extant in MHL), 83; and S. Yoder to L. Hartzler and D. Castillo (Chicago Home Mission folder), Feb. 20, 1936, IV-7-1, MBMC papers.

14. The concern was clearly present, for instance, in that special issue of *Missionary Messenger* (note 6). See also: *HT*, 35 (Jan. 15, 1898), 23; and American Mennonite Mission *Annual Report* (1926), 5.

15. S. Yoder to J. Mininger (Kansas City Mission folder), May 2, 1922, IV-7-1, MBMC papers.

16. Of course many Americans couched those self-help attitudes in biblical language and used biblical proof texts to support them—see Irvin G. Wyllie, *The Self-Made Man in America: The Myth of Rags to Riches* (New Brunswick, 1954).

17. *MM*, 11 (Nov. 29, 1934), 7; George Ronald Anchak, "An Experience in the Paradox of Indigenous Church Building: A History of the Eastern Mennonite Mission in Tanganyika, 1934-1961" (Michigan State University PhD dissertation, 1975), 138.

18. Reiff to A. Swartzentruber, May 18, 1927, IV-7-1, MBMC papers.

19. S. Yoder to R. Mishler (Los Angeles folder), July 8, 1933; Shank to V. Reiff, dated Feb. 5, 1930, but internal evidence dates it 1931, attached to Reiff to Shank, Mar. 28, 1931; IV-7-1, MBMC papers.

20. W. Lauver and C. Casares to S. Yoder, Apr. 6, 1931, IV-7-1, MBMC papers; T. K. Hershey, in Josephus W. Shank and others, *The Gospel Under the Southern Cross* (Scottdale, Pa., 1943), 156-159.

21. J. Kaufman to S. Yoder (India Mission Secretary folder), Jan. 7, 1931, and Dec. 14, 1933, IV-7-1; S. J. Hostetler, answers to 1935 Study & Revisions Committee questionnaire, Missionary Questionnaire folder, IV-25-3; MBMC papers.

22. Leaman to M. Steiner, Apr. 28, 1905, Steiner papers; *Building on the Rock* (Scottdale, Pa., 1926), 51, 52; *Gospel Witness*, 3 (July 10, 1907), 233; MBMC *Annual Report* (1941), 13.

23. Tobias K. Hershey, *I'd Do It Again* (Elkhart, Ind., 1961), 66; Hershey and E. V. Snyder, in Shank and others, *Gospel Under Southern Cross*, 86-87, 89. MBMC minutes, ann. bd. mtgs.: Apr. 30-May 3, 1927, p. 17; May 3-5, 1931, pp. 350-351. Hershey to S. Yoder and V. Reiff, Apr. 18, 1927, box 3, Hershey papers, AMC; Anchak, "An Experience in the Paradox" (note 17), 83.

24. Anchak, "An Experience in the Paradox" (note 17), 83 and ch. 3, *passim*.

25. Brunk in *GH*, 16 (Aug. 23, 1923), 420; Esch in *GH*, 13 (May 6, 1920), 118; Lapp to V. Reiff, May 4, 1933, IV-7-1, MBMC papers.

26. See for instance M. Lapp to V. Reiff, Dec. 8, 1922, IV-7-1, MBMC papers.

27. See for instance J. Kaufman to S. Yoder, Jan. 14, 1932; Graber to Yoder, May 16, 1939; India Mission Sec. folder, IV-7-1, MBMC papers. See also MBMC minutes, joint exec. and mission committees, May 16-17, 1941, pp. 2-3. Graber, answers to 1935 Study & Revisions Committee questionnaire (note 21).

28. J. Shank to S. Yoder (Sewing Circles folder), Apr. 22, 1935, IV-7-1, MBMC papers; Hershey, in Shank and others, *Gospel Under Southern Cross* (note 20), 159.

29. Hershey, in Shank and others, *Gospel Under Southern Cross* (note 20), 160; MBMC minutes, ann. bd. mtg., 1937, p. 338.

30. Nelson Litwiller, taped interview with John S. Miller, Dec. 29, 1972, AMC;

Hershey, in Shank and others, *Gospel Under Southern Cross* (note 20), 160-161.

31. Hershey, in Shank and others, *Gospel Under Southern Cross* (note 20), 43-44, 161.

32. J. Kaufman to S. Yoder (India Mission Sec. folder), Dec. 14, 1933; Kaufman to Yoder, dated Jan. 4, 1933, but internal evidence dates it 1934; IV-7-1, MBMC papers. Hostetler, answers to questionnaire (note 21); Graber, in MBMC *Annual Report* (1937), 121.

33. S. Yoder to A. Culp (Ontario folder), Mar. 19, 1931, IV-7-1, MBMC papers; city missions' answers to 1932 questionnaire (note 10); Hartzler to Yoder (Chicago Home Mission folder), Mar. 11, 1936, IV-7-1, MBMC papers.

34. "Peoria Mennonite Church 1941 Program of Self Support" (mimeographed pamphlet); S. Yoder to C. W. Long, Dec. 12, 1941; Peoria Mission folder, IV-7-1, MBMC papers. MBMC *Annual Report* (1940), 22-23; "Certified Copy of Authorization to Transfer Title of India Church Properties to India Mennonite Church Conference," Feb. 20, 1941, India Mission Sec. folder, IV-7-1, MBMC papers.

35. See David W. Shenk, *Mennonite Safari* (Scottdale, Pa., 1974), 107-111, for the demise of self-support dogma in Africa under such scrutiny in the late 1950s.

36. *HT*, 36 (July 15, 1899), 214.

37. Lapp to G. Bender, Apr. 29, 1914, IV-7-1, MBMC papers; S. Yoder to T. Hershey, May 6, 1920, and May 14, 1927, box 3, Hershey papers, AMC.

38. Harry A. Brunk, *History of Mennonites in Virginia* (Staunton and Verona, Va., 1959, 1972), I, 281, 286-287, and II, 179, 184, 191. S. Allgyer to V. Reiff, Feb. 11, 1921, Mar. 27, 1933; A. Kauffman to S. Yoder (Mexican border folder), Sept. 8, 1937; IV-7-1, MBMC papers. *GH*, 33 (Oct. 3, 1940), 586.

39. See Anchak, "An Experience in the Paradox" (note 17), ch. 3.

40. *GH*, 12 (Jan. 8, 1920), 774; Hershey, *I'd Do It Again* (note 23), 42-43.

41. *GH*, 6 (May 29, 1913), 133; J. Kaufman to T. Hershey, Jan. 8, 1920, box 3 T.K. and Mae Hershey papers, AMC; *GH*, 20 (June 16, 1927),244-245; American Mennonite Mission *Annual Report* (1927), 7. MBMC *Annual Reports*: (1932), 132-133, 139; (1940), 123.

42. T. and M. Hershey and J. and E. Shank to exec. and mission committees (South America Mission, misc. folder), Mar. 15, 1921, IV-7-1, MBMC papers; MBMC minutes, ann. bd. mtg., June 4-6, 1922, p. 25; Hershey and Snyder, in Shank and others, *Gospel Under Southern Cross* (note 23), 92-93; J. Shank to V. Reiff, Mar. 3, 1930, IV-7-1, MBMC papers; Nelson Litwiller, taped interview with John S. Miller, Dec. 28, 1972, AMC.

43. S. Yoder to T. Hershey, Feb. 22, 1927, Hershey to Yoder, Mar. 22, 1927; box 3, Hershey papers, AMC.

44. For a balanced treatment of this issue, see D. A. McGavran article in *International Review of Missions*, 22 (Jan., 1933). 33-49.

45. Lal, taped interview with Theron F. Schlabach, Aug. 21, 1973, AMC; Litwiller, interview (note 42); South America Mennonite Mission *Annual Report* (1926), 43; *HT*, 37 (Sept. 15, 1900), 278.

46. N. Litwiller to S. Yoder (South American Mission Sec. folder), Apr. 26, 1944, IV-7-1, MBMC papers.

47. N. Litwiller in MBMC *Annual Report* (1931), 225-226; *CM*, 34 (May, 1942), 143; Anchak, "An Experience in the Paradox" (note 17), 124-125; Shenk, *Mennonite Safari* (note 35), 53-54; MBMC *Annual Report* (1941), 72-73.

48. South America Mennonite Mission *Annual Report* (1929), 9; *HT*, 41 (Oct. 6, 1904), 326; N. Litwiller to S. Yoder, Apr. 20, 1935, IV-7-1, MBMC papers; *GH*, 35 (Oct., 1942), 578.

49. See, for instance, articles by Gascoyne-Cecil (note 3), 731-732, and C. Miao (note 1), 377.

50. Answers to questionnaire (note 10).
51. T. Hershey in South America Mennonite Mission *Annual Report* (1922), 14; Hershey to S. Yoder, June 17, 1922, IV-7-1, MBMC papers; *CM*, 14 (Dec., 1922), 746.
52. *MM*: 13 (Mar. 28, 1937), 3; 15 (Nov. 27, 1938), 14.
53. John A. Lapp, *The Mennonite Church in India: 1897-1962* (Scottdale, Pa., 1972), 162-163; Nelson Litwiller, in Shank and others, *Gospel Under Southern Cross* (note 20), 134-139; Shank, *Autobiographical Notes on the Life of Josephus Wenger Shank* (Hesston, Kan., 1969), 100, 108, 115; *MM*, 15 (Nov. 27, 1938), 14.
54. T. Brenneman to S. Yoder, May 20, 1943, box 25, S. C. Yoder papers, AMC.
55. *GH*, 6 (Sept. 11, 1913), 373; MBMC *Annual Report* (1938), 148.
56. Friesen, taped interview with John S. Miller, Mar. 2, 1973, AMC.
57. *GH*, 15 (Mar. 1, 1923), 946; Shank, "Central Argentine as a Background for Christian Evangelism" (Bethany Biblical Seminary, Chicago, BD thesis, 1933), 85; for mention of self-support and self-propagation but almost no reference to self-governance, see, e.g., the questionnaire sent to missionaries in 1932 by the board's Study & Revisions Committee, and replies (note 10); *GH*, 12 (May 29, 1919), 148-149.
58. MBMC minutes, ann. bd. mtg., May 2-6, 1924, p. 240; *Building on the Rock* (note 22), 50-51. Taped interviews with John S. Miller, AMC: Selena Gamber Shank, Nov. 15, 1972; Mina Esch, Nov. 16, 1972; Litwiller interview (note 42). American Mennonite Mission *Annual Reports*: (1921), 44-45; (1925), 23; see also S. Allgyer to MBMC exec. comm., Oct. 24, 1921, IV-7-1, MBMC papers. Shank and others, *Gospel Under Southern Cross* (note 20): Gorjón at 259; Weber at 254.
59. *Building on the Rock* (note 22), 44-46; American Mennonite Mission *Annual Report* (1922), 9; *CM*, 12 (Apr., 1920), 489-490. A. Brunk to S. Yoder, Oct. 12, 1934; Yoder to Brunk, Nov. 19, 1934; India Mission Sec. folder, IV-7-1, MBMC papers. MBMC *Annual Report* (1939), 91.
60. Hershey and Snyder, in Shank and others, *Gospel Under Southern Cross* (note 23), 88; *Convenciones de las Iglesias Menonitas de la República Argentina* (i.e. Conferences of Argentina Mennonite Churches), reports (1923), 1; *GH*, 16 (Nov. 8, 1923), 659; T. Hershey to J. Rutt, Nov. 30, 1932, IV-7-1, MBMC papers.
61. R. Mosemann in *MM*, 13 (Apr. 26, 1936), 13; Anchak, "An Experience in the Paradox" (note 17), 82. *MM*: 15 (Nov. 27, 1938), 15; 14 (Sept. 12, 1937), 5, 15; 16 (Oct, 22, 1939), 15. Shenk, *Mennonite Safari* (note 35), 90, 120.
62. Anchak, "An Experience in the Paradox" (note 17), 129.
63. For a few examples see *MM*: 7 (Dec. 7, 1930), 2; 11 (Mar. 31, 1935), 15; 15 (Feb. 5, 1939), 15; 16 (Oct. 22, 1939), 14. For more evidence see *MM*, 1930-1940, *passim*.
64. See, for instance, MBMC minutes: ann. bd. mtg., June 16-18, 1935, pp. 153, 155; joint exec. and mission committees, June 17-18, 1938, pp. 375-376. Garber in *MM*, 15 (Apr. 24, 1938), 2; Wenger, "A Study of Rural Missions" (note 12), 290-291.
65. See ch. 8 for some data on home mission congregations' achieving regular congregational status.
66. S. Yoder to E. Hallman, Kauffman, H. Reist, J. G. Hartzler, and A. Swartzendruber, Nov. 28, 1938; Kauffman to Yoder, Dec. 14, 1938; Mexican border folder, IV-7-1, MBMC papers. Paul Erb, *South Central Frontiers: A History of the South Central Mennonite Conference* (Scottdale, Pa., and Kitchener, Ont., 1974), 425-426, 439, 457, 458.
67. MBMC minutes, ann. bd. mtg., May 20-22, 1918, p. 36.
68. T. Hershey to S. Yoder, Jan. 21, 1929, Apr. 17 and Jan. 7, 1934, IV-7-1, MBMC papers; William Hallman, tel. convers. with Theron F. Schlabach, Aug. 1, 1977.
69. Lapp, *Mennonite Church in India* (note 53), 174.
70. *Building on the Rock* (note 22), 44, 45, 46; *Menonait Patrika* (Nov.-Dec., 1969), 20, (copy available in MHL); consultation with J. D. Graber, Dec. 12, 1977; M. Lapp in *Missionary Conference: Addresses Delivered at the First General Missionary Conference*

... *Dec. 24-26, 1917*, 63 (copy in MHL).
71. Lapp, *Mennonite Church in India* (note 53), 168. Graber to Millersville, Pa., Sunday School, Dec. 12, 1935; Graber to "Dear Fellow Missionaries on Furlough" (India Mission Sec. folder), Feb. 15, 1939; IV-7-1, MBMC papers.
72. MBMC minutes, exec. comm. mtg., Feb. 19, 1929, p. 146; MBMC *Annual Report* (1930), 62; *GH*, 20 (Apr. 28, 1927), 85; *CM*, 20 (June, 1928), 176-177; Miller to Yoder, Oct. 4, 1927, IV-7-1, MBMC papers; J.N. Kaufman, G. J. Lapp, E. E. Miller, *Report of the Committee on Transfer of Work to Indian Hands* (Dhamtari, C.P., India, 1928; copy in India Mission folder, IV-7-1, MBMC papers), 15-16; MBMC *Annual Report* (1929), 33-34.
73. Kaufman, Lapp, Miller, *Report*, 6-7, 13, 14, 15.
74. J. Kaufman to S. Yoder (India Mission Sec. folder), Feb. 29, 1928, IV-7-1, MBMC papers.
75. *Ibid.*
76. J. Kaufman to S. Yoder (India Mission Sec. folder), Jan. 7, 1931, IV-7-1, MBMC papers. MBMC minutes: bd. exec. session, May 2, 1931, p. 330; ann. bd. mtg., May 3-5, 1931, p. 346. E. Miller to V. Reiff, Jan. 24, 1931, IV-7-1, MBMC papers.
77. MBMC Annual *Reports*: (1933), 134; (1938), 9. J. Kaufman to "Dear Christian Workers," Sept. 22, 1933; E. Miller to V. Reiff, Jan. 24, 1931, Jan. 25, 1933; IV-7-1, MBMC papers.
78. MBMC *Annual Report* (1937), 121; MBMC minutes, ann. bd. mtg., June 13-15, 1937, p. 334.
79. Lauver to MBMC (South American Mission Sec. folder), Apr. 6, 1931, IV-7-1, MBMC papers; Litwiller, in MBMC *Annual Report* (1933), 174; Hershey and Snyder, and Hershey alone, in Shank and others, *Gospel Under Southern Cross* (note 23), 87-88, 159; Litwiller interview (note 42).
80. Litwiller interview (note 42).
81. J. Kaufman to S. Yoder, May 22, 1930; Yoder to Kaufman, July 11, 1930; India Mission Sec. folder, IV-7-1, MBMC papers. MBMC *Annual Reports*: (1940), 22-23; (1943), 14; (1944), 10. "Certified Copy of Authorization" (note 34). MBMC minutes: joint exec. and mission committees, May 16-17, 1941, May 14-15, 1943; exec. comm., Sept. 2, 1942. Lapp, *Mennonite Church in India* (note 53), 180.
82. See note 34.
83. Regarding Africa, see above at note 47. J. Shank to S. Yoder, Jan. 22, 1938, IV-7-1, MBMC papers. Duilio Bottaro to MBMC, Nov. 30, 1942; Yoder to Bottaro, Jan. 30, 1943; South America Mission, misc. folder, IV-7-1, MBMC papers. Hershey, in Shank and others, *Gospel Under Southern Cross* (note 20), 43-44; Hershey, *I'd Do It Again* (note 23), 122-125. Hershey's two accounts of the Battaglia affair come of course from one side only; and it is possible that missionary demands that Battaglia get into business to support himself, and then later that he get out of business (see above at notes 29-31), had something to do with his alienation.
84. Miller to Reiff (note 77, both letters); Graber to missionaries (note 71).
85. Graber to S. Yoder (India Mission Sec. folder), Jan. 7, 1939, IV-7-1, MBMC papers; S. King to Yoder, Mar. 16, 1939, box 29, S. C. Yoder papers, AMC; P. Friesen to Yoder, Mar. 23, 1939, IV-7-1, MBMC papers; Graber, in MBMC *Annual Report* (1939), 16-17.
86. Graber to Yoder (note 85).
87. Untitled document, n.d. (Graber to Yoder, note 88, dates it Nov., 1940), India Mission Sec. folder, IV-7-1, MBMC papers.
88. J. Graber to S. Yoder (India Mission Sec. folder), Jan. 30, 1940, IV-7-1, MBMC papers.
89. Document (note 87); see also MBMC *Annual Report* (1940), 17.
90. J. Graber to S. Yoder (India Mission Sec. folder), Dec. 16, 1940, IV-7-1, MBMC

papers; MBMC minutes, VIII, ann. bd. mtg., June 14-16, 1942, p. 30.
91. Graber to Yoder (note 88).
92. MBMC *Annual Report* (1943), 15.
93. Anchak, "An Experience in Paradox" (note 17), 126-133, 151-166.
94. American Mennonite Mission *Annual Report* (1924), 25.

Chapter 8. Gospel at Home (I)
1. In 1974 researcher John S. Miller spent several months gleaning home-mission information from various books, periodicals, etc., reducing the information to quantifiable form, recording it on computer tapes, and developing a program for using the computer to extract and correlate the data.

The periodicals Miller used were mainly newsletters of district conferences of the Mennonite Church, namely: *Allegheny Conference News*, 11-17 (1954-1960), continuing *Southwestern Pennsylvania Conference News*, 1-11 (1942-1954), superseding *Southwestern Pennsylvania Mission News*; (Franconia Conf.) *Mission News*, 1-24 (1937-1960); *The Illinois Conf.) Missionary Guide*, 1-16 (1944-1960); *The* (Indiana-Michigan Conf.) *Gospel Evangel*, 29-41 (1948-1960), continuing *Rural Evangel*, 1-28 (1919-1947); (Iowa-Nebraska Conf.) *Missionary Challenge*, 1-13 (1948-1960);(Lancaster Conf.) *Missionary Messenger*, 14-37 (1937-1960); *North Central Conference Bulletin*, 1-7 (1965-1971); *The* (Ohio and Eastern Conf.) *Ohio Evangel*, 7-14 (1953-1960), continuing *Ohio Mission Evangel*, 2-6 (1948-1952), continuing *Ohio Mission News Bulletin*, 1 (1943-1947); *Ontario Mennonite Evangel*, 1-5 (1956-1960), superseding *Church and Mission News*, 5-21 (1940-1956), continuing *Mission News Bulletin*, 1-4 (1936-1939); (Pacific Coast Conf.) *Missionary Evangel*, 1-16 (1945-1960); *The* (South Central) *Conference Messenger*, 1-16 (1945-1960); *Southwest Messenger*, 1-5 (1956-1960); and (Virginia Conf.) *Missionary Light*, 8-20 (1948-1960). In addition he included some data from *Gospel Herald*'s early years, i.e. vols. 1-3 (1908-1910), and from the non-conference paper of the (Colorado) Missionary Colportage Endeavor, *Colporteurs Messenger*, 1-3 (1937-1939).

Books, papers, etc., that Miller used were: Harry A. Brunk, *History of Mennonites in Virginia* (Staunton and Verona, Va., 1959, 1972); Lewis J. Burkholder, *A Brief History of the Mennonites in Ontario* (Markham, Ont., 1935); John L. Horst and Ammon Kaufman, *Seventy-fifth Anniversary of the Southwestern Pennsylvania Mennonite Conference* (n.p., 1951); Lee H. Kanagy, "Rural Missions in the Indiana-Michigan and South Central Conferences" (unpublished seminar paper, 1950; copy in MHL); John C. King, "History of the Ohio Mennonite Mission Board" (unpublished seminar paper, 1955; copy in MHL); Paul N. Kraybill, ed., *Called to Be Sent* (Scottdale, Pa., 1964); Ira D. Landis, *The Missionary Movement Among Lancaster Conference Mennonites* (Scottdale, 1937); Mennonite Board of Missions and Charities, *Directory: Mennonite Church District Mission Board and Congregational Home Missions, 1960* (Elkhart, Ind., 1960); *Mennonite Yearbook*, 1960, 1974; Carson Moyer, "Methods of Expansion for Mennonite Missions in Ontario" (unpublished seminar paper, 1954; copy in MHL); Samuel G. Shetler, *Church History of the Pacific Coast Mennonite Conference District* (Scottdale, n.d.); John R. Smucker, "The History of the Ohio Mennonite Mission Board and the Early Missions Concern of the Mennonites of Ohio" (unpublished seminar paper, 1958; copy in MHL); Grant M. Stoltzfus, *Mennonites of the Ohio and Eastern Conference: From the Colonial Period in Pennsylvania to 1968* (Scottdale, 1969); Robert L. Stoltzfus, "Mennonite Mission Work Among the American Negro" (unpublished seminar paper, 1950; copy in MHL); Harry F. Weber, *Centennial History of the Mennonites of Illinois* (Goshen, Ind., 1931); John C. Wenger, *History of the Mennonites of the Franconia Conference* (Telford, Pa., 1937); John C. Wenger, *Mennonites in Indiana and Michigan* (Scottdale, 1961); Glen and Lois Johns Yoder, *Building a Church at Culp, Arkansas* (Elkhart, n.d.).

Unfortunately, circumstances were such that Miller did not include data on missions from two district conferences—the Washington-Franklin Conference covering a region on the border of Pennsylvania and Maryland, and the Northwest (formerly Alberta-Saskatchewan) one. Nor had Linden M. Wenger's "A Study of Rural Missions in the Mennonite Church" (Union Theological Seminary ThM thesis, 1955) come to our attention by the time of Miller's research. The author has used Wenger's thesis to amplify the maps that appear in chapter 9, as Exhibit 9-6. But he found no reason to believe that inclusion of data from these sources would have altered any conclusions materially. Such inclusion would of course have altered some statistics a bit, but hardly enough to be of consequence in light of the margins one must allow already, due to the scattered nature of the data that got included. In other words, there seemed every reason to believe that there were uses for available research time and money far more fruitful than redoing the computer tapes.

2. John A. Hostetler, *The Sociology of Mennonite Evangelism* (Scottdale, Pa., 1954), 82-82a; Wenger, "A Study of Rural Missions" (note 1), 217, 224.

3. Bender, "The Anabaptist Vision," *Church History*, 13 (Mar., 1944), 3-24; for frequent reprints of that classic article, see ch. 4, n. 26.

4. Wenger, "A Study of Rural Missions" (note 1), 298.

5. For further confirmation of the grass-roots character of at least rural home missions, see Wenger, "A Study of Rural Missions" (note 1), 127-130.

6. Hubert R. Pellman, *Eastern Mennonite College, 1917-1967: A History* (Harrisonburg, Va., 1967), 63, 82, 118-119, 159-162; John S. Umble, *Goshen, College, 1894-1954: A Venture in Christian Higher Education* (Goshen, Ind., 1955), 197-212; Paul Erb, *South Central Frontiers: A History of the South Central Mennonite Conference* (Scottdale, Pa., and Kitchener, Ont., 1974), 209, 211-213.

7. Umble, *Goshen College*, 206-208; Wenger, *Mennonites in Indiana and Michigan* (note 1), 215, 217-218, 220; *Rural Evangel*: 14 (Jan. 1, 1933), 6; 14 (July 1, 1933), 4; 27 (Jan.-Feb., 1946), 6-7. *Gospel Evangel*, 30 (May-June, 1949), 3-4; Stoltzfus, "Mennonite Mission Work" (note 1), 12-15; Brunk, *History of Mennonites in Virginia*, II (note 1), 389-396, 399-409, 155-157, 159-162, 164-165, 232. *Mennonite Encyclopedia*: I, 433, 555; III, 758. *Missionary Light*, 9 (Jan., 1949), 15; Wenger, "A Study of Rural Missions" (note 1), 114-116. Erb, *South Central Frontiers*, 211-212; Mary Miller, *A Pillar of Cloud: The Story of Hesston College, 1909-1959* (North Newton, Kan., 1959), 117, 132, 150.

8. H. Raymond Charles, in Kraybill, ed., *Called to Be Sent* (note 1), 96-97; John Howard Yoder, *As You Go: The Old Mission in a New Day* (Scottdale, Pa., 1961), 7-9 and *passim*.

9. Indiana-Michigan Conf. *Minutes* (1905), 90.

10. Erb, *South Central Frontiers* (note 6), 110, 62.

11. Sauder in MBMC *Annual Report* (1933), 70; Graber to V. Reiff, Apr. 3, 1933, IV-7-1, MBMC papers. See especially Graber, *GH*, 39 (Jan., 1947), 929-930.

12. S. Yoder to T. Hershey, Oct. 23, 1936, IV-7-1, MBMC papers. *GH*, 48 (May 17, 1955), 473; 44 (Dec. 4, 1951), 1178.

13. Max Warren, *The Missionary Movement from Britain in Modern History* (London, 1965), 15.

14. Gideon G. Yoder, *The Nurture and Evangelism of Children* (Scottdale, Pa., 1959), 23-26. The Yoder book lays out quite well a Mennonite Church understanding of child evangelism at a time just beyond the scope of this study, and on pp. 63-66 prints an official 1955 Mennonite Church statement on the subject. The book is illuminating for understanding Mennonite Church responses in the 1930s and 1940s as well.

15. Robert W. Lynn and Elliott Wright, *The Big Little School: Sunday Child of American Protestantism* (New York, etc., 1971), *passim*, esp. 43-46; C. B. Eavey, *History of Christian Education* (Chicago, 1964), 378-379; Yoder, *The Nurture and Evangelism of Children*, 66-72; *Mennonite Encyclopedia*, IV, 654-656.

16. *HT*, 33 (Nov. 1, 1896), 329; A. M. Eash, *After Ten Years: A Brief Report of the*

Notes for Pages 242-255 327

... *Work of the Twenty-Sixth Street Mennonite Mission, 1906-1916* (Chicago, n.d.), 47.

17. See, e.g.: *HT*, 34 (Mar. 15, 1897), 81-82; *GH*, 2 (June 17, 1909), 179-180; *MM*, 5 (July 29, 1928), 8-9; J. Paul Sauder, in Kraybill, ed., *Called to Be Sent* (note 1), 36.

18. MBMC minutes, ann. bd. mtg., May 18-20, 1915, pp. 279-280; Swartzentruber to MBMC exec. comm. (Mennonite Orphans folder), Oct. 19, 1932, IV-7-1, MBMC papers.

19. Ressler diary, Nov. 18, 1894, AMC; Bressler in *Gospel Witness*, 1 (Dec. 20, 1905), 332; A. Metzler to M. Steiner, Mar. 13, 1905, Steiner papers. *GH*, 33 (Sept. 5, 1940); (Mininger at) 25 (Apr. 28, 1932), 85; 34 (July 3, 1941), 281.

20. J. S. Coffman to J. W. Coffman, Dec. 6, 1893, box 4, J. S. Coffman papers, AMC. E.g.: A. Metzler to M. Steiner, Nov. 24, 1903, Steiner papers; J. Liechty in *HT*, 42 (Apr. 20, 1905), 126. Yake in *CM*, 20 (July, 1928), 216-218; Sauder in *MM*, 16 (May 28, 1939), 4.

21. *GH*, 34 (May 22, 1941), 166, 172.

22. *CM*, 7 (Aug., 1915), 231-232; *MM*, 13 (Jan. 10, 1937), 8-9; for similar reasoning applied to vacation Bible schools, see *MM*, 9 (Aug. 14, 1932), 11. Thelma Lockwood and Lydia Burton, Feb. 25, 1973; Natty, Joe, and Esther Ventura, Feb. 3, 1973; taped interviews with John S. Miller, AMC.

23. See Constance E. Padwick, "Children and Missionary Societies in Great Britain," *International Review of Missions*, 6 (Oct., 1917), 561-575.

24. *CM*, 34 (June, 1942), 180, 192.

25. *MM*, 10 (May 28, 1933), 2-3.

26. A 1949 questionnaire tried to determine how many members of the Mennonite Church came from "non-Mennonite families," and got results ranging from a high of 37 percent in the Virginia Conference to a low of 8 percent in the Lancaster and several other conferences, with an overall figure of 12 percent. However, the question as asked was so ambiguous that it did not, for instance, make clear how many had come from Amish or other groups closely related to the Mennonite Church, how may with "non-Mennonite" surnames were first-generation Mennonites, and how many had come via "outreach" efforts rather than via intermarriage, etc. So as a test of success in mission, the results do not seem very useful. See *GH*, 42 (Mar. 29, 1949), 302-303.

27. *City Mission Quarterly Bulletin*, 1 (Aug. 19, 1944), 9 (copy in *CMQB* folder, IV-16-5, MBMC papers). *GH*, 34 (Feb. 19, 1942), 1005-1006, 1016, 1002.

28. *City Mission Quarterly Bulletin*, 2 (Apr. 19, 1945)—see note 27. Paul M. Lederach, "History of Religious Education in the Mennonite Church" (Southwestern Baptist Theological Seminary DRE dissertation, 1949); see also Lederach, "Planning for the Teaching Ministry" (mimeographed paper dated May 28, 1964; copy in MHL); and Lederach, "The Child in the Believers' Church," *Builder*, 23 (Dec., 1973), 6-14. Wenger, "A Study of Rural Missions" (note 1), 322, 325, 246, 294-295; Charles, in Kraybill, ed., *Called to Be Sent* (note 1), 96-97.

29. Kraybill, ed., *Called to Be Sent* (note 1), 97-98, 56.

30. MBMC minutes, ann. bd. mtg., May 7-11, 1926, p. 110; Landis, *Missionary Movement* (note 1), 73; Ivan Moyer in *Mennonite Historical Bulletin*, 18 (Apr., 1957), 2-3. For instance, regarding mobility and ethnic change in the neighborhoods surrounding the Mennonite Church's missions in Chicago by 1940, see J. Winfield Fretz, "A Study of Mennonite Religious Institutions in Chicago" (Chicago Theological Seminary BD thesis, 1940), 30, 70.

31. *HT*, 20 (July 1, 1883), 201; 21 (Dec. 1, 1884), 361; 40 (Mar. 15, 1903), 83. For the exchange with Virginians, see *HT*, 26 (Nov. 15, 1889), 341-343; 27 (Mar. 1, 1890), 74-75; 27 (Mar. 1, 1890), 75; 27 (Apr. 1, 1890), 106, Ressler diary, Feb. 17-May 31, 1893, *passim*, AMC.

32. Steiner to J. Coffman, Oct. 22, 1891, box 9, Coffman papers, AMC; *HT*, 33 (June 15, 1896), 179-180.

33. *GH*, 1 (May 2, 23, 1908) 76, 125; *MM*, 4 (Dec. 15, 1927), 12; L. Miller in MBMC *Annual Report* (1927), 122.

34. *HT*, 38 (Mar. 15, 1901), 86; *GH*, 13 (Apr. 1, 1920), 26; J. Faust in *MM*, 3 (June 15, 1926), 10-11.

35. References listed in note 34.

36. On Washington, see for example *HT*, 35 (Apr. 1, 1898), 98. On the Carlisle school, see Hazel Hertzberg, *The Search for an American Indian Identity* (Syracuse, 1971), 15-17. *CM*, 12 (Apr., 1920), 500.

37. *HT*, 35 (Nov. 15, 1898), 343; MBMC minutes, ann. bd. mtg., May 21-22, 1907, p. 44; J. I. Byler, *The Mennonite Mission Settlement, Youngstown, Ohio, January 1914 to December 1915* (printed booklet; copy in box 1, III-35-29, AMC), 11; S. Yoder to L. Hartzler (Chicago Home Mission folder), Feb. 10, 1937, IV-7-1, MBMC papers.

38. Yoder to Hartzler (note 37); Yoder to P. Friesen, Apr. 10, 1934, IV-7-1, MBMC papers. On southern mountain Whites, see unsigned (A. Wenger) to M. Steiner, Aug. 31, 1898, Steiner papers; Brunk, *History of Mennonites in Virginia* (note 1), II, 183; I. Horst in *GH*, 34 (Nov. 6, 1941), 687, 696. MBMC minutes, ann. bd. mtg., May 16-18, 1917, pp. 376-377.

39. MBMC minutes, ann. bd. mtg., May 2-6, 1924, p. 277.

40. Landis, *Missionary Movement* (note 1), 47-51. *MM*: 22 (June, 1945), 41; 22 (Jan., 1946), 5; (Good at) 16 (Apr. 16, 1939), 15.

41. Good (note 40), 15; on public and "scientific" attitudes of the time, see for instance Thomas F. Gossett, *Race: The History of an Idea in America* (Dallas, 1963), 366-369, 373-378, 424-430, 444.

42. Good (note 40), 14-15.

43. *Ibid.*, 15.

44. *MM*, 8 (Aug. 23, 1931), 1-2.

45. *Ibid.*, 2; Brunk, *History of Mennonites in Virginia*, (note 1), II, 389-390.

46. Regarding Argentina missionaries and militarism, see text of ch. 6 between note numbers 49 and 64. Weaver to S. Yoder, July 21, 1934; Friesen to MBMC exec. comm., Nov. 29, 1932; Chicago Home Mission folder, IV-7-1, MBMC papers.

47. Weaver to Yoder, and Friesen to exec. comm. (note 46); Yoder to Weaver (Chicago Home Mission folder), July 26, 1934, IV-7-1, MBMC papers. For evidence backing Friesen's charge, see: F. King to Yoder, Sept. 16, 1935; and L. Hartzler to Yoder, Aug. 20, 1936; Chicago Home Mission folder, IV-7-1, MBMC papers.

48. Good (note 40), 14-15; MBMC *Annual Report* (1926), 134, and *passim*.

49. *CM*, 6 (Jan., 1914), 399.

50. *MM*, 11 (July 8, 1934), 9; reports from Lancaster "Colored" Mission, *MM*, 1934-1940, *passim*.

51. V. and R. Harding, "Reflections on a Visit to Virginia," May, 1962, document attached to "Committee on Economic and Social Relations, Report of the Executive Secretary [Guy F. Hershberger]," Mar. 1, 1963, box 3, CESR papers, AMC; Hostetler, *Sociology of Mennonite Evangelism* (note 2), 107-108.

52. Hostetler, *Sociology of Mennonite Evangelism* (note 2,), 211.

Chapter 9. Gospel at Home (II): The Rural Gospel

1. For the Youngstown story, see ch. 3. For something of the Chicago troubles, see ch. 5, between note numbers 3 and 4.

2. Linden M. Wenger, "A Study of Rural Missions in the Mennonite Church" (Union Theological Seminary [Richmond, Virginia] ThM thesis, 1955), 98.

3. Linden Wenger set the watershed at 1930, "missions" for Mennonite Church people meaning primarily city work before that, primarily rural work thereafter. If one includes town efforts as city work (as my "urban" line indicates in Exhibits 9-2 and 9-3) the

lines for rural and city mission starts indeed cross very near to 1930. See Wenger, "A Study of Rural Missions," 107-108, 340.

4. Document No. 705, U.S. Senate, 60th Congress, 2nd Session; republished as *Report of the Commission on Country Life* (Chapel Hill, 1911, 1917, 1944).

5. Mark Rich, *The Rural Church Movement* (Columbia, 1957), 53-54, 64-67, 247-251.

6. *CM*: 1 (Mar., 1909), 93; 4 (Aug., 1912); 6 (May, 1914); 8 (July, 1916). *GH*, 5 (Oct. 10, 1912).

7. *CM*, 4 (Aug., 1912), 629-630, 631-632; Warren H. Wilson, *The Church of the Open Country: A Study of the Church for the Working Farmer* (Cincinnati and New York, 1911), esp. pp. 74-75, 162-163; *GH*, 5 (Oct. 10, 1912), 435; *CM*, 6 (May, 1914), 532-533.

8. *GH*, 5 (Oct. 10, 1912), 435; MBMC minutes, ann. bd. mtg., May 22-24, 1916, p. 343. *CM*: 11 (Nov., 1919), 324, 351; 13 (Oct., 1921), 294-295.

9. Rich, *Rural Church Movement*, 68. For sentiment that education was not necessary for rural missioners, see, e.g., *GH*, 6 (Oct. 30, 1913), 485; and MBMC minutes, joint mtg. of MBMC and members of district mission bds., May 20, 1918, p. 3. *CM*, 8 (July, 1916), 580; *GH*, 11 (Mar. 20, 1919), 910.

10. For claims of the relative effectiveness of rural missions, see. e.g.: *GH*, 5 (Oct. 10, 1912), 434-435; *CM*, 4 (May, Aug., 1912), 518-519, 613; and *GH*, 6 (Sept. 18, 1913). 389, 396-397. On economy, see: MBMC *Annual Report* (1926), 47; and *CM*, 4 (Aug., 1912), 623-624.

11. *GH*, 5 (Oct. 10, 1912), 434-435. *CM*: 4 (May, Aug., 1912), 518-519, 613; 6 (May, 1914), 532-533; 8 (July, 1916), 587-588; MBMC minutes, joint mtg. (note 9), p. 4.

12. MBMC minutes: ann. bd. mtg., June 4-6, 1919, p. 74; special bd. mtg., May 19, 1920, p. 126.

13. *Gospel Witness*, 1 (Jan. 3, 1906), 356.

14. *GH*, 6 (Sept. 18, 1913), 389, 396-397; *CM*, 6 (May, 1914), 541-542; N. Miller in *Missionary Conference: Addresses Delivered at the first General Missionary Conference ... Dec. 24-26, 1917*, 45; *CM*, 4 (Aug., 1912), 623-624; *GH*, 6 (Nov. 6, 13, 1913), 501, 516-517.

15. *CM*, 4 (Aug., 1912), 618-619; 11 (Mar., 1919), 68.

16. *CM*, 6 (May, 1914), 538; *GH*, 13 (Jan. 6, 1921), 816-817.

17. MBMC minutes, ann. bd. mtg., May 18-20, 1915, p. 291; see also *GH* (note 7); and Shoemaker (note 14).

18. MBMC minutes (note 17). *CM*, 4 (Aug., 1912), 623-624; 6 (May, 1914), 539.

19. See Timothy Smith, *Revivalism and Social Reform: American Protestantism on the Eve of the Civil War* (Nashville, 1957), esp. ch. 10.

20. See esp. Guy F. Hershberger, *The Way of the Cross in Human Relations* (Scottdale, Pa., 1958), ch. 5.

21. MBMC minutes, ann. bd. mtg., June 4-6, 1919, p. 58.

22. *CM*, 6 (May, 1914), 536-537; *GH*, 9 (Sept. 7, 1916), 435-437; MBMC minutes (note 8); *CM*, 7 (Apr., 1915), 108-109.

23. *Rural Evangel*, 1 (Jan. 1, 1920), 1. *CM*, 16 (Feb., 1924), 430; 17 (Oct., 1925), 301-302.

24. *CM*, 16 (Feb., 1924), 430, 477; 17 (Oct., 1925), 301-302.

25. For three good examples, see *CM*, 16: (Feb., 1924), 430, 477; (Mar., 1924), 460-462; (Oct., 1924), 684-685.

26. Guy F. Hershberger, "Nonresistance and Industrial Conflict," *MQR*, 13 (Apr., 1939), 135-154; reprinted in Mennonite [Church] General Conf. *Report* (1939), 101-117. See also: Hershberger, "Maintaining the Mennonite Rural Community," *MQR*, 14 (Oct., 1940), 214-223; and especially statements from the Committee on Industrial Relations, in the Mennonite [Church] General Conf. *Reports* of the 1940s. Theron F. Schlabach, "To

Focus a Mennonite Vision," in J. Richard Burkholder and Calvin Redekop, eds., *Kingdom, Cross, and Community: Essays on Mennonite Themes in Honor of Guy F. Hershoerger* (Scottdale, Pa., and Kitchener, Ont., 1976), 29-38.

27. See for example *The Mennonite Community*: 1 (Sept., 1947), 16; 2 (Jan., 1948), 6-7, 31; 3 (Oct., 1949), 26-27; 4 (June, 1950), 12-13; 5 (June, 1951), 14-15.

28. See the early pages of ch. 8.

29. See, e.g., MBMC *Annual Report* (1929), 16.

30. See ch. 5.

31. For Yoder's Protestant correspondents, see various letters in "Rural" folder, IV-7-1, MBMC papers—e.g., C. Vermilya to S. Yoder, May 12, June 4, 1925. For Jennings' quotations, see ch. 8 at note 48. For Yoder's and the committee's proposals, see Yoder to F. Brownlee, Oct. 30, 1925; Yoder to various Appalachia-area school officials, ca. Feb., 1926; Yoder to "Dear Brtheren [*sic*]," Oct. 21, 1928; J. Stauffer to Yoder, Oct. 30, 1928; J. R. Shank to Yoder, Oct. 29, 1928; Rural folder, IV-7-1, MBMC papers. Also MBMC *Annual Reports*: (Yoder, Shank, C. Derstine), (1926), 75-76; (S. Rhodes), (1928), 82-86. Yoder, in MBMC minutes, ann. bd. mtg., May 2-6, 1924, pp. 276-277.

32. MBMC minutes, ann. bd. mtg., May 3-5, 1925; Yoder to "Dear Brtheren" (note 31); Shank, *CM*, 9 (Nov., 1917), 333-334; Shank to Yoder (note 31).

33. Stauffer to Yoder (note 31).

34. S. Allgyer, in MBMC *Annual Report* (1930), 87-89.

35. MBMC minutes, ann. bd. mtgs.: May 21-23, 1933, pp. 36, 25; May 26-29, 1934, p. 94; June 16-18, 1935, p. 163.

36. MBMC minutes, VIII, joint exec. and mission committees, May 14-15, 1943.

37. Reiff to S. Allgyer, May 5, 1932, IV-7-1, MBMC papers.

38. *HT*, 28 (Nov. 15, 1892), 348; C. Hostetler to M. Steiner, Jan. 30, 1899; C. Yoder to Steiner, May 4, 1903; Steiner papers. *HT*, 43: (Sept. 13, 1906), 345; (Nov. 1, 1906), 417. MBMC minutes, ann. bd. mtg.,: May 16-18, 1917, p. 378; May 17-20, 1920, pp. 160-163. V. Reiff to Shoemaker (with penned answers in Shoemaker's handwriting), Feb. 8, 1921, treas. corr. Illinois, MBMC papers. MBMC minutes: exec. comm. mtg. Oct. 25, 1921, p. 265; joint exec. and mission committees, June 1-2, 1922, p. 4.

39. MBMC minutes, exec. comm. mtgs.: July 25, 1935, p. 196; Aug. 29, 1935, p. 197; Nov. 27, 1935, p. 201. MBMC minutes, joint exec. and mission committees: Feb. 18, 1936, p. 203; May 8, 1936, p. 213. MBMC *Annual Report* (1936), 16-20. W. and A. Detweiler to S. Yoder and D. Miller, Jan. 25, 1936; W. Detweiler to Yoder, Jan. 11, 1937; Yoder to W. Detweiler, Mar. 11, 1937; Canton folder, IV-7-1, MBMC papers. MBMC minutes, ann. bd. mtg., June 16-18, 1935, p. 190.

40. See ch. 5 at note 40, and ch. 7 at note 66.

41. Paul Erb, *South Central Frontiers: A History of the South Central Mennonite Conference* (Scottdale, Pa., and Kitchener, Ont., 1974), 137, 419, 421, 424, 438, 455, 132-133; Wenger, "A Study of Rural Missions" (note 2), 97-98; Magdalena Edelman Nice, taped interview with Theron F. Schlabach, Oct. 24, 1977, AMC.

42. Wenger, "A Study of Rural Missions" (note 2), 231-234.

43. *Ibid.*, 341-342, 292, 241-242, 233, 235-236, 243, 247, 293, 344, 294, 345-347.

44. *Ibid.*, 290.

ESSAY ON SOURCES

The notes on the various chapters of this study are ample, offering bibliographical information complete enough that to list all sources again would amount to repetition. Nonetheless, the collections of papers, the main printed primary sources, a series of taped interviews, and several of the secondary sources deserve fuller description. So also do some seminal, post-1944 pieces Mennonites have written about mission, showing directions after this book's story ends.

Collections of papers

Correspondence and other papers have formed the backbone of the present work; and of materials of that kind used, all but a very few are in the Archives of the Mennonite Church (cited as AMC in chapter notes), on the campus of Goshen College, Goshen, Indiana. Papers of M. S. Steiner and of course those of the Mennonite Board of Missions and Charities (now Mennonite Board of Missions) and its predecessors were most central of all. Some other collections supplemented those two.

Menno Simon Steiner (1866-1911) was the foremost leader among activists in the generation that actually succeeded in joining the Mennonite Church to the Protestant missionary cause. He became so through various roles, from bookseller to traveling evangelist to formulator of organizations and institutions. When he died, he was first president of the Mennonite Board of Missions and Charities, organized in 1906 as a capstone and a merger of many of his generation's activities. Beginning in 1884 and more systematically from about 1889 onward, and continuing until his rather early death, he collected from correspondents a substantial number of letters that remain extant, now filling some fifteen 3-inch boxes, i.e., amounting to 3.75 linear feet of storage space. In addition he kept diaries which still exist for the years 1890, 1893-1897, 1899-1904, and 1906 and 1907, plus some .75 linear feet of notebooks, clippings, sermon notes, and other material, on topics ranging from temperance, to missions and charities, to Antichrist. Virtually all of the correspondence is incoming, not his own writing. And the diary entries are those of a man of action, not extended or for the most part really deeply reflective and nuanced. Nevertheless, the material is most valuable, for Steiner was in touch not only with major Mennonite Church figures such as Funk or J. S. Coffman or G. L. Bender or Daniel Kauffman, but with numerous lesser ones as well, indeed with many fairly ordinary ministers, activity-minded youths, and others. Moreover, those who wrote to him often did elaborate and reflect at some length on events, reveal their inner feelings, etc., for he seemed somehow to attract such ruminations. And one can find good samples of his replies by consulting other collections mentioned below, especially those of Funk and of Coffman. As for the diaries, despite some brevity, the entries give very good record of Steiner's movements, of major meetings and events, and of texts he used in preaching; and they offer at least cryptic record even of his interpretations, personal feelings, and reactions. In all, the Steiner collection is a most valuable source of information on public events in the Mennonite Church of his time, along with excellent insights, to be sure mainly from one faction's point of view, into behind-the-scenes feelings and maneuverings. Only a small fraction of the papers are limited to purely personal or family affairs. The collection gets the researcher acquainted with the new kind of Mennonite who found the mission movement not just congenial but compelling.

Offering more material on actual mission development, practical issues on the field, etc., of course, is the MBMC collection. It is a vast resource—occupying somewhat more than 200 linear feet. Quite a bit less than half of it is pre-1944 materials; yet even within that fraction, the amount and also the redundancy are enough that the researcher, if sane, will be selective. Not quite all are actually MBMC papers, for some 1.5 linear feet are occupied with material from the MBMC's predecessors: Mennonite Evangelizing Committee (1882-1892), Mennonite Evangelizing Board of America (1892-1896), Benevolent Organization of Mennonites (1894-1896), Mennonite Evangelizing and Benevolent Board (1896-1906), Mennonite Board of Charitable Homes (1899-1903), and Mennonite Board of Charitable Homes and Missions (1903-1906). Extant from these agencies are legal papers, meeting reports and minutes, financial records, early foreign mission manual and examining board materials, and a limited amount of correspondence (in this case including some copies of outgoing documents, bound in letter-press volumes), especially of George (G. L.) Bender, treasurer and in effect chief business officer of several of the organizations. Much of this material was useful for the study.

Of actual MBMC materials, the research has made extensive use of (or at least selected extensively from) especially three segments: executive committee minutes (under AMC's classification IV-6-1), treasurers' correspondence (IV-8-10 and IV-8-11, especially the former), and executive office correspondence (IV-7-1). The executive committee minutes often cover, in addition to meetings of their own committee, joint meetings with the next most important sub-group of the board, the Missions Committee, plus meetings of the entire board. Typewritten and bound, they begin with sessions in 1906 in which representatives of the MEBB and the MBCHM met and approved merger, and carry on beyond the terminal date of this study. Because reporting was complete enough to offer more than just brief record of official actions, the researcher is able at most points to glean something of the discussion surrounding an issue. Sometimes, as is usual, the minutes include special investigative reports, etc., in toto. Also they preserve accounts, including at least the substance of addresses given, of the board's annual meetings—meetings which were a major public forum for Mennonite Church leaders and missioners to explicate their mission concepts. The annual meeting reports, however, are available also in printed form, as

Essay on Sources 333

indicated below in the discussion of printed primary sources.

Treasurers' correspondence, some 23 linear feet, was useful particularly for the early years of the MBMC and its activities, expecially up to 1921, when Sanford (S. C.) Yoder became the board's secretary and made his office more the dominant one, and when G. L. Bender, the original treasurer, died. As the first full-time official of the board, the treasurer was often in touch with matters that under a more professionalized system another executive might have seen to. Moreover Bender had the experience, the ability, and the confidence of church leaders to be far more than a functionary keeper of accounts. Nevertheless even Bender in his correspondence was often very naturally preoccupied with practical problems, to the point of having to constrain mission activities more than help develop them. Much, of course, in the treasurers' papers was highly routine, especially acknowledgments of gifts sent in. The nonroutine are valuable, especially for studying the institutionalizing process in mission. They are sometimes helpful, but less often so for studying the positive dynamics of the mission movement or underlying mission theology and theory.

Much more useful for the latter, and indeed for viewing very practical matters as well, is the executive office correspondence for the years under study, especially the years from 1921 to 1944 when S. C. Yoder was secretary. Those materials occupy about 8 linear feet and include both incoming documents and duplicates of outgoing ones, although for the early years the outgoing are by no means complete. For the years before 1921 much of the extant correspondence was to and from treasurer Bender rather than secretary Joseph (J. S.) Shoemaker; and here also even after 1921 there is a fair amount of treasurers' correspondence, especially with Vernon E. Reiff who was in office from 1921 to 1934. Yet it was Yoder's correspondence that, for this study, yielded the great bulk of interesting material. Although on the one hand Yoder was quite diplomatic, even a conciliator, on the other he often addressed himself to missionaries and others whom he trusted in surprisingly candid language, and he could be rather straightforward with missionaries and institutional workers under his jurisdiction when he thought they needed reprimand or blunt advice. Checked against other sources mentioned in this essay, Yoder's executive office papers seem to yield a fairly complete picture of issues and dynamics at work on the general board's foreign fields, and in some major home missions and institutions as well—although not for the decentralized district board and congregational efforts emphasized in chapters 8 and 9.

Among other MBMC papers, valuable at times but not used so extensively, were especially some Missions Committee materials classified under IV-6-1— materials such as statements of standards for missionaries, questionnaires filled out by would-be missionaries and workers, newsletters for missionaries under various titles, and some correspondence. Also useful were some MBMC legal papers, classified under IV-6-3.

Other AMC collections used and worthy of at least passing mention are those of G. L. and Elsie (Kolb) Bender (Hist Mss 1-392; 5.5 linear feet, but mostly family papers, with only a few inches relevant to this study); of John S. Coffman (Hist Mss 1-19; somewhat more than 3 linear feet); of John F. Funk (Hist Mss 1-1; about 35 linear feet); of T. K. and Mae Hershey (Hist Mss 1-114; 2.5 linear feet); of Daniel Kauffman (Hist Mss 1-20; 1 linear foot); of Jacob (J.A.) and Lina Zook Ressler (Hist Mss 1-117; 4 linear feet); and of S. C. Yoder (Hist Mss 1-162; nearly 7 linear feet). Funk's and Coffman's papers, although used herein more selectively than the papers of Steiner, were of course extremely helpful for the quickening period. Both of those collections include diaries. Funk's has, among other kinds of documents, quite a few article manuscripts, some unpublished and some published, that often help amplify the *Herald of Truth* as a source; also they include some materials even from Funk's youth, and from the time before he began the *Herald of Truth* in 1864. And there are diaries for all years 1852 to 1899, that is through all but the last several of the prime years of the quickening and of Funk's influence in the Mennonite Church, plus several scattered ones from later years. As for Funk's correspondence, it seems far from complete for years before 1887, then is quite ample until about 1902, and falls off in amount about 1911; fortunately again, the ample years are the prime ones of Funk's influence and of the quickening. Coffman's correspondence, also an exceptionally strong source of course for the quickening, is quite ample for years from about 1879 to his death in 1899; and he kept diaries, which are extant for the years 1871 and 1876-1899. Much the same generalizations hold true for Funk's and Coffman's diaries as made above for Steiner's—although Funk's seem even more sketchy at times, while of the three sets, that of Coffman seems generally the most informative and reflective.

J. A. Ressler's papers, used mainly as a further source for the quickening period (he gave detailed accounts of his early India mission activities in published articles), served to add first a Lancaster County and then in the latter 1890s a western Pennsylvania (Scottdale and vicinity) perspective to those of the Steiner, Funk, and Coffman collections. He kept diaries that were especially interesting as they revealed a young man who was in many ways surprisingly secular, yet who became for a time a major figure not only in beginning the India mission, but earlier in getting activity in Lancaster County. A journal of Lina Zook in the late 1890s, before she married Ressler and when she was a worker during trying days at the Chicago Home Mission, was also especially helpful for the present study—not only because it offered insight into that early city mission story, but also for the perspective of a very able young woman deep in the hard work of mission, and of a person struggling to keep her Mennonite Church identity and to accept church leaders' advice and discipline.

Other AMC collections mentioned above yielded less of benefit for this study—either because they were largely redundant after research in the MBMC papers (especially the Hershey and the Yoder papers, plus various collections not mentioned that would have been very useful had the MBMC papers not been available) or because only a limited amount of their material was directly relevant to the study (especially the Bender and the Kauffman papers).

Essay on Sources

In addition to papers in the Mennonite Church's archives, the study occasionally made use of various materials in other depositories: the files of the Eastern Mennonite Board of Missions and Charities at Salunga, Pennsylvania; documents in the Menno Simons Historical Library and its archives at Eastern Mennonite College, Harrisonburg, Virginia; items in the Eastern Pennsylvania Mennonite Historical Library located at Christopher Dock Mennonite High School near Lansdale, Pennsylvania; and others in the archives of the Lancaster Mennonite Conference Historical Society at Lancaster, Pennsylvania.

Printed primary sources

Of printed materials that protagonists in the Mennonite Church's early years of mission left for study, the most obvious of course are annual reports of mission organizations: the Mennonite Board of Missions and Charities; the MBMC's India mission, known as the American Mennonite Mission; and its Argentina one, or South America Mennonite Mission. Those of the India mission date from 1901, and continue uninterrupted beyond the years covered in this study. The MBMC began in 1907 to print its reports in the *Herald of Truth* and in the *Gospel Witness,* and then from 1908 onward in the *Gospel Herald*; also, it attached those of 1912 and 1915 as appendices to the India report. Actually, annual meetings of the mission boards, whose proceedings the reports largely consisted of, were not merely business sessions, but conventions for all mission-minded Mennonite Church people to attend. Finally from 1916 onward the board printed its annual reports as a record in its own right, reversing the order so that the India reports became attachments to the MBMC ones. In 1923 it added another attachment, annual reports of the Argentina mission. Typically MBMC reports from then until the mid-1940s run to 100 or more pages, India ones from 30 to 60, and South American ones from perhaps 25 to 40. While a substantial fraction of their space is taken up with financial summaries, resolutions, and other policy decisions, all the reports are much more than bare-bones accounts of business transacted, for a much larger fraction of content is articles, addresses, reports on developments or major issues, editorials and other reflective comments by secretaries of the missions or board officials, or similar statements by others. Much of the material is description, to be sure, more than idea or in-depth explanation. And where ideas are set forth, they are often quite conventional. The reports contain few surprises. Yet as public records of organizations' activities go, they are quite informative.

Journals published for Mennonite Church readership form another major set of printed primary sources. Those used in this study are all available for public use in the Mennonite Historical Library at Goshen College (cited as MHL, in the chapter notes). For early chapters, nothing else could quite have substituted for the *Herald of Truth* which John F. Funk and his privately owned Mennonite Publishing Company produced from 1864 to 1908. It gave hard information plus intangible feel not just about the growing mission concern, but about much of the context that fed that concern, from migrations of Mennonite people to their adoption of Sunday schools to their growing appetite for both Mennonite and non-Mennonite reading matter and beyond. The journal began as a monthly of four pages; in 1882 it became a semimonthly of sixteen pages, and in its very late years it became a weekly. In its early years, articles that were really sermons or sermon-like pieces set its tone, highly devotional and full of exhortation to walk carefully and avoid sin. Gradually, by the 1880s and 1890s, its spirit became much more that of extroversion and activism. Then about the late 1890s its exuberance fell off, because then and during the rest of its life, Funk was losing the confidence of the quickened among his people. So while in its last years Funk's paper still offered much information about mission and about other affairs of the Mennonite Church and its people, issues of those years are not the same quality source for study of the mission movement and its spirit as are earlier issues.

In 1905 younger quickened leaders—actually by then going into middle age—began to publish, through another privately owned company this time at Scottdale, Pennsylvania, what amounted to a rival journal, *The Gospel Witness*. In general it was the same kind of paper the *Herald of Truth* had been in its heyday, attempting to give news from communities where Mennonite Church people concentrated, accounts of conferences and other church events, limited commentary on national and world news, etc., as well as some teaching and exhortation for Mennonites' Christian lives. But Daniel Kauffman was its editor, and being product of the generation that was really joining Mennonite Church people to the missionary movement, it was especially full of mission news and concerns. Finally in 1908 the old paper of Funk and the new rival one ceased publication; and under a newly created denominational Mennonite Publishing Board and its new Mennonite Publishing House, Daniel Kauffman began to edit a more official organ, *Gospel Herald*. Kauffman continued as editor until 1943. A sixteen-page weekly, the new *Herald* too followed much the same format and functions as the *Herald of Truth* in that paper's heyday; yet, reflecting its times and its editor, it differed somewhat in two ways. (1) It had more of a doctrinal emphasis, and more broadly, tried harder to be an organ to create uniformity of belief and practice in the Mennonite Church. And (2) it gave expression to the Mennonite Church during decades when the assumptions and spirit of the quickening had thoroughly permeated her, and become axiomatic among her people. The *Gospel Herald* from 1908 to 1944 (and beyond) contains ample information on and discussion of Mennonite Church mission, indeed to the point of redundancy for the researcher—especially after the onset of Vol. 9 in April of 1916, when it began a monthly mission supplement of eight and eventually sixteen pages.

For more specialized study of how the mission spirit permeated, or how Mennonite Church people inculcated it into their offspring, or what certain subgroups or related groups were saying, one could mention various other journals—youth and children's papers; privately published organs, some of them brief, and others such as the Mennonite-Fundamentalist *Sword and*

Trumpet more lasting; etc. And there were the numerous district conference newssheets and papers mentioned in note 1 of chapter 8. Suffice it here to mention only two.

In 1909 the Mennonite Publication Board and its publishing house began the *Christian Monitor*, mastheading it "A Monthly Magazine for the Home." Geared more than the *Gospel Herald* to human interest and to day-to-day living, the *Monitor* shared the tasks of reporting and commenting on missions and the mission enterprise. And sometimes its emphasis could be rather different from that of the *Herald*, as for instance regarding rural reconstruction (see ch. 9). Complementing the *Herald* in a different way was also a monthly called *Missionary Messenger*, published from 1924 onward by the Lancaster Conference's Eastern Mennonite Board of Missions and Charities as its official organ. At first it had eight or ten pages per issue, eventually sixteen. It is an important source because the Eastern Board has been by all odds the most important of district conference mission boards, because it represented a very, very substantial segment of the Mennonite Church that was by no means entirely in tune with the MBMC-related sources mainly used in this study, because it served as the public record for the Eastern Board, its major meetings, and its missions, and because in some respects it was more than a missionary journal—more or less, it was also official church organ for the Eastern Board's constituency. That constituency, incidentally, spilled throughout eastern states well beyond the region of the Lancaster Conference, making the *Messenger* even more important as a source.

Finally, the study made fairly extensive use especially of two scholarly journals, some of whose articles are primary sources in the sense of being record left by the story's actors. *The Mennonite Quarterly Review* (cited in chapter notes as *MQR*) was intended to be a vehicle for scholarly interpretation of Anabaptist, Mennonite, and related history and affairs, by no means limited to Mennonite Church topics; yet people at a Mennonite Church college (Goshen) began it in 1926-1927 and edited it throughout the entire period under study. Occasionally they included articles touching Mennonite Church mission or charities, and of course they included many with implications for theological basis in mission. *The International Review of Missions* (more recently *of Mission*), published since 1912 by the International Missionary Council or the World Council of Churches, has of course been a major journal of Protestant missiology. Surveyed extensively as background for this study, the journal provided insights into the changing fashions of missionary concepts and language, and understandings and perceptions of mission against which to compare those that Mennonite Church people were using.

Still another kind of printed primary source, to be found referred to in chapter notes but whose examples are too numerous to begin listing here, have been books by Mennonite Church missionaries themselves. Directly, these have been valuable mainly for factual material. But of course they tell much also of the intangible outlook of the missionaries. And they provide insight into the process of educating Mennonite Church people in established North American congregations to support mission, since in virtually every case that was the book's purpose.

Taped interviews

An element of the larger mission history project of which this book is a part was to interview and collect oral history from people who had been connected with the Mennonite Church's pre-World War II mission effort. The purpose was partly to record the voices and reflections and styles of such people for their own sakes, and partly to provide additional resource for this study. In 1972-1973, therefore, the Mennonite Board of Missions employed a history graduate student, John S. Miller, to work for one year under the general supervision of the author, acquainting himself with issues and events and then traveling about North America collecting such oral records (and in fact some written ones as well). In addition, the author himself has occasionally either sat in with Miller and shared his interviewing task or conducted further interviews himself.

The result is tapes of conversation with some 56 persons or couples, most of them at least two hours long and some much longer. Persons interviewed were mainly retired missionaries, and included some from each major pre-World War II field, that is, from the home, the India, the Argentina, and the East Africa locations. A few persons included had been administrators or persons otherwise close to mission decision-making—Orie O. Miller, for instance, generally known for his Mennonite Central Committee leadership but important in the counsels of both the MBMC and the Eastern Board, contributed four reels' worth. Others interviewed had been sons or daughters of missionaries and had grown up on the fields. And a small sprinkling—too small, admittedly—was from the ranks of the "missioned" rather than of the missioners.

There are some 72 such tapes, most on four-inch reels, a few in cassettes, and they are deposited with the MBMC papers. Nobody has undertaken the expensive task of transcribing them, but for virtually all there exist rather extensive indexes, and it is rather easy to survey what is on them and locate segments especially interesting. With indexes the tapes were another highly useful primary resource for the study. To be sure, there really was no substitute (as the author became increasingly convinced) for careful examination of documents, when documents were as available as they were. The chapter notes indicate that for particular citations the written evidence usually served best. That was because they were almost always more specific and nuanced on a given question than oral evidence from even the best memory could possibly be. Yet the interviews were highly worthwhile for gaining general perspective and fairly often also for more specific evidence and interpretation; and the author wishes to use this opportunity to thank all those who cooperated.

Secondary studies

The two scholarly journals mentioned above, and of course various others, offered a number of articles of a secondary nature, that is, histories and analyses of events by nonparticipants, as well as offering those primary sources mentioned. Of course also, one could cite a vast number of books on the history and missiology of modern Protestant missions, for instance ones by Kenneth Scott Latourette, R. Pierce Beaver, Stephen Neill, and, in the case of missiology, especially of Roland Allen, Robert Speer, and Donald McGavran. This author would, somewhat arbitrarily, give special mention to three. Johannes van den Berg's *Constrained by Jesus' Love: An Inquiry into the Motives of the Missionary Awakening in Great Britain in the Period between 1698 and 1815* (Kampen, 1956) illuminates well the classic motives of modern mission—far, it would seem, beyond the time and geography that is the strict subject of the book. And two books by Max Warren, *The Missionary Movement from Britain in Modern History* (London, 1965), and *Social History and Christian Mission* (London, 1967), are much the same for illuminating contextual social-history background of the mission movement, such as class profile of missionaries, secular values they held, connection with cultural currents of the day and with political and economic expansion, and the like.

As for studies directly on Mennonite Church missions, or mission, thoroughgoing scholarly studies are few. Perhaps no more than a half-dozen deserve specific mention. Edmund G. Kaufman's *The Development of the Missionary and Philanthropic Interest Among the Mennonites of North America* (Berne, Ind., 1931) has large sections on Mennonite Church missions and charities along with others on those of different Mennonite branches. It is still very useful as a compendium of fact, despite my judgment, already argued in the text of chapter 5 at note number 18, that its interpretive remarks rest somewhat on two fallacies. John A. Hostetler has published *The Sociology of Mennonite Evangelism* (Scottdale, Pa., 1954), a book which despite its title deals with efforts only of the Mennonite Church, not of all Mennonite branches, and only with the home field. A limited-edition publication, produced by multilith only, it is nevertheless a fairly substantial one, in terms both of its factual research and its size (nearly 300 pages). Being a sociological study, it pertains most to the situation near the time of its publication, a period just beyond the scope of the present work. Yet Hostetler included much historical information as background, and offered many statistics reaching back to early-twentieth century. And of course he dealt not only with strictly mission activities, but more broadly with social forces and attitudes. A more complete book, indeed the fullest study to date devoted exclusively to a Mennonite Church mission topic, deals with a foreign field. The book is John A. Lapp's *The Mennonite Church in India, 1897-1962* (Scottdale, Pa., 1972). Telling its story from the beginning to a decade beyond the time when the mission was dissolved and the church became fully independent, Lapp's book is a well-synthesized description. Seemingly, in his style and organization, the author put such description first, ahead of analysis or the presentation of an interpretive framework for understanding Mennonite Church mission. Yet the book is, on nearly every page, rich in interpretive insight. And being so, it is most helpful even beyond the India story.

Well before Lapp wrote, J. Winfield Fretz produced a treatise which he labeled "A Study of Mennonite Religious Institutions in Chicago" (B.D. thesis, Chicago Theological Seminary, 1940). Some of Fretz's insights anticipate points of the present study: that Mennonites lacked much sense of offering gospel in a unique way, for instance, and that Mennonites really had no "philosophy of mission" (Fretz, pp. 163, 171-172, and *passim*). One feature very much limits Fretz's treatise as a study of mission, however: Fretz really was more concerned with attitudes and characteristics of country Mennonites transplanted in the city than with message, methods, underlying assumptions, or effects of mission *per se*. Moreover, since Fretz's generalizations often did not differentiate among the missions of the various Mennonite branches, they were not always directly useful for a work such as the present one. Much more to the point on that latter count was another treatise, concerned with Mennonite Church efforts, namely Linden M. Wenger's "A Study of Rural Missions in the Mennonite Church" (ThM thesis, Union Theological Seminary [Richmond, Va.], 1955). The study is especially valuable for identifying and detailing the rural efforts, and for categorizing them according to type of origin or type of work. Also, Wenger offered many helpful comments on missioners' outlook(s), and on problems and prospects of further development. It would seem that his study of Mennonite missionary language was not quite intensive enough really to deal extensively with underlying assumptions. In fact, often his interpretive comment is as valuable as primary source, showing what one thoughtful Mennonite commentator on mission was saying in the mid-1950s, as it is as secondary source for earlier Mennonite developments. Yet, as text and notes especially of chapter 9 of the present study indicate, Wenger's work was informative and generally provocative for this book.

Finally, a more recent treatise is George Ronald Anchak's "An Experience in the Paradox of Indigenous Church Building: A History of Eastern Mennonite Mission in Tanganyika, 1934-1961" (PhD dissertation, Michigan State University, 1975). Anchak seems to have brought to his subject what might be termed "secular-anthropology" assumptions quite alien to the group of missioners he was dealing with, concerning the nature and value of fusing Christianity and missioned peoples' cultures. While his assumptions at some points served as useful tools of analysis, at others they seem to have prevented him from coming fully to terms with and from fully understanding (regardless of any questions of approval or disapproval) the thought patterns and ingrained cultural responses of those Eastern Board missioners. Moreover, he seems to have promised analysis, when most of his discussion is more in the nature of description colored by editorial comment. Nevertheless, he brought to his study a most worthwhile question, and offered valuable insights; and he has summarized the major events and developments on that first field of the Eastern Board's foreign work. Chapter notes indicate that his dissertation was often the source of information for this study's references to Eastern Board work.

The present work notwithstanding, there will in the future be ample room

Essay on Sources 341

for further scholarly study and analyses of Mennonite Church experience in mission.

Post-1944, more reflective Mennonite Church writings on mission

Implicitly or explicitly, this study has variously made the point that the Mennonite Church's missionary movement proceeded in the late nineteenth and early twentieth centuries more by uncritical borrowing of assumptions and methods than by reflection on the meaning, for mission, of Mennonites' understandings of gospel and of God's hope for His children. Since about 1960 a few in the Mennonite Church have offered more reflection of that latter kind. Interestingly, most have done it in cryptic little thought-pieces; none has yet produced a fully developed treatise that amounts to a weighty book. Nevertheless, anyone interested in further study of the Mennonite Church in mission will surely want to know the directions of such thought.

As an outgrowth of Conrad Grebel Lectures for the year 1959, Joseph (J. D.) Graber published *The Church Apostolic: A Discussion of Modern Missions* (Scottdale, Pa., 1960). The book still breathes much of pre-World War II Mennonite Church ways of approaching mission. It is an intelligent work, highly aware of political and social changes of its time, cognizant of pitfalls such as aligning mission with forces of injustice in the world or failing to join words with deeds, and in all very much a credit to its author and his church. Yet for the most part its business is to update the Mennonites' borrowing of the modern missionary approach, and to translate the latest Protestant missionary thinking for a Mennonite audience. It deals creditably with questions such as emphasis on soul-saving versus church-planting, relation of words and deeds, proper concepts of missionary giving, and mission as colonialism gives way to nationalism. Yet it does so in a way to guide the existing mission impulse into proper channels more than to examine basic understandings and assumptions behind the impulse and its resultant strategies.

A small booklet (36 pp.) in the Focal Pamphlet series, John Howard Yoder's *As You Go: The Old Mission in a New Day* (Scottdale, Pa., 1961), is much more forthrightly a call for breaking with the modern missionary movement's patterns. To be sure, Yoder in one sense did no more than continue Graber's line of thought. In his book Graber had written of decisions of some denominations' boards (whom he hoped Mennonites might emulate) to move away from "elaborate and powerful foreign mission organizations on the mission fields." Such organizations, Graber said, had been "inevitable in the colonial period" but were now outmoded because "such foreign power centers in countries with an awakened nationalism are severely resented" (p. 123). And in an introduction to Yoder's booklet, Graber effectively tied Yoder's offering to his own line of thought.

Nevertheless, Yoder called for that break in a way that Graber had not. On the one hand he asked explicitly whether it were not possible for today's church to grow by a "method which has been most effective down through the centuries rather than that of the [modern] foreign missionary movement" (p. 17). On the other he elaborated on what he considered to be the time-tested, centuries-old method: "migration evangelism." Through most of history, Yoder argued, Christians have spread the gospel merely as they have moved about, usually on their own financial resources. Much evangelism in the past has come about through peoples' moving naturally; nevertheless, Yoder called for deliberate strategy, especially one of having developed-world Christians equip themselves with skills the developing world needs, and then going as servants of the peoples and institutions in developing nations. Actually it is not clear why Yoder assumed that nations in development would, before long, want foreign specialists any more than foreign power organizations. Nor of course was the idea of preparing oneself with such skills anything uniquely Yoder's. The seminal point Yoder made was his explicit turning away from modern missionary traditions. And that in turn proceeded implicitly from a certain vision of how the church is church—church being church in mission not by marshaling special resources and special machinery with a special order of people conducting a highly specialized cause, but rather just by having its people truly make being God's people in the world their ordinary business. Carrying the gospel would be a large but only an integral part of simply being God's people.

John Driver has developed that understanding of church in mission much further in a small, much more recent book, *Community and Commitment* (Scottdale, Pa., 1976), a revision of his Spanish-language *Communidad y Compromiso: Estudios sobre la Renovación de la Iglesia* (Buenos Aires, 1974). Writing in a day when liberation theology has been challenging both traditional Protestant missionary concepts of gospel and more particularly Mennonite ideas of relation of gospel and peace, Driver has also thoroughly integrated the view of church with a *shalom*-oriented understanding of the gospel's message. Thus his emphasis thoroughly incorporates concern for social and economic justice. Actually, only the final chapter (ch. 6) of *Community and Commitment* is explicitly about mission; but it is very much the chapter toward which Driver's whole discussion moves. The book is still too brief and succinct to supply Mennonites with a fully elaborated statement of mission. But it is a powerful little treatise, and shows the direction of flow in at least one vein of Mennonite Church mission thinking.

Another channel where such thinking has flowed is sessions of a "Mennonite Missionary Study Fellowship," occurring annually since 1971 under the auspices of the Institute of Mennonite Studies headquartered at Associated Mennonite Biblical Seminaries, Elkhart, Indiana. The sessions are a forum to which missionaries, mission officials, scholars, and other interested persons from the various Mennonite branches and occasionally elsewhere have come for unofficial sharing and discussion of their ideas. Participants have produced a number of unpublished papers, some of them still available through the Institute, plus a half-dozen published or soon-to-be published books. Of those books, one edited by Wilbert Shenk, *The Challenge of Church Growth: A*

Symposium (Elkhart, Ind., 1973) is a series of papers offering Mennonite responses to the theories of Donald McGavran and his followers. Samuel Escobar and John Driver's *Christian Mission and Social Justice* (Scottdale, Pa., 1978) takes up the question its title suggests. And a forthcoming one edited by Robert Ramseyer will offer essays on theology of mission. Of a rather different nature is a book by Edwin and Irene Weaver, *From Kuku Hill: Among Indigenous Churches in West Africa* (Elkhart, Ind., 1975); and that in turn is a companion to another by the same authors but published by the Mennonite Board of Missions, entitled *The Uyo Story* (Elkhart, Ind., 1970). The Weavers' books are different in that they are highly personal accounts. And more importantly, they are evidence of a different vein in recent Mennonite mission development: work with the independent, highly indigenous Christian churches that flourish in Africa.

Finally, a very convenient source of reflective thought in the Mennonite Church of the 1970s on the question of mission is a small bimonthly release of the Mennonite Board of Missions entitled *Mission Focus*, published since 1972 and often carrying quick thought-piece articles that are kernels of fresh thought. *Mission-Focus* and other recent literature show clearly that Mennonite Church missioners have begun to think more deliberately about how people with Mennonites' understandings and characteristics should go about proclaiming gospel. Yet such evidence does not necessarily signal arrival of some new Golden Age of Mennonite mission. The sobering fact is that it has appeared only after the curve of mission starts, at least on the home field, has taken its sharply downward turn.

INDEX

Africa, 20, 22, 36, 49, 160.
Allen, Roland, 173, 195-196.
Allgyer, Samuel E., 107, 206, 278, 279; quoted, 107, 155, 167-168, 174, 244, 270-271.
Altoona (Pa.) mission, 100, 153, 156.
American Board of Commissioners for Foreign Missions, 20, 23, 195.
American Mennonite Mission (in India), 34, 94-96, 127, 174, 175, 178, 199, 202-203, 219, 230; origins of, 78-82, 88, 93-94, 197; financial problems, 95-96, 133; under attack, 132-147; relations with National Christian Council of India and Protestant missions, 139-144, 149, 173. See also: India; Mennonite Church in India.
Amish, and Amish Mennonites, 27-32, *passim;* 39-45, *passim;* 47; 55-58, *passim;* 63, 69; 84-90, *passim;* 102, 103, 114, 156, 233, 246; Sunday schools of, 34 ff., 46-47.
Amstutz, Daniel and Fannie, 87. See also: Old people's home (Ohio).
Anabaptists, 23-30, 44, 48, 53, 116, 152, 170, 182, 188, 190; missionary zeal of, 24-26, 44, 49; "Anabaptist vision" in the twentieth century, 116, 146, 175, 227-228, 247.
Anderson, Rufus, 22, 195.
Anglicans, 20, 21, 195.
Argentina, 99, 101, 106, 107, 127-132. See also: South American Mennonite Mission.
Argentina Mennonite Church (and Conference), 188, 191, 213.
Arkansas, 121-122. See also: Southern highlands.
Attire. See: Dress.

Balodgahan, India, 94, 95-96, 202.
Baptism, believer's, 24, 171, 243, 246, 247; Anabaptists and, 23-25, 172.
Baptists, 20, 21; 29, 68, 136, 160, 187.
Battaglia, Santiago, 203, 219-220.
Beaver, R. Pierce, 181.
Bender, Daniel H., 80, 89, 168, 173, 177, 279.

Bender, George L., 51-52, 87, 92; quoted, 43, 52, 69, 98, 104, 107.
Bender, Harold S., 25, 190, 227.
Benevolent Organization of Mennonites, 64, 65, 68, 78. See also: Mennonite Evangelizing and Benevolent Board.
Berkey, Edward J., 60, 68.
Bible Institute of Los Angeles, 131.
Blacks, 20, 74-78, 100, 106, 154, 163, 206, 233, 247-262; tables, 248-252; graph, 253.
Bixler, Jacob K., 268, 272-273, 277.
Boelke, Otto, 65, 67.
Brackbill, Christian M., 69, 70, 77.
Brenneman, Daniel, 33, 36.
Brenneman, Fred, 141, 175.
Brenneman, John M., 31-56, *passim.*
Bressler, John F., 243.
British and Foreign Bible Society, 20, 201.
Brubacher, Jacob N., 62, 70, 73, 74.
Brunk, Aldine C., 135-136, 202.
Brunk, George R. (Sr.), 114, 137.
Buckingham, Maude, 121-122.
Burkhard, Jacob, 96, 230.
Burkhard, Mary, 142, 158-159, 230.
Byers, Noah H., 89-90, 102.
Byler, John I., 103-106.

Calvinism, Calvinists, 19-24, 46, 114.
Canton (Ohio) mission, 152, 182.
Carey, William, 21-23, 36.
Catholicism, 115, 116; in Argentina, 131, 163, 190, 202.
Cavadore family, 203, 207, 210, 213.
Chicago Home Mission, 41, 43, 49, 54-68, 73, 82, 88, 119, 150, 155, 173, 201, 204, 242, 259, 265; beginnings of, 56-65; temporarily closed, 65-66.
Child evangelism, 73, 238-247, 262. See also: Fresh Air.
Children's homes. See: Orphans'.
China, 29, 35, 49, 75, 158, 181, 201.
Christian Monitor, 153, 155, 158, 256; quoted, 153, 172; ruralism in, 267 ff., 277.
Christolear, John, 54-56.
Christian and Missionary Alliance, 29, 207.
Church
—concept of: Anabaptists', 24-28, 37, 170, 176; Mennonites', 64, 67, 72, 96, 102-

Index 345

103, 116-118, 176, 199-200.
—as practiced and taught in Mennonite mission, 110, 145-146, 161, 167, 170-179, 192, 205, 223.
—and culture, 196-197, 270; in Argentina, 131.
Church-planting, 67, 74-77, 95, 108, 131, 136, 170-179, 195, ff., 214-215, 221. See also: Three-self formula.
Church of the Brethren, 45, 105, 142.
Church Missionary Society, 20, 22, 195.
City missions, 28, 49, 54, 56, ff., 62, 73, 100-108, 198, 204 ff., 206 ff., 224 ff., 260-265, 269, 270, 287-289; tables, 264, 286-287; graphs, 265, 280. See also names of specific cities.
Coffman, John S., 33, 41, 50, 56, 64, 70, 84, 243, 254; quoted, 38, 42, 43, 49, 59-60, 61, 66, 71-72, 84, 85, 102, 112.
Coffman, Samuel, 30, 31, 33.
Coffman, Samuel Frederick, 59, 60, 62, 65, 67, 168; quoted, 120, 142.
Colonization (by Mennonites), 232, 254; as strategy for mission, 40-41, 234 (tables, 232, 235, 236).
Covering. See: Prayer veiling.
Cressman, Una, 130.
Crook, Andrew and Mary, 55-56, 263, 289.

Del Bosque, Simon, 206.
Denlinger, Mary, 65.
Derstine, Clayton F., 136, 176, 273.
Detroit mission, 154-155, 244.
Detweiler, Joseph, 106.
Detweiler, William D., 279-280.
Devolution, 196. See also: Self-goverance.
Discipleship: Anabaptists' emphasis on, 24, 25, 48, 171; Mennonites' emphasis on, 27, 149, 153, 171; as part of the missionary message, 66, 68, 166, 171, 177, 194; discipline in new churches, 178, 213.
Dress standards, 27, 51-52, 57-58, 68, 99, 106, 115, 118, 121, 134, 146, 149-151, 153-155, 194; in India, 136, 139, 164; in Argentina, 144-145, 164, 179; in home missions, 61, 150, 152, 155, 156, 164, 238. See also Prayer veiling; wedding bands.

Eash, Amos M., 156, 242.
East Africa Revival, 185, 221.

Eastern Mennonite Board of Missions and Charities, 126-127, 164; origin, 69, 74; opens foreign work, 144-145 (see also: Africa); policies of, 145, 186, 211, 214 ff., 247, 260.
Eastern Mennonite School, College, Seminary, 114, 133, 136, 151, 162, 230-233, 259.
Ebersole, Melinda, 65.
Ebersole, Solomon D., 43, 49, 56-60, 66.
Eby, Isaac, 70-71.
Education, 64, 122; as a missionary method, 19, 22, 29, 75, 109, 136, 138, 145; higher (among Mennonite Church and Amish Mennonites), 34, 42-43, 133, 200; of missionaries, 64, 86, 135, 138, 139, 158-159, 160, 197, 202, 230; of missionary children, 150, 191. See also: Schools, mission; Leadership, training of.
"Elkhart" board. See: Mennonite Board of Missions and Charities.
English language: Mennonites' use of, 28, 30, 31, 33, 42, 44, 69; taught by missionaries, 22, 103, 136, 145, 198.
Erb, Allen, 44, 98, 99, 120-122, 130, 135, 183.
Erb, Alta Mae, 246.
Erb, Paul, 111, 119, 246.
Esch, Christian D., 202, 211-212.
Evangelism.
—methods, general, 169-170, 228.
—methods, in Mennonite Church missions, 128; in Argentina, 131-132; in India, 136; in home missions (tables, 239, 245; graph, 240).
—to scattered Mennonites, 37-40.
—"direct," 22, 95, 99, 107-108, 147; ch. IV, *passim;* 126, 128, 130, 131-147, 202, 271, 272, 278.
—See also: Mass-movement; Literature; Radio; Child.
Excommunication, 179. See also: Discipleship, discipline in new churches.

Farming (in Argentina), 128-130, 198, 203.
Foot washing rite, 115, 163, 193.
Fort Wayne (Ind.) mission, 89, 206, 243, 269.
Franconia Mennonite Conference, 83, 84, 133, 226, 238.
Fresh-Air programs, 73, 242.
Friends, Society of, 45, 124, 126, 138.
Friesen, John, 176, 179, 212.

Friesen, Peter A., 133, 137, 216, 259.
Fundamentalism (in Protestantism), 109-115, 127, 134, 145, 180, 270. See also: Mennonite Church, and Fundamentalism.
Funk, John F., 31-36, 39, 42-46, 54-56, 61-65, 80, 85-88, 112; biographical data, 32, 33, 46, 47; quoted, 35, 36, 60, 65, 66.

Gamber, Selena. See: Shank, Selena (Gamber).
Gandhi, Mahatma, 160, 184.
Garber, David, 87.
Garber, Henry F., 145, 214.
"General" board. See Mennonite Board of Missions and Charities.
General Conference Mennonite Church (GC), 29, 41-42, 58, 69, 75, 78-80, 83-84, 97, 117, 155, 156.
General Conference of the Mennonite Church, 32, 80, 81, 90, 92, 97, 110, 114, 115, 118, 144, 150, 182; formed, 84.
Godshall, J. R., 29.
Good, Allan, 169.
Good, Noah, 257-258.
Gorjón, Feliciano, 189-191, 210, 213.
Goshen College, 87-89, 101, 103, 110, 114, 117, 133-134, 137, 138, 219, 230-233; begun (as Elkhart Institute), 34, 43.
Gospel Herald, 32, 111, 114, 116, 136, 154, 158, 267; quoted, 151, 152, 199, 238, 243, 255, 267.
Governments. See: Political.
Graber, Joseph D., 79, 146, 150, 159, 172, 180, 184, 197, 216, 238; quoted, 160, 169-170, 172, 173, 180, 203, 204, 220, 238.
Graber, Minnie, 150, 159.
Great Commission, 22, 34-37, 42, 147, 149, 157, 193, 194, 212; Anabaptists' acceptance of, 24.

Haider, John, 216.
Hallman, William and Beatrice (Hershey), 175, 189.
Hartman, Emanuel M., 63, 65.
Hartzler, Jonas, S., 57, 59, 76, 91, 133, 216.
Hartzler, Jonathan K., 36, 49, 256.
Hartzler, Levi C., 126, 205, 238.
Herald of Truth, 36, 38, 41, 45, 54, 55, 58, 71, 80, 87, 102, 113, 254, 256, 279; begun, 32; quoted, 35-37, 40, 56, 57, 75, 76, 84-85, 153. See also: John F. Funk.
Heatwole, Reuben J., 57, 279.

Hershberger, Guy F., 127, 170, 183, 190, 273.
Hershey, Eusebius, 29.
Hershey, Isaac, 45-46, 59, 70, 73; quoted, 43, 73.
Hershey, Tobias K. (and Mae), 100-106, 118, 127-132, 144, 160, 179, 187-193, 207-208, 214-216; quoted, 132, 152, 157, 169, 178, 198, 204, 220; helps open mission in Texas, 279.
Hesston College, 122, 230-233.
Hinduism, 21, 135, 159, 178.
Hispanics, mission work among, 215, 244, 256, 259, 279-281; begun, 206, 215, 238, 277, 279 ff.; tables, 248, 250-252; graph, 253.
Holdeman, Calvin, 130.
Home missions. See: City; Rural Missions, congregational.
Horsch, John, 44, 113, 114, 119, 155-156, 190.
Hostetler, Christian K., 62, 80, 89-90, 182, 255; as superintendent of Youngstown mission, 105-107.
Hostetler, S. Jay, 204.
Humility theme, 33, 36, 37, 43, 45, 46, 47-48, 62, 117, 182, 226, 268.

Iglesias Menonitas de la República Argentina. See: Argentine Mennonite Church.
Illinois Mennonite Conference, 62, 63.
Imperialism, and missions, 21, 22. See also: Missions, cultural attitudes in.
India, 21, 29, 49, 127, 153. See also: American Mennonite Mission; Mennonite Church in India.
India Mennonite Conference. See: Mennonite Church in India.
Indiana-Michigan Mennonite Conference, 33, 38, 62-63, 113, 164, 226, 237, 272.
Indians (Native Americans), 19, 26, 42, 247-251, 254-256, 261; tables, 248, 250-252; graph, 253.
Indigenization, 22, 192, 195-197, 221. See also: Three-self formula; Replica churches; Missions, cultural attitudes in.
Industrial mission, and industrial work in missions, 129, 159, 274; in India, 135, 202. See also: Welsh Mountain Mission; Social service; Washington, Booker T.

Index

Instruction of new believers, 177-180, 187.

Jennings, Selina, 159-160, 260, 277.
Jews, mission work among, 153, 247-251; tables, 248, 250-252; graph, 253.

Kansas City mission, 100, 107-108, 200, 243.
Kansas-Missouri, and Kansas-Nebraska-Oklahoma Mennonite Conferences, 85, 99, 118, 163.
Kauffman, Amsa H. (and Nona), 215, 280.
Kauffman, Daniel, 76, 110-111, 113, 115-117, 136, 150, 157-158, 162; quoted, 40, 80, 91-92, 137, 154, 168, 177, 181, 199.
Kaufman, Edmund G., 155-156.
Kaufman, James Norman, 95, 96, 137, 140, 146, 199, 217.
King, Benjamin B., 99-100, 269.

Labor unions, 151, 271.
La Junta (Colo.) Sanitarium and Hospital, 96-99, 120, 123, 127, 130.
La Voz Menonita, 188, 189.
Lal, Obadiah P., 208.
Lambert, George, 79-80.
Lancaster Mennonite Conference, and Lancaster (Pa.) area Mennonites, 59, 61-63, 67, 85, 90, 126-127, 129, 132-147, 162, 172, 186 ff., 200, 226; mission effort begins, 68-78, 82; home missions of, 173, 183, 237, 242, 247, 251, 257. See also: Eastern Mennonite Board of Missions and Charities.
Lantz, D. Parke, 126, 131-132, 213.
Lantz, Peter R., 182.
Lapp, George, 136, 137, 143, 211, 217; quoted, 96, 163, 199, 202-203, 206, 268.
Lapp, Mahlon C., 96, 132, 172, 216.
Lauver, William, 210.
Laymen and laywomen, 38, 40, 72, 73.
Leadership, national and indigenous (of missions and mission-created churches), 196, 206 ff.; in Africa, 207 ff., 214 ff., 221; in Argentina, 129, 188 ff., 213 ff., 215-216, 219, 221; in India, 202, 207, 213, 216; in home missions, 206-207; 244; training of, 129-130, 207, 210 ff.; pay of, 203-204, 208-210, 219-220; ordination of, 207, 214. See also: Three-self formula.
Leaman, A. Hershey, 67, 119, 201, 257.
Leatherman, John, 186.

Lehman, Jacob S., 100-101.
Lehman, M. Clifford (and Lydia), 133-135, 153, 159, 178, 182, 202; quoted, 156, 157, 210.
Leprosaria (in India), 94, 135, 136.
Liberalism, theological. See: Modernism.
Liechty, John A., 152.
Life insurance, 149, 151, 153, 155, 270.
Lima (Ohio) mission, 199, 206.
Lind, Marcus, 183.
Literature evangelism, 20, 131, 201.
Litwiller, Nelson (and Ada), 150, 179, 210, 218; quoted, 130-131, 208-209, 219.
Livingstone, David, 21-22.
Long, C. Warren, 183.
Los Angeles Bible Institute. See: Bible Institute of Los Angeles.
Los Angeles mission, 151, 163, 201, 244.
Loucks, Aaron, 60, 80-81, 85, 107.
Luayza, Albano, 203, 207, 208, 213, 216.
Lutz, Henry E., 174, 175.

McGavran, Donald, 171-173.
Mack, Noah H. (and Elizabeth), 75-77, 91, 173.
Mack, Noah K., 165.
Marriage, polygamy, etc., 164-165.
Martyrs' synod, 25, 26, 44.
Mass-movement evangelism, 135, 143, 171, 203.
Medical mission work, 58-59, 68, 108, 109, 120, 278; in Argentina, 129-130; in India, 81, 94, 135. See also: La Junta.
Mellinger, Jacob, 71, 75, 255, 256.
Mellinger, John H., 69, 71, 73, 77, 88, 89, 91, 93, 144, 145, 258-259.
Mennonite Board of Charitable Homes, of Charitable Homes and Missions, 34, 91, 92; formed, 88-89.
Mennonite Board of Guardians, 84, 124.
Mennonite Board of Missions and Charities (later, of Missions), 76, 92-93, 107, 117, 118, 140-142, 193, 220, 279; formed, 80, 89-92; policy pronouncements, 128, 137-141, 143-146, 151-152, 161, 163, 168, 278; home mission initiatives, 234, 236, 269, 276, 277 ff. (tables, 232, 235; graphs, 236, 237, 280).
Mennonite boards of mission, local and district, 233-236, 259, 261-262, 268, 272, 276; tables, 232, 235; graphs, 236, 237, 274, 280.

Mennonite Brethren (MB), 28, 29.
Mennonite Brethren in Christ, 29.
Mennonite Central Committee, 124-126, 228.
Mennonite Church (MC), 193, 254.
—and missions, pre-1890, 29-31, 34 ff., 54 ff., 224 ff.
—opponents of missions, 60-62, 70-73.
—"quickening" in. See: Quickening.
—relation to its missions, 60 ff., 65-69, 72, 80, 81-82, 86-87, 175.
—and Fundamentalism, 112-117, 132, 144, 146, 150, 151, 179, 270, 275-276. See also: Missions, Fundamentalist impact upon.
—doctrinal statements, 110-111, 114, 117-118, 144, 175.
—See also: Mennonites.
Mennonite Church in India, 95, 132, 184-185, 203, 216, 220-221; organized, 213. See also: American Mennonite Mission; India.
Mennonite Evangelizing Committee, Mennonite Evangelizing Board of America, Mennonite Evangelizing and Benevolent Board, 34, 40, 41, 64-65, 78-81, 84, 88-92, 125; formed, 38-40, 65. See also: Benevolent Organization of Mennonites; Mennonite Board of Missions and Charities.
Mennonite Home and Foreign Relief Committee (or Commission), 34, 79-81, 124.
Mennonite Home Mission Advocates, 70-74. See also: Mennonite Sunday School Mission.
Mennonite Publishing Company, 32, 44, 89. See also: John F. Funk; *Herald of Truth*.
Mennonite Relief Commisson for War Suffers, 125. See also: Relief Committee.
Mennonite Service Units, 127. See also: Voluntary Service.
Mennonite Sunday School Mission, 73 ff. See also: Mennonite Home Mission Advocates.
Mennonites, 100, 154, 175 ff.; origins, 23 ff.; doctrinal statements of, 110, 114, 118, 144, 175; early attitudes toward mission, 23, 26-29, 35. See also: Anabaptists; General Conference Mennonite Church (GC); Evangelical Mennonites; Mennonite Brethren (MB); Mennonite Brethren in Christ; Mennonite Church (MC).
Methodists, 20, 21, 30, 33, 46, 50, 58, 61, 77, 80, 101, 135, 138, 143, 152, 267.
Metzler, Abram, Jr., 69, 75; quoted, 70, 71, 97-98.
Mexican-Americans, 163. See also: Hispanics.
Miller, Daniel D., 162.
Miller, Earl, 152.
Miller, Ernest E., 137, 141, 160-161, 172-176, 178, 184, 217-218, 220.
Miller, Menno S., 56, 58.
Miller, Orie O., 186.
Mininger, Jacob D., 107-108, 156, 244.
Missionaries. See: Missions.
Missionary Church. See: Mennonite Brethren in Christ.
Missionary Messenger, 186, 244, 255-256.
Missions
—early: Protestant, 19 ff.; Anabaptist, 24-25, 25, 27.
—motives for, 22, 35, 42, 48, 82, 230; table, 231.
—strategies, 40-41, 44-45, 54 ff., 58, 60, 65-68, 71, 72, 98; ch.IV, 127, 128 ff., 168, 195 ff., 206 ff., 212, 223, 224 ff., 228 ff., 229 ff., 272-273, 277-278 ff. See also: Church-planting; Youngstown.
—relation to church, 26, 31, 40, 58, 60 ff., 63-66, 81-82, 96, 107.
—"faith", 26, 63-65, 78, 95-96, 171, 230.
—Mennonite, Fundamentalist impact upon, 117-123, 125, 127, 128, 132-147, 159, 186, 188, 190, 227, 273, 275, 276, 289.
—foreign, of the Mennonite Church, 57, 64. See also: India; Argentina; Africa.
—organization and government of, 37, 81-82, 83 ff., 86-87, 88-92, 104, 105, 110, 128, 157, 196, 203-204, 209-210, 212-222, 229. See also: Self-governance.
—financing of, 38, 64-65, 73, 78, 85-87, 93, 97, 98, 101, 104, 106, 107, 128-129, 133, 136-138, 142, 145, 210, 208, 218. See also: Three-self formula.
—professionalization and, 83, 87, 89, 90, 92, 98-99, 199-205, 262.
—cultural attitudes in, 19, 22, 29, 49, 74, 76, 77, 86, 87, 100-109, 119, 121, 130-131, 143, 145, 148-149, 152-154, 157-161, 174-175, 181, 191, 196, 198, 199, 202, 203, 208 ff., 223, 227, 256, 257, 261,

Index

269-270, 287, 288. See also: Racism.
—congregation-initiated, 227, 230, 234 ff., 261, 275-277, 281; tables, 232, 235; graphs, 236, 237, 274, 280.
—political contexts and attitudes. See: Political.
Modernism (theological), 114-116, 119, 132, 136, 144, 151, 159; in Protestant missions, 119, 158; accusations of, in Mennonite Church missions, 144. See also: American Mennonite Mission, under attack.
Moody, Dwight L., and Moody Bible Institute, 32, 43, 56, 59-62.
Moseman, Philip, 35-36, 50.
Mosemann, John H., Jr. (and Ruth), 145, 186.
Mosemann, John H., Sr., 114, 117, 133-134, 137, 140, 186.
Music, and musical instruments, 74, 149, 150, 157, 161-162.
Musselman, Samuel H., 77, 93, 128, 130, 187.
Mutual aid, 84, 123-124, 126, 129, 131, 199, 223. See also: Life insurance.

Nissley, Peter, 34, 35, 46.
Nonconformity doctrine, 34, 45, 57-58, 66, 68, 69, 74, 120, 132, 148-149, 151, 168, 174, 176, 177, 188, 222, 227, 288. See also: Dress.
Nonjuring, 151.
Nonresistance doctrine, 45, 48-51, 93, 105-106, 113, 123, 129, 134, 141, 148-149, 150, 152, 160, 168, 176, 180-194, 226, 265; in home missions, 183; in Argentina, 179, 186-194; in India, 184-185; in Africa, 185-186. See also: Peace.
Nunemaker, William, 279.
Nurses' training, 64, 91, 97, 98, 122-123; in Argentina, 130. See also: La Junta.

Oath-taking. See: Nonjuring.
Oberholtzer, John, 83, 84.
O'Connell, Maurice, 206.
Old people's homes, and aid, 34, 84; in Ohio, 65, 87-88; in Illinois, 88; in Lancaster Conference, 74, 88; in Maryland, 88; in Argentina, 130.
Orphans' homes, children's homes, children's aid, 34, 84-87, 120, 243; in Ohio, 65, 87, 88, 243; in Lancaster Conference, 74; in Kansas City, 88, 108;

in India, 80, 94, 135; in Argentina, 127, 129, 130.

Page, William and Alice (Thut), 58, 61, 81, 93-94, 206.
Peace message, 24, 27, 46, 49-51, 55, 57, 86, 93, 112, 122, 126, 134; and missions, 21, 35, 105, 167, 176, 180-194, 228, 259, 289. See also: Nonresistance.
Peace Problems Committee, 182, 183, 185, 188, 193.
Pehuajó, Argentina, 129, 189, 214.
Peoria (Ill.) mission, 152, 183, 205, 219.
Philadelphia, 28, 73.
Pickett, J. Waskom, 135, 143, 171.
Pietism, 19, 20, 25, 27, 28, 172, 181, 182.
Political contexts and attitudes, 19, 21-22, 131, 152, 153, 160, 161, 182, 196, 222-223, 267; in India, 94-96, 99, 174, 177, 220; in Argentina, 131, 174, 188, 189-193; in Africa, 185; at Youngstown, 100 ff., 105, 108; church-state separation, 24, 45, 48, 115, 119, 189, 190.
Polygamy. See: Marriage.
Portland (Ore.) mission, 169, 183, 257.
Prayer veiling, 118, 139-140, 149, 151, 162-163.
Premillennialism, 110-112; in the Mennonite Church, 99, 113, 114; among Mennonite Church missionaries, 131, 186.
Presbyterians, 32, 33, 46, 58, 61, 70, 77, 107, 134, 267.
Printing and publishing; by Mennonites in Argentina, 130, 187-190, 202, 220. See also: John F. Funk; Mennonite Publishing Company; *Herald of Truth;* *Gospel Herald;* Literature evangelism.
Protestant missions, 19 ff., 29, 41, 53, 54, 56, 58, 63-64, 66, 70, 71, 79, 80, 82, 83, 88, 93, 100 ff., 134-135, 150, 156, 158, 171-172, 180-181, 187, 195-197, 204, 205, 210, 212, 221, 224, 238, 241-242, 244, 265, 267, 269, 278. See also: American Mennonite Mission, relations with.
"Protracted" meetings. See: Revivalism.

Quakers. See: Friends, Society of.
"Quickening" in Mennonite and Amish Mennonite Churches, late-nineteenth century, 31 ff., 42-52, 110, 112, 134, 154, 156, 179, 227.

Raber, Frank, 154-155.
Racism, 160, 174, 181, 196, 251-261, 262.
Radio evangelism, 279.
Reading (Pa.) mission, 154, 257.
Reformation, 23 ff., 51; missions and, 25.
Regeneration, understanding of. See: Salvation.
Reiff, Vernon, 136, 200, 279.
Reist, H. Frank, 268, 273.
Relief Committee, of Mennonite Board of Missions and Charities (later, Relief and Service Committee), 125-127, 182; formed, 125. See also: Mennonite Relief.
Relief work, 84, 103, 123-127, 150, 174, 201, 228, 244; in India, 78-80, 94, 124; in Spain, 132; by Eastern Mennonite Board of Missions and Charities, 186; relation to mission, 80. See also: Mennonite Board of Guardians; Mennonite Home and Foreign Relief Committee; Mennonite Relief Commission for War Sufferers; Mennonite Central Committee; Relief Committee; Social service.
"Replica" churches, 157-161, 196.
Ressler, Jacob A., 45-46, 59, 70, 254, 256; biographical material on, 44; as missionary, 81 ff., 93-94, 158, 267; quoted, 40, 70, 72, 85, 89, 90, 112, 177, 206, 209, 210, 212, 243.
Ressler, Lina (Zook), 65, 68.
"Restrictions," 51, 157, 184, 187, 190.
Revivalism, 32, 37, 45, 50-51, 148, 152, 156, 169, 176, 181, 182, 241; begun, among Mennonite Church and Amish Mennonites, 33. See also: "Quickening."
Riehl, Mabel, 106.
Rural mission work, and ruralism, 100, 104, 107, 122, 128-129, 151, 159-160, 198; in home missions, 146, 154, 175, 199, 224 ff., 227, 260, 262 (table, 264; graphs, 265-266, 280); in India, 143. See also: Farming; Southern highlands.
Rutt, Mary, 168-169.

Salvation, understanding of, 45, 51-52, 109, 111, 119, 120, 133-134, 154, 228; Anabaptists' v. Reformers', 25; by Mennonite Church missionaries, 135, 136, 226, 270; as transmitted in mission, 167-170, 194, 172, 176, 177, 179, 183, 186, 194, 203.

Sauder, J. Paul, 186, 237, 243, 247.
Schertz, Henry R., 173.
Schertz, Lydia Ellen, 158.
Schools, mission: in India, 94, 96, 120, 128, 135-136 (reorganized, 142), 184, 200, 201, 202, 211; in Argentina, 128-130, 188, 201; in Africa, 145, 200. See also: Education; Leadership, training of.
Self-governance, 201, 204, 213-222, 281; of home missions, 228 (table, 229). See also: Missions, organization and governance.
Self-propagation, 205-212, 222-223.
Self-support, 197-205, 209-210, 222. See also: Missions, financing.
Seventh-Day Adventists, 87.
Sewing Circles and sewing classes, 73, 75, 103; in Argentina, 129.
Shank, Charles L., 202, 267.
Shank, Crissie (Yoder), 267.
Shank, Emma, 128, 144, 150, 259.
Shank, John R., 159, 237, 278, 281.
Shank, Josephus W., 118-121, 159, 259; investigative trip to South America, 118, 127, 187; as missionary in Argentina, 127-131, 144, 187, 191, 193, 198, 203, 207, 213.
Shank, Selena (Gamber), 99, 122, 129-130.
Shenk, John, 55, 65.
Shoemaker, Joseph S., 68, 92, 104, 216, 279.
Simons, Menno, 23, 24, 26, 44, 123, 190.
Smith, Jacob B., 84-85, 114, 161, 162.
Smucker, Jonathan, 55-57.
Snyder, Elvin, 189, 191.
Social Gospel, 99, 112, 170, 182, 268, 270-271, 289; and Mennonite Church missions, 119, 120, 123, 127, 131, 135, 146, 190. See also: Social service.
Social service, in mission, 20, 66, 74-78, 97, 100, 107-108, ch.IV, *passim*, 168, 228, 271, ff., 287; benevolent institutions for, 83-88, 143; at Youngstown, 100-108; on foreign fields, 127 ff., 202, 203; as means of beginning missions (tables, 239, 245; graph, 240). See also: Relief; Medical; Education; Industrial; La Junta; Rural; Old people's; Orphans'.
South American Mennonite Mission, 127-132, 144, 157, 160, 174, 176, 178, 179, 259; beginnings of, 118, 127-128, 150, 152, 198. See also: Argentina; Argentine.

Index

Southern highlands, 159-160, 160, 233, 260, 277-279, 281. See also: Shank, John R.; Buckingham, Maude; Jennings, Selina.
Southwestern Pennsylvania Mennonite Conference (later, Allegheny), 63, 81, 86-87.
Spanish Civil War, 126.
Spanish-language work. See: Hispanics; South American.
Sprunger, John A., 58, 97.
Stauffer, Elam, 165.
Stauffer, John L., 133, 136, 141, 153, 278.
Steiner, Menno S., 46, 50, 56, 58-62, 64-66, 69, 71, 81, 82, 84, 85, 90, 91, 93, 97, 102, 105, 110, 113; biographical data on, 43, 60; clash with John F. Funk, 88 ff., 92; as mission board president, 92; quoted, 37-38, 41, 43, 57, 85-86, 93, 113, 172, 182, 254.
Student Volunteer Movement, 22, 80-81, 230.
Summer Bible schools. See: Vacation.
Sunday school conferences, 32-33, 49, 58, 60.
Sunday schools, 20, 23, 41, 226; beginnings of, among Mennonite Church and Amish Mennonites, 32 ff., 69, 73; Mennonites and interdenominational; 46-47; as strategy of mission, 58, 59, 62, 73, 122, 128, 131, 224, 238, 242, 243, 247 (tables, 239, 245; graph, 240); in Mennonite Church missions, 66, 77, 94, 101, 157, 233.
Swartzentruber, Amos and Edna, 106-107.
Swartzentruber, Laban, 243.
Swartzentruber, Orley, 175-177.
Swiss Brethren, 23, 24. See also: Anabaptists.

Tampa (Fla.) mission, 244, 259.
Tanganyika, 145. See also: Africa.
Texas, 267. See also Hispanics.
"Three-self" formula, 23, 135, 145, ch. VII. See also: Self-governance; Self-propagation; Self-support.
Thut, Alice. See: Page.
Toronto Bible College, 103, 142.
Toronto mission, 155, 160.
Tract distribution. See: Literature.
Troyer, Sara Alice, 29.
Twenty-sixth Street Mission (Chicago), 156, 242.

United Brethren (Church of the United Brethren in Christ), 46, 70.

Vacation Bible schools, 122, 206, 224, 233, 238 ff., 243, 247; tables 239, 245; graph, 240.
Venn, Henry, 22, 195.
Ventura family, 244.
Village work, 96, 136. See also: Balodgahan, India.
Virginia Mennonite Conference, 31, 114, 115, 137, 139, 146, 226, 259, 279.
Virginia Mennonites, 46, 54, 61, 132, 136, 254; and early mission, 29-31, 206, 263.
Voluntary Service, 127, 228.

War—and Mennonite mission and relief, 125, 126.
Washington, Booker T., 74, 135, 202, 256.
Watkins, Robert, 136.
Weaver, David S., 98, 104.
Weaver, Edwin, 259.
Weber, Lewis, 160, 174.
Wedding bands, and bangles, 150, 164.
Welsh Mountain Mission (later, and Samaritan Home), 74-78, 88, 251, 255, 274.
Wenger, Amos D., 114, 137, 151.
Wenger, Linden, 214 ff., 226, 247, 281 ff.
Wenger, Solomon B., 90, 198.
West Virginia missions, 30-31, 55, 156, 206, 233.
Whitaker, Glenn, 163, 244.
Women, 113; and missions, 26, 59, 61, 64, 65, 67, 68, 86-87, 97, 100-101, 247; Bible women, 136, 204, 207, 210. See also: Nurses' training; Sewing circles.

Yoder, Christian Z., 106, 172, 269.
Yoder, John Howard, 171, 192.
Yoder, Sanford C., 99, 114, 119, 128, 137, 140-142, 162, 187, 191, 200, 206, 207, 257, 278-279; difficult position of, 146; quoted, 140, 150, 151, 157, 176, 177, 193, 201, 204 ff., 238.
Young Men's Christian Association, 32, 46, 105, 143, 230, 268.
Young People's Meetings, 34, 157.
Youngstown (Ohio) mission, 99-108, 128, 154, 257, 265, 289.

Zook, J. K., 86, 113.
Zook, Lina. See: Ressler, Lina.

Theron F. Schlabach is professor of history at Goshen College, Goshen, Indiana, where he teaches United States history and the history of Mennonites in America.

He serves on the editorial board of *The Mennonite Quarterly Review* and is secretary of the Mennonite Historical Society. He is a member of the Organization of American Historians, the American Historical Association, and the Mennonite Mission Study Fellowship.

Schlabach received the BA degree from Goshen College, the MS and PhD degrees from the University of Wisconsin, and was a National Endowment for the Humanities Fellow at Princeton, 1976-77.

He has written for the State Historical Society of Wisconsin, Mennonite Board of Missions, *The Mennonite Quarterly Review,* and other publications.

Theron and Sara Ann (Kauffman) Schlabach are members of the College Mennonite Church, Goshen, Indiana. They are the parents of Gerald, Carlyle, Roderic, and Kristina.

www.ingramcontent.com/pod-product-compliance
Lightning Source LLC
Chambersburg PA
CBHW071228230426
43668CB00011B/1344